Rebels

FEARGHAL McGARRY

Rebels

Voices from the Easter Rising

PENGUIN
IRELAND

PENGUIN IRELAND

Published by the Penguin Group
Penguin Ireland, 25 St Stephen's Green, Dublin 2, Ireland (a division of Penguin Books Ltd)
Penguin Books Ltd, 80 Strand, London WC2R 0RL, England
Penguin Group (USA) Inc., 375 Hudson Street, New York, New York 10014, USA
Penguin Group (Australia), 250 Camberwell Road, Camberwell, Victoria 3124, Australia
(a division of Pearson Australia Group Pty Ltd)
Penguin Group (Canada), 90 Eglinton Avenue East, Suite 700, Toronto, Ontario, Canada M4P 2Y3
(a division of Pearson Penguin Canada Inc.)
Penguin Books India Pvt Ltd, 11 Community Centre, Panchsheel Park, New Delhi – 110 017, India
Penguin Group (NZ), 67 Apollo Drive, Rosedale, Auckland 0632, New Zealand
(a division of Pearson New Zealand Ltd)
Penguin Books (South Africa) (Pty) Ltd, 24 Sturdee Avenue, Rosebank, Johannesburg 2196, South Africa

Penguin Books Ltd, Registered Offices: 80 Strand, London WC2R 0RL, England

www.penguin.com

First published 2011
1

Set in 10.5/14 pt Sabon LT Std
Typeset by Palimpsest Book Production Limited, Falkirk, Stirlingshire
Printed in Great Britain by Clays Ltd, St Ives plc

A CIP catalogue record for this book is available from the British Library

ISBN: 978-1-844-88203-8

www.greenpenguin.co.uk

Penguin Books is committed to a sustainable future for our business, our readers and our planet. This book is made from paper certified by the Forest Stewardship Council.

For my father, Des, whose father participated in the gun-running at Howth in July 1914, and my mother, Ita, whose mother witnessed what followed on Easter Monday, 1916

Contents

Introduction

Shortly before noon on 24 April 1916, Easter Monday, over thirty men drawn from the ranks of the Irish Volunteers, Fianna Éireann and the Irish Citizen Army crowded into a small house off Rutland Street in Dublin's north inner city. The men, who had been mobilised at short notice, were instructed to remove their uniforms and exchange their rifles for automatic pistols. Their mission was the destruction of the Magazine Fort in the Phoenix Park, site of the British Army's principal armoury in the city. One group set off for the Park by bicycle, while two other sections travelled by tram.

In his witness statement to the Bureau of Military History, Gary Holohan described how he and Paddy O'Daly, who would lead the attack, stopped at a shop on Ormond Quay to purchase a football before joining their comrades in the Park.[1] There, Tom Leahy remembered, the men paused before the attack to say a decade of the Rosary and shake hands – 'in case we should never meet again'.[2] Holohan, a Fianna veteran, described what happened next: 'After a few minutes' chat together, as if we were a football team with followers, we moved around to the front of the Fort in a casual way, some of the lads kicking the ball from one to the other.' The sole sentry on the gate was overwhelmed as the rebels rushed the fort. Ten soldiers in the guard room were quickly captured, leaving Holohan to confront the remaining sentry on the parapet of the fort: 'He came towards me with his bayonet pointed towards me. I fired a shot and he fell . . . The poor sentry was crying, "Oh, sir, sir, don't shoot me. I'm an Irishman and the father of seven children."' Despite the ease with which they breached the fort's defences, the rebels found themselves unable to enter the high-explosives store; the officer in charge, it transpired, had left for the Fairyhouse races with the key in his pocket. Although they succeeded in mining the small-arms ammunition store, the dull explosions that followed – which could not be heard beyond the Park – did not provide the desired dramatic prelude to the Rising. Undeterred, the rebels – clutching their captured rifles and singing 'The Soldiers' Song' – raced to the city centre to join their comrades in the GPO.

Although the Rising would come to be seen as an unequal battle between chivalrous rebels and the might of the British Empire, the violence of Easter Week was sometimes less clear cut. The soldiers encountered by the rebels in the Magazine Fort were frightened youths; 'one was weeping copiously'.[3] The sole fatality of the raid was an unarmed 14-year-old civilian, Gerald Playfair, the son of the fort's commandant, who was shot three times as he attempted to enter a house near the Park to raise the alarm. 'I jumped off my bicycle,' Holohan recalled, 'and just as the door opened I shot him from the gate.' The rebellion pitted Irish rebels against Irish servants of the Crown as well as British soldiers, and the majority of those who lost their lives in Dublin that week were civilians. Ultimately, the failure of the raid – like the military failure of the Rising itself – proved irrelevant. The scale and audacity of what was attempted transcended the strategic limitations and often inept execution of the insurrection. Easter 1916 – and the ill-judged response that it provoked from the British government – demonstrated the tremendous power of political violence, even when deployed on a small scale in a militarily ineffective way by an unrepresentative minority, to change the course of Irish history. After the Rising, nothing would be the same again.

No event did more to shape the politics of modern Ireland than the Easter Rising. Before 1916, Irish nationalism was dominated by a moderate constitutional tradition represented by John Redmond's Irish Parliamentary Party. A devolved 'Home Rule' parliament – a constitutional settlement that would keep Ireland within the United Kingdom – appeared by far the most likely outcome of the political crisis that had intermittently convulsed Ireland and Britain since the introduction of the Government of Ireland Bill in 1912. That alternative future was destroyed, along with much of the centre of Dublin, in April 1916. The scale, timing and impact of the Rising shocked contemporaries, even those – such as the chief secretary, Augustine Birrell

– whose role it was to guard against just such an event: 'in my wildest dreams I never contemplated the possibility of what actually happened.'[4] In killing Home Rule, the rebels transformed Ireland, reviving a moribund physical force tradition and establishing republicanism as the dominant element in Irish politics. By January 1919 a revolutionary government had secured a democratic mandate to bring into being the Republic that the Easter rebels had died to proclaim. The next five years brought guerrilla war, partition, secession and civil war.

The Rising not only altered the course of Ireland's history; it shaped its politics over the decades that followed. The emergence of popular support for a republic – the most extreme of the competing objectives advocated by militant nationalists before 1916 – led inexorably to the War of Independence. As W. B. Yeats had recognised as early as 1917 when he wrote 'Sixteen Dead Men': 'who can talk of give and take . . . While those dead men are loitering there . . .?' The acceptance in 1922 of the Anglo-Irish Treaty by a majority of Sinn Féin deputies, a political settlement that fell substantially short of republican objectives, made inevitable the civil war that followed. Opposition to the Treaty was based less on its political flaws than on what those who remained loyal to the Republic notionally established in 1916 saw as its moral and spiritual illegitimacy. For these republicans, this consideration outweighed the wishes of the Irish electorate; as Éamon de Valera, the only surviving commandant of the Rising, declared: 'the people had never a right to do wrong.'[5] Despite the cessation of revolutionary violence in 1923, the politics of independent Ireland long remained polarised around the question of the Republic. The legacy of the Rising proved no less contentious in Northern Ireland, where it served to legitimise the violence of the Provisional IRA during the Troubles and continues to provide a rationale – or pretext – for the actions of dissident republican paramilitaries to this day.

We now know a great deal about the events of 1916, and yet there remains much disagreement about fundamental aspects of the Easter Rising. Did the rebels think they had any chance of success, or was their insurrection intended as a symbolic act of sacrifice? What sort of society did they wish to bring about? Why did the actions of an initially unpopular conspiratorial elite generate mass support? Such debates arise in part from the continuing political potency of the Rising, but also from the fact that while we know an enormous amount about leaders such as Patrick Pearse and James Connolly, the motivations and experiences of the rank and file – 'ordinary' men such as Gary Holohan and Tom Leahy, without whom there would not have been an Irish revolution – have remained obscure. Reconstructing the Rising from within and from below, this book presents the story of these people in their own words.

It is only with the release of the records of the Bureau of Military History – whose witness statements provide the source material for this book – that historians have been provided with the raw material necessary to explore this dimension of the Rising in any great detail. Established in 1947 by the Irish government in collaboration with a committee of professional historians and former Irish Volunteers, the Bureau aimed 'to assemble and co-ordinate material to form the basis for the compilation of the history of the movement for Independence from the formation of the Irish Volunteers on 25th November 1913, to the 11th July 1921'.[6] The negotiations leading to the Anglo-Irish Treaty and the events of the Irish Civil War were deliberately excluded from the Bureau's remit, a pragmatic decision given the project's ambition to secure contributions from both sides of the Civil War divide and a widely shared reluctance to revive memories of a conflict that continued to divide Irish society. Its investigators (predominantly army officers) were tasked with gathering detailed statements from veterans of the revolution. In some cases the statements were written by the witnesses; more frequently, they were based on oral testimony and composed into a coherent statement by the investigators before being submitted to the witness for verification and signed approval. By the time it was wound down a decade later, the Bureau had accumulated 1,773 statements, mainly by members of the Irish Republican Brotherhood (IRB), Sinn Féin, Fianna Éireann, the Irish Citizen Army, the Irish Volunteers and Cumann na mBan. Ranging widely in terms of accuracy, detail and interest, its 36,000 pages of evidence illuminate almost every aspect of the struggle for independence. It forms one of the richest and most comprehensive oral history archives devoted to any modern revolution.

To the dismay of the historians who cooperated with the project, the remarkable archive gathered by the Bureau was sealed within eighty-three steel boxes in the strong-room of Government Buildings in March 1959, where it remained unavailable for public or scholarly scrutiny. This decision was justified on the grounds of the controversial nature of the statements: 'If every Sean and Seamus from Ballythis and Ballythat who took major or minor or no part at all in the national movement . . . has free access to the material,' a member of the Bureau's advisory committee claimed, 'it may result in local civil warfare in every second town and village in the country.' The archive was finally opened in 2003, following the death of the last witness.

The purpose of this book is to bring the remarkable but unwieldy riches of the Bureau of Military History's witness statements to a wider audience. It seeks to distil the vast testimony of the statements into a coherent, readable narrative without sacrificing its variety or complexity. A central aim is to highlight the range of viewpoints that coexisted within the revolutionary movement, including those that were excluded from the popular historical narrative that emerged after the Rising. In this book the voices of the 'losers' – figures such as Bulmer Hobson, whose reputation was blackened by his efforts to prevent the Rising, and the many provincial Volunteers who failed to rise – can be heard alongside those whose reputations were made (often posthumously) by their decision to fight. Aside from selecting extracts and providing brief contextual links, editorial intervention has been kept to a minimum. Where the witnesses disagree on issues – such as whether the IRB's Military Council was entitled to mount a rising without informing the Volunteer leadership, or whether the rebels thought that such a rising could succeed – readers can form their own judgements based on the first-hand testimony.

The statements vary considerably in content and style. Some are egocentric, self-serving or otherwise unconvincing in tone. A few seek to shift blame, justify actions or settle scores. Some recall events and conversations in implausible detail. A small number, such as those of Desmond Ryan, are clearly literary constructs fashioned from previously published accounts.[7] The lengthy statements of prominent political figures such as Seán MacEntee, Ernest Blythe and Bulmer Hobson were clearly written (and often disseminated elsewhere in other forms) with broader considerations in mind. These men were not so much recording their recollections of the past as making appeals to posterity. The vast bulk of the Bureau's statements, however, are spare, measured accounts in plain language that carry an air of authenticity. They are the product of unknown veterans who believed in the importance of recording the minor role they played in an event that most of them regarded as the most important of their lives. They make no great claims as to the wider significance of their actions and are characterised by modesty rather than by vanity or self-interest. Some place on record doubts and regrets about past actions or decisions.

Like any historical source, the witness statements must be evaluated carefully. Those that deal with the Easter Rising were created over thirty years after the events recollected. They record not the events of that time but the witnesses' imperfect memory of them from a remove of several decades. In his statement, an ageing Jack Plunkett recalled how, reunited in Richmond barracks with his brother Joseph after the Rising, the chief military strategist who had planned the Rising with absolute secrecy finally 'dropped his reticence and spoke openly' about the rebellion: 'He said to me, "Here are some things you must remember."' Plunkett, alas, had by then forgotten whatever it was his brother felt compelled to reveal.[8] Unsurprisingly, dates, places, numbers and other details are often inaccurate. And some (intriguing but unverifiable) claims seem less plausible than others: did Father Flanagan of Ringsend invent the sawn-off shotgun?[9] Did the provisional government's members, as Desmond Ryan claimed, really spend the first night of the Republic under the influence of opium?[10]

The passage of time also meant that a considerable number of veterans were no longer alive to record their memories. (Indeed, a growing realisation of this fact had added to the pressure on the government to sanction the project, which had been under consideration in different forms since the early 1930s.) Nor does the archive include statements from all who were requested to participate. Some veterans, unwilling to betray confidences or simply wishing to forget the past, refused. One member of an IRA flying column explained that his memories of the period were tainted 'with a feeling of aversion and self-disgust'.[11] Even among those veterans who felt no such ambivalence about their actions, an unwillingness to discuss the past – even with family members – was far from unusual. Prominent among those who refused to provide statements were individuals who had gone on to successful political careers, including Éamon de Valera, the head of the government that established the Bureau and the most eminent surviving rebel, and Richard Mulcahy, former IRA chief of staff and veteran of the battle of Ashbourne. Some politicians may have been reluctant to place formally on record their precise actions during the period: de Valera, for example, was notably preoccupied with his place in history.[12] The willingness of his long-time political rival, W. T. Cosgrave, to contribute a statement – one that criticised aspects of the Rising he participated in – presents a striking contrast. Other former revolutionaries refused because of their distrust of the project or of the government responsible for establishing it. Elizabeth Farrell, who achieved fame by conveying Patrick Pearse's offer of surrender to Brigadier General Lowe, declined on the grounds that 'all governments since 1921 had betrayed the Republic.' The Civil War inevitably cast a long shadow: an official from the Bureau recorded how one veteran, refusing their request, had sarcastically observed that they should have secured a statement from a former comrade 'before we shot him'.[13] Pauline Keating, who did submit a statement, was surprised by the attitude of other former members of Cumann na mBan: 'some of them said they would rather burn anything they had than give it to the Bureau . . . I suggested that the information might be of interest to future generations, but I did not succeed in convincing them.'[14]

Some witnesses' recollections were distorted by subjectivity, bias or the subsequent accumulation of knowledge. A more subtle difficulty is posed by the influence of political factors, particularly the legacy of the Civil War. These problems were compounded by the nature of the project itself. The Bureau's statements represent a heavily mediated form of oral history, recording those aspects of the past that interviewees were able or willing to recall, reflected through the lens of a state-sponsored historical project. The Bureau's investigators, for their part, determined who would be interviewed and who would not. Interpreting their remit to record 'the history of the movement for Independence' in a more narrow fashion than would have been the case had the project occurred later, they invited relatively few constitutional nationalists, unionists, members of the Crown forces and

British officials to submit statements.[15] Those who were urged to do so did not always prove cooperative. Alfred Cope, a former Dublin Castle assistant under-secretary who played an important role in bringing an end to the conflict, refused to submit a statement on the grounds that he regarded the period as

> the most discreditable of your country's history – it is preferable to forget it: to let sleeping dogs lie. It is not possible for this history to be truthful although I am sure Mr McDunphy [the director of the Bureau of Military History] will do his utmost to make it so – the job is beyond human skill. The IRA must be shown as national heroes and the British forces as brutal oppressors . . . What a travesty it will be and must be. Read by future generations of Irish children, it will simply perpetuate the long-standing hatred of England and continue the miserable work of self-seeking politicians who, for their own aggrandisement, have not permitted the Christian virtues of forgiveness and brotherhood to take its place. Ireland has too many histories: she deserves a rest.[16]

Although Cope's reservations would have been shared by many, the failure to record more non-republican voices represents a missed opportunity, as does the under-representation of the important role played by female activists. Although the Bureau provides a valuable insight into Irish women's participation in the struggle for independence, only 8 per cent of its statements were contributed by women, a considerable number of whom were interviewed as widows or relations of the leading men rather than as activists in their own right. This reflected, in part, unconscious assumptions about the relative importance of the contribution made by women that were evident in the titles of popular accounts of the period such as *Dublin's Fighting Story 1913–1921: Told by the Men Who Made It*.[17]

Notwithstanding these flaws, the Bureau of Military History remains the single most important source for enhancing our understanding of the political revolution in Ireland. In the absence of substantial written records of the military plans for the insurrection or the inner workings of the IRB's Military Council, the witness statements provide vital historical evidence. Conventional sources, moreover, can be just as susceptible to bias. Much of what was known about the Rising at the time came from sources hostile to the rebels –

particularly newspapers owned by supporters of the Irish Party and police reports – complicating assessments of how public opinion changed during and after the rebellion. The witness statements leave little doubt as to the (often disputed) hostility of many ordinary Dubliners to the rebellion at the time, but they also chart the transformation of opinion over the weeks and months that followed.

To their credit, the Bureau's investigators – and the historians who advised them – viewed their task as the collection and preservation of evidence rather than its interpretation.[18] Given that much of the value of the statements lies in the insight into the day-to-day experiences of the rank and file that they provide, the Bureau's long-suffering director, Michael McDunphy, deserves praise for resisting pressure to focus on the role of the revolutionary elite. He contended that 'an ordinary volunteer who served in the ranks and then returned to private life may often have a clearer and perhaps much more important story to tell than one who served with a titular rank.'[19] Nor was the Bureau blind to the pitfalls of oral history. Detailed instructions were issued to its investigators in an attempt to solicit accurate accounts:

> In listening to and recording his story you should keep an open mind. Your aim at all times must be to get from him an objective, factual record of events based on his own experiences. To that end he should be tactfully questioned on every point, to ensure that what he tells is, in fact, what he knows and not something which he has imagined, read or heard from someone else . . . a witness must, under no circumstances, be persuaded to agree to anything which does not accord with his own personal recollection. There must be no attempt to smooth out or adjust a story, in order to make it more plausible or readable.[20]

And, given their vast number, statements can be cross-checked for accuracy and consistency. Many ostensible discrepancies result from divergent experiences rather than from poor memory or unreliable narratives. Individuals encountering much the same circumstances – whether enduring the bombardment of the General Post Office or suffering the privations of imprisonment – frequently experienced them in very different ways.

Much of the particular value of oral sources lies precisely in their subjectivity. Few other sources provide meaningful insights into the motivations and experiences of rank-and-file separatists, people largely from lower-middle-class or working-class backgrounds who rarely recorded their thoughts in letters, diaries or memoirs. The views expressed by many witnesses are clearly biased – Irish Party supporters are caricatured as venal and opportunistic, Britain is presented as a malign and tyrannical entity – but these perceptions are part of the story their statements have to tell us. In seeking to understand how separatists viewed themselves, and how they justified their own actions within the world they lived in, subjective perceptions are more important than empirical realities.

Although the statements were made long after the Rising, they provide a window into the mentality and experiences of separatists during a period when most people regarded republicanism as a hopeless cause advocated by cranks and wreckers. They offer a hint of what it felt like to be there at the time without knowing what would happen next, and it is our knowledge of the latter which forms the greatest obstacle to understanding the past. The statements restore the all-important dimension of contingency to history, reminding us, for example, how aspects of the Rising presumed to be central to the event were more peripheral for many: the proclamation of the Irish Republic by Patrick Pearse, for example, was barely noticed by most rank-and-file rebels, and came as a surprise to many of those who did take notice of it.

The witness statements provide a wealth of obscure but rich detail, preserving some of the texture of the past rarely recorded by conventional sources: they describe the clothes that people wore (tweed deerstalker hats represented defiance for Sinn Féiners, while evening suits aroused their suspicion), how they moved about (would Enniscorthy have risen or Ashe's column triumphed at Ashbourne without the bicycle?), and what they ate (a new invention of the food industry, the Oxo cube, kept many rebels going during Easter Week, while their less fortunate comrades contemplated eating horses). They tell us what the rebels actually did during the Rising: surprisingly little fighting for the most part, but much praying and the occasional song and dance. They describe the weather during Easter Week: beautiful in Dublin (hastening the decomposition of the many corpses and carcasses littering its streets by the end of the week) and atrocious in

Cork (compounding the dismal impact of the failed mobilisation). They remind us how different Dublin's streets looked under British rule and reveal how deeply this was resented by republicans.

They tell us why people joined the Irish Republican Brotherhood or the Irish Volunteers and give us a sense of what it meant, in practical terms, to be a member of these organisations. Gary Holohan's account, for example, vividly conveys his excitement on 'getting a real gun in my hands for the first time', and the process of radicalisation that occurred as a result of his Fianna activism ('a sacred duty'). The statements provide a wealth of information on rudimentary but important questions: how did the Volunteers go about training, securing weapons and manufacturing ammunition? What did they see as the purpose of their activism? Did they know that it would culminate in a rebellion against British rule? They describe also the obstacles to this activism, whether parental disapproval, clerical censure or the fear of ridicule. The Catholic Church – from individual bishops to local curates – was less hostile towards separatism than is often assumed; the accounts also reveal how Volunteers and Fenians sought to accommodate or disarm clerical authority.

Less tangibly, the statements provide insights into the importance of contemporary social, class and gender distinctions. A close reading highlights the conservative social and cultural influences of the Edwardian era. Even within James Connolly's socialist Irish Citizen Army, women were excluded from playing a full role, and differences arising from social status remained significant. The unwillingness of many women to accept their subordinate roles – whether by demanding the right to learn how to shoot, refusing to be kept out of rebel garrisons or insisting on their right to be arrested at the end of Easter Week – is equally striking. Éamon de Valera, who notoriously refused to allow women to serve in Boland's bakery, would have been shocked by Áine Heron's decision to fight in the Rising while expecting her third child.[21]

Collectively, the statements challenge the notion of the rebellion as an ideologically coherent project, an idea that owed much to its powerful contemporary impact and the sudden centrality of the Proclamation, tricolour (a flag which was unfamiliar to many 1916 rebels) and iconography of republicanism. In describing their own politicisation, many witnesses spoke of fighting for Irish freedom and a hatred of British rule rather than of the more complex ideological influences that motivated many prominent activists. The influence of social and communal tensions is more evident than the radical ideals of the Proclamation – and this sheds light on the ultimately conservative nature of the Irish state that the rebels succeeded in bringing about.

The importance of local factors is striking: small numbers of separatist families and local traditions of radicalism often made the difference between the success or failure of separatism in a particular village or townland. The divergence between attitudes in Dublin and those in provincial Ireland are particularly striking in accounts of the Rising. Sectarian tensions and clerical involvement feature more prominently in the accounts of Volunteers from Ulster, while agrarian factors are emphasised by those from the west of Ireland. The various detailed accounts of provincial Ireland's failure to rise suggest that the importance of Britain's interception of the German arms ship, the *Aud*, and of Eoin MacNeill's countermanding order has been overestimated. Volunteers and Fenians throughout much of Ireland differed significantly from the Military Council in Dublin when it came to their understanding of the purpose, rationale and potential of the Rising; and the socialist Irish Citizen Army's involvement in the Rising provoked suspicion among Volunteers and the IRB in rural Ireland.

Ultimately, the witness statements will settle few arguments. Individually, they are inconclusive, contradictory and fragmentary. Much of their value lies precisely in demonstrating the difficulty of generalising about the divergent beliefs of the rebels, or imposing a single narrative on the events of the Rising. In this respect, they restore some welcome complexity to the most polarising event in modern Irish history. Those seeking evidence of British malice will find it, but perhaps more striking – because surprising – are the shades of grey: the mutual respect and acts of kindness between British soldiers and Irish rebels, and the painful ambivalence of many Irish-born members of the Crown forces and police. Collectively, the witness statements offer an unmatched insight into the process by which a society was transformed by revolutionary violence. They help us to understand why, against the odds, this generation of young men and women succeeded in changing the course of Irish history, and they stand testament to their idealism and integrity.

NOTES

1. B[ureau of] M[ilitary] H[istory] W[itness] S[tatement] 328 (Gary Holohan).
2. BMH WS 660 (Thomas Leahy).
3. Max Caulfield, *The Easter Rebellion: Dublin 1916* (Colorado, 1995 ed.), p. 48.
4. Augustine Birrell, *Things Past Redress* (London, 1937), p. 217.
5. *Irish Independent*, 20 March 1922.
6. Cited in Jennifer Doyle, Frances Clarke, Eibhlis Connaughton and Orna Somerville, *An Introduction to the Bureau of Military History 1913–1921* (Dublin, 2002), p. 1.
7. BMH WS 724 (Desmond Ryan). In fairness to Ryan, his statement, while clearly the product of literary endeavour, was – like those of many rebels – based on notes that he made while imprisoned after the Rising.
8. BMH WS 488 (Jack Plunkett).
9. BMH WS 129 (Seán O'Shea).
10. BMH WS 724 (Desmond Ryan).
11. Gerard O'Brien, *Irish Governments and the Guardianship of Historical Records, 1922–1972* (Dublin, 2004), p. 142.
12. Patrick Murray, 'Obsessive Historian: Éamon de Valera and the Policing of His Reputation', in *Proceedings of the Royal Irish Academy*, section C, 101:2 (2001), pp. 37–65.
13. O'Brien, *Irish Governments*, p. 142.
14. BMH WS 432 (Pauline Keating).
15. Doyle et al., *Bureau of Military History*, p. 1.
16. BMH WS 469 (Alfred Cope).
17. *Dublin's Fighting Story 1913–1921: Told by the Men Who Made It* (Tralee, 1949). See Eve Morrison, 'The Bureau of Military History and Female Republican Activism, 1913–1921', in Maryann Valiulis (ed.), *Gender and Power in Irish History* (Dublin, 2009).
18. For the Bureau's administrative history and working practices, see O'Brien, *Irish Governments*, pp. 130–53.
19. Cited in Diarmaid Ferriter, '"In such deadly earnest": The Bureau of Military History', *Dublin Review*, 6 (Winter 2001/2).
20. Cited in Doyle et al., *Bureau of Military History*, p. 3. It should be noted that the Bureau's advisory committee was critical of many aspects of the project (O'Brien, *Irish Governments*, pp. 130–53).
21. BMH WS 293 (Áine Heron).

Conventions

Silent minor editorial amendments have been made to the text of witness statements to enhance clarity and consistency: typographical and other obvious errors have been corrected; some abbreviations have been provided in full; capitalisation has been standardised; and – where possible – witnesses are identified by the name by which they were commonly known during the period described in the extract. Female witnesses, for example, are identified by maiden name rather than by any subsequent married name, while some witnesses are identified by their familiar English name rather than by the Gaelic form with which they signed their witness statements. The affiliations provided after witness names are those considered most relevant to the particular extract. Where more than one affiliation is identified, efforts have been made to list older affiliations first. Geographical descriptions refer to the witnesses' place of residence during the period described in the extract rather than to their place of birth. From Chapter 4 onwards, Volunteer affiliation is generally signified only by reference to a particular battalion (in Dublin) or company (outside Dublin). During the period of the Rising, witnesses are generally identified by garrison rather than by unit, while organisational affiliations are listed only for witnesses who were not members of the Irish Volunteers.

The original witness statements can be consulted in the Military Archives (Dublin) and the National Archives of Ireland. I am grateful to the staff of both institutions, particularly Commandant Victor Laing of the Military Archives, for access to the witness statements of the Bureau of Military History. All quotations are reproduced courtesy of the Military Archives.

I

Unknown Depths: Politicisation

Why were a minority of young Irish men and women drawn to separatist movements in the decades before the Easter Rising? How significant were childhood influences such as family background and education? What role did class, religion, locality and other social factors play? How did the experience of growing up under British rule shape an awareness of national identity? The following accounts illustrate the diverse influences cited by Irish revolutionaries to explain their own politicisation.

*

Many revolutionaries emphasised the importance of family influences as a source of radicalisation. Some could attribute specific grievances – real or imagined – to British rule, recalling parents, grandparents or more distant forebears who had been prosecuted, exiled or dispossessed. Conversely, some recalled their parents' opposition to their militancy, and the theme of intergenerational tensions recurs often.

Tomás Ó Cléirigh, Volunteers, Waterford

I had no use for England, as my mother told me that they exiled her great-grandfather from the country. My father was a member of the Fenian Brotherhood and his great-grandfather, O'Brien of Knockavelish, Woodstown, had his land taken from him. My mother always said: 'Don't join the British Army. Let them do their own work.'

Séamus Robinson, Fianna Éireann, Volunteers, IRB, Belfast and Glasgow

There was a national tradition in my family back to the time of both of my grandparents. My paternal grandfather, a Fenian, escaped to France in 1867 . . . I was told that he left the Fenians and then he swore he'd never shave again till Ireland was free – he had a luxurious beard when I saw him last. He was then about 84 years old and I, 4. My parents were ordinary typical Catholic nationalists of their day. Their sympathy was with Parnell but they couldn't take sides against the bishops. They had become convinced that the British Empire was invincible. They had all the arguments against us young people. Then the '98 centenary celebrations set us youngsters agog and enquiring. We wanted to prepare for another fight but we were told not to be foolish. 'It would be lovely if it could be done,' we were told, 'but your grandfathers failed and your great-grandfathers failed, all better men than you could ever hope to be, and besides England has become much stronger and is just as ruthless.' I think it was Joe, my brother, who first pointed out to me that we should be ashamed of our father's generation. They were the first generation of Irishmen who had not struck a blow for Ireland.

My brother always seemed anxious to keep me away from militant activities. He had the idea that I should stay at home to care for the old people, thus relieving him of anxiety and responsibility. I believe Joe himself was prepared for a life of hardship and excitement with a hangman's rope likely at the end. However, I had my own ideas and didn't mention them to Joe. I was always anxious to know how serious the [Fianna] movement was and I learned by trial and error a method to find out. The only way I could get Joe to talk was to throw cold water on their bona fides. Then he told me in so positive, cool, matter-of-fact [a] way that a fight would come off, not only in our time but very shortly, that I believed him. I prepared myself mentally and physically. I trained myself to be supple, not muscle-bound, and I found my strength increasing markedly. I learned to jump my own height – only 5'6", but it was tough going. I learned to sprint with all my clothes on in short bursts of twenty to thirty yards. I learned to shoot. My father had already taught me the theory of shooting and Joe had an air rifle from our Belfast days and I took every opportunity of practice at circus and show grounds and at rifle ranges. I was very proud the first time I hit the ball dancing on the water fountain. I became quite good, judging by what I saw round about me. I discovered with secret delight that the average British Tommy was quite a poor shot. I may have been unfortunate in those I came across. I had gained a confidence that later experience showed was not quite justified.

John Kenny, Volunteers, Dublin

My parents had strong national tendencies, especially my mother, who regarded the English as responsible for the fall of man.

Joseph Gleeson, Sinn Féin and IRB, Liverpool

I was born in Liverpool of Irish parents. My father and my uncle were Fenians. My earliest remembrance is being brought as a small boy to a lecture by O'Donovan Rossa in the Picton Lecture Hall, alongside the Museum and Art Gallery in Liverpool. The lecture was the usual thing about vengeance on England and it made a deep impression on me. I was about 12 or 14 years of age at this time.

Edward O'Neill, IRB, Sinn Féin and Volunteers, Dublin

I had a good Irish home atmosphere, as my mother was an old Co. Wicklow lady and an admirer of the Fenians up to the time of her death. My father's grandfather was a '67 man from Tallaght, but my father himself was always a parliamentarian. It was due to my mother's influence that I joined Sinn Féin and the Irish-Ireland movement.

Seán Boylan, Volunteers, Dunboyne, Co. Meath

My ancestors took a prominent part in the '98 rebellion and also in the Fenian rising. Some of them were transported to Van Diemen's Land. My parents told me this and infused a patriotic spirit into me from my earliest days. My father often said to me that nothing good ever came from England. 'Even the wind', he would say, 'that blows from there is a foul one.' He meant of course the east wind. My uncle took a particular pride in asserting that during his whole life, which was a long one, he never spoke to a policeman. This was the atmosphere in which I was reared.

Patrick Kelly, Volunteers, Dublin

I was born on the 23 February 1891, at 44A Chamber Street, Dublin. My father, James Kelly, came from Gleann-na-Smole, Bohernabreena, Co. Dublin. He was the descendant of the 'Rebel Kellys' of Knockraheen, Roundwood, Co. Wicklow, who are reputed to have fought with Michael Dwyer and General Holt. When I was a small boy my father told me many stories of his father and grandfather, and used to boast that none of his family ever served the British Crown in any capacity.

Máire Fitzpatrick, Cumann na mBan, Enniscorthy, Co. Wexford

I was born in a house in Church Street, Enniscorthy, fourth of a family of six. My father carried on a tailor's business and what a father! When we were kids we used to say of Dad – Ireland first, Ireland last, Ireland over all. Other children had fairy stories; we had history and ballads. We said our prayers in Irish. At that time there was no Irish spoken in Enniscorthy or taught at school, but knowing your prayers in Irish got you a lot of respect from the nuns who taught us . . . Dad was a member of all organisations that helped to free Ireland . . . Dad and Mum saw to it that we six spoke, read and thought all for Ireland. Everything we wore was made in Ireland.

Seán Whelan, Volunteers, Enniscorthy, Co. Wexford

My mother's father, James Tomkins, Tombrick, Ballycarney, was a member of the Fenian Brotherhood, and was waiting, with his Schneider rifle, in 1867 for the call that never came . . . Thanks to my mother's great fund of Irish songs and ballads, I was familiar with Ireland's struggle for independence long before I could read or write.

Eamon Price, Volunteers, Dublin

My parents were staunch nationalists and I remember with pleasure how my father on Sunday around Dublin would lead me to the historic spots and relate the deeds of glory of the past and so the seed was sown. That, however, did not make me a revolutionary. Far from it, I did not believe in physical force as a weapon. The failures of '98, '48 and '67 had impressed themselves too deeply upon my mind to permit me to indulge in such wild dreams, however pleasant, as the overthrow of Britain's might by force.

Michael Hynes, Volunteers, Kinvara, Co. Galway

I was born in Dungora in the parish of Kinvara on 28 August 1896. I went to Northampton National School until I reached the age of 15. Neither the Irish language nor the Irish history was taught in the school. My grandfather was a native Irish speaker. He was prosecuted and fined for having his name in Irish on a common cart. The fine was one penny and it was never paid. My father was a member of the Land League and later of the United Irish League. He was very keen on the Irish language and on Irish history. He often spoke to us about Emmet, Wolfe Tone, Mitchel and other Irish patriots, and always hoped that eventually we would be free from English tyranny. He was very keen on the fight put up by the Boers and watched the progress of their struggles day by day . . . It was through the teaching of my father in my own house that I learned something of the history of Ireland, and my interest was sustained by the national newspapers which he was always purchasing and bringing home to the family.

Many separatists regarded education as a radical influence. Conscious of this, the commissioners of national education initially excluded both Irish history and Gaelic from the curriculum. The subsequent introduction of a choice between Irish or British history, and state funding for Irish lessons outside school hours, failed to placate some nationalists. Other potentially radicalising influences included teachers, a profession often associated with Fenianism, and the Irish Christian Brothers, whose schools inculcated a patriotic Gaelic ethos. An emotive 'faith and fatherland' history was also popularised by poems, ballads, stories and other forms of popular and print culture.

Marie Perolz, Inghinidhe na hÉireann, Cumann na mBan, Dublin

It was the Presentation nuns who made a rebel of me, Sister Bonaventure especially.

Seán Gibbons, Fianna Éireann, Volunteers, Westport, Co. Mayo

In 1912 I came home to Westport from my grandfather's place, where I was reared, and I went to the Christian Brothers' School. The Brothers, of course, in those days were violently patriotic. Brother Toomey, I remember, said one time to a class of us, 'God help poor Ireland if you are the sons she has to depend on when she is in danger!'

John Quilty, Volunteers, Limerick

I naturally imbibed at home a very clear concept of Irish national aspirations, which my father insisted upon instilling into me. At the Christian Brothers, this was further developed, and at the Jesuit College my recollection is that Father Kirwan did a lot to continue the shaping of my national outlook.

Joseph Furlong, IRB and Volunteers, Co. Wexford

My grandfathers on both sides of my family were in the Fenian movement. My father did a period in jail during the Land League days. My mother was a separatist. I went to school with the Christian Brothers in Wexford Town. Brother Collins, who was one of our teachers there, instructed and explained Irish history to us and made us study it. Through him and my parents I grew up a rebel.

Nora Ashe, sister of Volunteers leader Thomas Ashe

He [Thomas Ashe] taught Irish in the Corduff school. He was fond of the language and started branches of the Gaelic League in Skerries and other neighbouring villages. In the school, when children marched out to recreation, he used to get them to march over a Union Jack which he had provided for the purpose.

Denis Madden, Volunteers, Tralee, Co. Kerry

One of my uncles, Denis Murphy, who was a teacher in the city, went out in '67. He had to clear out of the country when that movement fizzled. I remember my people talking about it and especially to the effect that the men were not properly armed. I went to the National School at Ballinlough . . . The teacher, John Dennehy, was a good Irishman. I remember he told us that we should be ashamed if we did not know 'Who Fears to Speak of '98'. It would be about 1896, he told us he would give us lessons in Irish *after* school hours if we stayed on. The British did not allow Irish to be taught during school hours.

Thomas Markey, Christian Brothers schoolboy and Volunteers, Finglas, Co. Dublin

There was nothing in the subjects then taught at school which would develop any pupil's patriotic sense.

Patrick Kelly, Volunteers, Dublin

I was educated at the National Schools in Dublin and was never taught Irish history. When I was about 8 years old I began to take a keen interest in books and stories of Ireland's fight for freedom, and particularly the treatment of the people by the British garrison. I began to hate everything English, but what really made a rebel of me was a book called *Croppies Lie Down*, which dealt with the Yeomen, North Corks and the Pitch Caps. After reading this book I vowed that if ever there was an Irish army I would join it and help beat the British out of Ireland. At 14 I was taking a keen interest in shooting and military training. I spent many hours watching soldiers at drill in some of the city commands and listening to the words of command. I did my shooting practice with a 'Daisy air gun' and considered myself a good shot.

Seán Prendergast, Fianna Éireann, Dublin

Though quite young at the time I possessed not a little knowledge of Irish history, which I had acquired by reading various books and tracts, such as *Speeches from the Dock*, stories of Sarsfield and the Wild Geese, books on the insurrection of '98 and various accounts of '48 and '67 . . . My father too had often related stories of Parnell; he himself was a Parnellite and a member of the Irish National Foresters. These had made deep impressions on me.

Peadar Bracken, Volunteers, Tullamore, King's Co.

It was a study of the history of my country and the stories told to me by the old people that gave me a national outlook.

Thomas Reidy, Volunteers, Kinvara, Co. Galway

I remember in my young days that the old men at social gatherings clasped hands and sang Irish songs together. In the winter time dances were held regularly in our townland. Patriotic songs like 'Michael Dwyer' and 'The Bold Fenian Men' were sung at these gatherings. I heard stories of the Fenians and so became aware of Ireland's struggle for her freedom. In addition, I read all the books on Ireland I could lay my hands on. Amongst the books I read were A. M. Sullivan's *Story of Ireland*, *The Green Cockade* and *The Forge of Clohogue*.

Edmond O'Brien, Volunteers, Galbally, Co. Limerick

From my earliest years I was always a very keen student of Irish history, and the struggles through the ages to shake off the rule of the foreigner made a very deep impression on me. The national ballads of all kinds, and the writings of such men as Thomas Davis, Charles Kickham, Michael Doheny (*The Felon's Track*) and several others, had their effect on a very receptive mind for this type of literature.

Elizabeth Bloxham, Cumann na mBan, Dublin

I was one of the younger members of a large family living in the west of Ireland. Being Protestants, we were, as a matter of course, unionists. I have no recollection of any political discussion in the family; it was just taken for granted that we joined in the singing of 'God Save the King' at the end of our concerts and temperance meetings, just as we took it for granted that the local brass bands played 'God Save Ireland' and 'A Nation Once Again' . . . On looking back, I am inclined to think that a good deal of the unionism in the west is largely due to an invincible ignorance of the history of their country and for that form of ignorance allowance is always made. The poorest and least educated Catholics had their symbols of nationality. At that time you rarely entered a house that had not a picture of Wolfe Tone and Robert Emmet. *Speeches from the Dock*, in its green paper cover, was well thumbed by some member of the family. There was talk of the Land War and of 'old unhappy far-off things and battles long ago' and there was the telling of folk tales. The Protestant mind had no such hinterland.

Séamus Reader, Fianna Éireann, IRB, Volunteers, Glasgow

As long as I can remember from my earliest years I had a good national background. I remember hearing rebel songs such as 'The Wearing of the Green', 'Who Fears to Speak of '98', etc., being sung. In my home and the homes of my boy companions were pictures of Robert Emmet and of the Irish Brigade at Fontenoy.

Many separatists attributed their politicisation to the late-nineteenth-century cultural revival. While an influential elite participated in the literary revival, people from ordinary backgrounds were more influenced by involvement in the Gaelic Athletic Association (founded in 1884) and Gaelic League (1893), which became mass movements. Although most were attracted by their recreational, rather than ideological, appeal, their promotion of Gaelic culture and opposition to 'Anglicisation' created a more assertive sense of national identity. Separatists also described the radicalising influence of political newspapers.

Dorothy Macardle, Cumann na mBan, Dublin

I was awakened to an awareness of Irish nationality, like so many others of my generation, by the poetry of Yeats, especially *Cathleen ní Houlihan*, the Irish legends collected by Standish O'Grady, Lady Gregory and others, the Abbey plays and all the writings of the Celtic Twilight school.

P. S. O'Hegarty, IRB, Cork

Sometime in the early spring of 1902, I was walking along the South Mall, in Cork, on my way to the Free Library, and, as I passed the Assembly Rooms, my eye was caught by a large poster advertising the Munster Feis of the Gaelic League, and sounds of music could be heard faintly in the street. I stopped for a moment debating with myself whether to go in . . . I arrived in at one of the senior competitions, and heard for the first time Irish songs properly sung . . . Something in the songs – though I could understand only a few of the words – something in the music – something in the atmosphere – gripped me, and I seemed to be put into touch with something far back in the race. Unknown depths in me were stirred

. . . I understood, accepted and felt myself to be one with the Gael. For the first time I saw the whole of Ireland.

Gary Holohan, Fianna Éireann, Dublin

It was during the weekends in Bulmer Hobson's cottage that I first read Ethna Carbery's poems. I think they were only published about that time, and I can assure you they did much to fan the fires of patriotism to white heat. From now on my outlook on life was completely changed. The Fianna was no longer a mere pastime or social function. It became a sacred duty, and I started to bend my every effort towards the freeing of Ireland. No task was too great or time too long.

Elizabeth Bloxham, Cumann na mBan, Dublin

Among my friends were two brothers, Martin and John Moran, who were boat-builders . . . One evening I found the brothers pleasurably excited because they had found in a paper a poem which they thought I would like. It was 'Clare Coast' by Emily Lawless. They asked me to read it and beamed with pleasure when they found I was as moved as they were by its poignancy . . . 'We'll give you the poem,' said Martin; 'get the scissors, John, and cut it out.' I demurred at the cutting out. I said I'd take the whole paper and return it safely to them. They looked at each other questioningly and then Martin said, 'I think we'd better cut it out because this is the sort of paper ye wouldn't like in your house.' The paper was Griffith's *United Irishman*, so they were showing delicate consideration for the susceptibilities of our household. I laughingly said I thought we could stand it and took the paper home with me. It was the first copy of the *United Irishman* which I had seen. In a very short time I was writing articles for it, which seems to justify Martin and John's conviction that it was an unsettling paper to let loose in a Protestant household. It would, no doubt, be of interest if I could recall a struggle before accepting the outlook of such a paper. The fact is that I had no such experience. That one's first loyalty is to one's own country seemed to me then, as it does now, to be unquestionable.

Thomas Doyle, IRB centre and Volunteers, Enniscorthy, Co. Wexford

Miley Wilde stopped me. He got talking to me about politics. After a while, he gave me a paper called *Irish Freedom* and told me, if I liked, I could read it. Sometime later I met him again. He asked me what I thought of it. I said: 'If you have any more copies I would be glad to get them.' It was not long until I was approached by Paddy Tobin, senior, to join the Irish Republican Brotherhood; the aims of the organisation were explained to me and what it stood for. I agreed to join, and on the following night I was sworn in as a member by Larry de Lacey. That was the start of my political career.

Min Ryan, Cumann na mBan, Dublin

My family were first attracted to the national movement through my eldest brother – later Father Martin Ryan – who was then in Maynooth College as a student. At that time (1902–6) Maynooth was a leader of young opinion, especially regarding the language, and afterwards regarding Sinn Féin . . . He would come home at holiday time and talk tremendously about the language movement and Sinn Féin. We started to read papers about every single thing that was said by Arthur Griffith in connection with the Sinn Féin movement. Griffith was *the* man at that time. We used to read every paper he was connected with, from cover to cover. That was the origin of our coming into the movement.

Muriel Frances Murphy, Cumann na mBan, Cork

I think reading Sinn Féin and Irish Volunteer newspapers was what enlightened me, and also the wonderful principles and high moral standing and self-sacrifice of all men and women in the nationalist Sinn Féin movement. This contrasted very favourably with the people I had been brought up with . . . I had suffered since the age of 4 from seeing the appalling social conditions, especially among the children. The Irish movement, besides fulfilling my nationalist aspirations, seemed to me at that time to also solve that great wrong. I got to know the MacSwineys and others in the movement about '14 and '15, but I think it was the newspapers more than everything else which converted me to the Irish nationalist movement. I read

[James] Connolly's *Workers' Republic*, Arthur Griffith's *Nationality*, *Scissors and Paste*, *The Spark*, and [Eoin] MacNeill's *Irish Volunteer* every week. I also became immediately interested in the Irish language and got Norma Borthwick's wonderful little [series of] books *Ceachta Beaga Gaedhilge*. It was in Liam Russell's shop in the Grand Parade that I got these papers and books. You met everybody there.

Michael Manning, Sinn Féin and Volunteers, Mullagh, Co. Galway

In the years before 1916, the spark of nationality was kept alive in this area by *Sinn Féin* and later by Seán Mac Diarmada's paper *Irish Freedom*.

Kevin O'Shiel, Sinn Féin, Dublin

My particular set of friends and acquaintances felt ourselves being more and more influenced by Arthur Griffith's famous paper *Nationality*. We read it eagerly, column by column; its sharp hammer-like sentences sinking into our minds and staying there.

Denis Madden, Volunteers, Tralee, Co. Kerry

Reading Griffith's papers was something entirely new too. *Sinn Féin* was a magical voice to us young people. It seemed to bring back, to the more intelligent young people, a call which had been heard long ago. Fermoy was then a stronghold of the British Army, but even here, under the shadow of the military barracks, we were asking questions. The unanswerable one was 'Why have not the Irish people as much right to freedom as the English, or any other people?' The politicians here were fighting verbal battles on the floor of the British House of Commons. They were losing ground. It came to this in the end, that [John] Redmond assured the British parliament that 'separation was unthinkable' and [John] Dillon and others referred to 'our army and our navy'.

The centenary of the 1798 rebellion, two royal visits (in 1900 and 1903) and the Boer War (1899–1902) provided opportunities for a period of extended agitation around the turn of the century.

Joseph O'Connor, Volunteers, Dublin

In 1898 the centenary commemoration of the insurrection of 1798 occupied all our minds and attention. The newspapers and periodicals were literally filled with accounts of the many battles of that time and with poems and songs about that period. On 15 August 1898, a great national commemoration was held in Dublin City at which I attended. The foundation stone for the memorial to Tone and his comrades was laid at the top of Grafton Street . . . In 1897 the Queen of England celebrated her diamond jubilee and the decoration and general conduct of a section of the people was very annoying. Trinity College students protected by the authorities demonstrated very roughly in favour of the jubilee and, of course, against the citizens. This culminated in a fierce riot in College Green. In that one night I saw upwards of 200 people and at least sixteen or twenty police carried out of the street to hospital . . . When the French delegation arrived for the '98 commemoration I was in the party to receive them and when we had reached the outside of a hotel at the corner of Nassau Street and South Frederick Street, the police intervened. We called them 'jubilee butchers' and they beat us up.

Seán Murphy, IRB, Dublin

My first introduction to national affairs was the commemoration of '98, when I was present at the laying of the foundation stone in St Stephen's Green to Wolfe Tone.

Leslie Price, Cumann na mBan, Dublin

My first recollections of nationality came through my mother's keen Parnellism and her and my father's pro-Boerism in the British attack on the Afrikaners. These were strengthened later when she became a member of Sinn Féin. As a young child I remember my eldest brother, Eamon Price, and I were taken to a children's party organised by Miss Maud Gonne at Clonturk Park [on 1 July 1900]. This, I think, was an opposition party to that organised by loyalists of the children of Dublin on the occasion of the visit of some British royalty [Queen Victoria].

Séamus Robinson, Fianna Éireann, Volunteers, IRB, Belfast and Glasgow

. . . the arguments were all on our parents' side, until the Boer War. Heavens! What thrills we got out of that great struggle. Bonfires in the streets on the news of a Boer victory, complete disbelief in Boer reverses! The Irish Boer Brigade! How we wished we were old enough to be with them.

Augustine Ingoldsby, IRB and Cumann na nGaedheal, Dublin

One year during the Boer War, Alice Milligan, who was very enthusiastic, put on a tableau about the Boers showing dead British soldiers in uniforms with Boer soldiers of the Irish Brigade standing over them. On that occasion I fired some blank cartridges from a six-chamber revolver and frightened the life out of all the women, including Alice herself.

P. S. Doyle, Volunteers, Dublin

The policy of physical force had been preached for centuries in Ireland . . . but it was only after the Boer War that militant nationalists created an impression that there was little or no hope of Ireland gaining her freedom unless they armed themselves.

Augustine Ingoldsby, IRB and Cumann na nGaedheal, Dublin

We must not forget it was only a very small majority of the Dublin population kept the nationalist spirit alive. On every occasion, such as the King's visit, all the shopkeepers, merchants, officials of the Corporation etc. were ready to wave the Union Jack. Of course, it was in the interest of their pocket that they did this. Anyone who sold a hat or a pair of shoes to the Castle people put up over their doors, 'Hatters to His Excellency the Lord Lieutenant', 'Shoemakers to the Lord Lieutenant', etc. For that reason great credit is due to [William] Rooney, [Arthur] Griffith and their followers for keeping up the opposition to the shoneenism and Union Jackery of the vast majority of the population. The Bar was particularly rotten in this respect, because any hint of sympathy with nationalism was a certain hindrance to promotion in their profession.

Gerald Byrne, IRB and Volunteers, Dublin

I remember the King's visit to Dublin. The streets were decorated with poles draped in red, white and blue. We went around with bottles of paraffin oil setting the drapings on fire. The people were generally hostile to anyone who displayed any patriotic symptoms.

P. J. Murphy, Volunteers, Cork

The 'Rebel City' of today was not known as such during the early part of this century. It was known throughout the length and breadth of the land as 'Rotten Cork' and 'Khaki Cork' – names which made every honest nationalist in the city blush with shame. There was little or no political activity at the time but displays of loyalty to England were everywhere.

Although separatists almost invariably attributed their radicalisation to exclusively patriotic motives, social and economic factors often played some role. Agrarian tensions remained important, particularly in Connacht, where small farmers scraped a living from inadequate landholdings. Conflict between former tenant farmers and the remnants of the landed class was exacerbated by sectarian tensions. Sectarianism also proved a radicalising force in rural and urban Ulster. While accounts of conflict with the police feature in many statements, surprisingly few revolutionaries cite poverty or class struggle as a politicising influence.

Tom Hales, Volunteers, Ballinadee, Co. Cork

The men of Ballinadee who gave such an inspiring lead to West Cork were animated by the traditional Fenian spirit and doctrine, which had been handed down to us by my father, Robert Hales, and other older men from 1900 onwards. The spirit of the Land League days lived on in the district and it was revived in 1907 when the fight against the local landlords reached peak point. In that year attempted seizures of cattle by the sheriff were an everyday occurrence. The farmers combined and organised to defeat the bailiffs . . . On one occasion two of my father's cows were in Bandon pound, behind locked gates and guarded by twenty RIC men. The sheriff had arrived to proceed with the sale and removal to Cork.

About twenty Ballinadee men, armed with ash plants, in a sudden organised attack, scattered the policemen, broke open the gate and rescued the cattle. The police used their batons freely, but the reliable ash plants, wielded by the powerful Ballinadee men, proved better weapons and soon rendered their hands and arms useless. The cattle were, by a prearranged plan, driven off to a destination from which the sheriff never afterwards recovered them. This was an example of combined organisation and physical courage unequalled in those days. The plan was organised by my brother, Seán Hales, in cooperation with the O'Donoghues, Finns, McCarthys, Collins, etc., all of whom were afterwards the leading men in the Ballinadee [Irish Volunteer] Company.

Patrick Crowley, Volunteers, Gurteen and Tinkers Cross, Co. Cork

My family had been evicted out of our land in 1890 and were out of it for seventeen years. We were hostile to everything British and the police were always watching us. We had a family tradition reaching back to 1798 ... Bandon and its neighbourhood were strongly Protestant and they were very much against the Catholics.

Gilbert Morrissey, IRB, Craughwell, Co. Galway

I think [IRB leader Thomas] Kenny's main concern was to keep the spark of nationality alive in us until the opportunity came. This was not so difficult in Co. Galway because, in a sense, arms were never put away. If the people were not fighting against British forces proper, they were making a fair stand against its henchmen, the tyrant landlord class, their agents and bailiffs, who were backed up and protected by the Royal Irish Constabulary.

Thomas Courtney, IRB and Volunteers, Galway

I also remember a man speaking at Eyre Square, Galway. One or two policemen were always in attendance. On this occasion, the evening of a fair day, he was telling the crowd to buy nothing but Irish goods even if it were only a box of matches. The police method was staring into the faces of the people, who drifted away until there was one man and three boys, including myself, left. I was given to understand afterwards that the speaker was Arthur Griffith, which at the time did not convey much to me. I remember distinctly the RIC sergeant saying to the man who was speaking, 'Why are you staying, there is nobody to listen to you,' and his answer: 'While there is one I won't go.' This was my first clash with the RIC as, when I was told to move, I refused. They spoke to me as I was a telegraph messenger and likely to obey, but I could not do so as my companions remained firm. For this the police tried to get me dismissed.

Thomas Leahy, Irish Citizen Army, Dublin

I was active in the labour movement from 1912 and learned, through it, the way the workers of Ireland were being treated. With wages and working conditions and long hours of employment forced on them by the employers, somewhere and somehow, if these were not changed or improved, revolt against some employers must come. I attended all meetings, lectures and talks by James Connolly, Jim Larkin, P. T. Daly and other labour leaders and well-known leaders in the republican movement.

Patrick Colgan, Volunteers, Maynooth, Co. Kildare

One thing that helped me along the right lines was the fight put up by the Dublin workers in 1913. It was the first time I commenced thinking along physical force lines.

Linda Kearns, Cumann na mBan, Co. Sligo

The first thing that made me interested in national politics was a visit I paid, about 1911 or 1912, as a trained nurse to the typhus hospital in Belmullet. There was an epidemic of that disease in Mayo and I was horrified at the conditions prevailing in the hospital. It was not a hospital at all; it was only an old barn that was converted to this purpose. You could see the sky through the ceiling and walls, and the patients were lying in filth on the floor. It occurred to me that it was time the government that was responsible for that state of affairs should be expelled from the country.

Thomas McNally, Volunteers, Belfast

My parents were country-bred folk who had drifted to the city for a living. The struggle for a reasonably comfortable existence was so acute that there was no time for national discussions. My parents had the usual detestation of the RIC . . . My early impressions of life in the city were influenced by riots, police-baton charges, calling out the military – more charges – the reading of the Riot Act (a most vindictive element of British law); some unfortunates, usually innocent people, shot; Orange processions, Catholic counter-demonstrations with huge bonfires on each side; provocative arches strung across the street from chimney to chimney; AOH – Foresters and election struggles with torchlight processions . . . These then were the conditions under which a great majority of the Belfast youth were reared – an unreasoned hatred of Protestants, a detestation of police and a more or less neutral feeling towards soldiers.

John McCoy, Volunteers, South Armagh

I was born on a farm of about seventy acres in a bowl-shaped valley surrounded with mountains in South Armagh . . . My earliest recollection of my mother was her recounting to me the successes and adventures of her famous forebear, who returned to Ulster to drive the Sassenach out and deal in particular with the undertakers who had murdered his Ulster kith and kin and taken possession of his family lands in the neighbourhood of Tanderagee, Co. Armagh . . . My grandfather, who was alive when I was a small boy, was habitually telling us stories around the kitchen fire on winter nights, of Redmond Count O'Hanlon, [John] Johnston of the Fews, a famous priest-hunter, his own recollections of the 1848 rising and the local activities of the Fenian days . . . I was also told of the attempt made in the last decade of the 1700s to plant the valley covered by our parish with men redundant in other areas further north, which had been exclusively planted during the previous one hundred and fifty years . . . Several prospective planters who came into the valley to view particular holdings were intercepted and killed, while others, who were installed in holdings by force of arms and were being guarded by soldiers, were watched and when opportunity offered they killed and, in some cases, mutilated the new settlers, their wives and families . . . Such methods broke the efforts to plant the area, and in my day the mountain districts stretching from Newry to Crossmaglen near the Monaghan border contained a concentrated area composed of the old Gaelic people unmixed with foreign blood . . . I am giving this history of my childhood days, as its influence must have had unpredictable results and helped to mould my later actions.

2
White Heat: Revolutionary Politics

The decades before the Rising are often considered a period of malaise. Disillusioned by the fall of Parnell, which split the Irish Parliamentary Party at great cost to the cause of Home Rule, a younger generation turned away from conventional politics, devoting its energies to the cultural nationalist revival. In time, the profound changes wrought by this 'long gestation', as W. B. Yeats later described it, would lead to the events of 1916. However, this interpretation owes much to hindsight. In reality, the reunited Irish Party resumed its traditional dominance of nationalist politics in 1900, marginalising its militant rivals. The accounts in this chapter convey the enthusiasm and idealism of separatism during this era, as well as the divisions and failures that characterised the movement at its lowest ebb.

*

Formed in 1858 with the aim of establishing an Irish republic by revolutionary means, the Irish Republican Brotherhood proved the Irish Party's most enduring rival. Although a mass movement during the 1860s, and a powerful force in the 'new departure' of 1879 that preceded the Land War, Fenianism no longer posed a meaningful threat to the Irish Party or British rule by the early twentieth century. It continued to attract small numbers of enthusiastic young men, although some were disillusioned by what they found once they joined.

Denis McCullough, IRB, Belfast

My grandfather and father [Daniel McCullough] were Fenians and my father was later treasurer of the Parnell Leadership Committee, so I was brought up in a nationalist and separatist atmosphere ... About this time [*c.* 1900], as I was approaching 18 years of age, my father suggested that I should join 'the Organisation', meaning the IRB. Accordingly he brought me to the side door of a public house owned by a man named Donnelly – it was afterwards called 'The Republican Bar' on the Falls Road – and I was duly sworn in by a large, obese man, a tailor by trade, named Ibbotson, evidently a good and steady customer of Donnelly's. I was disappointed and shocked by the whole surrounds of this, to me, very important event and by the type of men I found controlling the Organisation; they were mostly effete and many of them addicted to drink. In a year or two, after I had organised one or two new circles of young men to support me, I got most of these older men retired out of the organisation, which had been split up into about three factions by their personal squabbles.

Joe Barrett, IRB, Darragh, Ennis, Co. Clare

I was sworn into the Fenian Brotherhood on 15 August 1908 ... At the time I joined, it was the practice in our part of Clare to invite the eldest son of all the old Fenians to become members of the Brotherhood, and my father was an old Fenian at the time. I was sworn in by Peter McInerney of Lisheen, Ballynacally, Co. Clare, at an unoccupied house at Drumquin. There were fifteen of us, mostly the eldest sons of old Fenians, sworn in on the same night. The fifteen formed the nucleus of a circle which represented three or four parishes.

Ernest Blythe, IRB, Dublin

Shortly afterwards I joined the central branch hurling club and in it became friendly with Seán O'Casey, the future dramatist. After we had known one another for some months, both of us being very bad hurlers and never getting on the team but practising zealously in the Phoenix Park every Saturday and going together to see the matches in which the club team played, Seán began to talk to me about the Fenians. One Saturday evening, coming home on the tram from the Phoenix Park, he said to me that it was a great pity that the Fenian organisation had not survived. I agreed. When we came to the end of Blessington Street he asked me to leave the tram as he wanted to talk to me. We walked up Hardwicke Street and he proceeded to inform me that the Fenian organisation was still alive and was again recruiting young men. He asked me if I would join. Having read something about the Invincibles, I told him that I did not favour assassination and would have nothing to do with an organisation which countenanced it. Seán said that the Fenians were completely against assassination, and that their policy was to prepare to make open war on England. I thereupon told him that I should give him my answer the following week. Within a couple of days, however, I had made up my mind to join. When I told Seán I was willing, he said that, as I was a stranger to Dublin and unknown to the people with authority in the organisation, I should be kept under observation for some months. I discovered afterwards that Seán had spoken to me in a moment of impulse [without having the authority to do so], and that [during] the so-called period of observation . . . he was endeavouring to get [the] authority to speak to me. After a delay of several months Seán finally told me that I might now be sworn in. I met him in O'Connell Street [as Sackville Street was later renamed] and was taken to a house on the western side of Parnell Square. A number of people were going up the stairs. I was introduced to Michael MacAmhlaidh and taken by him into a back room, where he administered the oath to me. Afterwards I went with Seán into the front room while Michael MacAmhlaidh was swearing in some other new recruits. The front room was packed, I should say there were over a hundred people in it. When, at one point in the proceedings, new members were asked to stand up and let themselves be seen by the meeting, four or five of us arose.

Eamon Bulfin, IRB, Dublin

In the summer of 1912, on Wolfe Tone's grave in Bodenstown Churchyard, I was sworn into the IRB by Art O'Connor of Elm Hall, Celbridge.

Liam Walsh, IRB, Co. Waterford

I came of Fenian stock, my grandfather being an old Fenian. My first connection with the national movement was through the

Gaelic Athletic Association and the Gaelic League, which I joined about the year 1909. About the year 1909, I was at a hurling match in Maryborough [now Portlaoise] when I met M. F. Crowe of Limerick, a prominent GAA official at the time. He was an organiser for the Irish Republican Brotherhood and he had a chat with me about joining. I agreed to join so he swore me in there and then, gave me a copy of the oath and told me to start enrolling new members down in the Waterford area.

The cultural revival provided the IRB with potential recruits, a forum for disseminating republican values and a cover for its activities. The IRB nonetheless continued to decline owing to clerical opposition, state repression, infighting, public apathy and the popularity of constitutional nationalism.

Gary Holohan, Fianna Éireann leader and IRB, Dublin

I remember attending a dramatic performance organised by the Dramatic and Choral Society that used the Fianna rooms at 10 Beresford Place. It was held in the Molesworth Hall in Molesworth Street in the winter of 1911. The first play depicted a scene in the Fenian rising of 1867 in Collooney Wood and the shooting of a Fenian leader ... These activities were only a cloak to keep the members of the IRB together.

Christopher Byrne, IRB, Dublin

I joined the Lord Edward Circle ... We met in Parnell Square every month, we called it our 'Sodality'; we would say 'Tonight is our Sodality night.'

Dan Dennehy, IRB, Rathmore, Co. Kerry

For a number of years before the formation of the Volunteers we had been using the Total Abstinence Hall and the Total Abstinence Association in Rathmore to inculcate our ideas by endeavouring to instil patriotism in the members. We had occasional plays ... I was a subscriber to *Sinn Féin* and got the paper regularly, so that the members in the hall were being gradually enlightened.

Albert Cotton, IRB organiser, Sligo

I was only a week in Dublin when I was transferred to Sligo Labour Exchange [in 1912]. When leaving Dublin Seán MacDermott appointed me IRB organiser . . . The first thing I did was to join the Dramatic Society in the Temperance Hall. I thought there would be likely material there, but it was very poor – all shoneens. I objected to the production of any but Irish plays, and I got the backing of Father [Bernard] Crehan, which was very useful. I was the only Protestant among them. Father Crehan had attempted to form a pipers' band . . . I succeeded in getting him a few good young lads. I got in touch with Séamus McGowan, a brother of Paddy McGowan, and with Joseph Neilon and also with a lad named J. Keaveny. He was not brought into the circle at the time, but was ripening fast. These boys brought a few more along and we formed a pipers' band. We also organised a Freedom Club, which was an open organisation. The members of the circle were in it and dominated its activities, but it had some non-IRB members also. A lecture which we arranged for the Manchester Martyrs' Anniversary in 1913 gave a much needed fillip to national feeling in the town . . . With the assistance of Father Crehan I got a branch of the Gaelic League organised in the town, with about forty members.

Thomas Doyle, IRB, Enniscorthy, Co. Wexford

That year [1912] the new members took over club-rooms, had the club repaired and painted, as it was in a bad state. Our first job was to start amusements for all the young members. A dancing class was got going and other games. A dance was run twice a week, and we would have a couple of all-night dances in the year. A good many young fellows were let join the club, but they would not know anything about the IRB. The reason was, when the police would see them all going in, they thought that the club was only a dancing club. The reason we made them members was to cover up our activities.

Francis McQuillan, IRB, Dundalk, Co. Louth

From the time I joined the organisation, we used the GAA functions as a cover for our meetings. In the early days before I joined the IRB I heard that coursing meetings were used generally as a cover for the meetings of our members. All prominent men were encouraged to take an interest in dogs and usually kept one.

Robert Kelly, IRB centre, Newry, and chairman of the GAA County Board, Co. Down

In GAA circles I found some very good lads whom I knew would make good soldiers of Ireland and they did give their best in the fight later, but very few of them would join the IRB. As for labour, it was not very hard to get to be chairman of the local trades council. All that was necessary was to play a straight game with the worker and when you did so – even [if] the worker did not agree with you politically – he would not let you down.

Bulmer Hobson, IRB leader, Belfast and Dublin

The membership of the whole IRB at this time, 1911, was, I think, about 600–700 in Dublin and about 300–400 elsewhere, the total being probably about 1,000 and certainly not more than 1,500.

Diarmuid Lynch, IRB leader, Dublin

In January 1914 Thomas Ashe and myself went on a mission to the United States to raise money for the Gaelic League . . . I stayed on as I had another and a secret mission, viz., that of IRB envoy to the biennial convention of the Clan [na Gael]. In the latter capacity I had no contact with the convention proper, the regular procedure being: first the envoy consulted with the 'RD' (Revolutionary Directory), which then comprised John T. Keating of Chicago, John Devoy and Joseph McGarrity; next day to appear before and confer with the 'Committee on Foreign Relations'. One of my duties was to report on the 'Home Organisation'. On stating its strength to be approximately 2,000, I recollect an outburst of amazement on the part of an American-born member of the committee. He evidently had been under the impression from previous reports that we had a much larger membership – coupled with the feeling that the heads of the Home Organisation were lax in recruiting . . . this particular committee-man – a veteran in the Clan – had no conception of the conditions under which we at this side laboured. He probably had a recollection of a much earlier period when the

Home Organisation included perhaps thousands – the remnant of the very large IRB membership in the early days of the early Land League. Meantime, of course, death had taken toll of that remnant, and the great majority of the survivors had been diverted from their republican allegiance by the overpowering growth of the Home Rule movement under Parnell and his successors.

Bulmer Hobson, IRB leader, Belfast and Dublin

The method of recruiting was as follows. When a member became acquainted with someone who was likely to prove a good member, he was not at liberty to approach him until he had obtained permission. He proposed the name at his circle meeting. The names proposed were taken by the secretary of the circle to a meeting at which all the secretaries of other circles attended. The secretaries exchanged the names and came back and read the list of men proposed in all the other circles at their next circle meeting, so that every name proposed was open to comment in every circle meeting, and any opposition which was not frivolous was sufficient to prevent the matter being proceeded with in any particular case. Only after a prospective candidate's name had survived this scrutiny was permission given to the man who originally proposed him to speak to him on the subject. This made recruiting slow, but it also made it virtually certain that undesirable people did not gain admission into the IRB, and it ensured that the police had not the remotest chance of getting people introduced into the organisation.

Diarmuid Lynch, IRB leader, Dublin

Local [IRB cell] centres and even unattached members were definite focal points from which to do recruiting. But where neither existed the location of a likely prospect was more difficult than the proverbial 'looking for a needle in a haystack' – the needle *was* in the stack but in those days of denationalisation there may not have been in a whole district a single man imbued with republican ideas! Even in cases where one was assured that a certain man was a likely prospect, the official responsible for his induction had not alone to be certain that such 'prospect' entertained the republican viewpoint but that his probity and tact were beyond question. And, often when after tedious investigation a man was deemed fit in every respect, the inquisitor found himself 'up against a stone wall' – that of religious scruples in the matter of numerical progress.

Simon Donnelly, IRB, Dublin

I joined the IRB about April 1914. The meetings of the IRB at that time mainly consisted of recruiting for the organisation . . . At that time the first function of the IRB to my mind was to instruct its members to get control in as many groups and organisations as possible. It was a policy of peaceful penetration in order to wield the widest possible authority in all groups, trade unions being concentrated on, as well as sports and athletic organisations and the Gaelic League.

James Haverty, IRB, Moylough, Co. Galway

Once we were suspected [of IRB membership] the RIC adopted two ways of trying to undermine us. One was to warn our parents that we were embarking on dangerous seas and to ask them to advise us differently, with of course the usual predictions of what was likely to happen to us if we did continue in our bad ways. The other way was to warn the parish priest that we were organising secret societies in the parish.

Diarmuid Lynch, IRB leader, Dublin

The religious ban . . . to my personal knowledge prevented many men from joining. Even some enrolled members occasionally developed uneasiness on that point.

Charles Donnelly, IRB, Dublin

I introduced a very reliable person into the [Fintan Lalor] Circle. Shortly after his initiation [in 1912], the bishops made a pronouncement on secret societies. This man's conscience was troubled and he confided in me. I brought him to Seán MacDermott, who took him aside and, following their talk, the man was released from his oath.

James Cullen, IRB, Enniscorthy, Co. Wexford

About 1912 or 1913, with two or three other delegates from Enniscorthy, I attended an IRB meeting in a house in [41] Parnell Square,

Dublin . . . The meeting was addressed by Reverend Father Sheehy. Some members had been uneasy about the attitude of the Church in connection with the IRB oath and their membership of an oath-bound secret society. The gist of Father Sheehy's talk was that the IRB oath was not contrary to the teachings of the Church. When we returned to Enniscorthy we explained the position to the members and they all appeared to be satisfied.

Dan Corkery, IRB, Macroom, Co. Cork

The IRB organisation in Macroom and the districts adjoining it died out as an active body in the years 1910–12. The main reason was that most of the members were suspended, one by one, for taking part in politics; some on the Redmondite and some on the O'Brienite side.

Patrick Rankin, IRB, Newry, Co. Down

Very little progress was made during these years 1907 to 1913. Our officer's reason was precaution and build[ing] up the IRB either by good men or none, so from my own experience, the slow but sure medium was adopted . . . The people did not seem to care about such things, and there did not seem to be any meetings of these organisations.

Kevin O'Shiel, Sinn Féin, Dublin

Though separatism was, in those days, dead, or nearly dead, nearly every sizeable town possessed a tiny sprinkling of diehard separatists – generally old Fenians or their sons. They were, of course, a very insignificant element in the community, hardly an element at all; but they were respected as idealists, living in a world and an age to which they did not belong.

Thomas Wilson, IRB, Belfast

The majority of the nationalists in Belfast were indifferent, if they were not hostile. All Irish-Ireland movements were, in those years, at a very low ebb. The people working on separatist ideas were small in numbers, and if a person was known to be active, the authorities would detail a detective to watch his movements. Even in those early days I had my special detective watching my movements. Our numbers were so small, it was easy for the police to have a man on each of us.

While awaiting the next revolutionary opportunity, the IRB devoted much of its effort to recruitment, propaganda and often mundane forms of activism. Some Fenians found its activities lacking in purpose during this period. Factionalism and land hunger, rather than insurrectionary republicanism, accounted for its appeal to some. However, the ascendancy of Tom Clarke and a younger generation of activists put in place a more radical leadership on the eve of the Volunteering crisis.

Diarmuid Lynch, IRB Supreme Council, Cork

Supreme Council meetings at that time [1912] were largely devoted to reports on the state of the organisation in the several divisions: on finance, on publications; on such events as the Wolfe Tone and Emmet commemorations; on possibilities for the advancement of the Irish republican doctrine and contrariwise to defeat [of] denationalising schemes.

Luke Kennedy, IRB Supreme Council, Dublin

At meetings of the IRB [Nally Club] circle the usual procedure was – the roll was called by the secretary first; then the chairman (who was the centre) declared the meeting open and the treasurer took the subscriptions. The secretary recorded these as well as the chairman. The usual questions then came up for discussion – arms procurement, and so on. In the case of absentees, the section master had to give an explanation, which was recorded by the chairman. Then any other matters bearing on the work of the organisation were brought up and discussed.

Liam Walsh, IRB, Waterford

We held our meetings at intervals of six months or so in the old Sinn Féin rooms in Colbeck Street, Waterford . . . At these meetings we used to discuss ways and means of contacting Irish-Ireland organisations with a view to swearing in likely candidates, so that when a favourable opportunity arose an armed rising would be started in Ireland.

Joe Barrett, IRB, Darragh, Ennis, Co. Clare

We held meetings about every two months or so, where the ways and means of procuring arms and ammunition were discussed and, so far as we were able, we did our best to acquire what arms we could.

Séamus Connelly, IRB, Co. Clare

The IRB meetings for the North Clare area were generally held in McCormack's Hotel about once every three months. Each member paid a small subscription, *6d.* or *1s.*, I forget which. The principal business transacted at the meeting was to listen to Tomás O'Loughlin's appeals to make ready for the fight against British rule and to endeavour to collect arms wherever the opportunity presented itself.

Donal O'Hannigan, IRB, Dublin

The principal activities at this time were the posting up of anti-enlisting posters and destroying all British recruiting posters, which were usually exhibited outside the RIC barracks. On many occasions all the members of the RIC of Santry and Raheny stations spent several hours nightly trying to catch us in the act of posting up the leaflets, leaving only the orderly in the barracks. They would return to find the windows and doors of the barracks plastered with our literature.

Michael Newell, IRB, Castlegar, Co. Galway

The principal matters discussed at the meetings were the recruiting of new members and land division. At this time [*c.* 1908] there was a great deal of agitation for the division of land. The IRB took a leading part in the agitation and carried out numerous cattle drives, also the breaking down of walls on the farms of landlords and land-grabbers, whose houses were fired into.

Joe Barrett, IRB, Darragh, Ennis, Co. Clare

We took an active part in the local agitation for the acquisition of ranches by the Land Commission [Congested Districts Board] and, in the division of such lands, we tried to ensure that our members would get preference. These large estates had been in the hands of landlords against whom there was a traditional hostility; they were mostly of planter stock and invariably were opposed to every Irish national movement.

Rory Haskin, IRB, Belfast

The policy of the IRB in the early days of my membership was mainly an anti-recruiting effort against the British Army, and the effort to get the proper type of recruits for the IRB. The activities of the IRB after I joined looked to me as rather futile . . . The meetings of the IRB were mainly taken up with discussing ways and means of furthering republican principles in Belfast and the purchase of arms.

Arthur Greene, IRB, Co. Louth

I could see little use in it. We were constantly 'hatching' and nothing came out of our plans. A lot of the IRB were old men and were useless as a physical force body.

Ernest Blythe, IRB organiser, Dublin

The only thing that the IRB did there [rural Ulster] was to keep alive a feeling of dislike and distrust of the Hibernians and of the parliamentary movement, and to cause a few young people to read *Sinn Féin*.

Augustine Ingoldsby, IRB, Dublin

I had not a very high opinion of the IRB and I did not think they were men of ability apart from Tom Clarke and a few of the younger men.

Bulmer Hobson, IRB leader, Belfast and Dublin

In 1911, the IRB in Dublin was practically controlled by three members of the Supreme Council – Jack O'Hanlon, Fred Allan, who was secretary of the Supreme Council, and P. T. Daly, and their influence almost stifled all activities . . . Tom Clarke returned from America to Ireland in 1908, and was co-opted a member of the

Supreme Council sometime after. He always demanded a more active policy and supported the younger men.

Seán McGarry, IRB leader, Dublin

Shortly after his return he was co-opted to the Supreme Council of the IRB, but he was dissatisfied with what he found there. The members were not alive. He felt that the organisation was still in the rut out of which it could not see in 1900 and turned his attention to the younger men in whom he could see a spirit of restlessness and impatience . . .

Denis McCullough, IRB leader, Belfast

It was only after the advent of Tom Clarke into the movement that it really shaped like taking serious action. His reputation enabled the younger men on the Supreme Council, like Seán MacDermott, P. S. O'Hegarty, Diarmuid Lynch and Bulmer Hobson, to move forward with his backing in organising, preaching and teaching the value and necessity of a physical force meeting. It protected them from the usual charges of youthful overenthusiasm and of insincerity. I say with every confidence that Tom Clarke's person and Seán MacDermott's energy and organising ability were the principal factors in creating a group and guiding events to make the Rising possible.

Seán McGarry, IRB leader, Dublin

I had thought [re Tom Clarke] of an old man who was in gaol for Ireland some years before I was born. I was surprised, surprised by his youthful demeanour and the enthusiasm with which he spoke of the future, the eagerness with which he spoke of the work to be done for the Fenian cause. To him the Irish nation was very real. He spoke of fighting for Ireland as casually as he did about any item of the day's news. To fight England was to him the most natural thing in the world for an Irishman. He had wonderful energy, a great power of concentration and a tremendous [capacity] for mastering details and a quick judgement. He made friends rather slowly and had few intimates but his friendship once given was solid and enduring. He was slow to condemn, always ready to hear the other side, and was perhaps rather over-tolerant to his friends. His solitary confinement in prison made him a man of few words, which made people think him abrupt. He had no hankering after the limelight and any prominence was distasteful. He was always content to do the work and get it done; the credit could go anywhere. He had an exquisite sense of humour and entered into a joke with boyish enthusiasm.

Patrick McCartan, IRB leader, Co. Tyrone

In the February 1911 issue of *Irish Freedom* I wrote an editorial stating that resolutions dealing with the proposed visit by the King of England would be submitted to the meeting to be held in the Rotunda to commemorate the birth of Robert Emmet. Sometime later Tom Clarke told me that the Wolfe Tone Memorial Committee decided that there would be no resolutions, as such would be political. Both Tom and I were disgusted . . . The orator on the occasion was Pádraig Pearse and Major MacBride presided . . . In the course of his speech Pearse said, 'Dublin would have to do some great act to atone for the shame of not producing a man to dash his head against a stone wall in an effort to rescue Robert Emmet.' I was thinking of the lost chance of dealing with the coming royal visit and the above sentence gripped me . . . I jumped up on the stage as the band was leaving it and proposed my resolution. I knew I was dashing my head against the stone wall of the discipline of the IRB but Pearse's words were still ringing in my ears. After I read the resolution, Tom Clarke, to my surprise, jumped up on the stage also and seconded it. It, of course, was passed with a whoop . . . My breach of discipline was raised at the next meeting of my circle, and I indiscreetly said it was strange that a member who had misspent some of the organisation's money was immune while I was to be censured for opposing a loyal address to the King of England . . . I was therefore summoned to appear before the Supreme Council and asked where I got my information and I replied from Joe McGarrity, who was a member of the Executive of the Clan na Gael. [Fred] Allan, [Jack] O'Hanlon and some others resigned and with Tom Clarke the young men got control of both the paper and the organisation. A short time afterwards Pádraig Pearse was taken into the organisation.

Seán McGarry, IRB leader, Dublin

... the fight was on for the control of the organisation and the paper. It ended in about three months in complete victory; the old crowd, as they were called, was completely routed.

Bulmer Hobson, IRB leader, Belfast and Dublin

The conflict was the recurring one between an older generation who wished to go slowly and quietly, and the younger generation eager to get things done.

Gary Holohan, Fianna Éireann and IRB, Dublin

At the time I joined there had been a split – that Christmas 1912 – which was very harmless. There had been a kind of a clean-up. While a number of the men had done a good deal of work in their younger days, I think they were inclined to lean on their laurels and use the organisations as a means for getting into the [Dublin] Corporation, as Fred Allan had good influence. However, Tom Clarke, Seán MacDermott and Bulmer Hobson had the reins when I joined, and it was not long until things started to move.

In light of the ineffectiveness of Fenianism during this period, many contemporaries regarded cultural nationalism as a greater challenge to the status quo. The following accounts demonstrate how cultural activism exerted a radicalising influence. However, both the GAA and the Gaelic League described themselves as non-political organisations, and only a small proportion of their members were separatists before 1916.

Áine Ceannt, Gaelic League, Dublin

After the Parnell split, there was no interest taken in politics by the young folk. There were too many divisions. The Gaelic League, where there were no politics spoken, was a Mecca for everyone. The people learned that they had a country with a language; they learned the music, the dancing and the games. They were encouraged to use Irish-manufactured goods, and in the competitions at the Oireachtas of the Gaelic League the competitors would not be awarded a prize unless they could guarantee that they were dressed in Irish materials.

Frank Drohan, Gaelic League and IRB, Clonmel, Co. Tipperary

We had all kinds in the Gaelic League at that time, all kinds of political shades, but all of them were enthusiastic learners of the language. We started to organise historical debates, taking phases and incidents of Irish history for discussion, and thus encouraged the study of Irish history.

Maeve Cavanagh, Gaelic League, Dublin

At this time I was in Derry. I was in the Gaelic League there too. I thought that branch snobbish, as some of the members did not take kindly to the idea of factory girls coming in as members, so we founded another branch, at the second meeting of which I read a paper. A reporter off the *Derry People* asked me for permission to publish it in his paper. He gave it a great splash although I thought it immature. As it was an attack on parliamentarianism it struck a new note up there . . .

Patrick Higgins, Gaelic League, Cork

James Connolly came to Cork and was given the Dún for a lecture. The priests who were in the Gaelic League objected strongly to this action by the League. Connolly . . . was talking straight socialism at the time. The priests objected to socialism, but Connolly got the hall. One result of this action was that the priests tried to get control of the Gaelic League, but the result of their effort was that they were thrown out. Even the mildest Gaelic Leaguers would not have it.

Thomas Harris, IRB and Volunteers, Prosperous, Co. Kildare

About 1913 we had an Irish teacher named Seán O'Connor . . . He began by bringing *Irish Freedom* and other national papers to his classes. We would read these papers in the classroom and discuss the political situation of the time. In this way we became more absorbed in political discussion than in our pursuit of the language.

James Ryan, Gaelic League, Clonmel, Co. Tipperary

About the year 1914 a small number of young men, all members of the Gaelic League, used to meet in a room in the Temperance Hall,

Irishtown, Clonmel. Here, under our leader, Frank Drohan, we studied the language, history and music of our country. We organised feiseanna, céilidhí, and learned all the Irish dances. About this time the RIC were getting suspicious of our meetings and kept a close eye on all our members. A few of our members were summoned for collecting money for the League, others for giving their names in Irish to [the] RIC sergeant.

Cornelius Murphy, Volunteers and IRB, Cork

The members of these bodies were not, generally speaking, revolutionaries. 90 per cent of the GAA was just GAA, the other 10 per cent was good . . . With the exception of the O'Growney branch, the Gaelic League branches in Cork were interested in the revival of the language and nothing more.

Patrick Higgins, Volunteers, Cork

Between 1900 and 1913 the Gaelic League was an active and growing organisation, which had numerous branches in the city. It was a body that anyone could go into, and people with only the mildest interest in national affairs did come into it. There were a number of small organisations with limited membership and slight resources, such as the Young Ireland Society, the Celtic Literary Society, Inghinidhe na hÉireann, the Industrial Development Association, Sinn Féin, the Fianna, and the AOH [Ancient Order of Hibernians] American alliance. Somewhere in these organisations, in the Gaelic League and, to a lesser extent, in the GAA, and often in more than one or two of them, a small group was active and forward in every activity . . . They were particularly strong in the O'Growney branch of the Gaelic League.

Joe Good, Volunteers, London

I attended Gaelic League classes at a branch which had its headquarters in Maiden Lane. The Gaelic League in London impressed me as being a purely cultural organisation, with no pretence whatsoever to the application of physical force as a means of obtaining freedom in Ireland.

An important consequence of the cultural nationalist revival was the politicisation of its ideals by a host of radical organisations that emerged during the early twentieth century. Women played a relatively prominent role within this milieu, as is evidenced by the formation of Inghinidhe na hÉireann.

Helena Molony, Inghinidhe na hÉireann, Dublin

The Inghinidhe had come into being in the year 1900, at the time of the last royal visit of Queen Victoria . . . as a counterblast to the orgy of flunkeyism which was displayed on that occasion, including the exploitation of the school children – to provide demonstrations of 'loyalty' on behalf of the Irish natives . . . The Inghinidhe grew out of that, and formed itself into a permanent society of Irishwomen pledged to fight for the complete separation of Ireland from England, and the re-establishment of her ancient culture. The means decided upon for the achievement of this object was the formation of evening classes for children, for Irish language, Irish history – social as well as political – the restoration of Irish customs to everyday life, Irish games, dancing and music. The chief work of the society was the teaching of children's classes in the above subjects. The children were mostly recruited from the poorer quarters of the city, where, at that time, the British Army got its most valuable recruits.

Maire O'Brolchain, Inghinidhe na hÉireann, Dublin

I was in the Celtic Literary Society from 1896. They did not admit ladies as members, but they had certain functions such as Irish classes and special literary meetings that ladies were allowed to attend . . . Then Maud Gonne suggested that we form a society – that was agreed upon – and the name [Inghinidhe na hÉireann] – and we took the same objects as the Celtic Literary Society – fostering of Irish language, literature, music, history and industries – adding 'among the young'. William Rooney, acting editor of the *United Irishman*, was in the outer room . . . Maud Gonne proposed that we give effect to his suggestion in the *United Irishman* that a treat be given to the patriotic children who had refused to attend at the treat given when Queen Victoria had visited Ireland seeking recruits for [the] South African war . . . 30,000 children marched [on 1 July 1900], according to press reports. Children's classes were held in 32 Lower Abbey Street and at other centres through the city – one in a hayloft was a great success. Monthly literary meetings for members and their friends – papers on famous Irishwomen were read and discussed over tea . . . Perhaps the whole youth movement of this century began with the Patriotic Children's Treat.

Maud Gonne MacBride, Inghinidhe na hÉireann, Dublin

Disrespectfully and affectionately our friends often called Inghinidhe 'the Ninnies', and the Ninnies would have been indignant had they been told they were not to do national work because they might be arrested.

Maire O'Brolchain, Inghinidhe na hÉireann, Dublin

The Inghini was unique amongst women's associations in that it took no interest whatever in women's rights or suffrage – just did what was most urgent for Ireland.

Margaret Keogh, Inghinidhe na hÉireann, Dublin

We used to go into the public houses with our anti-recruiting leaflets and had things thrown at us and very vile language sometimes. We tried to get the soldiers off the streets. We did not succeed fully in this. We got them, however, confined to certain areas. They could only walk on one side of O'Connell Street. Our main object was to save the young Irish girls from falling into their hands. A decent girl could not walk down the Post Office side without being molested. Then such girls got the name of a 'soldier's totty'.

Helena Molony, Inghinidhe na hÉireann, Dublin

[The leaflets] were in all cases addressed to Irish girls appealing to them not to consort with the armed and uniformed enemies of their country, telling them that we were at war with England, and that all our political and social ills were due to her occupation of our country. It is difficult for people today to realise the atmosphere of our capital city in the early years of this century . . . many thousands of innocent young country girls, up in Dublin, in domestic service mostly, were dazzled by these handsome and brilliant uniforms, with polite young men with English accents inside them – and dazzled often with disastrous results to themselves . . . These young girls had not the faintest idea of the moral, social or political implications of their associations with the 'red coats'. Of course the publication and distribution of these bills was illegal . . . and soldiers at that time had the habit of taking off their belts and attacking civilians with them if they thought there was any hostility to them.

Helena Molony, Inghinidhe na hÉireann, Dublin

In the year 1907 we decided to start a woman's journal. I think that we Irishwomen, in common with the women of the rest of the civilised world, felt that the time had come when the point of view of women on the many aspects of social and national life had to be expressed definitely. But we had another reason for wishing to do this. Arthur Griffith had founded Sinn Féin, based on the entirely new idea of achieving freedom by passive resistance – a policy of extreme non-cooperation, and obstruction of foreign governments. It gradually captured the imagination of the country, and certainly overshadowed the old physical force party, as Sinn Féin was definitely and explicitly against physical force. Thousands of young Irishmen profoundly disagreed with this policy, or rather with the repudiation of any idea of physical force. Of course Inghinidhe na hÉireann emphatically disagreed. While we encouraged and carried out the Sinn Féin policy as far as supporting everything Irish – language, games, manufactures etc. – and sabotaging and obstructing British government wherever opportunity offered, we could not see any virtue in joining a mere repeal movement, for the original object of Sinn Féin was to restore the Irish parliament of 1782. We considered that the ideals of Tone, Davis, Mitchel and Fintan Lalor were being pushed into the background. We thought that Sinn Féin was a movement to attract the 'moderate' nationalists, and the anglicised or more peace-loving section of our people . . . it was an odd kind of woman's paper. It was a mixture of guns and chiffon. The national position and international politics were front-page news. But we also had fashion notes (written in the interest of Irish-manufactured fabrics), gardening notes, written by Countess Markievicz, and a children's corner, with a serial fairy story, anti-recruiting articles (some from Arthur Griffith) and good original poems from Pearse ... It was a funny hotch-potch of blood and thunder, high thinking and home-made bread ...

It is a curious thing that many men seem to be unable to believe that any woman can embrace an ideal – accept it intellectually, feel it as a profound emotion, and then calmly decide to make a vocation of working for its realisation. They give themselves endless pains to prove that every serious thing a woman does (outside nursing babies or washing pots) is the result of being in love with some man, or disappointed in love of some man, or looking for excitement, or limelight, or indulging their vanity ... We were writing about labour conditions – women's labour in particular – years before Larkin came to Ireland ...

Fusing Irish-Ireland and advanced nationalist ideals, new organisations such as Cumann na nGaedheal and its rivals – Arthur Griffith's National Council and the IRB-backed Dungannon Clubs – emerged to revive militant politics in early-twentieth-century Ireland. Their small support base remained divided by ideological disputes, but, despite tensions between admirers of Griffith's 'dual monarchy' policy and republican separatists such as Bulmer Hobson, the three organisations gradually merged to form Sinn Féin in 1907.

Maud Gonne MacBride, Inghinidhe na hÉireann and Cumann na nGaedheal, Dublin

We had lost faith in a secret society for freeing Ireland, but we felt an open revolutionary movement could create an atmosphere out of which armed revolution could develop. Cumann [na nGaedheal] was the society from which the Sinn Féin movement developed ... We started at once to appeal to Young Ireland Societies, who needed some central direction to galvanise them into activity, and all the numerous '98 Clubs, who, after the centenary of '98 was passed, had little to occupy them. In fact, we accepted the affiliation of any club or society, literary, dramatic, social, athletic, whose members accepted the ideal of complete national independence and who agreed to send delegates to annual conventions which at first were to be held in Dublin . . .

Augustine Ingoldsby, Cumann na nGaedheal and IRB, Dublin

Our little society [Cumann na nGaedheal] organised concerts with the express purpose of . . . making the people familiar with decent national songs and music. After one such concert in Clontarf we presented a tableau showing specimens of Irish manufacture and the event was a great success . . . At the time you could hardly get any articles of Irish manufacture in the shops and the general opinion was that Irish-manufactured goods could not be as good as English. On St Patrick's Day we had what we called an Irish-language procession and we induced all the Dublin manufacturers of goods to take part in it. Every firm sent their vans decorated showily and displaying their goods. It was our organisation that induced the publicans to close their pubs on that day. Seán O'Casey and myself visited the publicans on the north side. Many of them favoured the idea and said, 'God bless the work.' Others objected naturally because it would hit their pockets and said why should the hotels get the benefit of the money that would circulate on that day? All the assistants were on our side and we succeeded in having the pubs closed . . . In the Irish-Ireland movement there was a sort of honour among the fellows. We advocated general good conduct, respect for women, etc., and I never saw the sign of drink on anyone at any of our céilidhes . . . There is no question that this campaign, conducted by the Gaelic League, Cumann na nGaedheal, sowed the seeds of the republican struggles that led to the Rising and the subsequent struggle for independence, though most of us did not realise the fight was so near.

Bulmer Hobson, IRB leader, Belfast and Dublin

I first heard Griffith expound his policy at the annual convention of Cumann na nGaedheal on 30 October 1904. Griffith, however, was dissatisfied with the inactivity of Cumann na nGaedheal and founded a new body, called the National Council, to push his new policy. Dissatisfied with the lack of activity of both groups in Dublin, Denis McCullough and I started the Dungannon Club in Belfast in March 1905. We were at a loss what to call the new organisation, and the name Dungannon Club was reminiscent of the Irish Volunteer movement in 1782 . . . It consisted of thirty or forty young men at a white heat of enthusiasm. They undertook anti-recruiting activities on a large scale, and, as it was easier to print illegal literature in Belfast than in other parts of Ireland, we printed anti-enlistment leaflets wholesale, and retailed them at so much a thousand to people all over the country. The club published postcards and pamphlets, and in 1906 I founded and edited a weekly paper called *The Republic.*

Bulmer Hobson, IRB leader, Belfast and Dublin

In the Dungannon Clubs we advocated the policy of abstention from the British parliament, on the same lines as Griffith in Dublin. We were violently attacked by Tom Kettle and other parliamentarians, who accused Griffith of falsifying Hungarian history. I was much too busy to find out whether Griffith's account was entirely accurate or not, but I declared at public meetings that the issue was not one of accuracy or inaccuracy about Hungarian history, but whether the policy of abstention was the right one for the Irish people to pursue. Griffith was very indignant at my taking this line.

Patrick McCartan, IRB leader, Co. Tyrone

Griffith was never hostile to a republic nor republicanism, but a republic did not appeal to the masses, as they considered its attainment impossible. Hence Griffith in Sinn Féin demanded repeal of the union and took his stand on the Renunciation Act. He believed this policy would appeal more to the people as an alternative to parliamentarianism. Though the Dungannon Clubs openly preached republicanism I was associated with both. The immediate aim of both was to withdraw the MPs from Westminster and meet in Dublin. Outside the IRB there were few republicans and Griffith knew it and so did we. We were mere propagandists and we realised it.

Bulmer Hobson, IRB leader, Belfast and Dublin

Griffith was an excellent propagandist, but was extremely dogmatic and I found him difficult to work with. He did not appear to want cooperation but obedience.

Denis McCullough, IRB leader, Belfast

The fact is that [Bulmer] Hobson was a very headstrong and somewhat egotistical person, and being much younger than Griffith, the latter naturally resented Hobson's endeavouring to force his or our opinion on Griffith and his friends.

Bulmer Hobson, IRB leader, Belfast and Dublin

Our friends in America felt strongly that it was absurd to have three small organisations in Ireland all advocating the Sinn Féin policy, and, as I agreed with them, I endeavoured on my return to arrange for an amalgamation. We arranged a meeting in Dundalk in the autumn of 1907 . . . Cumann na nGaedheal were quite ready to join in an amalgamation, but [Arthur] Griffith and [Walter] Cole would not agree on any conditions. As a result, the Cumann na nGaedheal and the Dungannon Club amalgamated and became the Sinn Féin League, and in the following year we out-voted Griffith in the National Council and the resultant union of the three organisations became known as Sinn Féin. As far as I recollect, the membership of the different organisations overlapped a great deal.

Helena Molony, Inghinidhe na hÉireann, Dublin

The social ideals of Sinn Féin did not appeal to us. They wished to see Irish society (as their official organ once expressed it) 'a progressive and enlightened aristocracy, a prosperous middle class, and a happy and contented working-class'. It all sounded dull, and a little bit vulgar to us, and certainly a big comedown from the Gaelic Ireland of Maedhbh, Cuchulain and the Red Branch Knights, which was the sort of society we wished to revive. Well, we did not quarrel, and Arthur Griffith made the unique and paradoxical achievement of compelling tens of thousands of people, who disagreed with his object, to carry out his policy with the greatest enthusiasm.

Although it did contest elections, Sinn Féin focused more on propaganda and agitation than conventional politics. The extent to which many ordinary members were preoccupied with cultural and moral concerns is striking. Despite some initial progress, the party fell into decline after 1908.

Peter Kieran, Sinn Féin and Volunteers, Dundalk, Co. Louth

The start of Sinn Féin in Dundalk was in the year 1906 . . . The principal activities of Sinn Féin in Dundalk were producing dramas such as *Robert Emmet*, etc.

Edward O'Neill, Inchicore Sinn Féin branch, Dublin

We learned the Irish language, did Irish dancing and singing, and produced several Irish dramas. Meetings were held at regular intervals.

Robert Kelly, IRB centre, Newry, and chairman of GAA County Board, Co. Down

From the time Sinn Féin got going it drove foreign dancing completely out of Newry and district.

Sidney Gifford, Cumann na mBan, Dublin

It became almost evidence of your political opinions to be seen wearing Irish tweed garments. The tweed deerstalker hat became almost the badge of the true Sinn Féin man and to appear at any function in the regulation evening suit was to arouse lively suspicions of your political opinions. I remember, for instance, the first time O'Rahilly lectured for Sinn Féin at some hall in Upper O'Connell Street he arrived in full evening dress, as was the custom in America, and there was a gasp of horror from the audience.

Nancy Wyse Power, Cumann na mBan leader, Dublin

A great deal of its activity in the early days was devoted to raising the standard of local administration, and municipal elections were regarded as issues of major political importance. In Dublin the standard-bearers of Sinn Féin were Tom Kelly, Seán T. O'Kelly and Walter Cole. When a man was prosecuted for having his name in Irish on a cart, the Dublin Corporation put Irish inscriptions on all their vehicles . . . In such minor ways the Sinn Féiners fought every step of the road in an effort to combat the national apathy which was almost universal after the Liberal Party had come to power in England in 1906 . . .

Practically everyone was benefiting in one way or another [from the Irish Party's access to Castle patronage], and there was almost universal resentment of the Sinn Féin policy, which was that no Irishman should serve an alien government in any capacity. Accordingly, the Sinn Féiners were always in the minority on local councils and had usually a hard fight to be elected at all. Many enlightened persons who approved of the constructive side of the movement, industrial development, etc., were unable to support its political side, above all the suggestion that the Irish representatives should withdraw from Westminster. At a time when, for the first time in history, patronage had passed to the hands of Irishmen! The term 'Sinn Féiner' in those days was almost as opprobrious as the word 'communist' is today.

Min Ryan, Cumann na mBan, Dublin

It was purely a small intellectual crowd who were interested in these new ideas – particularly priests. It was a new movement, with very little following. The bulk of the people were satisfied with the Irish Parliamentary Party and with their efforts to get Home Rule. If you talked about Sinn Féin and tried to bring up a new idea, people looked on you as being a bit queer, with 'notions'.

John McCoy, South Armagh

When Sinn Féin started in South Armagh about this time I read their periodicals and books such as Griffith's *The Resurrection of Hungary* and Connolly's *Labour in Irish History*. The active propagandists for Sinn Féin were few in number. In fact I do not think there was one person in our parish trying to propagate the new movement. In the towns of Dundalk and Newry there might be to my knowledge about a dozen in each trying hard to make an impression on the lukewarm supporters of the parliamentarians. The Gaelic League at this time was very active and had classes organised in almost every parish, and their influence had much more effect than the strange new departure which Sinn Féin advocated. It did not appear to me then that anything could be achieved worthwhile by starting a policy of passive resistance as Sinn Féin advocated.

Patrick McHugh, Sinn Féin, Dundalk, Co. Louth

At 16 years of age [*c.* 1909] I became a member of Sinn Féin ... The membership of Sinn Féin [in Dundalk] was indeed very small, not numbering more than twenty. Its members were looked upon as cranks and dreamers, whose ideals were hopeless and impossible of fulfilment. Although not a military organisation it acted as an outlet for the feelings of those who favoured force as a means towards the end and covered their thoughts.

Patrick McCartan, IRB leader, Co. Tyrone

It was the failure of the North Leitrim election in 1907 [*recte* 1908], where Cha[rle]s J. Dolan of Manorhamilton resigned from the House of Commons and contested his seat as a Sinn Féin candidate, that was partly responsible for the collapse of the National Council to my mind. The failure of the *Sinn Féin* daily also contributed.

Bulmer Hobson, IRB leader, Belfast and Dublin

In the following two years [1908–10] we were busy with meetings in the various parts of the country, forming new branches of the Sinn Féin organisation, and had endless committee meetings which went on night after night, but a good many of us were very dissatisfied with the progress we were making, and we felt that many of the committees in Dublin were far more interested in winning a few seats in the Dublin Corporation than they were in getting the country organised. In 1910, feeling that these endless Dublin committees were becoming more and more futile, a number of us, including [P. S.] O'Hegarty, [Denis] McCullough and myself, decided to quietly drop out of the Sinn Féin organisation, and, as we could not run it with [Arthur] Griffith, we thought he had better try and run it alone. When we left there were about 135 branches in the country, in the following year there were six, and a year later there was one.

3
An Army of Boys: Na Fianna Éireann

Formed in opposition to Baden-Powell's new scouting movement, Na Fianna Éireann promoted similar values of militarism and manliness but in a republican, rather than imperial, context. Aiming 'to train the boys of Ireland to fight Ireland's battle when they are men', the organisation provided a bridge between the separatist revival of the early twentieth century and the later Volunteer movement.

*

Fianna Éireann was founded in 1909 by Countess Constance Markievicz, a member of the landed Protestant Gore-Booth family, and Bulmer Hobson, an Ulster-born Fenian and cultural nationalist from a Quaker family background. Combining Irish-Ireland and militarist influences within an explicitly republican framework, Fianna Éireann anticipated the ideological trajectory of Irish separatism.

Joseph Lawless, Fianna Éireann, Dublin

The first excuse for the formation of an Irish semi-military organisation was provided by Sir Robert Baden-Powell, in his Boy Scout movement, which the English element in Dublin sought to establish there. The counter-movement, Na Fianna Éireann, brought together all the boys of nationally minded parents to form sluaighte in the city wards.

Eamon Martin, Fianna Éireann, Dublin

I had left school for about two years, in 1909, but I had continued to pay a weekly visit to the home of my former schoolmaster. It was he, Mr William O'Neill of St Andrew's National School, Brunswick

Street, who informed me of a new organisation which was about to be launched. He told me he had been approached by Countess Markievicz, who had asked him to recommend the organisation to his pupils and explain that it was to be national in outlook and purpose. He told me that he had been very much impressed by the Countess – who was an Irish lady – and he thought I should go along and find out more about the organisation for myself. Accordingly, I went to the meeting which was held in what I learned later was a small theatrical hall at 34 Lower Camden Street. At the time we were attending the Gaelic League together and were also members of the same hurling club. As the meeting had been advertised in the columns of *An Claidheamh Soluis*, there was a fairly large attendance, I would say about one hundred boys.

Michael Lonergan, Fianna Éireann, Dublin

I attended that first organisation meeting of the Fianna, being then about 15 years of age. There were fifty or sixty boys present, mostly adventurers from the Coombe and neighbourhood.

Eamon Martin, Fianna Éireann, Dublin

The chair was taken by Bulmer Hobson, who opened the meeting and explained the purpose of the organisation. It was to be national in character and having for its ultimate objective the complete independence of Ireland. It would be organised on a semi-military basis following the pattern of the Baden-Powell scouts, which had been founded the year before, and one of the immediate aims would be to counteract the influence of this pro-British body. Madame Markievicz also spoke – in a patriotic strain – and she laid particular stress on the point that the organisation would be governed by the boys themselves, who would elect the Executive Council at a general meeting. The name by which the organisation was to be known, 'Na Fianna Éireann', was proposed and adopted. This, as is known, was the name of the army of ancient Ireland, commanded by Finn MacCumhaill and it had been chosen by Hobson for a somewhat similar association which he had organised seven years before in Belfast but which had not survived. The meeting then proceeded to elect the Executive Council. Bulmer Hobson was elected president; Madame, vice-president, and Pádraic Ó Riain, honorary general secretary. A few weeks later Hobson had to go to Belfast, where he lived for almost a year – with only occasional visits to Dublin – and Madame was elected president in his place.

Helena Molony, Inghinidhe na hÉireann, Dublin

I was more or less political mentor to the Countess at that time. She was groping at first. She read, and read, and read . . . it seemed the right thing, to her direct mind, to begin founding an army of boys, who would grow up to know what they were fighting for.

Seán Prendergast, Fianna Éireann, Dublin

Madame was in our minds a truly strange lady. Some of us might think she was forward – even her smoking in our presence often shocked some who themselves thought no lady should smoke, at least not in public. Sometimes some of the boys were not even pleased at her wearing our uniform tunics. She generally walked beside us and not in the ranks. Yet withal she was a truly unique, distinctive personality, full of energy, talented, brimming over with enthusiasm for the Fianna idea.

Helena Molony, Inghinidhe na hÉireann, Dublin

They were all young children. It meant getting their parents' consent and confidence about letting them out for the weekend. Madame Markievicz did it. No one else could. No mother would let her 10-year-old child out like that, unless she was sure that good care would be taken of him . . . Madame Markievicz did not start anything for girls. She did not like girls and there were, of course, those classes in the Inghinidhe for them. You would see a group of boys and girls, who were living in the same laneway; the girls would come out and pull the boys' hair, and that sort of thing; the boys would get sort of shy. Madame used to say: 'They always confuse me – those dreadful girls.' She never liked them.

Molly Reynolds, Cumann na mBan, Dublin

When my three brothers were old enough they joined Na Fianna Éireann and among their other activities learned first-aid and fencing, which they practised at home. Watching them, I often wished there was a similar organisation for girls. One day early in 1913, I asked Mr Bulmer Hobson, who was, I believe, one of the founders of the Fianna, if they would start a girls' section in the Fianna and he replied that if I started it, they would give me all the assistance I needed. I had neither the self-confidence nor initiative to do this and so the matter was dropped.

Liam Brady, Fianna Éireann, Derry City

The desire for drilling and marching got into my blood, and, without knowing the reason why, I kept looking for somewhere I could drill, drill, drill. At school a chum of mine told me that drilling was taught at a Sunday School held by the Irish Christian Brothers, so I went at three o'clock each Sunday to attend these classes. A man named Séamus Kavanagh was our drill instructor and Paddy Hegarty would give lectures on Ireland's glorious past. He told us of Finn McCoole and the daring exploits of the Fianna; of the coming of the English and their destruction of our Irish industries, and the methods they had been using for almost 750 years to destroy our Irish language and culture. He also told us that the spirit of the Fianna of old was alive today in Fianna na hÉireann (Boy Scouts of Ireland). At last, I thought to myself, this is what I have been dreaming about.

Séamus Reader, Fianna Éireann, Glasgow

In Glasgow there were a number of Boy Scout troops and patrols, also the Clarion Scouts. I joined the 7th Group and later transferred to the 56th Group of the Baden-Powell Scouts and eventually was promoted patrol leader . . . In 1911 my young brother came to me and told me he had joined a scouts' organisation better than I had joined, and he said they had swords. It was Na Fianna Éireann. These scouts met in Anne Street. At first my brother did not know much about them, but after a few weeks he told me what they were doing. He also told me about their uniforms and soon I went down to the Fianna.

Roger McCorley, Fianna Éireann, Belfast

The tradition of my family leaned rather towards armed insurrection, and I had been taught some day when I grew up I would have the honour of 'striking a blow for Ireland'. It was natural, therefore, that I should join the Fianna.

Felix O'Doherty, Fianna Éireann, Blarney, Co. Cork

Early in the summer of 1911 I was attracted by an advertisement in the Cork *Evening Echo*. It was to the effect that anyone who desired to form a branch (sluagh) of Na Fianna Éireann, Irish National Boy Scouts, could get all particulars if they called at An Dún, 19 Queen Street, Cork, on any Monday, Wednesday or Friday, between 8 p.m. and 9 p.m. Many of us boys had often discussed amongst ourselves the Boy Scout movement. However, the troops of scouts that, from time to time, camped near our village, Blarney, did not appeal to us. There was something about the khaki shirt and hat that bore close resemblance to the army of occupation. We knew, also, that the founder of these khaki-clad scouts, Sir Robert Baden-Powell, had fought against the Boers in the South African War. Now, here at last was something that would appeal to an Irish boy, here was the opportunity he had been waiting for.

Seán Prendergast, Fianna Éireann, Dublin

The personnel of our sluaigh consisted of mainly working-class boys, many of them apprentices to various trades, carpentry, plumbing, electrical, painting, printing, etc. Our captain, Mick Lonergan, seemed to be the best placed of the lot, and apparently living comfortably.

Felix O'Doherty, Fianna Éireann, Blarney, Co. Cork

The uniform consisted of a green hat, with thin strap, bound with very thin brown leather and turned up at the left side; green tunic shirt and dark blue shorts. Equipment: leather belt, haversack, water-bottle with sling, mess-tin, knife and fork, whistle. Training: Irish history and Irish language and the support of home manufacture; scouting; signalling; squad, section and company drill; first-aid; physical drill; marching; topography; map reading, etc. The badge was designed thus – a sunburst through which was a croppy pike surrounded with the inscription in Irish 'Remember Limerick and the treachery of the English'. On joining, each boy made and signed a declaration 'To work for the independence of Ireland, never to join any of England's armed forces and to obey my superior officers'.

Seán Kennedy, Fianna Éireann and Dublin Guards, Dublin

At this time [1912] a dispute arose in the Fianna higher councils regarding the manufacture of the Fianna uniform. While some of the garments were made in Ireland by Irish craftsmen and, as far as possible, of Irish material, the hats which we wore were made in and imported from England. This gave rise to a good deal of dissatisfaction. As a result a large number of us broke away, formed and joined the unit known as the Dublin Guards . . . we had a special hat made of Irish tweed designed and manufactured for us. As the material was soft, an attempt was made to stiffen it by several rows of stitching, but we found that, after a few showers of rain, it shrunk to unwearable size and lost its shape.

Séamus Kavanagh, Fianna Éireann, Dublin

There was a bookshop, owned by a firm called Ponsonby's, in Grafton Street where British Army manuals of every description could be purchased. I spent most of my spare cash and time buying and studying these books. We were encouraged to do this by our officers.

Helena Molony, Inghinidhe na hÉireann, Dublin

We made use of Baden-Powell's scout book for training them . . . The boys loved playing at soldiers.

Eamon Martin, Fianna Éireann, Dublin

We then secured the voluntary service of Kavanagh, who, I believe, was ex-British Army, and an excellent instructor. Then, too, among the young men who had joined, it was soon discovered we had a natural instructor in the person of Micheál Lonergan from Tipperary, and at this time working in Clery's of Dublin. Micheál had the figure and walk – the dapper style of dress, the typical crisp voice of command and all the mannerisms, without the slightest sign of embarrassment, which add up to the making of the perfect officer.

Seán Prendergast, Fianna Éireann, Dublin

He was so neatly, so tidily dressed, indeed he was outstanding, not so much because of his dress but because of his military bearing and generally good form and make-up. He was a very active, dashing type of character, especially when he was dressed in his neat and evenly fitting uniform – so distinctive, so elegant, so truly military.

Gary Holohan, Fianna Éireann, Dublin

It was usual for the Fianna to salute each other in Irish from the first. Con Colbert was a great enthusiast and used the little he had on every occasion. We used the form of salute later used by Hitler in Germany. I understand that this was an old Irish form of saluting.

Eamon Martin, Fianna Éireann, Dublin

In a comparatively short time we had left the 'form fours' stage behind us, and had advanced to section and company formations, to signalling and all the rest of a fairly comprehensive course.

Seán Prendergast, Fianna Éireann, Dublin

Our programme of training consisted of military drill, first-aid, signalling, scouting and map reading. We also indulged in physical and Swedish drill . . . The outdoor exercises were the practical application of scouting, reconnaissance and tracking. In the winter we had route marches, in the summer camping out and manoeuvres.

Seán Healy and Liam O'Callaghan, Fianna Éireann, Cork

Training was given in map reading, knots, Morse, semaphore, first-aid, tent-pitching, tracking and scoutcraft generally. Tests were held at intervals and the scoutmaster was very strict in maintaining a high standard in them. A badge was issued in first-aid. This badge was a Red Cross emblem on the sleeve. Boys who had qualified for it also carried a belt pouch containing a first-aid outfit. Irish and history classes were held in An Dún . . . Discipline was strict. There was an order that members of the Fianna would not appear on the streets in uniform in company with girls.

Peadar O'Mara, Fianna Éireann, Dublin

Meetings were held twice a week, with marches or exercises carried out on Sundays. The subjects taught on week nights included Irish history, Irish language, foot drill, arms drill with hurleys or broomsticks, first-aid and signalling. Games were also encouraged. Occasionally in the summer months route marches and exercises were carried out from Camden Street and the various sluagh halls to Belcamp, Raheny, where Madame Markievicz had a house and an estate. Exercises usually terminated with a high tea at which plenty of home-made jam was supplied.

Eamon Martin, Fianna Éireann, Dublin

Special attention was given to the language . . . Irish history was also a special feature and particularly the phases recording Irish battles and the many insurrections against the British occupation. In this way the boys were being given a reason for their own military training.

Gary Holohan, Fianna Éireann, Dublin

If we were not camping we usually went for route marches to the mountain or to St Enda's College, Rathfarnham. We would go to Kilmashogue Mountain, to Hell Fire Club, Glendubh, or to the Three Rock Mountain. We usually went to St Enda's, or Scoil Éanna's as we called it, if the weather was bad so that we could get shelter. Pádraig Pearse was very good to us and used to give us every facility. We had permission to swim in the pool he had constructed for his boys.

William Mullins, Fianna Éireann, Tralee, Co. Kerry

Joe Melinn taught us step dancing and many of the boys competed at feiseanna.

Seán Healy and Liam O'Callaghan, Fianna Éireann, Cork

In 1912 and 1913 we helped in carrying out an anti-recruiting campaign. Seán O'Hegarty supplied us with the posters and paste, and we put up the posters all over the city. Tomás MacCurtain used to get us to go round the shops asking for specific articles of Irish manufacture, which he knew were available but not stocked, in order to create a demand for them. Almost from the start of the organisation in Cork the Fianna acted as Guard of Honour for the Blessed Sacrament at Wilton Church on the occasion of the annual public procession . . . Another annual function performed by the Fianna was the laying of laurel wreaths on the Fenian graves at Aghabullogue, Rathcooney, St Joseph's and St Finbarr's cemeteries on the morning of the day of the Manchester Martyrs' Commemoration.

Felix O'Doherty, Fianna Éireann, Blarney, Co. Cork

On one occasion, at Ballincollig, the boys were preparing a meal after field exercises on what appeared to be a bit of waste ground. Suddenly, out from some trees that screened the place, came a man on horseback with hunting crop and riding boots. He was typical of the tyrants of the Land War days. 'Who gave you permission to camp here?' he said in a stern voice. Tomás MacCurtain, Bob Langford and Donal O'Callaghan, who were present, answered in the native tongue. It could easily be seen that he was hostile to everything Irish and the fact of being spoken to in the Irish language was not in favour of a peaceful settlement. He threatened to call the police. This only brought more retorts in Irish, to our great delight. He was one of those who expected people to bow before him. He could not understand his orders being disobeyed, he, a Justice of the Peace. He did not know that a new spirit had been born and that the Irish nation had awakened from its slumber. Eventually, giving one anxious look around, he turned his horse and rode away.

Gary Holohan, Fianna Éireann, Dublin

Eamon Martin, Liam Mellows, the Reynoldses [Frank and Jack] and myself used to go to 5 Findlater Place to the *Irish Freedom* office to fold the papers and stamp them for the post. We would then carry them to the GPO and post them . . . I remember one night we were folding the papers when we heard a band playing and Eamon Martin and I rushed into O'Connell Street. At that time strikes were becoming more frequent, and you could feel the air electrified with revolution.

Felix O'Doherty, Fianna Éireann, Blarney, Co. Cork

At this period the paper *Irish Freedom* was a tower of strength to the cause of freedom. So as to increase circulation of this valuable journal, I put up posters in the district and distributed specimen copies. I remember some of the posters had the words 'Be ready for the Word'.

Fianna Éireann radicalised a small but committed activist core that would play a leading role in the Easter Rising. The militaristic and revolutionary dimensions of the movement became more evident during the Home Rule crisis. Inevitably coming under the control of the IRB, Fianna Éireann facilitated Fenian efforts to gain control of the Irish Volunteers.

Eamon Martin, Fianna Éireann, Dublin

Between 1909 and 1913 the Fianna grew slowly but steadily. By 1910 sluaighte had been formed in other parts of the city and county, and the organisation had extended to Cork and Limerick (where Seán Heuston joined) and to Belfast and Derry. The first ard-fheis was held this year. By the next ard-fheis, in 1911, sluaighte had been formed in Clonmel, Waterford, Dundalk and Newry . . . It was during this early period that the Fianna had been attracting to its ranks the many young men who were later to become prominently identified with the struggle for independence. In 1913 Liam Mellows, now holding the rank of captain, went on the road as a full-time organiser, and, in the short space of six months, by the time the Irish Volunteers were founded, he had covered almost every city, town and village in Ireland, and I believe there was no county that was not represented in the organisation.

Michael Lonergan, Fianna Éireann and IRB, Dublin

Out of the Fianna grew a circle of the IRB and out of this circle's initiative grew the active military training of the members of the IRB. This was carried on for a year or two before the open organisation of the Volunteers at the Rotunda Rink in 1912, I believe. So that it can really and truly be said that this first organisation meeting of the Fianna was the beginning of the military history of recent times. Previous to that, nothing whatever was being done by any organisation in a military way.

Alfred White, Fianna Éireann, Dublin

The majority of the Fianna officers were already in or subsequently enlisted in the IRB, but the influence of Madame Markievicz was sufficient to offset the obvious wire-pulling of caucus groups, sincerely motivated though the latter were; to her it owes, perhaps, the voluntary independent character which it kept to the end.

Eamon Martin, Fianna Éireann and IRB, Dublin

While it is true that there was no positive directive there was unquestionably IRB influence. I believe that the possibilities for the IRB were very much in Hobson's mind when the Fianna was launched . . . [By 1913] I would say every senior officer throughout the country had become a member. Of the Headquarters' Staff, seven in number, all were members. In 1912 a separate circle for the Fianna, known as the John Mitchel Circle, was formed with Con Colbert as centre . . . The practice was to hold a meeting of this circle with the country delegates attending on the eve of the ard-fheis and at this meeting all matters of policy were decided. The agenda of the ard-fheis was examined and discussed and decisions were arrived at before the ard-fheis met. Certain resolutions of no great importance were left open for free voting, but, apart from the discussion arising out of these, the rest was all so much eye-wash. It can be seen, therefore, that while, as I have already said, it was expedient to leave Madame [Markievicz] as president, she really had no voice in shaping policy and was overruled or outvoted whenever her ideas ran counter to the decisions of this group. Let me say that I entirely approved of this caucus control . . . Let it not be thought that I am detracting from Madame's part in the founding and development of the Fianna. While it is true she was 'used', it is nevertheless true I believe that without her it is doubtful if Bulmer Hobson or anyone else would have embarked upon the project. I believe it needed Madame's enthusiasm, her tremendous energy and above all the abiding faith of such a noble character to have brought the dream to fruition. In recording this inner history I find

I have destroyed two myths: one that the organisation was governed by the boys themselves, and two, that Madame Markievicz controlled the organisation.

Joseph Lawless, Fianna Éireann, Dublin

Small boys are natural radicals, and the boys, given a uniform and some semblance of a military organisation, needed no encouragement to declare themselves openly as revolutionaries who looked forward to the day when they might strike a blow in another fight for freedom. Of course, adults smiled tolerantly at this, not realising that the boy will soon be a man, and that the sentiments imbibed in his formative years are likely to remain with him in after life . . .

Roger McCorley, Fianna Éireann, Belfast

In the Fianna I was taught that Ireland had never got anything and never could expect to get anything from England except by physical force; that the parliamentary campaign was doomed to failure and it was, therefore, the duty of the boys in the Fianna to make themselves proficient in the use of arms so as to be in a position to form the spearhead of the revolution when the country eventually came to its senses.

Thomas Dwyer, Fianna Éireann, Enniscorthy, Co. Wexford

This club was the breeding ground of rebellion, for here was instilled into our youthful minds the hatred of the Sassenach, and there grew in us a burning desire to see our country freed from the chains of bondage. We were told how other Irishmen down through the centuries had fought against overwhelming odds and died in a glorious attempt to rid Irish soil of a foreign foe. We learned of the rebellions of Owen Roe, of Wolfe Tone and the United Irishmen, of Rossa and the Fenians, and we longed for the day when we too might join in the fight against the common enemy.

Seán O'Shea, Fianna Phádraig, Ringsend, Dublin

Father [Patrick] Flanagan by his teaching and example inspired us, from our earliest days, with love of country. He was not the ordinary type of popular curate but I would venture to say that his influence in the Ringsend–Beggars Bush area is felt to this day. Without ever raising his voice from the pulpit, he succeeded in stamping out drunkenness and loutishness from Ringsend. His chief weapon was the Fianna, a well-trained body with its own pipe band. He took the Fianna, on winter's evenings, through the history of the Boer War, and showed us that war had been imposed on a peaceful people by a bullying empire. He told us how the Boers fought and how they could have won. He understood guerrilla warfare and passed his knowledge on to us. We imbibed all this for four or five years before the Rising. We were the first Fianna unit to carry arms openly. This was the year before the Rising. He borrowed .22 rifles from all quarters so that we could march to the tattoo we held in Shelbourne Park in the summer of that year . . . He was a fine man. Would it be indiscreet to mention that he was the inventor of the sawn-off shotgun? I know he conveyed the idea to the IRA GHQ, complete with tapes inside the greatcoat so that the arms could be swung and suspicion of carrying the other kind of arms avoided! But perhaps it would be better to keep that off the record.

Gary Holohan, Fianna Éireann, Dublin

At that time they made a collection of threepence each at each meeting for a draw for a rifle, and it took two months to get the price of one rifle and 100 rounds of ammunition. A rifle at that time cost about £7.

Felix O'Doherty, Fianna Éireann, Blarney, Co. Cork

The most important matter discussed was arms for the older boys and rifle practice. At the time the officers of the Blarney sluagh carried side arms, French Army sword bayonets . . . As the months went by, the boys advanced in military matters and were gradually being moulded into a young Republican Army.

Gary Holohan, Fianna Éireann, Dublin

I remember getting a real gun in my hands for the first time while on sentry duty. It was a great sensation . . . It was at Belcamp I first got lessons and practice in shooting, from the Countess. She had two .22 rifles and always kept a liberal supply of ammunition . . . The Fianna were supposed to be non-political. We simply promised to work for the independence of Ireland. However, I soon found myself moving towards everything that was Irish-Ireland. We were taught to be aggressive to the RIC, and the boys in Camden Street would avail of every opportunity to attack the Protestant Church Boys Brigade, who at that time were very strong and would carry the Union Jack.

Eamon Martin, Fianna Éireann and IRB, Dublin

A short time before this [the formation of the Volunteers] the IRB had decided upon the military training of its younger members, and four senior officers of the Fianna – Pádraic Ó Riain, Con Colbert, Micheál Lonergan and myself – were assigned as instructors. Needless to say these officers were themselves members of the IRB. The training was carried out, in secret of course, at various halls, but principally at the Foresters' Hall, Parnell Square.

Seán Healy and Liam O'Callaghan, Fianna Éireann, Cork

Members of the Fianna in uniform were on the platform in the City Hall on the night of the meeting for the inauguration of the Volunteers. They did their best to prevent the hostile crowd getting on to the platform when the row started. In fact, Christy Monahan saved the chairman, J. J. Walsh, from more serious injury by breaking a blow intended for him.

Eamon Martin, Fianna Éireann and IRB, Dublin

With the founding of the Irish Volunteers in 1913 the contributory value of the Fianna was immediately recognised. Wherever a company was formed the Fianna was in a position to, and did, supply an officer as instructor . . . It was only to be expected that the members of the IRB who had received the earlier training were, for the most part, selected as NCOs.

Eamon Martin, Fianna Éireann and IRB, Dublin

From the formation of the Volunteers, the Fianna, while it retained its separate identity, worked in close union with this new body, and no step involving policy or action was taken by either without consultation with the other . . . Joint parades, route marches and camps became a normal feature, and it was at this time that the Fianna commando was formed. This was an active service unit designed to operate in conjunction with the Volunteers and comprising selected officers and specially picked boys.

4
Armed at Last: Volunteering

Following three decades of campaigning, the Irish Party stood on the verge of securing Home Rule when the Liberal government introduced the Government of Ireland Bill in April 1912. Ironically, this achievement unleashed the violent forces that would ultimately destroy the party. Opposition to Home Rule was led by Ulster's unionists, backed by the Conservative Party and other influential sections of the British establishment. The formation in January 1913 of the Ulster Volunteer Force, a citizen militia prepared to use violence to achieve its objectives, provided the opportunity for a nationalist counterforce. The emergence of this new force, the Irish Volunteers, undermined the Irish Party's grip over popular nationalism.

*

The Irish Volunteers was only one of several militias to emerge on the eve of the Great War. It was preceded by the nationalist Hibernian Rifles, the loyalist Ulster Volunteer Force and the socialist Irish Citizen Army. Launched at the Rotunda in Dublin on 25 November 1913, the Irish Volunteers attracted a broad spectrum of nationalist opinion including Fenians, cultural nationalists, Home Rulers and Sinn Féiners. Although an ostensibly defensive movement, open to Irishmen 'of every creed and of every party', it was regarded with suspicion by the British authorities and Irish Party leadership.

John Hanratty, Irish Citizen Army, Dublin

Early in October 1913, about six weeks prior to the meeting on 25 November 1913 in the Rotunda, at which the Irish Volunteers were inaugurated, I attended an open-air meeting of strikers in Beresford

Place, Dublin . . . I was then an oven-hand in Jacob's biscuit factory, the staff of which were on strike, and a member of the [ITGWU] committee of No. 16 branch . . . The meeting was addressed by James Larkin, general secretary of the Irish Transport and General Workers' Union. He spoke about the need for workers organising to protect themselves against the savage attacks by the police, in many cases unprovoked . . . and signified his intention of forming a Citizen Army. He introduced Captain Jack White and spoke of him as the son of General George White, and told the meeting that Captain White had offered to place his military training at the disposal of the workers. All those desirous of joining the new Citizen Army were to attend at Croydon Park the following night . . . About 8 p.m. I was in Croydon Park with about forty others, including Robert de Coeur. Neither James Larkin nor Captain White was there. We waited an hour, but there was nobody to take our name. Among those present there was a man named Kavanagh . . . Reacting to his Fianna training, he lined those present on the gravel drive in front of Croydon House and put them through some foot drill. He took no names and there was no enrolment, but we regarded the army as formed.

Seán McGarry, IRB leader and Volunteers, Dublin

I have heard several statements and claims made as to who first thought of starting a Volunteer organisation. I do not know anything of them but I do know that while the idea was in the air and everybody was talking about it the decision to write the letter which was brought by Séamus O'Connor to *The Leader* was taken in Tom Clarke's shop and that to the day of his death the late D. P. Moran believed that the credit was due to himself and Séamus O'Connor.

Seán Fitzgibbon, Sinn Féin and Executive, Volunteers, Dublin

One evening in the autumn of 1913, [Éamonn] Ceannt informed me that a meeting was to be held within a day or so in Wynn's Hotel of a number of people from national organisations to consider the advisability of starting an Irish Volunteer force, and that I was invited to attend. I was verbally invited by Ceannt . . . In my position in the national movement I was chairman of the central branch of Sinn Féin headquarters at 6 Harcourt Street. I attended the first meeting and Professor [Eoin] MacNeill was in the chair . . . After general agreement was reached on the advisability of the proposal, it was then pointed out by some of the members that all those present were broadly speaking of the one school of thought, i.e. Sinn Féin, Gaelic League, IRB, and it was agreed to by all that the basis of the Provisional Committee should be widened and suitable people known as supporters of the Irish Parliamentary Party should be asked to join the committee . . . Arthur Griffith was not asked on the Provisional Committee because his presence would be considered as linking the thing too definitely with the Sinn Féin organisation and with the opposition to Mr Redmond. The object of the Volunteers was while securing that there should be a preponderance of men of separatist tendencies, at the same time the organisation should be sufficiently broad to include supporters of the Irish Parliamentary Party, otherwise it would lose its national appeal and become a sectional organisation.

Michael Ó Cuill, Gaelic League, IRB and Volunteers, Cork

For some time before the actual start of the Volunteers the idea was in the minds of many people in one form or another . . . The Ulster Volunteers and the Citizen Army were in existence. Something was done about forming Volunteers at Athlone, and finally articles appeared in *An Claidheamh Soluis* . . . This was followed by [Eoin] MacNeill's article advocating the formation of a Volunteer force. The men in Cork immediately fell in with the spirit of the time.

Diarmuid Ó Donneabhain, Provisional Committee, Cork City Corps, Volunteers

The initiative in calling the first meeting for the formation of the Volunteers in Cork was taken by the small group of Sinn Féiners who in 1911 opposed the loyal address by the Corporation.

J. J. Walsh, GAA County Board and Provisional Committee, Cork City Corps, Volunteers

Immediately after the start of the Volunteer movement in Dublin, the formation of a corps in Cork was seriously discussed between

Diarmuid Fawsitt, Liam de Róiste and myself . . . I wrote to Eoin MacNeill and Roger Casement. Both of them agreed to attend and speak at our meeting. We arranged the meeting for the City Hall on Sunday night, 14 December 1913, had cards of invitation printed and distributed in bundles to GAA clubs, Gaelic League branches and every national or political society and organisation in the city and neighbourhood. These early meetings were not attended by anyone closely identified with Sinn Féin or extreme national views.

Cornelius Murphy, B Company, Cork City Battalion, and IRB

The whole movement for national revival in Cork between 1900 and the organisation of the Volunteers started with, and depended upon, the activities of from twelve to twenty families. Even after the start of the Volunteers that organisation depended mainly upon the same people for leadership, policy and morale. They went into everything that looked like being national – the Gaelic League, the GAA, the Fianna, the Celtic Literary Society, the Industrial Development Association and the AOH American Alliance . . . The start of the Volunteers in Cork was spontaneous after the Rotunda Meeting in Dublin. The situation was ripe for it.

Patrick Higgins, Brigade Council, Cork City Corps, Volunteers

I suspect that the IRB men in these bodies were the prime movers in starting the Volunteers in Cork. They brought in men well known to them in the existing organisations to make it look representative, men such as J. J. Walsh, then chairman of the Cork County Board, GAA; Jerry Fawsitt, then secretary of the Industrial Development Association, and Seán Jennings, who was a strong and respected member of the AOH.

Michael Ó Cuill, Gaelic League, IRB and Volunteers, Cork

The committee was obviously selected with care . . . How far the selection was influenced by the IRB I do not know. In the result they were strongly represented on the committee and it would be in accord with the normal IRB policy to place their men as far as possible in positions of influence and responsibility.

J. J. Walsh, Provisional Committee, Cork City Corps, Volunteers

At eight o'clock there was a fair attendance at the City Hall. At 8.30, when MacNeill, Casement, Fawsitt, de Róiste and myself went out on the platform, the hall was filled to capacity. The side passages and the space at the end of the hall were crowded. There were some Fianna boys on the stage and a crowd of about fifty, mainly Gaelic Leaguers, at the back of the platform. These had come spontaneously and had not been organised by us. I spoke first and was followed by Fawsitt, who read the manifesto of the Dublin committee. This was enthusiastically received and the meeting appeared to be going well. Then MacNeill spoke and, concluding his address, called for cheers for Sir Edward Carson's Volunteers. A signal was given to the organised group of Hibernians in the Hall. The whole audience stood up. There was confusion, hooting, hissing and shouting for a few minutes; then the lights were put out and a crowd charged with a rush on to the platform. I was struck with a chair on the head and taken away to the South Infirmary for treatment . . . the Cork corps of Irish Volunteers was formally inaugurated.

The Volunteers were widely regarded as a product of the Irish-Ireland movement. Its organisers were often prominent cultural nationalists, and Volunteer companies frequently emerged out of Gaelic League branches. But cultural nationalists often remained aloof from the new organisation and many of the Irish-Irelanders who formed Volunteer companies – including Michael Leahy, Frank Drohan and An Seabhac mentioned below – were often secretly working on behalf of the IRB.

Patrick Higgins, Brigade Council, Cork City Corps, Volunteers

The Dublin meeting for the formation of the Volunteers electrified all Gaelic League and Irish-Ireland circles in Cork, especially because MacNeill and Pearse were associated with it.

Michael Leahy, IRB and Cobh Company, Co. Cork

Immediately after the public meeting for the formation of the Volunteers in Dublin in November 1913, and before the public meeting in the City Hall, Cork, on 14 December 1913, a group of us who were attending a Gaelic League class in a room in the AOH Hall, Cobh, decided to hold a meeting to form a Volunteer corps . . . All who attended were members of the Gaelic League class . . . MacNeill's article, 'The North Began', was read, and it was decided to form a Volunteer corps.

Thomas Halpin, Gaelic League and Volunteers, Clonmel, Co. Tipperary

The Volunteer force was started in Clonmel by Frank Drohan, who had always been an outstanding Irish-Irelander throughout his life.

Michael Spillane and Michael Sullivan, Volunteers and IRB, Killarney, Co. Kerry

On 28 November 1913, when a meeting of the Gaelic League was in progress in An Dún, High Street, Killarney, a stranger arrived and was met by An Seabhac (Mr P. Sugrue), who was one of the Irish teachers at the classes. The stranger was, we believe, a Donegal man, but we do not know his name. An Seabhac knew him and introduced him to those present. He said that he came on behalf of the headquarters of the Irish Volunteers to ask that a company be formed in Killarney. He said that it was their object to have one formed in every town and village in Ireland. There and then all present decided to join and the company was formed.

John Shouldice, F Company, 1st Battalion

Half of the company were members of the Gaelic League and about one third were members of the GAA.

Joe Good, Volunteers, London

I attended various functions and sports meetings of the Gaelic Athletic Association. This association impressed me as having behind it, or in it, the driving force of Michael Collins. He was a participant in most of the sports, and he obviously had something to do with organising such sports. The organisation of which he was a member attracted quite a number of young men, many of whom seemed to be attached to him. I think the GAA was the driving force behind the revolutionary spirit in the Volunteers in London.

Thomas Peppard, Lusk Company, 5th Battalion

In July 1914, companies of the Irish Volunteers were started in Lusk. I say companies, because from the outset there were two companies. One company was started by the Rooneys and had its origin in the hurling and football club, and the other club was started by the Taylors and Murtaghs . . . There was a local dispute between the Rooney family and the Taylors and Murtagh family and an amount of jealousy, and this gave rise to the formation of two companies of Volunteers in a small district where there was room for really only one.

Cornelius Murphy, B Company, Cork City Battalion, and IRB

I belonged to two GAA clubs when the Volunteers started, and I was the only member of either of the two clubs who joined the Volunteers.

Liam Jones, Patrick McCarthy and Cornelius O'Regan, Mourne Abbey Company, Co. Cork

There was a small branch of the Gaelic League, but it contributed nothing to the start of the Volunteers, none of its members joining up. There was a GAA organisation also, but it did not influence the start in any way.

Michael Ó Cuill, Gaelic League, IRB and Volunteers, Cork

In regard to the attitude of the Gaelic League to the Volunteers, it was that generally of not interfering with the freedom of decision by the members individually. All branches had members who favoured the Volunteer movement and participated in it from the start. They also had members who did not take a physical force movement seriously. Individual members held different views and were free to hold them.

From the outset the Irish Republican Brotherhood regarded the Volunteers (whose formation it had discreetly encouraged) as a potential insurrectionary force. In many places IRB members were responsible for the formation of Volunteer companies. Elsewhere, it sought secretly to gain control of them by placing its members in positions of authority.

Bulmer Hobson, IRB leader and general secretary, Volunteers, Dublin

As a result of the steps taken by the IRB earlier in the year, those members of the Volunteers who were members of the IRB were mostly all well drilled . . . The result was that the trained members of the IRB came into prominence and became officers. The control of the IRB was not apparent in this or suspected, but it operated in practice.

Diarmuid Lynch, IRB Supreme Council and Volunteers leader, Dublin

The only other [IRB] general meeting of which I have any knowledge was that held in the Foresters' Hall, Parnell Square, Dublin, early in December 1913 . . . the purpose on this occasion was to emphasise the duty of IRB men to cooperate to the fullest extent in the formation of Irish Volunteer companies, and of choosing IRB men as officers where possible.

Seán McGarry, IRB leader and Volunteers, Dublin

It had been already decided that no prominent member of the IRB should accept office, but Hobson allowed himself to be appointed honorary secretary. This had to be accepted as a fait accompli, though with bad grace, and everything went well for a while.

Gerald Byrne, IRB and C Company, 4th Battalion

On the formation of the Irish Volunteers we were instructed by the IRB to join and to do everything possible to get hold of the key positions in the Volunteers. It was now perceived by the members of the IRB that this was a chance to do openly what we had previously to do in secret.

Peter Galligan, IRB and C Company, 2nd Battalion

As we had some previous military experience we were soon picked out to fill the key positions.

Cornelius Murphy, B Company, Cork City Battalion, and IRB

The IRB ordered its members into the movement . . . even though there was an election of a committee later, the nominations were arranged. The IRB had effective control and exercised it in all appointments to Volunteer positions.

Liam Murphy, D Company, Cork City Battalion, and IRB centre

There was a case in which a vacancy for brigade adjutant occurred in 1915 ... An examination was set and a man named Liam Rabette, adjutant of 'D' Company, and Seán Nolan sat for it. It was stated at the time that although Rabette got the highest marks, Nolan was appointed because he was an IRB man.

Patrick Harris, B Company, Cork City Battalion, and IRB

Although the influence of the IRB was not obvious to me at that time, I saw later, when I became a member in 1915, that the IRB men, largely on their merit as individuals, did, in fact, exercise an unseen control over the Volunteer organisation.

Thomas Wilson, IRB and Executive Committee, Volunteers, Belfast

The Irish Volunteer Executive was not entirely in the hands of, or controlled by, the IRB but I believe the IRB had sufficient influence on the Executive to have their reliable men appointed in charge of each important county district. In Belfast, before the split took place, the IRB had virtual control of both the Volunteer committees and was able to exercise control in matters of policy without question from the Volunteers who were non-members of the IRB.

Patrick O'Mahoney, IRB and Dungarvan Company, Co. Tipperary

The general line of policy in regard to it was that the IRB would not take too prominent a part, or show their hands completely in the formation of the organisation. It was desirable that the Volunteer movement should be fully representative of Irishmen of all political creeds, and it was felt that IRB men on their own merits would secure sufficient voice in the effects of the organisation to enable them to keep its national policy on the right lines.

Joe Melinn, IRB and Tralee Company, Co. Kerry

The IRB worked quietly in the preparations for the formation of the Volunteers in Tralee and in the organising work that preceded the public meeting. The members approached clubs and individual friends and ensured a favourable atmosphere for the start. I think Tom Slattery presided at the public meeting for the inauguration of the Volunteers, though he was not an IRB man. People of all shades of political opinion attended and joined the Volunteers. The IRB was quite satisfied to let the organisation develop in a natural way; we were well represented and felt that if the necessity arose we could direct and influence the national policy of the new body.

John Shields, Benburb Company, Co. Tyrone

The IRB took the initiative in organising the Irish Volunteers . . . Generally there was a circle of the IRB in each Irish Volunteer company area and the IRB held the controlling influence in each Volunteer company. It was not considered essential that an Irish Volunteer officer should be a member of the IRB. Most of the officers were, however, in the IRB. Only [that] I was a member of the IRB I would not have been selected as a representative at the Irish Volunteer convention.

Although Volunteering was a response to the Home Rule crisis, non-political factors such as the appeal of drilling, militarism and camaraderie encouraged many to join. Regional variations were also evident, with sectarian tensions and clerical involvement more pronounced in Ulster. Many nationalists saw the movement as a means of countering the Ulster Volunteer Force; others echoed Eoin MacNeill's depiction of the loyalist force as an empowering model for Irish nationalists.

Eamon Morkan, A Company, 1st Battalion

What prompted me to associate myself with the Irish Volunteers in the first place was that I had been reared in a household with strong national leanings and had from childhood heard Home Rule discussed. Under such influence I became an enthusiastic Home Ruler and was dissatisfied with the progress being made by the Irish Parliamentary Party. In common with other young men, I felt that a more active policy would be needed if anything was to be achieved in the line of independence for the country.

Henry Murray, A Company, 4th Battalion

When I joined the Irish Volunteers I had no particular affiliations with any political party or association with any cultural or social organisation. I had always believed in my country's right to complete independence and considered that the extent to which that right could be secured depended on the amount of force that the men of the country were prepared to exert.

Bernard McAllister, Swords Company, 5th Battalion

I had joined the Irish Volunteers because I had seen a chance in them of doing something to attain the freedom of our country and breaking the connection with England. In following Redmond I could see no hope of this.

Liam Tannam, E Company, 3rd Battalion

It was Éamonn Ceannt who induced me to join the Irish Volunteers. His office was next door to mine in the Municipal Buildings, Castle Street. One day he asked me to buy a ticket for a Sinn Féin concert and he asked me did I belong to the Volunteers. I said, 'No.' They were then referred to as the Sinn Féin Volunteers and many of us thought that Sinn Féin did not go quite far enough. I had read Griffith's *Resurrection of Hungary*. I thought Griffith was in a sense satisfied if the country were similarly placed to Hungary in coming under a dual monarchy, and it seemed to me that Sinn Féin would be satisfied with getting back the parliament that once sat in College Green, i.e. subservient to the British. I declined to buy the ticket. Ceannt asked me the reason and told me that the Volunteers should not be referred to as the Sinn Féin Volunteers, that they meant to go much further than Sinn Féin. He said, 'Suppose I tell you that we'll fight, would you join?' I said, 'Yes.'

Patrick Twomey, Kilmona Company, Co. Cork

Like my father, I could not follow Redmond . . . I remember attending an entertainment at the Opera House, Cork, held under the auspices of the Irish Volunteers. A lady gave a recitation, standing in front of the curtain. I remember the part of it, 'The men who died for Ireland, who will stand and take their place?' The curtain went up showing a party of twenty or thirty Irish Volunteers on the stage with their rifles at the slope. I decided that this was my party.

Robert Kelly, IRB and Newry Company, Co. Down

We joined the Volunteers in 1914 believing that if we got guns it would not be long until a good few who joined would want to know when they were going to use them.

Thomas Walsh, B Company, 5th Battalion

One of my pals had already joined a company which had its headquarters in Sandymount Castle, and he gave me a very fine description of his first drill night. He told me about the marching men and the orders of Captain Condron, and I made an appointment to go to Sandymount Castle on the next parade night . . . I was the first Volunteer in this company to wear a uniform.

George Staunton, Volunteers, Prospect Hill, Galway

Ever since I was 10 or 12 years of age I was very anxious to know everything in connection with firearms . . . I was just as fond of drill books – I somehow got possession of a British training manual through some militia men from the village. I used to keep this safe in my school bag. I valued this drill book much more than I did my schoolbooks and religiously studied it from cover to cover. I had always the ambition of becoming a soldier but not a British soldier – somehow I never had any grádh for anything British, and the RIC, I disliked them.

Nicholas Smyth, Volunteers, Co. Tyrone

As far as I understood, the object of the Volunteers in 1914 was to oppose and, if necessary, fight Carson's Ulster Volunteers.

James Tomney, IRB centre and Dungannon Company, Co. Tyrone

In the autumn of 1913 I joined the Irish Volunteers at its organisation in the Dungannon district. I cannot give credit to any particular person for organising the Volunteers, as the movement was a spontaneous answer to the plans of Sir E. Carson's Ulster Volunteers.

Séamus Dobbyn, IRB and Volunteers, Belfast

The Belfast section of the Irish Volunteers was formed in St Mary's Hall, Belfast . . . At the meeting it was indicated that we were got together for the purpose of fighting the Ulster Volunteers. I remember that I and some others disagreed with this policy, as we believed that the Ulster Volunteers should not be our target, but our old traditional enemy, England. It was stressed that our main task was to get the Volunteers formed, and that the UVF would only be our enemy insofar as they helped England.

Father Eugene Coyle, Volunteers leader, Co. Tyrone

Sir Edward Carson's Ulster Volunteers were well organised in Fintona and paraded the town carrying arms two or three times a week. Fintona is a Catholic town and I felt that the arming of the Ulster Volunteers was a great danger to the safety of the Catholic population. It struck me forcibly that if the Carsonite section of the population could with impunity ignore the law, the Catholic section should take similar action and provide the means to defend themselves . . . I went to Dublin and called on The O'Rahilly and explained to him my people's situation in Fintona and my determination to help, as far as I could possibly do it, in getting our people armed. I gave him a cheque out of my private means, which at that time were limited, for £150 for rifles for my parishioners. He [O'Rahilly] supplied me with sixty rifles, a bayonet for each rifle and a supply of suitable ammunition . . . Shortly after this sixty young Fintona Volunteers paraded on the streets of our town all armed with serviceable rifles, each rifle having attached a fixed bayonet. At the time we got the rifles the Unionist Volunteers had only forty rifles in Fintona and they had no bayonets for them, so they ceased parading on the streets.

John McCoy, Newry Company, Co. Down

The prevailing idea was that the organisation of the Ulster Volunteers was a game of political bluff . . . I had no clear idea in my mind at this time, if arms were made available, against whom we should use them. I could not then visualise their use against the Ulster Volunteers, as I had many good friends among young unionists in Newry and district.

Patrick Crowley, Gurteen and Tinkers Cross Company, Co. Cork

Our incentive was opposition to the Ulster Volunteers, and we had no policy apart from this until we fell into line with the all-Ireland organisation when it started.

The demands of Volunteering were considerable. Volunteers drilled twice weekly and devoted their weekends to route marches and field exercises. As with the Fianna, the degree to which Volunteers emulated the conventional training methods and militaristic ethos of the British Army is striking. The significance of the movement in this period lay less in its insurrectionary potential than its radicalising impact.

J. J. Walsh, Provisional Committee chairman, Cork City Corps, Volunteers

In January or February 1914, a store in Fisher Street was rented as a drill hall. An ex-artillery sergeant-major named Goodwin gave his services free as a drill instructor. Later we got ex-Sergeant-Major Donovan, who was paid a small fee and was an excellent instructor.

Thomas Doyle, IRB centre and Enniscorthy Company, Co. Wexford

It was not long until we got a drill instructor, an ex-British recruiting sergeant named Darcy. He was delighted to be drilling us; he thought in his own mind he was preparing us for the British Army.

Liam Murphy, D Company, Cork City Battalion, and IRB centre

Parades were held three nights a week and route marches every Sunday. The first drill instructors were all ex-servicemen . . .

Denis Lordan, Kilbrittain Company, Co. Cork

Weekday parades were sometimes as frequent as three a week. These, of course, were held at night – the only time they could be held in an agricultural district – and men often travelled on foot three to six miles to the place of parade.

Cornelius O'Mahony, Ahiohill Company, Co. Cork

Police were always present at these parades, usually following each company for the day, and returning with them in the evening.

Daniel O'Keefe, Mitchelstown Company, Co. Cork

We looked upon them as good days out, enjoyed ourselves and were amused by the way people thronged to their doors and windows to stare at us as we marched by.

Liam Carroll, A Company, 1st Battalion

We worked more or less on the lines of normal British Army training – extended lines and that – and we did use all the British Army books.

Felix O'Doherty, Volunteers, Cork

In my opinion, the Volunteers were far better trained than the soldiers of the British Army. The reason for this was that the Volunteer officer had a very good knowledge of military matters in general – squad, section, company drill, military engineering, signalling – Morse and semaphore; explosives; army – rifles, revolvers, automatics, refilling of cartridges, making of bombs and many other things.

Michael Leahy, IRB and Cobh Company, Co. Cork

We had no arms at first but used staves.

John McCoy, Mullaghbawn Company, Co. Down

We had no rifles or other military equipment. We did not possess in our ranks even a competent military instructor. We had a preponderance of manpower, from men of advanced years who wished to give the movement their approval, down to boys just after leaving school. Arms drill was carried out with pitchfork and shovel handles. There did not seem to be much efficient direction either in the local organisation of the Volunteers or in their efforts to set up a progressive drilling and training scheme. Our absolute deficiency in arms made our efforts at training seem unreal and not worth the effort.

Patrick Twomey, Kilmona Company, Co. Cork

The men paid 3*d.* a week into a fund for the purchase of equipment. Out of this fund we purchased haversacks, bandoliers, belts and puttees. There was only one Volunteer cap in the company – mine. We had only one uniform – mine. By Easter 1916, all the men in the company were equipped with haversacks, bandoliers, belts and puttees.

Frank Robbins, Irish Citizen Army, Dublin

We set about organising rifle and revolver clubs, as well as uniform clubs. This was accomplished by paying a subscription of one shilling per week to the rifle club and sixpence per week to the revolver club. By this means a number of us became the proud owners of what was known as the Boer Mauser, which had a magazine for five bullets and one in the breech. We were the envy of our less fortunate comrades, whose lack of means prevented them from doing as we had done . . . The rifles, revolvers and other equipment were obtained through Messrs Lawlors of Fownes Street.

Joseph O'Connor, A Company, 3rd Battalion

The men had to pay threepence a week towards the cost of rent and light. They had to pay for the ammunition they used in practice. They had to pay for their own rifle ammunition and equipment. In addition to that the companies had to form a company fund to provide themselves with such things as first-aid, field dressings, stretchers, signalling flags and lamps, and a reserve of ammunition, and where possible, training tools, i.e. picks and shovels. The sacrifices made at the time, both by officers and men, were very great . . .

Séamus Kenny, B Company, 4th Battalion

I devoted all my time to Larkfield, between drilling and training and all. I put my heart and soul into it.

Diarmuid Ó Donneabhain, Provisional Committee, Cork City Corps, Volunteers

There was a shooting hall in Sheares Street . . . where we had target practice with miniature rifles. We strolled in when we felt like it and paid for our ammunition.

Dick Balfe, D Company, 1st Battalion

In the competitions held in St Enda's sometime in 1915, D Company obtained third place. A Company of the 4th Battalion got first and the Citizen Army got second with only a half mark between each . . . We staged a display of company and section ordinary drill and extended movements. We gave a bayonet charge that was very realistic and had arranged for one man with a French bayonet to cover himself with sheep's blood. We had to prevent doctors from interfering, it was so realistic, in order to allow our men to carry out first-aid. Tents were erected within a minute and communication was opened up by ordinary telegraphy, visual and audible, and by semaphore and Morse.

Laurence Nugent, K Company, 3rd Battalion

The company was about the best trained in the Co. Dublin. We won several shooting competitions.

Liam Tannam, O/C, E Company, 3rd Battalion, and IRB

About this time [1915] a series of lectures for officers was arranged and started at 41 Kildare Street and was continued at headquarters, Dawson Street, which I attended. Most of the lectures were given by Tomás MacDonagh. MacDonagh was a very good lecturer. He started, I think, at the Campaign of Xerxes and went on to the South African War. After the lectures there were examinations held in tactics. My examination took place at Greenhills, I think Ginger O'Connell was the referee . . . After this I was gazetted in the *Irish Volunteer,* dated 4 December 1915. It was given out at the time that anybody who failed to pass this test would not be confirmed in rank.

Although it had become a significant presence by early 1914, the Volunteers had not yet become a mass movement due to the hostility of the Irish Party, and its lack of credibility as a military force.

J. J. Walsh, Provisional Committee chairman, Cork City Corps, Volunteers

A large number of men – 400 or 500 – had signed the enrolment forms which had been distributed at the City Hall meeting. These were invited to a meeting in the Dún in Queen Street before Christmas 1913; about 150 attended ... Arrangements were made for drills in the Dún on two or three nights a week. For a considerable time, perhaps six months, after that the position was that we had a large number of men enrolled but poor and irregular attendance at drill.

Diarmuid Ó Donneabhain, Provisional Committee, Cork City Corps, Volunteers

I understand about 130 joined at that first meeting, but only about twenty turned up at the first drill at the Dún subsequently.

Liam Murphy, D Company, Cork City Battalion, and IRB centre

At that parade there were only nine men drilling, viz.: Tomás MacCurtain, Seán O'Hegarty, Martin Donovan, Paddy Corkery, Seán O'Sullivan, Jack Lane, Tadg Barry and myself ... At the next and subsequent parades more men came in and the strength started to grow steadily.

Patrick Higgins, Brigade Council, Cork City Corps, Volunteers

We were doing serious and important work in the Gaelic League; we felt a sense of responsibility to that organisation; it was a big job and some of the work would have to be dropped if we went into the Volunteers. Volunteering was a bit of a joke at first. We were not hostile but we were critical.

J. J. Walsh, Provisional Committee chairman, Cork City Corps, Volunteers

The paucity of public support for the Volunteer movement was evidenced by the hostility we encountered. In these first marches bottles and other missiles were thrown at us by the mob.

Daniel O'Keefe, Mitchelstown Company, Co. Cork

The novelty of forming fours and parading soon wore off for many, including our instructors, and in a few months our strength dwindled to between fifty and seventy men.

Patrick Looney, Donoughmore Company, Co. Cork

I went to Beeing and put up notices and gave out leaflets explaining the objects of the Volunteers. A number of men joined nominally, but the people generally thought us mad. They had nothing to say against me personally; the politicians gave the advice – 'Take no notice of him, he's mad.' . . . I called a meeting for New Tipperary but no one turned up. I felt like giving them up forever.

Timothy O'Leary, Ballyhar Company, Co. Kerry

The Ballyhar Company was started in the spring of 1914. A few Volunteers came out from Killarney Company and tried to get a number of local men to form a company, but the first effort was not successful. Then Michael Spillane and Michael J. O'Sullivan came out and addressed a meeting on a Sunday after Mass and a start was made with four Volunteers . . . Strength increased slowly at first. There was no hostility but the lads were shy about coming out in public. When they heard of companies forming in other areas they joined in larger numbers . . .

Tom Hales, Ballinadee Company, Co. Cork

Parades were held on two evenings a week and a route march on Sundays. These marches were usually to neighbouring towns or villages, and one of their objects was to encourage recruiting for the Volunteers. In this way sections, some of which afterwards developed into companies, were organised at Bandon, Kilbrittain, Gaggin, Kilpatrick, Farnivane and Newcestown, Ahiohill and Ballinspittle. RIC men usually accompanied these marches.

The Irish Volunteers transcended class, geographical and political divisions, but primarily appealed to young Catholic nationalists. Although discussion of party politics was discouraged, the movement's militaristic rhetoric reflected a well-established Fenian discourse on the virtues of armed citizenship and the inadequacy of relying on parliamentary methods as a means of securing independence.

Charlie Cullinane, Lyre Company, Co. Cork

All the men in the company were young, with the exception of Jim Walsh, the captain, who was about 40; all the others were in the twenties.

Liam Carroll, A Company, 1st Battalion

We had a number of tradesmen in our company; we also had Post Office workers, labourers, a painter, a butcher; we had clerical workers and students . . .

Liam O'Brien, F Company, 1st Battalion, and IRB

The rank and file were of the Dublin artisan class, with many clerks, shopmen, civil servants and students. The democracy was complete. If anything, the higher a man's social status, the more he had to do and the sterner the discipline.

Father Eugene Coyle, Volunteers leader, Tyrone

We had about 700 men available in Co. Tyrone in districts where the Volunteers were organised. All those boys were poor farmers' sons . . .

Denis Lordan, Kilbrittain Company, Co. Cork

The Volunteer movement was strong in the rural districts of West Cork and weak in the towns. Conversely the towns were the chief sources of recruitment for the British forces . . . Their earnestness and enthusiasm spread a new spirit in the countryside; papers like the *Irish Volunteer*, *Irish Freedom* and *The Spark* were introduced into many homes, and the principles and policies they advocated became subjects of discussion and comment.

Joseph O'Connor, A Company, 3rd Battalion

I heard the company behind mine singing a very fine marching song. That was the first occasion on which 'The Soldiers' Song' was sung in public, certainly as a marching song. It caught on and in a few days' time every Volunteer in Dublin was whistling or singing it.

Diarmuid Ó Donneabhain, Provisional Committee, Cork City Corps, Volunteers

Seán Scanlon and, I think, some others attended the training camp in Wicklow in August 1915. The first time I heard 'The Soldiers' Song' was when he returned . . . In the country they sang songs on the march: 'Step Together', 'Ireland Boys Hurrah', 'God Save Ireland', 'Clare's Dragoons' were the most popular. Later 'The Soldiers' Song'. We often held smoking concerts at Sheares Street Hall, where 'Phil the Fluter's Ball', etc. were mingled with patriotic songs and recitations. While at Fisher Street we organised a pipers' band . . . The first time we carried a flag was on a route march from Fisher Street Hall (upstairs in a corn loft) and that was the green flag with gold harp. It was some time afterwards before we rose to a tricolour. However, about 1914 we began to wear small tricolour badges in our hats, or caps.

Joseph Lawless, C Company, 1st Battalion

Scarcely a Sunday passed through the summer and autumn of 1915 that there was not a muster of Volunteers for some parade, exercise, or to attend a football match or aeriocht. Generally these were followed by a céilí in Swords, Lusk, St Margaret's or somewhere. We did not mind how far we cycled for such entertainment; and we sang and danced all night to the music of a lone violin; occasionally a piano might make its appearance. The rebel songs of those gatherings had more than a little to do with the fostering of a rebel spirit in those who listened to them. The national poets and ballad writers such as Davis, John Kells Ingram and Paddy Archer sowed many a seed that bloomed on the battlefield in the years that followed . . .

Gary Holohan, Fianna Éireann and D Company, 1st Battalion

On almost every Sunday aeridheachta or concerts were held for the purpose of raising funds for arms and equipment. They were also availed of to spread the gospel of physical force, as the only way of winning back our country from England . . . It would be impossible to estimate the effect of this singing in reviving the spirit of the nation.

Daniel O'Keefe, Mitchelstown Company, Co. Cork

We paid a weekly subscription of 6*d*. per man per week towards an arms fund, and I must say that each and every man looked forward to the day when he would own a rifle.

Thomas Meldon, C Company, 2nd Battalion

In one corner of the room was a stack of rifles and on a table a pile of typewritten forms, one of which we each signed as we received our rifles. We then fell in outside, formed up and marched back to the hall, a silent body of soldiers, there to be received by our less lucky comrades with that respect and awe which only the possession of arms in the hands of earnest men can inspire.

William Daly, E Company, 2nd Battalion

The 2nd Battalion O/C, Tom Hunter, was marching in front with his adjutant and second in command, and, on nearing the British party, gave orders to the pipers to strike up a quick march tune, which they did with such effect as to throw the British out of step with their own band. I felt a thrill of delight when this happened. I should have mentioned that we were with full equipment on the parade and I was proud of my short Lee-Enfield, which was the latest pattern . . .

J. J. Walsh, Provisional Committee chairman, Cork City Corps, Volunteers

On this occasion I was dressed in the first Volunteer uniform worn in this Volunteer movement. The O'Rahilly had given an order to Messrs Mahony of Blarney for the grey-green cloth. The Mahony firm, which I knew well, obliged me with a length which I had made into a uniform by Messrs T. Lyons & Co. The first appearance of the new garment created something of a sensation.

Liam Tannam, O/C, E Company, 3rd Battalion, and IRB

I changed into uniform after dinner for swank, I think, to meet my girl.

Joseph O'Connor, A Company, 3rd Battalion

. . . it was the desire of every officer or Volunteer to have a uniform of what he considered to be the first Army of Ireland for years.

John Joseph Scollan, Hibernian Rifles, Dublin

At this time [*c.* 1915] we had lost a number of our men to the Irish Volunteers. The Volunteer force was more attractive, as they had uniforms.

Laurence Nugent, K Company, 3rd Battalion

In business houses, workshops, offices and various professions, a feeling of comradeship which never previously existed sprung up. Men who had only a nodding acquaintance shook hands when they met in the street. The young men clicked their heels when they met their pals and actually hugged and pulled each other around: all were joining up . . . Tonight we were no longer a mob. We looked forward to long lines of well-trained armed marching men. We were Volunteers . . . We could hold our heads up; we could drill; we could march. We were taught what discipline meant and we knew how to obey orders . . . discipline became a matter of honour with every man.

James O'Shea, Irish Citizen Army, Dublin

It was drill, drill, most of the time and we were becoming experts with rifles . . . We also had something that was worth more than anything else since or before – a peculiar comradeship that had no limits . . . We were like a big family when you got the swing of it. Home or nothing else mattered . . . It made for a carelessness in danger and a happy-go-lucky devil-may-care comradeship that I had never experienced before.

Volunteering appealed to young women as well as men. The membership of Cumann na mBan, established in 1914, was disproportionately drawn from committed republican families and middle-class women of independent means. Like Inghinidhe na hÉireann, the organisation prioritised patriotic rather than feminist issues, and its subordinate status and gendered functions disappointed some of its more radical members.

Elizabeth Bloxham, Cumann na mBan, Dublin

The actual founding of Cumann na mBan was the result of a conversation with Mrs Wyse Power and, I think, Molly McGuire and some others . . . Mrs Power spoke of an Executive and I asked how is an Executive elected. She said, 'We elect ourselves; that is the way an Executive has to be elected' . . . I rarely met any of the members of the Executive because I was straight away chosen as an organiser, having some experience as a public speaker at literary and suffragette meetings . . . I started branches at various places, among them the following: Carrigaholt, Kildysart, Kilkee, Tipperary town, Clonmel, Galway, Athy, Maryborough, Athenry. There would be some contact before I would visit these places. A Volunteer might be up in town and ask Mrs Wyse Power to form a branch. I would always have some place to go and someone to meet me when I arrived at the town. We appointed a president and a secretary from among the women or girls who attended. The meeting would be in a room off some hall perhaps.

Áine O'Rahilly, Cumann na mBan, Dublin

I was present at Wynn's Hotel at the foundation meeting of Cumann na mBan in the early part of 1914 . . . There were not more than a dozen women present but they represented all shades of nationalist opinion . . . the objects of the organisation were as set out by Mrs Wyse Power . . . namely, (1) to advance the cause of Irish liberty (2) to organise Irish women in furtherance of this object (3) to assist in arming and equipping a body of Irishmen for the defence of Ireland and (4) to form a fund for these purposes to be called a Defence of Ireland Fund. At that first meeting one of the women present, Miss Agnes O'Farrelly, suggested that we should start making puttees for the Volunteers. I was disgusted.

Nancy Wyse Power, Cumann na mBan, Dublin

I understand that the idea of such an organisation emanated from Thomas MacDonagh. Miss O'Farrelly was the first president. The promoters may have had in mind an auxiliary association of women acting under the general instructions of the Volunteer Executive but the organisation immediately declared itself to be an independent organisation of women determined to makes its own decisions.

Min Ryan, Cumann na mBan, Dublin

People like Mrs Wyse Power and others used to maintain that we were not an auxiliary to the Volunteers, but an independent body; but the fact of the matter was that our activities consisted of service to the Volunteers. We had it straight in our constitution – that we were an independent organisation working for the freedom of Ireland . . . we were not formed as an auxiliary, but we looked on ourselves as such.

Elizabeth O'Brien, Cumann na mBan, Tralee, Co. Kerry

We worked on our initiative trying to do the best we could to help the Volunteers in every way possible.

Nora Thornton, Cumann na mBan, Liverpool

We started Cumann na mBan in 1915 in Liverpool where my family – my father and three brothers and sisters lived . . . We joined the Gaelic League and started the branch of Cumann na mBan about the same time as my brother Frank started the Volunteers.

Eily O'Hanrahan, Cumann na mBan, Dublin

I joined Cumann na mBan at the instigation of my brother [Michael] in 1914.

Máire Fitzpatrick, Cumann na mBan, Enniscorthy, Co. Wexford

Liam Mellows came to stay with us while he was organising Na Fianna Éireann. Seán [her brother] helped him to establish the first branch in town. I was allowed to help with the organising, but Liam Mellows wouldn't let a girl join. Seán got the loan of a revolver and I was allowed to learn to use it, until one day I shot a hen belonging to Mum, so I had to stop . . . Then came the Volunteers. Seán and my brother Liam went into the Volunteer movement, and Dad also. Then Cumann na mBan was formed in Dublin and I formed a branch in Enniscorthy. Mrs Wyse Power addressed the first meeting; it was a great success; we had a hundred members. Dr Kelly and Nurse Hardy gave first-aid lectures. My elder sister,

Sighle, was drill instructor. During this time I left school; I hated it anyway. Mum didn't want me to leave, but Dad backed me up. I had lots of work to do for the movement. I was organising Cumann na mBan, giving lectures and holding first-aid classes.

Elizabeth Corr, Cumann na mBan, Belfast

We never had been attached to any Irish association, but were so disgusted with the pro-British feeling in Belfast that we felt that we must do something about it. My brother (Harry) had become a Volunteer some time previously, and he proposed us for Cumann na mBan.

Elizabeth O'Brien, Cumann na mBan, Tralee, Co. Kerry

Parades were held regularly twice a week at the Rink from the start up to Easter 1916, either for drills or for classes. Drill instruction was given by Volunteer officers. First-aid classes and sewing classes were in constant operation. We made all the haversacks for the Tralee Volunteers; also a number of canvas bandoliers and a number of sleeping bags. We made thousands of green and gold ribbon badges and sold them. We ran dances, concerts and collections at races and sports meetings, as well as carrying out a house-to-house collection in the town for the Volunteers. We did all the catering for the Volunteer dances. We held two bazaars, all the material for which we collected free in the town.

Elizabeth Corr, Cumann na mBan, Belfast

We were taught first-aid and military drill. Rory Haskin trained us in rifle shooting at a stationary target . . . I won a second prize for rifle shooting just before Christmas . . . We were followed around by police and G-men who, strangely enough, did not interfere with any of our activities. One girl (Nora Kelly) on her first visit to the [Willowbank] huts on a very dark night asked the policeman (who was evidently keeping an eye on us) where Cumann na mBan met, and he escorted her to the hut, most politely.

Molly Reynolds, Cumann na mBan, Dublin

. . . we carried out the usual activities of first-aid, signalling, drill and marching. In addition, we learned to clean, cool and load rifles and revolvers. The idea in teaching us the latter subjects – as explained by our instructor, Commandant F[rank] Henderson – was not that we would use arms, but that we could assist the men by being able to carry out these duties.

Kathleen Murphy, Cumann na mBan, Belfast

It was impossible for us to obtain any central premises to rent, as our organisation was not popular, not considered respectable in Belfast.

Molly Reynolds, Cumann na mBan, Dublin

I was getting into trouble at home for being out late at night, as the classes didn't finish before eleven o'clock.

Annie Cooney, Cumann na mBan, Dublin

He [Con Colbert] took two photographs out of his pocket and asked me: 'Would you care to have one of these?' One of the photos was of himself alone and the other of himself and Liam Clarke. I said I would be delighted and he actually gave me both and I have brought in one of them to show you. I was charmed because, to tell the truth, I thought an awful lot of him and, of course, he must have known it. He was not, however, at all interested in girls; he was entirely engrossed in his work for Ireland and devoted all his time to it.

Bridget Lyons, Cumann na mBan, Dublin

I was thrilled with him [Ned Daly] and felt that although he was quiet he was very forceful. What I felt about him the first time I met him the previous summer, and also about Séamus Sullivan – they probably would not care to be told this – was that they were the nearest approach to British officers in appearance and inspired us girls with feelings of enthusiasm and caused us many heart throbs. I met Frank Fahy and Peadar Clancy. He was fascinating and epitomised for me all the attractive heroes in Irish history.

Marie Perolz, Cumann na mBan and Irish Citizen Army, Dublin

That time we did not think about sex or anything else. We were all soldiers and I was only bothered about what I could do for Kate Houlihan.

Although the Volunteers were regarded with suspicion by the British authorities, rank-and-file members of the Royal Irish Constabulary and Dublin Metropolitan Police – many of whom were Catholic nationalists – were more ambivalent or even sympathetic.

Constable Eugene Bratton, Royal Irish Constabulary

I joined the RIC on 15 June 1898 and did my training at the RIC depot in the Phoenix Park, Dublin . . . There was no instruction given to us on intelligence work or on political duties . . . During the Home Rule movement the police were generally disinterested, and I would say that the majority of them were in favour of Home Rule. Right from the start of the Irish Volunteers a close watch was kept on them. When meetings were held we were instructed to have a pencil and notebook under our capes and to make notes of what had been said. Police were detailed to attend all parades of the Volunteers and to record who was present when they returned to their barracks. In some cases the police actually assisted in the training of the Volunteers for a short period, but not for long.

Constable Patrick Meehan, Royal Irish Constabulary

When the Irish Volunteers were started I was stationed in Ballinabrackey and there we assisted in drilling and training the Volunteers. Most of the RIC, that is the rank and file, were in favour of Home Rule. Generally I think that it could be taken that the majority of the officer class were opposed to Home Rule.

Frank Hynes, Athenry Company, Co. Galway

The police, instead of preventing us from carrying rifles, used to stand at the barrack door as we marched past, and even shouted words of encouragement to us. We knew what the idea was – the English government thought that we would be available when they wanted us.

James Maguire, Glenidan Company, Co. Westmeath

The RIC from the local barracks always paid us a visit and would have long chats with John Keane. The sergeant used to say, 'I must go up and visit this little republic,' and would have to walk two and a half miles to see us.

Thomas Reidy, Kinvara Company, Co. Galway

Two members of the RIC stationed at Kinvara followed us wherever we went, whether it was along the public road or across the fields. Sometimes we lost them in the fields and they laughed when they caught up with us . . . One thing especially I remember about Father O'Meehan is that he always told us not to insult the RIC, as he was of the opinion that they would change over and join with us when the time came to fight.

Marie Perolz, Irish Citizen Army, Dublin

I had told [James] Connolly once that Myles, a policeman in the Castle, had offered to be of use to us . . . Myles used to give me a lot of information walking along the street without [letting on] we knew each other.

Volunteer companies were often formed after Sunday Mass and collections were held outside churches. Priests could indicate their disapproval at the pulpit or merely by declining to be associated with the movement, but the hierarchy chose not to denounce the Volunteers as it had the IRB, because it was neither an openly subversive nor an oath-bound organisation. Although many clergy remained aloof, a minority – whether motivated by patriotism or a desire to exercise a moderating influence – lent their support.

Paud O'Donoghue, Carriganima Company, Co. Cork

Seán Nolan and I interviewed the local curate, the late Reverend John Casey, brother of the late Bishop Casey of Ross. He agreed to support the movement, and arrangements were made for a public meeting after Mass on the first Sunday in September. At Mass on that Sunday, Father Casey appealed strongly to the young men to join . . . and about twenty-five men joined afterwards.

Bob Kinsella, Ferns Company, Co. Wexford

Early in 1914 a company of the Irish Volunteers was started in Ferns. Father Michael Murphy, who was CC [curate] of Ballyduff, a half-parish of Ferns, took a prominent part in the formation of the company . . . A collection for the Volunteers was held outside the chapel gate and £200 was subscribed.

Felix O'Doherty, Volunteers, Cork

About this time a national collection for the Defence of Ireland Fund was held. For this collection I was ordered to see the local P[arish] P[riest] (Canon Higgins, later Dean of Cloyne) to obtain permission to collect at the church gates. On my way to his house I met him on the road and told him of the collection and the required permission. 'What is the object of the Volunteers?' he asked. 'Well, Canon,' I replied, 'it's to drive the British out of Ireland.' 'Wouldn't it be great if we could do it,' said he. 'By all means hold the collection.' . . . The collection was carried out and realised a good sum.

Edward O'Neill, IRB and F Company, 4th Battalion

Father Matthew used to be out with us at night during training exercises, but he was not a Volunteer.

Father Eugene Coyle, Volunteers leader, Co. Tyrone

I was not an official member of the [IRB] organisation; my priestly calling would not allow my joining an oath-bound society. I attended these [Volunteer] meetings and in this way I hoped to give the country boys the feeling that they were working on the right lines by organising, arming and training for the defence of our country.

John McGahey, Rockcorry Company, Co. Monaghan

Our local company – Rockcorry Company – was organised by our local parish priest, Father Laurence O'Ceiran . . . In the summer of 1914, our company received thirteen rifles, two of which were magazine rifles and eleven were Martini-Henry single-shot rifles. I don't know where the rifles actually came from but I expect we got them through Father O'Ceiran's great influence.

Martin Newell, IRB and Clarenbridge Company, Co. Galway

Some time in 1915, Father Henry Feeney was appointed CC of Clarenbridge and he threw himself wholeheartedly into the advancement of the Volunteers and did everything in his power to encourage us. Meetings of the officers were held in his house, and even bombs were manufactured there. He always attended our parades.

Michael Hynes, Kinvara Company, Co. Galway

I was recruited into the company by Reverend Father O'Meehan, CC, Kinvara . . . Father O'Meehan was our inspiration. He supplied us every week with papers like *Scissors and Paste* and *Nationality* free of charge. He also supplied green uniform hats at his own expense.

The political crisis triggered in the spring of 1914 by the revelation of the unwillingness of British Army officers in the Curragh to impose Home Rule on Ulster, and the successful importation of 25,000 German rifles into Larne by the Ulster Volunteer Force, inflamed nationalist opinion. As moderate nationalists turned to the Volunteers, the Irish Party was forced to shift its position. Encouraging his supporters to join the movement, John Redmond secured the appointment of twenty-five Irish Party nominees to the Volunteers Executive, infuriating Fenians like Tom Clarke.

Gary Holohan, Fianna Éireann and D Company, 1st Battalion

When the Irish Parliamentary Party saw the Volunteer movement embraced by the young people of Ireland, they became alarmed and at once set about gaining control of the organisation.

Joseph Connolly, Volunteers, Belfast

At the beginning recruitment was slow, but due to some sudden change in policy and the word received by the UIL [United Irish League] and AOH branches we were shortly flooded out by members until at the peak point the Belfast regiment must have numbered between four and five thousand . . . Up to a point we succeeded in keeping the Volunteers entirely free from political control, though it became evident early in 1914 that many – but not all – of the Devlinite supporters who were members were working to get control.

Liam Murphy, D Company, Cork City Battalion, and IRB centre
In June 1914, the strength of the Cork City companies was about 400. When the Redmond supporters came in, the strength went up to about 2,000.

Bulmer Hobson, IRB leader and general secretary, Volunteers, Dublin
MacNeill made no secret of what he was doing, but he never brought any phase of it before the committee until forced to do so by Redmond's press ultimatum of 9 June 1914. MacNeill was a straightforward honourable man, incapable of deliberately deceiving anybody, whether his own committee or John Redmond. But it is possible that John Redmond believed that MacNeill, who was chairman of the Provisional Committee, was acting with the full approval of that committee, and that MacNeill failed to make the true position clear.

Seán Fitzgibbon, Provisional Committee, Volunteers
The Provisional Committee met in a strained atmosphere. MacNeill presided at the meeting in the Volunteer office . . . and the committee were arranged around the table. Colonel Moore, [Roger] Casement, being on MacNeill's left, followed by myself, Eamon Martin and Liam Mellows, who was secretary of the organisation. The position on MacNeill's right was occupied by [Bulmer] Hobson. He told me that he deliberately took up that position so that he would be able to wind up the debate, as MacNeill asked each member of the committee in rotation, starting on his left, for his views. MacNeill read a statement in which he proposed the admission of Mr Redmond's nominees, but it was clear that it was with his reluctance and with the intention of avoiding a split at a very critical stage in the national movement . . .

The vote was taken and the proposal passed by a large majority, Hobson winding up the debate in a speech in which he made it clear their decision was being taken not merely for the purpose of avoiding a national split at this time, but leaving nobody under any illusion as to his views on Mr Redmond's dictatorial attitude.

Eamon Martin, Fianna leader and Provisional Committee, Volunteers

When John Redmond issued his ultimatum that twenty-five of his nominees be co-opted to the Volunteer committee, and the majority, swayed by Hobson's appeal to accept the 'bitter pill' and save the organisation, acceded to Redmond's demand, I was among the nine, with our old friend Piaras Béaslaí, who opposed it. I did so for the reason, which I stated at the meeting, that as the Home Rule Party was already fairly well represented in numbers on the committee of thirty, a further twenty-five of Redmond's nominees would simply have meant out-and-out control. Hobson argued that Redmond wanted us to reject his demand – that he would be a very disappointed man if we accepted it and thereby kept the Volunteers intact. But his acceptance, and his persuading of the majority to accept, earned for him very bitter criticism from Tom Clarke and MacDermott and many others. But, thinking back, I have often wondered what would have happened had Hobson's view been rejected. There is, in my opinion, no doubt that the organisation would have been split from top to bottom throughout the country. I agree that the split was inevitable, but I cannot share the view that when it came it was only after irreparable harm had been done by the acceptance of Redmond's ultimatum . . . when the split did occur it was on a more vital issue – one which was to favour and in time greatly strengthen the Sinn Féin element in the Volunteers and in the same due time was to almost completely wipe out the Redmondite faction . . .

Seán McGarry, IRB leader and Volunteers, Dublin

I was with Tom [Clarke] when the news came and to say he was astounded is understating it. I never saw him so moved. He regarded it from the beginning as cold-blooded and contemplated treachery likely to bring about the destruction of the only movement in a century which brought promise of the fulfilment of all his hopes.

Gary Holohan, Fianna Éireann and D Company, 1st Battalion

Hobson was accused of favouring the agreement for the purpose of making a job for himself, but I do not believe that such an accusation should ever have been made. I believe he was quite sincere in his belief that if the Redmondites did not get some representation at the time, they were in a position to split the movement in such a way that the result would be disastrous. I am also satisfied that his action justified itself, and gave the IRB an opportunity of contacting some of the finest patriots that Ireland is proud of. However, the position between Tom Clarke, Seán MacDermott and Bulmer Hobson was never the same.

Thomas Wilson, IRB and Executive Committee, Volunteers, Belfast

When Mr Devlin's nominees came on the committee we were practically swamped with recruits. New companies were formed. The original Volunteers lost control, or had their authority weakened in the appointment of company officers. The Executive Committee remained soundly republican. Friction started on the Executive Committee with Devlin's nominees, which did much harm but did not effect any change in policy.

Séamus Dobbyn, IRB and Volunteers, Belfast

Shortly after the admission of the Devlinite representatives . . . we were supplied with about 800 rifles which were of Italian make but which – unknown to the rank and file – were entirely useless, and for which there was no ammunition. These were nicknamed afterwards, when we realised their uselessness, 'Gaspipes'.

Bulmer Hobson, IRB leader and general secretary, Volunteers, Dublin

As I had anticipated, the Redmondite control proved completely illusory. The work was carried on by the officers and people who had started the movement. Except that the wrangling in the Provisional Committee [with Redmond's nominees] was a waste of time and a nuisance, it had hardly any effect on the development of the movement.

Gary Holohan, Fianna Éireann and D Company, 1st Battalion

. . . the new arrangement was only an unholy alliance. The Redmondites had no intention of building up a strong effective military force. Their mentality was to control everything in the interests of the Irish Party, whose approach to the British government was diametrically opposed to physical force.

Laurence Nugent, K Company, 3rd Battalion

In the majority of companies in the city and county a large number of the Volunteers were members of the AOH or United Irish League. But in actual training, no political opinions were expressed and training went on smoothly . . . The ordinary Volunteer knew little of the squabbles that were going on at the top, but they hoped for the best . . . after the Irish Parliamentary Party got control, a large number of wealthy men, some of the lords, earls, etc., and quite a few ex-British officers who were apparently opposed to the Orange Volunteers, joined up.

James Kavanagh, C Company, 3rd Battalion, and secretary, Defence of Ireland Fund

All the seóiníní flocked into their ranks. Lord this and that would call in to the office to see the secretary.

J. J. Walsh, Provisional Committee chairman, Cork City Corps, Volunteers

At Bantry there was the unique spectacle of no less than three potential armies. At the entrance we met and addressed the O'Brienites. In the middle of the great square were a few Sinn Féiners, while at the other end we addressed the Redmondites. These groups would not work together as one body, and it was the same in many parts of the county . . . Men of different political affiliations worked together in the organisation, but their party allegiance was not altered.

Redmond's takeover of the Volunteers reasserted his grip over popular nationalism, but at a cost to his moderate image in Britain and Ireland. His party's efforts to absorb the vitality of the movement while divesting it of its radicalism met with limited success. The Volunteers continued to expand – peaking at 190,000 men (nearly a fifth of all Irish Catholic males) – but Irish Party activity slumped and Redmond was embarrassed by the separatist faction's coup in smuggling 900 German rifles into Howth on 26 July 1914. The heavy-handed response of the British Army, which killed three protestors at Bachelor's Walk on the same day, further radicalised nationalist opinion.

Bulmer Hobson, IRB leader and general secretary, Volunteers, Dublin

When the Volunteers were started in 1913, we very rapidly got an enormous number of members, variously estimated to be between 100,000 and 150,000. It was this fact which probably impelled Mr Redmond to seek control, but, while we had this vast membership, we had very little funds, and virtually no arms. In order to try and end this deadlock, which was endangering the whole Volunteer position, Casement, on his own initiative, went to London in the early part of 1914 and got together a few friends who between them advanced £1,500 ... The first I heard of this project must have been in June 1914, when Casement asked me if I could make arrangements for the landing of the two cargoes ... On thinking the matter over, I decided that 1,500 rifles would not go very far in solving our problems, but that if we could bring them in in a sufficiently spectacular manner we should probably solve our financial problem and the problem of arming the Volunteers as well. With this in mind I decided to bring the guns in in daylight, in the most open manner and as near as possible to Dublin as possible.

Seán Fitzgibbon, Provisional Committee, Volunteers

The Howth landing was deliberately organised in a spectacular way to win the utmost publicity for the Volunteers and to wake up the country. The Kilcoole cargo, which was as big as the first one, was deliberately organised as a secret operation.

Gary Holohan, Fianna Éireann and D Company, 1st Battalion

I will never forget that march to Howth. We had collected the batons – they were to be used against the police if they gave any trouble – from Thompson's garage in Shaw Street that morning. I knew there was going to be a load of guns landed but I had no idea of where the place would be. We proceeded along the Clontarf Road, past the Bull Wall and Dollymount, and all the time I had my eyes skinned to see if I could notice any suspicious craft on the sea.

Joseph Dolan, A Company, 4th Battalion

When we arrived at the railway station, Howth, we were halted, and saw a little white yacht moving into the harbour. Immediately the yacht went in, we got the order to 'double-quick march'. The leading companies went up to the pier at the double. When we reached the pier Éamonn Ceannt halted us and gave the command: 'Allow no person either to enter or leave this pier.' After about four minutes a police sergeant and two constables came along to the pier and were refused admission. They then demanded admittance in the King's name, but Éamonn Ceannt laughed at them, saying: 'In the name of the Republic you will not be admitted until this little operation is over.'

Seán Prendergast, Fianna Éireann, Dublin

Then a movement from the yacht when a man and a woman commenced handing out articles wrapped in straw, which when torn away revealed to our astonished gaze rifles, rifles, and still more rifles. Oh, the thrill of it! We were gun-running! Who could blame us for being excited? We were frantic, hysterical with joy at the drama that was being enacted at that moment; the indescribable scene of pent-up emotion at first sight of that precious cargo. Some men cheered, some wept with joy; some others too overcome by emotion went pale with excitement . . . At last we were armed. Irish nationalists were armed at last.

Felix O'Doherty, Volunteers, Cork

You would think the fellows would go mad. They started wringing each other's hands and shouting – they were wild with delight. We marched home, every man with a rifle – about 1,500 in all – and we were told not to give them up to anybody, except the Provisional Committee. On our way back we were cheered on all sides. A priest – standing bareheaded on a tram-car – with tears in his eyes – shouted, 'Go on, now, I have given you an old man's blessing.'

Joseph Dolan, A Company, 4th Battalion

When we came to Fairview the military and police held the road against us . . . The next thing we heard was a police officer giving the order to the police to disarm us. The police were not armed. About four or five of them refused to obey the order. They told the police officer that they would not disarm us and refused to stir from where they stood.

Constable Patrick Bermingham, Dublin Metropolitan Police

I mentioned to my comrade Andy O'Neill, 'I wonder if this is anything to do with the nationalist Volunteers because the Ulster Volunteers were allowed to land arms at Larne some months ago and no action was taken against them.' O'Neill answered, 'If they are trying to rush us against the nationalist Volunteers here is one who will have nothing to do with it.' I replied, 'I am with you in that.'

Liam O'Doherty, Volunteers, Dublin

Suddenly, there was a wild stampede. We were forced back, as the line of the Volunteers had given way. There was nobody to lead – Kettle was missing and the commanders couldn't give instructions because they didn't know what to do. Then shots rent the air – I believe they were only blank cartridges – but that served to frighten some of the men who fled in every direction. You will be delighted to hear that the only people who behaved splendidly were the Boy Scouts who were with us. One young fellow halfway up a lamp-post shouted, 'Give me a rifle and I'll do for the whole of them.' They behaved like heroes and stood their ground . . . We were standing like fools at the back and although they had plenty of ammunition they wouldn't give it out. In five minutes we would have shot or routed every soldier on the road. I heard the Peelers absolutely refused to do their duty. In any case they stood lazily by the side and didn't move at any time ... A Volunteer named O'Doherty from the north of Ireland ... broke away and nearly killed a soldier with the butt end of his rifle. Another Volunteer had a revolver which he used mercilessly, and unless he is a very bad shot he must have done some damage. It was a pity they didn't give us the ammunition as we would have taught the soldiers and Dublin Castle a lesson they would never forget.

Bulmer Hobson, IRB leader and general secretary, Volunteers, Dublin

[DMP Assistant Commissioner Harrel] said that we were an illegal body, illegally importing arms which he was about to seize, and before I had time to reply he turned to the police and ordered them to seize the arms. A considerable number of the police did not move and disobeyed the order, while the remainder made a rush for the front company of the Volunteers and a free fight ensued, in which clubbed rifles and batons were freely used. This fight lasted probably less than a minute, when the police withdrew to the footpath of their own accord and without orders. Meanwhile I had been standing with Mr Harrel and was a spectator of the mêlée. At this point I told Mr Harrel that these men, although they had rifles, had no ammunition, that they were peacefully going to their homes, but that there was ammunition in the column and that if he attacked again I could not prevent the distribution, that a great many of his men and my men would be killed, packed in that narrow road, and that the sole responsibility would be his. I had already suspected that he might have gone out without orders, and I rapidly saw that his nerve was visibly ebbing and that he realised the impossibility of taking rifles from 900 men with eighty reluctant policemen.

Patrick Egan, C Company, 4th Battalion

The police were then withdrawn, and the Scottish Borderers moved up. I saw Commandants Éamonn Ceannt and Thomas MacDonagh in front; both officers knelt down; Ceannt rested his Mauser pistol on MacDonagh's shoulder and opened fire. Charlie and I ran back to the trek wagon which contained the ammunition. Several Fianna lads were standing around the car with drawn revolvers. I think

Eamon Martin was one of them. The road was jammed with Volunteers roaring and shouting for ammunition, while the Fianna threatened us if we advanced a step nearer. Lying along the top of a wall bordering the road was a young Fianna lad emptying his revolver over the heads of the men on the roadway into the Scottish Borderers. An order was quietly passed around the men to slip across the fields of O'Brien Institute.

Seán Prendergast, Fianna Éireann, Dublin

Shots were ringing out. I could see some of our Fianna officers on the wall of the O'Brien Institute, which stretched along the right side of the road down to Fairview, firing revolvers. Pandemonium reigned. In the midst of this we Fianna boys had a stiff time to keep off the Volunteers who were clamouring for the ammunition from the trek-cart. The police menacingly were approaching our group. We had to beat them off as best we could with our clubbed rifles, which for many caused quite an effort.

Gary Holohan, Fianna Éireann and D Company, 1st Battalion

The soldiers who were sent out to disarm us were very angry, having failed in their task, and were determined to have revenge on the citizens. That evening when they (the King's Own Scottish Borderers) were returning to the Royal barracks (now Collins barracks), they fired on the people at Bachelor's Walk. Two [three] men were killed and several others wounded. It was decided to give them a public funeral . . . Imagine my amazement when I saw a party of men parading with Howth guns.

Michael William O'Reilly, B Company, 2nd Battalion

The events of Bachelor's Walk brought recruits pouring into the Volunteers and we were kept extremely busy getting our new men into check.

Liam O'Brien, F Company, 1st Battalion, and IRB

When the first big consignment was landed at Howth, the Redmond nominees knew nothing of it. This was the beginning of that necessary double-dealing which was to play such an important part in the events of Easter Week. After the Howth affair the joint committee was doomed.

Bulmer Hobson, IRB leader and general secretary, Volunteers, Dublin

We got £1,000 from America the day after, and thereafter we received help from different organisations in America at the rate of about £1,000 a month. Money also came in from various parts of Ireland, and after the gun-running we never had any serious financial worries.

Liam Tobin, C Company, 1st Battalion

I joined the Volunteers immediately after the Howth gun-running. Previous to that I had been rather critical of the then Irish Volunteers ... That incident convinced us that the Volunteers meant business.

5
England's Difficulty: War

The Home Rule crisis, and the possibility of sectarian violence in Ulster, were put into suspension by the outbreak of the Great War on 3 August 1914. The subsequent transformation of the political atmosphere appeared to vindicate Redmond's decision to support the British war effort. In the longer term, however, the formation of a Westminster coalition government comprising conservative and unionist opponents of Home Rule in May 1915, and growing fears about conscription, created a more favourable atmosphere for separatists as they prepared for a wartime insurrection.

*

On the outbreak of the war 58,000 Irish military personnel and reservists were mobilised, while around 32,000 Irish Volunteers served in the British forces in total. This enthusiastic response, which contrasted with the far more ambivalent response to the Boer War, highlighted the strikingly moderate nature of popular nationalism – and the marginal status of separatism – in the summer of 1914.

Thomas Courtney, Castlegar Company, Co. Galway

When the war started in August 1914 the town of Galway went recruiting mad. It was not a question of 'Will you join up?' but 'What regiment are you joining?'

Laurence Nugent, K Company, 3rd Battalion

British propaganda at that time was extraordinary and there was little opportunity of counteracting it. Men of Sinn Féin and the

Volunteers who spoke against recruiting were jailed. The country generally had lost its old national spirit.

Kevin O'Shiel, Volunteers, Dublin

In those days of constant surprises and crises, the event that excited and stirred the country most deeply was the invasion of Belgium. And not so much the invasion itself as the burnings, shootings and lootings that the newspapers told us followed in the wake of the conquerors. I can still remember those lurid reports and their profound reactions on our feelings . . . For example, after the destruction of Louvain, the Dublin mob rose up and, in its anger and indignation, sacked and looted the German-owned pork shops in the city, and the DMP had the greatest difficulty in preventing those premises from being set on fire . . . In those days, Ireland was nearer the English point of view than she has ever been before or since.

Jim O'Shea, Irish Citizen Army, Dublin

No matter where you looked there was khaki. Every bit of wall space seemed papered with one kind of recruiting appeal. Between the soldiers and their women it seemed as if we were getting more English than the English themselves and that there would soon be no room for anything but khaki in the city.

Gary Holohan, D Company, 1st Battalion

The number of men who went away was colossal . . . They were carried away in the mail boats and in liners escorted by destroyers. There would be troops packed everywhere, in the lifeboats, on the bridge, from stern to stern. All the other ships in the harbour would blow their sirens, while everybody sang 'Rule Britannia, Britannia Rules the Waves' and 'God Save the King' . . . There was hardly a family in Dublin that was not affected, with the exception of the extreme nationalists, and even these were affected in some cases.

Kevin O'Shiel, Volunteers, Dublin

The average young nationalist was, for a time, torn between conflicting ideals of duty, conflicting appeals and conflicting emotions. In my own case, I hardly knew where I stood. On the one hand, I found every day more and more of my contemporaries, my fellow students of yesterday, donning the khaki, drawn to the army by the appeals of John Redmond, and, much more so, by the sufferings of invaded Belgium . . . The streets were full of uniforms – soldiers, naval men and those new curiosities that Irish eyes found it difficult to get used to – the WAACs and WRNSs and other types of female warriors . . . Companies, detachments and, now and again, whole regiments of troops were constantly marching along the streets to their various assignments. The latter, led by a band and fully equipped, were for the docks, en route for the front, accompanied by crowds of friends and supporters, cheering them off . . . Nearly every dead wall in the city had an enormous outsize picture of Kitchener's forbidding countenance pointing a huge forefinger at us with the single pronoun in huge capitals: 'YOU!'

John McCoy, Mullaghbawn Company, Co. Down

The fact that the Home Rule Act was on the statute book was used as an argument to encourage young nationalists to join up and do their part in fighting for small nations on the European Continent. I attended recruiting meetings and got a certain amount of thrill listening to a good military band playing traditional Irish war marches. I was not enthusiastic about the war. I was not against it. I had no feeling of resentment against acquaintances who joined the army or navy. I resented the British government's attitude towards the antics of the Ulster Volunteers in 1912–14 and their quibbling on the question of Home Rule. I looked on John Redmond as weak when England was in her hour of difficulty at the outbreak of the war and I distrusted his promises to have Home Rule put into operation at the end of the war . . . In our locality and, I may say, all over South Armagh a spirit of at least tolerance of the British war effort was everywhere apparent. Dances and entertainments were frequently held for the British Red Cross and a lot of 'nationalists' attended. Announcements were frequently made of locals killed in action or missing at the war fronts. There was generally a feeling of disinterestedness in every phase of political life at this time. Prices for all classes of farm produce were high and the farmers were making money.

Joseph O'Connor, A Company, 3rd Battalion

People who were what one would have thought rebels on Sunday were completely pro-British the following Sunday . . . One of the sickening things in all this pre-'16 period was the inconstancy of the ordinary people . . .

Felix O'Doherty, Volunteers, Cork

It was a sickening sight in those days for anyone who loved Ireland: the hoardings plastered with recruiting posters – 'Your King and Country need you', 'Join an Irish Regiment today', 'Come, boy, and lend a hand', 'You can be a rebel and still join in the fight'. With the exception of the faithful few – the Irish Volunteers – the country was reeking with imperialism. The majority were influenced by the crowd: they were too weak-willed to follow the dictates of their conscience.

Although the outbreak of war initially spurred volunteering in some quarters, the mobilisation of the Volunteers' reservist drill sergeants and the recruitment of large numbers of urban men depleted the movement. John Redmond's call for Irishmen to serve in the British Army, made at Woodenbridge on 20 September, inevitably split the Volunteers. Over 90 per cent joined the Redmondite National Volunteers, reducing the militant Irish Volunteer minority to a marginal rump.

Peadar Doyle, F Company, 4th Battalion

In the hectic excitement of that early war period, volunteering became suddenly fashionable . . . The Volunteer movement was inundated by members who at the time had no real sympathy with the real ideas of the Volunteers. Rapidly the Volunteer movement was being converted into a recruiting instrument for the British Army.

Bulmer Hobson, IRB Supreme Council and general secretary, Volunteers, Dublin

Lord Powerscourt announced his adhesion to the movement and turned up at a parade of the Bray Company and tried to present them with a Union Jack.

George Berkeley, chief inspecting officer, Volunteers, Belfast

As far as I could reckon we had lost at least 700 men, either as reservists or through enlistment, during the first ten days – there may have been more.

David McGuinness, Volunteers, Belfast

The course of the war . . . diverted people's minds from the early national aspects of our struggle for Home Rule, and amongst the extreme crowd of nationalists, from the Republic . . . and so the Volunteer movement fell into a feeling of apathy and indifference.

David O'Callaghan, Castletownroche Company, Co. Cork

Sullivan and Jones – the drill instructors – were British Army reservists and were called up in August 1914. This and the difference of opinion on the question of Redmond's recruiting campaign finished any organisation that existed and the company faded out.

Patrick Houlihan, Annascaul Company, Co. Kerry

The Great War had just started and we had a parade of Volunteers. We were addressed by Thomas O'Donnell, MP, and the McGillycuddy of the Reeks . . . They spoke to us about joining up in the British Army and told us we were fine fellows. We had joined the Volunteers to fight for Ireland and when we heard the recruiting speech a group of us walked out.

Cornelius Meany, IRB and Mushera Company, Co. Cork

Captain [Talbot] Crosbie proceeded to address the [Millstreet] committee and, in the course of his remarks, spoke somewhat as follows: 'We are actually at war with Germany and the boom of her guns may at any moment be heard on our shores.' At this point he was interrupted by a member of the committee who said, 'We are not at war with Germany; England is, but we are not.' Crosbie replied, 'That is all very well, but if we are invaded and you tell that story to a German soldier his answer would be a crack of a rifle butt across your head, and what would our women and children do?' The interrupter answered, 'Our women and children could not fare worse than they recently did at the hands of the British at

Bachelor's Walk.' When the captain found that he could not make any progress he stated that further discussion would not serve any purpose, and said he was about to take a certain course which he would not state then, but that he would make a public announcement in a day or two. On the following night [30 August] in Cork he publicly announced his intention of joining the British Army.

Patrick O'Sullivan, Kilnamartyra Company, Co. Cork

We were to go to Cork next day for an inspection which was to be carried out by Captain Talbot Crosbie . . . My uncle, Dan Harrington, asked if Captain Talbot Crosbie was an officer of the British Army, and if our attendance in Cork next day [30 August] would pledge us to support England's war effort. Not receiving any satisfactory reply, my uncle and I and two others stepped out of the ranks, indicating our disapproval of any attempt to identify the Volunteers with England's war. That finished the company.

Liam Murphy, D Company, Cork City Battalion

About 2,000 Volunteers were present at the Cornmarket meeting on 30 August 1914 . . . Captain Talbot Crosbie had no connection with the Volunteers before he was appointed chief inspecting officer for Cork county after the Redmond followers came in. At the parade on 30 August he read a telegram he had sent to the War Office offering the services of the Cork Volunteers to the British government, and said he had received a reply. The Volunteers, he said, would have to decide that day between him and the committee . . . No formal vote was taken, the parade just divided in support of one side or the other. About sixty or seventy officers and men followed the committee, the remainder accepted Crosbie's leadership.

Liam Tannam, E Company, 3rd Battalion

I was present at the Redmondite split. As far as I can recollect the company was about 130 strong. The majority were present on the night of the split. Éamon de Valera put the matter bluntly that the parting of the ways had come, and he explained the situation and he said, 'Those who side with Ireland will go to that side of the hall, and those who would like to support the British Empire will take the other.' As far as I remember there was no count but I was almost certain that there were two or three of a majority remained with the Irish Volunteers. The drill hall belonged to the AOH . . . and, therefore, we had to march out.

Michael Leahy, Cobh Company, Co. Cork

The split came in September 1914, at a meeting called by the committee at the Baths Hall (now the Tower Cinema). Joseph Healy was chairman and he put the Redmondite point of view to the meeting. It was to the effect that the Volunteers would join the British Army. The meeting seemed unanimous. I attempted to speak but was struck by a man named Charlie Finn. The chairman, however, secured me a hearing and I was put upon a seat. I objected to recruiting the Volunteers for the British Empire, and said they had been established to fight for the freedom of Ireland. I asked any man who believed as I did to follow me out of the hall. Fifteen of us walked out. We were jeered and hissed, and barely escaped being beaten up.

Thomas Treacy, Kilkenny Company

Peter De Loughry called on all those who stood for Ireland and the green flag to fall out and line up at a point indicated by him, near the poultry sheds in the market place; and all those who stood for England and the Union Jack to stand where they were. Twenty-eight men left the ranks and lined up at the point indicated for those who stood for Ireland and the green flag; and the balance on parade (over 600) stood on the Redmondite side . . . I formed them into company formation and marched them out of the market amidst a most hostile demonstration. Tempers on both sides were very frayed and a feather could have turned it into a riot.

James Maguire, Glenidan Company, Co. Westmeath

. . . our whole company fell asunder. They were not going to fight Ulster, they were not going to France, and the whole thing collapsed.

Joseph Connolly, Volunteers, Belfast

Of that meeting it will suffice to say that Mr Devlin took over complete control of the Belfast regiment and organisation. No hearing was given to any of us. Denis McCullough made a futile effort to state our point of view but it was quite evident that the vast majority had been organised to howl down any person who was opposed to the new departure and recruitment for the British Army. We were ejected from the meeting . . . only about 200 remained loyal to the original Volunteers, the remainder – the vast majority – lining up behind Devlin.

Nancy Wyse Power, Executive Committee, Cumann na mBan

After the Volunteer split on the outbreak of the war, a convention of Cumann na mBan was held to determine the future of the organisation. There was a strong element which was anxious not to involve itself in the split; they desired to remain neutral and to assist both Volunteer bodies. The convention, however, voted that the resources of the society should be pledged to the Irish Volunteers . . . Miss O'Farrelly resigned with a number of others and when the convention decision was conveyed to the branches, many members followed suit, whole branches disappearing in some cases.

Máire Fitzpatrick, Cumann na mBan, Enniscorthy, Co. Wexford

I gave my speech and asked any member that was against Redmond to stand on my side of the hall, but Mrs Green and I were standing alone. It was my first big disappointment. I was heartbroken.

The decline of the Irish Volunteers continued after the split, even in Dublin where it had initially retained significant support. Although falling under the renewed suspicion of most nationalists, the Volunteers' retention of its most militant members strengthened its resolve and the IRB's influence over the movement.

Liam Tannam, E Company, 3rd Battalion

About fifty on our side were mostly juveniles, and their fathers and mothers advised them to keep away from the Irish Volunteers because the old people at the time had been backing Redmond. The next parade mustered about twenty-five. The parade was held in a field opposite Donnybrook Catholic Church. In a few weeks' time our numbers had declined to seven, i.e. de Valera plus seven men. Even with that small number de Valera carried on as if he had a full company and solemnly issued orders to form fours with the seven men.

Laurence Nugent, K Company, 3rd Battalion

During the period after the split in many districts the men began to fall away. The early enthusiasm was disappearing and this applied to both sections of the Volunteers.

Diarmuid Ó Donneabhain, Executive Committee, Cork City Corps, Volunteers

After the split there were not more than seventy Irish Volunteers in the city.

Liam Gaynor, IRB and Volunteers, Belfast

The physical force body, who were in a very small minority, gathered and held weekly drills in old military huts at Willowbank, Falls Road, Belfast. At these drill parades about forty-five Volunteers attended regularly.

Séamus Dobbyn, IRB and Volunteers, Belfast

We were actually afraid to appear in public, afraid of our own people, because we were informed that if we appeared we would be attacked by the people themselves, the Hibernian people.

Francis McQuillan, IRB and Dundalk Company, Co. Louth

For some time after the split it would be difficult to get more than half a dozen to attend a meeting.

Cornelius Murphy, B Company, Cork City Battalion, and IRB

We were ostracised by our neighbours, by our bosses and by some of our priests. We were jeered at in public and spat upon. Men's employment was jeopardised by membership of the Volunteers and some lost their jobs when they would not give up membership.

There were incidents when people spat into our collection boxes. There was one solitary Volunteer in Douglas; he was almost a pariah and dare not wear his equipment when leaving home. It required great moral courage to continue in face of this opposition.

Eamon O'Connor, A Company, Tralee Battalion, Co. Kerry

Later on considerable pressure was put on many Volunteers by their employers, as a result of which they either fell out altogether or went over to the National Volunteers . . . My own company was, in fact, practically wiped out in this way . . . During 1915 the attitude of a section of employers in the town hardened against the Volunteers. A number of men lost their employment. [Austin] Stack was dismissed from his post as income tax collector in March; [Alf] Cotton lost his job in the employment exchange in April; and in May, Joe Melinn was dismissed by Slattery's.

Thomas O'Donovan, Dunmanway Company, Co. Cork

The people generally took no interest, even men who turned out good afterwards. They said we were only leading the boys into trouble. Some were hostile and set the dogs on us when we were collecting.

Seán McGarry, IRB and Volunteers, Dublin

There was some consolation in the fact that those who remained in the Irish Volunteers after the split meant business.

Henry Murray, A Company, 4th Battalion

It was at this stage that A Company commenced to become an efficient military unit. The officers were no longer burdened with the handling of a large body of men, many of whom were strangers to them, and for the first time felt that they had the full confidence of the men. In consequence the officers were accepted by the men as leaders in a movement that had a serious purpose and personal associations were formed which were invaluable to efficiency and esprit de corps.

In late 1915, as the war grew unpopular, the Irish Volunteers began to revive. While the Redmondite Volunteers disintegrated amidst fears of conscription, the Irish Volunteers' opposition to the war provided it with a sense of purpose. The resumption of drilling, parades and demonstrations – most notably the funeral of veteran Fenian Jeremiah O'Donovan Rossa – asserted the movement's growing confidence and presented a challenge which Dublin Castle chose not to confront.

Frank Drohan, Clonmel Company, Co. Tipperary

A lot of Redmondite Volunteers were by this time becoming shaken in their allegiance as they saw that the only outlook for that organisation was to provide recruits for the British Army, and so the organisation had begun to dwindle away.

John McCoy, Mullaghbawn Company, Co. Down

The majority of Mullaghbawn Company were then followers of the Redmondite party but they did not like the idea of taking part in England's war effort. Drilling ceased at this period.

Cornelius Meany, IRB and Mushera Company, Co. Cork

Immediately after Messrs Redmond and O'Brien offered the services of the Irish Volunteers to the British military authorities, both corps of Volunteers in Millstreet ceased to exist.

Michael Ó Cuill, Volunteers, Cork

All the AOH element did not approve of offering the Volunteers to the British War Office. One of them came to me to help distribute handbills prepared by Pat Ahern. These were against enlistment in the British Army.

Kevin O'Shiel, Volunteers, Dublin

The Sinn Féin and advanced nationalist papers were then beginning to expand and to influence bodies of nationalists, mostly young, who, a few months previously, would have nothing to say to them. Subtly, clearly and constantly, they appealed to and drew out the latent and nationalist separatism inherent in nearly every young Irishman, thereby developing in us an extremely critical attitude towards the [Irish] Party and the Liberal government . . . My battalion, though one of the first after the split to proclaim its allegiance to John Redmond, through its captain, J. M. Muldoon, just withered away and vanished into thin air.

Kevin O'Shiel, Volunteers, Dublin

The hoardings and dead walls were papered over with posters and informing [Irish] youth that 'England expects every man to do his duty' . . . separatists altered the slogan to read: 'England expects every Irishman to do *her* duty'.

Thomas Doyle, IRB and Enniscorthy Company, Co. Wexford

Mick Kelly, the chemist, was one of them [who enlisted]. He was not out long until he lost his arm. At this time the British government had posters put up around the town with the photo of a soldier on them. The wording on the poster was 'Join the army and lend a hand'. Some member of the IRB had slips printed and put under the poster: 'Mike Kelly lent a hand but never got it back'.

Eamonn Ahern, Dungourney Company, Co. Cork

The immediate circumstances which gave rise to the formation of the company were that Tom and David Kent of Castlelyons came to Dungourney on a Sunday in October 1915 . . . I got five or six of the local lads to go through the congregation to ask the men to assemble at the Tallow side of the village after Mass. About 100 men, young and old, assembled. We put them in fours and told them what we proposed to do. They were instructed that they were to hold their formation whatever happened and not break ranks. I went down to the village to see if the recruiting meeting was on – it was. Captain Donnellan, Major Hallinan and a few other speakers from Cork were present. There were no military or police. I went back and we then marched our body of men right through the meeting. When Captain Donnellan saw us coming, he said, 'Here are the boys'; he thought we were National Volunteers. We marched on to the end of the village, then turned about and marched back. When we got back in a few minutes, the meeting had broken up and the people scattered. Captain Donnellan went to the parish priest. We then adjourned to an old library building on the Mount

Uniake road, where we held a meeting and decided to form a company of Volunteers.

Michael Spillane and Michael Sullivan, Killarney Company and IRB, Co. Kerry

Later the same year [1915] Tom O'Donnell MP was the principal speaker at a recruiting meeting for the British Army in College Square, Killarney, surrounded by soldiers and RIC. The Volunteers pipers' band of Killarney, followed by . . . a fully armed company marched up and down through the recruiting meeting, and all present, except military and police, followed the Volunteers, and this finished all active recruiting in this area.

Edward Moane, Westport Company, Co. Mayo

At the end of November 1915 Captain Balfe and Lord Sligo addressed a big recruiting meeting from the balcony of the town hall . . . It was a very big meeting, as such meetings usually were, and elaborate arrangements had been made to receive recruits. Not even one recruit did they get. That night we paraded the Volunteers, about 150 strong, and marched through the town. Arising out of this parade, twelve of us were arrested by the RIC and brought to Castlebar and tried before Judge Doyle at the Quarter Sessions . . . We were put on bail. I walked out of court without signing anything, and I believe others did the same . . . This incident sent our stock soaring amongst the people of Westport . . .

Dermot O'Sullivan, Fianna Éireann, Dublin

Limerick city at that time [May 1915] was recognised as very anti-Irish in its outlook and it was felt that by a show of strength on the part of the Volunteers it might change the feelings and outlook of the people there.

Alphonsus O'Halloran, Volunteers, Limerick

The march along the Boherbuidhe district was through a barrage of abuse from thousands of excited females, who hurled at the Volunteers such taunts, jeers and reproaches as only the fertile wit of womankind can coin, but the men marched on with scarce a glance to right or left. It was not until the head of the column reached Irishtown that signs of a more malignant hostility became apparent. Mungret Street, its chief thoroughfare, is one of the oldest streets in the city, and behind it on either side lie the slum areas of Watergate and Palmerstown, which were wont to furnish some of the finest fighting material of the famous Munster Fusiliers. The inhabitants, whose banked masses on either side of the street scarcely confided a passage for the marching men, were not content with verbal compliments, but brought bottles, stones and other missiles to reinforce them. They had been told that these men had cheered and gloated over every disaster that had befallen the Munsters in the war which was then raging, and so their hearts were filled with bitter hatred of the pro-German Sinn Féiners, as they called the Irish Volunteers.

Father Michael Curran, secretary to Archbishop William Walsh, Dublin
The funeral of O'Donovan Rossa on 1 August 1915 was to my mind the date that publicly revealed that a new political era had begun. It was the prelude to the 1916 Rising . . . I arrived at Glasnevin as the crowds were returning. The funeral was most impressive, skilfully organised and carried out. It was a challenge to Dublin Castle and a deeply significant lesson to the Irish people. The Irish Volunteers and a detachment of the Citizen Army marched in uniform, some with arms. Besides the various organisations allied to Sinn Féin, many municipal and local government bodies took part. So too did the GAA in large numbers, and the National Volunteers, but these without arms. Pearse's graveside oration has become a classic, but the supremely impressive moment was the triple volley fired by the Volunteers. It was more than a farewell to an old Fenian. It was a defiance to England by a new generation in Ireland. I heard the volleys as I hurried up Iona Road.

Peter Galligan, Enniscorthy Company, Co. Wexford
On the day of the funeral, [Thomas] MacDonagh established his HQ on Grattan Bridge in a cab and my orders were to keep a clear passage from Grattan Bridge to the City Hall. He placed a company of Volunteers at my disposal to do this and I lined the route with

them. A superintendent of the DMP approached me in a furious temper . . . He had an argument with MacDonagh and he ordered me to put him under arrest, which I did, and he was detained until the funeral passed.

Leslie Price, Cumann na mBan, Dublin

When the armed Volunteers passed I then suddenly realised that the men I had seen – Tom Clarke, The O'Rahilly, Seán McGarry – looked as if they meant serious business. This aspect of the funeral and the reading of Pearse's oration the following day made such a deep impression on my mind that on the following Thursday night I joined the Árd Craobh of the Cumann na mBan. I joined from conviction and on my own volition.

Seán Cody, G Company, 1st Battalion

On St Patrick's Day 1916 the Dublin Brigade, practically fully armed, uniformed and equipped, paraded through the city of Dublin and held that portion of Dame Street from the City Hall to the Bank of Ireland for over an hour, during which no traffic was allowed to break the ranks of the Volunteers, Citizen Army and Cumann na mBan. I remember seeing on that day British soldiers with horse-drawn vehicles conveying war material from the North Wall under heavy armed guards being stopped and ordered to proceed on alternative routes and having no choice but to obey the directions of our men. A large force of armed policemen were simply powerless to intervene . . . it was felt by all that soon something big would take place.

William Daly, E Company, 2nd Battalion

We received orders drawing us to attention, were filed into SS Michael and John's to attend the special Mass held for the benefit of the Irish Volunteers. The Reverend Father Nevin, I believe, officiated and the scene had a profound effect on me which will never leave my mind. A guard of honour in full uniform had been drawn up around the altar and the chapel packed to its utmost capacity with Volunteers. At the elevation the guard of honour drew their swords to the salute while the bugles rang out with a clarity that was astounding owing to the packed condition of the chapel; in the immediate silence that took place the priest on the altar, with the guard in the attitude of salute, looked like a vision from another world and in the faces of those near me was the appearance that they also were looking into something wonderful. Patrick Pearse, The O'Rahilly, Seán MacDermott and the Executive, who were in close attendance near the altar, appeared to look in their uniforms as if receiving a special blessing from God, and undoubtedly every man attending that Mass received such a blessing. Suddenly a rich baritone voice burst into the hymn to our patron saint, 'Hail Glorious St Patrick', and it was taken up by the whole congregation in such a fervent manner that a lump rose in my throat and I wanted to burst out crying or do something to prove that I was worthy of being in their company.

Jim O'Shea, Irish Citizen Army, Dublin

There was a great protest meeting held on St Stephen's Green and the ICA was mobilised for duty. It was a stirring affair and we got a lot of wholesome respect out of it as we faced the cream of RIC, armed with carbines that night, also DMP. There was no speaking but a thoroughly disciplined armed workers' army in batches facing the police. Wherever there was a squad of police that night there was a squad of Citizen Army facing them. It was turn about with a vengeance and they did not move. The meeting was a success and Dublin Castle knuckled under after proclaiming the meeting.

Efforts to arm the Irish Volunteers were now stepped up. Guns were purchased, stolen or smuggled into the country, and weapons and ammunition were manufactured. But, despite such ingenuity, the movement remained dependent on the arrival of German arms to mount a mass insurrection.

Gary Holohan, D Company, 1st Battalion

I carried a Howth gun for a short period, but I was given one of the first long Lee-Enfield magazine rifles that came into the country for the Volunteers. I paid five guineas for it and one hundred rounds of

.303 ammunition. I also bought a Savage automatic pistol, .32 I think, for £2.5*s*.0*d*. and one hundred rounds of ammunition. I paid for these by instalments to Bulmer Hobson, and they were fully paid for before the Rising. I got my rifle from Seán Murphy; he had a shop in Clanbrassil Street at the time.

Michael Staines, quartermaster, A, D and G companies, 1st Battalion

Every man in the three companies had a rifle . . . I obtained rifles from The O'Rahilly, from members of the IRB, revolvers and shotguns from Henshaw's, where I was employed, shotguns and ammunition from Garnett's and Keegan's gunsmiths. In addition I obtained them from Peadar Breslin and Jack Shaw, who got them from British soldiers by purchase. My brother, Humphrey, who was employed on the liner *Baltic*, used to bring from America about twenty revolvers on each trip to Liverpool.

George Berkeley, chief inspecting officer, Volunteers, Belfast

The position of the gunsmiths was peculiar; nominally the importation of arms was forbidden, but actually it was in full swing. In Belfast the only restriction was that nationalists could not get them.

Cornelius Murphy, B Company, Cork City Battalion

The first rifles that came to Cork in bulk were purchased from D. T. O'Sullivan, Cook Street, in 1915. I think that lot was fifty Lee-Enfield rifles and they cost £5 each. They were the last free imports; the prohibition against the importation of arms came into force just after they arrived.

Michael O'Flanagan, Volunteers and IRB, Glasgow

My job as a public-house manager brought me into contact with many Irishmen, particularly natives of Donegal, who were employed in the mining areas surrounding Glasgow. They were all native Irish speakers . . . These men by reason of their employment had access to explosives such as gelignite, detonators and fuses, etc., which they brought me in small quantities from time to time and which I handed over to my quartermaster, Liam Gribben.

Séamus Robinson, IRB and Volunteers, Glasgow

Towards the end of 1915 I began to notice a suppressed excitement among the Fianna lads; they were holding their heads high, becoming self-confident with an elated seriousness. They were raiding continually for munitions. This activity increased as 1916 approached. The raids had become almost 'barefaced' – they had got away with so much for so long without detection. At last a sort of grand finale was planned and carried out at Uddington, I think it was, when a big haul of explosives was captured. An exodus of all able-bodied Volunteers [to Ireland] was to follow this.

Séamus Reader, IRB and Volunteers, Glasgow

On 1 January 1916, with Eamon Murray and Alec Carmichael, I arrived in Belfast from Glasgow with one portmanteau and two small cases containing 150 rounds of .303 and 200 rounds of assorted revolver ammunition, eight short .45 and eight .32 revolvers, 40 feet of strum or fuse, 200 detonators and one stone of explosive.

Liam Murphy, D Company, Cork City Battalion, and IRB centre

We got 6,000 rounds of .303 off a train at Kilbarry in 1915. Four boxes of it containing 1,000 rounds each were brought to my house . . . They were painted red and had geranium pots placed on them on windowsills.

Seán O'Keefe, B Company, 3rd Battalion

In some cases soldiers whom we knew gave us their rifles; in others, we bought them. The price we paid varied between £1 and £3 for each rifle. In a few cases where soldiers were not prepared to give them or sell a row was picked and in the mêlée which followed the rifle disappeared.

Liam O'Carroll, A Company, 1st Battalion

As a matter of fact, my father bought quite a quantity. He had a shop in Manor Street. These fellows, when they wanted a few drinks, would take anything out of the barracks.

Luke Bradley, Irish Citizen Army

At that time publicans were forbidden by the authorities to serve soldiers with drink if they were carrying rifles. Soldiers on leave lost many a rifle when they handed them to someone who obligingly offered to look after them while they had a drink in one of the pubs on the quays.

Gary Holohan, Fianna Éireann and D Company, 1st Battalion

These soldiers were always short of money and they would sell their shirts, socks, boots and brushes to get drink . . . After a time, there were so many guns missing, it was arranged to disarm the soldiers in England before they took the boat.

Sergeant Edward Handley, 4th Battalion, Royal Dublin Fusiliers

The authorities knew that rifles were being taken but I was never suspected . . . A military policeman who had been transferred from Portobello with me knew what I was doing and was sympathetic. I always chose the time he was on duty at the back gate to pass out the rifles. In Wellington barracks there were huts where men used to go for lectures on wet days. They often left their rifles outside the huts and it was an easy matter to take a few.

Dick Balfe, D Company, 3rd Battalion

Through our intelligence system we heard that they were to hold a display before Lord Wimborne at Trinity College. D Company, with the assistance of members of the Fianna, equipped ourselves with caps and armlets marked 'G. R.' We went to Beggars Bush barracks and said we were sent there and were equipped. There were about twenty of us in it. We were equipped with the best Lee-Enfields together with haversacks and belts. We marched from Beggars Bush barracks to Trinity College and took part in a display before the Lord Lieutenant. I was section commander. We were complimented by the Lord Lieutenant on our efficiency and display, which consisted of ordinary foot and arms drill. When it was over we left Trinity College and took a wrong turn.

Michael Walsh, Gaggin Company, Co. Cork

We had plenty of cartridges, as we had made our own buckshot and filled a number of cartridges with them. I had a machine for filling cartridges. I had also about ten pounds of gelignite, which I used in my own business, and some fuse.

Peter Galligan, Enniscorthy Company, Co. Wexford

During the latter end of 1915 and early 1916 the Enniscorthy Battalion had decided to start making pikeheads owing to the shortage of other arms. The pikes were made on the '98 pattern and fitted with six-foot shafts.

Joseph Lawless, C Company, 1st Battalion

. . . I found myself confronted with a problem. Most of the gelignite was frozen, and my knowledge of this explosive extended far enough to realise that it was dangerous and uncertain in this state. How to thaw it out in the one day available was not so easy with facilities available in a farmyard, so I spread it out in the sun on a rick cover at the back of a ditch, while I hovered around to keep off stray-comers who might be too inquisitive. But the April sun was not very warm and the process seemed too slow. A lot of it was oozing nitroglycerine, but nevertheless I packed a lot around my body, carrying it around so that the heat of my body helped the thawing process. Finally, I decided to take a chance by spreading it near the kitchen range while I sat and watched over it. Perhaps I was lucky, but at any rate it appeared to be all right by tea-time, and I packed it away to await the morrow.

Desmond Ryan, E Company, 4th Battalion

For some months before the Rising, I helped in the manufacture of tin-can hand grenades and the filling of shotgun cartridges in the Hermitage, Rathfarnham, a work which was spread over three months, to the best of my knowledge. This work was undertaken at the request of P. H. Pearse, and was done under the directions of Peter Slattery, then a science master in St Enda's . . . When raids for ammunition became frequent before the Rising about 1915, Pearse made us carry around several hundred rounds of .303 concealed on our persons all day, on trams, in the streets, everywhere till the alarm died down. The grenades were stored in a room in the basement of St Enda's, and our work on the bombs was carried out in our study room – we were all NUI students in an upper room of the Hermitage.

Joe Good, 'Kimmage Garrison'

Mick Collins ordered me to go to Larkfield, Kimmage. This place was 4th Battalion HQ, where they had a miniature range. When I arrived there I found thirty or forty men, mainly Liverpool men, occupying a derelict mill, part of some property belonging to Count Plunkett, whose residence adjoined the old mill . . . The number in Kimmage swelled to sixty-four or eighty-four, composed of men from Manchester, London, Liverpool and Glasgow, the majority of whom were born in England . . . We behaved as disciplined troops, and when not drilling we were engaged in making ammunition. The ammunition consisted of shotgun cartridges filled with large slugs, larger than peas. We sometimes worked a 24-hour shift. We also made hand grenades.

Matthew Connolly, Irish Citizen Army, Dublin

The 'armour room', on the first floor [of Liberty Hall], was a busy place. Improvised hand grenades were being manufactured. Cartridges were being altered to fit rifles and guns for which they were meant. Bayonets, of an old French type, were being heated over a blow-lamp and bent or reshaped, to fit an old German Mauser rifle. It was quite a common thing, on entering the armoury room, to find a man sitting over the fire, brewing a can of tea on one side of it, while melting a pot of lead on the other side; two or three men at a bench, making some repairs to a rifle, while, at the same time, two or three others were stretched on the bare floor, snoring, fast asleep.

Despite the devastating impact of the Volunteers split, the IRB Supreme Council resolved, in September 1914, to mount a wartime rising. Although some leading Fenians, notably Bulmer Hobson, opposed an unprovoked rebellion, Tom Clarke's militant faction argued that the credibility of Fenianism depended on a wartime insurrection. A secret Military Council, later joined by ICA leader James Connolly, was put in place to plan the Rising.

Dick Connolly, IRB Supreme Council, London

The hottest meeting of the whole lot was in the end of September 1914, when [Bulmer] Hobson was 'on the carpet' over the Volunteers, and [Tom] Clarke threatened to resign because there was an idea of how far they would be able to use the Volunteers. He put forward his view that something should be done before the war ended. Clarke said definitely that, Volunteers or no Volunteers, he was going to let out some force during the occasion, that if they did not strike during the war, they were damned for posterity . . . That meeting finished up by agreeing with Clarke that before the war finished, the [Supreme] Council should take war action. I was quite certain Hobson was at that meeting. At the September 1914 meeting he tendered his resignation and he was allowed out.

Denis McCullough, IRB Supreme Council, Belfast

I know that I was in the chair when Dr Patrick McCartan pointed out that we were taking a great responsibility in committing the country to war, without having, at least, a considerable section of the population behind us. I had to quieten the protests of at least two of those present [who were] enthusiastically in favour of a fight by pointing out that McCartan's contention was a very just and reasonable one and in accordance with the IRB constitution and must be considered calmly. Against that I stated that we had been organising and planning for years for the purpose of a protest in arms when an opportunity occurred, and if ever such an opportunity was to arrive, I didn't think any better time would present itself in our day. The whole matter was discussed calmly and seriously and the unanimous decision arrived at was that preparations for a rising were to be pushed forward and a date arranged in any of the three following contingencies, viz.: (1) any attempt at a general arrest of Volunteers, especially the leaders (2) any attempt to enforce conscription on our people and (3) if an early termination of war appeared likely . . . I think it was at the same meeting, after the above decision, that it was decided to set up a military committee to take charge of the preparations and plans.

Dick Connolly, IRB Supreme Council, London

The only curb on the Military Committee was the Executive. The Supreme Council did not count so much at all in 1914 and 1915 – it was the Executive that counted.

P. S. O'Hegarty, IRB Supreme Council, Wales

When they [the Military Council] met they found that Joe Plunkett had plans prepared, on which he was working for a long time, and they adopted them practically without alteration, and the Supreme Council accepted their recommendation.

Jack Plunkett, Volunteers staff officer, Dublin, and brother of Joseph Plunkett

Joe was not himself a really practical person, but he was able to produce plans and schemes that could be put into practice by other people and, in work done at military headquarters, he was very keenly critical of proposals put forward, including his own.

Charles J. MacAuley, Joseph Plunkett's surgeon

The first time I saw him he was living at Larkfield, Kimmage. I went out there to see him. He was very thin and highly strung and was suffering from abscesses in his neck. I remember in the course of examining him he asked me did I see a G-man at the gate and I said I did not notice anyone at the gate. He said I would know one by his feet. He seemed rather disappointed that I had not seen one. As he required an operation I sent him into Miss Quinn's nursing home in Mountjoy Square . . . While he was there quite a number of young men visited him. I remember once finding a group of them seated round his bed with notebooks and pencils in their hands, while he was sitting up in bed, apparently giving them instructions. I, frankly, did not take this at all seriously and remarked: 'Napoleon dictating to his marshals' – a remark which was not well received. On another occasion I joked with him, saying: 'I suppose you sleep with a revolver under your pillow' and, to my surprise, he said: 'I do' and pulled one out.

Madge Daly, Cumann na mBan, Dublin, and sister of Edward Daly

They all thought Joe Plunkett the cleverest from the point of view of military organisation.

Jack Plunkett, Volunteers staff officer, Dublin, and brother of Joseph Plunkett

Secrecy was the characteristic of all the important things connected with the movement at that time and all along up to the Rising.

Bulmer Hobson, IRB centre and general secretary, Volunteers, Dublin

As I was the officer in charge of the IRB in Dublin, and had to be kept in ignorance of these proceedings, extraordinary precautions and a great deal of duplicity were practised. Such a policy was, of course, a violation of the constitution of the IRB.

Denis McCullough, IRB Supreme Council and Volunteers leader, Belfast

. . . after the Rising was decided on, I was deputed to tell Hobson that a rising was inevitable, as he had been promulgating once or twice amongst the younger men that that period was not Ireland's opportunity. I definitely informed Hobson of this, before my return to Belfast, after the meeting at which this decision was taken, and he undertook not to proceed further on the lines he had been following, in view of this position, as I pointed out that divided counsels would only weaken any action taken, and as a responsible member of the organisation he was bound to obedience.

Diarmuid Lynch, IRB Supreme Council and Volunteers

Clarke and Mac Diarmada – accepted as leaders and known to be the two members of the Executive resident in Dublin and in closest contact with events which would govern decisions of the IRB – had the entire confidence of the council . . . To me, possessed as I was of knowledge of many of their moves, it was evident that [none] of these three [Clarke, MacDermott and Pearse] desired to report the full extent of their progress ... for the obvious reason that the secret decisions and plans of the Military Council had better be kept within as narrow a circle as possible ... Mac Diarmada's motion that 'we fight at the earliest date possible' was in line with that attitude, and the council as a whole was fully justified in being satisfied with that decision.

Denis McCullough, IRB Supreme Council and Volunteers leader, Belfast

It may be appropriate at this stage to record my view that ... all details of the Rising, and all its plans and preparations, were in the hands of Seán MacDermott and Joseph Mary Plunkett and that the Military Committee, the Supreme Council, the Executive of the Volunteers, and all of us were used by them to bring the Rising about. I have heard them criticised for their actions in this regard, but I have no complaint for what they did and the way they did it. A rising had been decided on. The fewer who were aware of the arrangements, the less chance there was of any leakage of information.

Bulmer Hobson, IRB centre and general secretary, Volunteers, Dublin

The great majority of the Irish Volunteers, and the great majority of the members of the IRB, would have been definitely hostile to a demonstration like the 1916 insurrection had it been possible to consult them. An overwhelming majority of the Irish Volunteer Executive supported MacNeill and me in our design to build up the Volunteers into a powerful organisation, and to resort to guerrilla tactics if and when we were attacked. The 1916 men were unable to challenge this policy successfully in the Executive Committee and were, therefore, driven to misuse their position as officers in the Volunteers to order men into action in pursuance of a policy different from the one they were publicly pledged to maintain.

Seán Fitzgibbon, Executive Committee, Volunteers

The Rising was not planned, organised, or even discussed by the Executive of the Volunteers, which was the governing body of that organisation.

John MacDonagh, 2nd Battalion, and brother of Thomas MacDonagh

The Military Council have been blamed for not informing Eoin MacNeill, who was chief of staff of the Volunteers, of their plans for a rising. They had reason to fear, however, that he was opposed to such extreme measures, unless the Volunteers were first attacked by the British. They were men exalted by their mission to strike once more with arms, as had been done in every generation against the British oppressor, and this purpose was so all-embracing that it completely dominated their lives, and no consideration, such as family or strict adherence to any formal procedure, could be allowed to interfere with their accepted destiny, to which they gladly dedicated their lives.

Eamon Martin, Fianna Éireann and Executive Committee, Volunteers

. . . [Hobson's advocacy of defensive guerrilla warfare] seemed to be quite sound and practicable. This is not to say its soundness or practicability would have diverted my own course. I believe that Pearse's doctrine, no matter how impracticable from the military aspect, had a greater appeal for those who had become tired of waiting for favourable opportunities. And I think it was generally felt that the European war, which had been going on for eighteen months, might end without any attempt being made to take advantage of England's difficulty, that this would be shameful and disastrous, and that even a glorious failure would be better than no attempt at all.

Seán McGarry, IRB and Volunteers, Dublin

As editor of the Rossa funeral souvenir I called to Liberty Hall to ask [James Connolly] for an article on the Citizen Army. I had known him for several years and had given him a weekly article during the Dublin strike so we were friendly. He looked at me for a while then almost shouted, 'What's the good of talking about Rossa? Rossa wanted to fight England when England was at peace. You fellows won't fight when she is at war.' . . . I told Tom Clarke how Connolly was feeling. Tom saw him and shortly afterwards he became a member of our [Military] committee.

Helena Molony, Irish Citizen Army, Dublin

I think what transpired [when Connolly was allegedly kidnapped in January 1916] was that the Volunteer leaders wanted to talk seriously to Connolly, to get him to stop his propaganda in the *Workers' Republic*. Of course, Connolly never would; he would rather die. He would never have stopped unless they convinced him – as I think they did – that they were not 'Fan go fóills' and that they did not share the ideas held by Bulmer Hobson, who, I think, exercised a great influence over Eoin MacNeill . . . I was staying at Madame Markievicz's Surrey House [in Rathmines]. One evening I went into the kitchen and there was Connolly. The Fianna boys were all round the house as scouts. When they went to bed Madame said, 'Where have you been, in the name of Heaven?' He smiled and said, 'I have been through hell!' 'But what happened?' said we. 'I don't like to talk about it. I have been through hell, but I have converted my enemies.' We did not pursue the conversation, as he did not seem to want to . . . The attacks on the Volunteers ceased immediately, because Connolly knew they meant business.

Seán McGarry, IRB and Volunteers, Dublin

Connolly was a man of massive intellect, of great resource and courage and of immense value to the committee, but he was as temperamental as a prima donna. He was impatient, irritable and petulant . . . His method of revolution differed from that of Tom Clarke. He wanted to shout it from the housetops, did not care how soon it started or with how many men. He believed that once the standard of revolt was raised the people – his people – would rally to it and he was afraid of a sudden collapse of the war. He was wrong in both assumptions. Tom, who had infinite patience in a matter of this kind, had his hands full at times and Connolly was successfully humoured.

The Military Council was composed of men of very different backgrounds, including the veteran Fenian Tom Clarke, the cultural-nationalist intellectual Patrick Pearse and the working-class socialist James Connolly. Frustrated by the passivity of Ireland, they were united by a belief in the necessity for action. The Great War provided them with a compelling rationale to act despite their acceptance of the likelihood of military failure. In contrast, many ordinary rebels believed that a military (rather than simply a moral) victory could be achieved.

Seán McGarry, IRB and Volunteers, Dublin

. . . one of his [Tom Clarke's] greatest disappointments after his release was that there was no thought of a rising during the Boer War. He never understood it and never gave up thinking of it . . . The old feeling of humiliation at the failure of his generation (as he called it) during the Boer War was still with him and he wanted to do all that one man could do to assure that should another war come, it would be proved to the world that there were still in Ireland men who were willing to fight and die for Irish freedom.

Liam Gaynor, IRB and Volunteers, Belfast

About two months before Easter 1916 we were addressed by James Connolly at our headquarters at Willowbank. He spoke very strongly about periods in Irish history when the Irish people had opportunities of fighting for freedom and did not avail of them. He said that the first of such opportunities occurred when the Boer War broke out in 1899. The second occurred when the World War commenced in 1914, and the third, in his opinion, was offering itself in the near future. He felt so strongly about this that he stated, in my hearing, 'If the Irish people don't fight, then by G[od] I'll go out and fight myself.'

Desmond Ryan, E Company, 4th Battalion

On a couple of occasions in 1915–16 we did discuss the question of a rising or not. 'Consider how we would look,' said Pearse, 'and what would the people think of us after all our talk and promises if we said, "Well, after all the British are too strong and we don't feel like fighting them." The people would just laugh at us and our movements would collapse in laughter.' Pearse thought his speeches and conduct had committed him to action.

Dan McCarthy, IRB and D Company, 4th Battalion

In my opinion, the 1916 rebellion was a blood sacrifice. The men who signed the Proclamation knew that they were finished. Nationality was at a low ebb at the time. The war was on, and Dublin citizens cheered the fellows going away at the North Wall. These men, I think, came to the conclusion that something must be done to save the soul of the nation. Of course, there were some of our lads who believed they were going to drive the British into the sea, but I don't think that was in the minds of the men who signed the Proclamation. It was not on my mind, I can assure you.

Liam O'Brien, F Company, 1st Battalion, and IRB

The main idea was that of Robert Emmet, which also was based on a dramatic seizure of Dublin Castle as a means of firing the whole country into action. Simultaneously, a landing of arms in Kerry would arm the south and west, and we would have had in 1916 the guerrilla warfare of 1920–21. And what results were to be hoped? The Republic? Hardly! It was expected that the Rising, if it coincided with a big German offensive in France, would divert large British forces, and later on compel the enemy to negotiate.

Joseph Lawless, C Company, 1st Battalion

I remember discussing the probabilities in this way with Joe Taylor of Swords, who was my constant companion at the time, and, while there was a certain pitch of anticipation in the air, there was a considerable confidence that victory was within our grasp ... The younger ones of us never doubted, of course, that arms would be made available at the right moment. We had a supreme confidence in the leaders of our organisation, and surely it would be in the interests of Germany to see that we were armed. Also, we were conscious of influential friends in the USA who were equally anxious for our success, and who, we trusted, could surely find means to send arms once the flag was raised in battle.

Joseph O'Connor, A Company, 3rd Battalion

I knew that there was to be a rising, and with outside help I thought it could be successful; I thought that every man would rush in to help.

Denis McCullough, IRB president and Volunteers leader, Belfast

On the following morning (Monday [17 April]) I found Seán MacDermott at the office in D'Olier Street. He tried to avoid me and to put me off, but eventually I got him into a room, locked the door and told him that he must talk to me. Seán laughed and said all right, he would tell me all I wanted to know, which was everything. He told me of the plans for Dublin and of the coming of the German arms to Clare or Kerry. He also said that they expected a ship to Dublin, with German officers to lead the Rising. I put little faith in this statement and I don't think Seán did either. I can't decide in my own mind even yet, whether or not he was trying to deceive me or was deceiving himself.

Gary Holohan, D Company, 1st Battalion

Eamon [Martin] and I went into the pavilion [on Good Friday], where we met Thomas MacDonagh, and he gave a short address to about a dozen of us. He told us we were about to rise and that if we were able to stand up against the British for one week as a uniformed disciplined force we would be able to claim recognition at the Peace Conference that would be held at the end of the war.

Bulmer Hobson, IRB centre and general secretary, Volunteers, Dublin

Pearse's development towards left-wing nationalism was remarkably rapid. As late as 1912 he spoke at a Redmondite meeting in Dublin, and a little over a year later he became a member of the IRB. Six months after I swore him in to the IRB he was writing to people in America, to whom I had introduced him, telling them that I was not sufficiently reliable, from a revolutionary point of view, to be entrusted with funds or given support . . . He was a sentimental egotist, full of curious Old Testament theories about being the scapegoat for the people, and he became convinced of the necessity for a periodic blood sacrifice to keep the national spirit alive. There was a certain strain of abnormality in all this. He did not contribute greatly to the hard grinding work of building up the movement, but as soon as we had succeeded in getting a small organisation and a handful of arms he seized the opportunity to bring about the blood sacrifice.

Claire Gregan, fiancée of Bulmer Hobson

I . . . felt that a long life did not interest him [Seán MacDermott] much, as he was not a strong man and was due for another operation.

Bulmer Hobson, IRB centre and general secretary, Volunteers, Dublin

It must . . . be remembered that he [Joseph Plunkett] was in a very advanced stage of TB and that his condition was far from normal.

Seán Fitzgibbon, Executive Committee, Volunteers

The main argument he [Seán MacDermott] mentioned was that in our day the national movement was kept alive by the sacrifices of the Manchester Martyrs, and that the national sentiment voted by that act should be reinforced by action in our day. The idea that the national movement in my time should be merely one to provide further martyrs instead of being directed to a successful termination of our struggle for independence did not appeal to me.

Josephine MacNeill, Volunteers sympathiser, Dublin

[Ginger O'Connell] talked to me about the Volunteers and he frequently spoke to me about the two tendencies that prevailed among the Executive of the Volunteers. He wished that Eoin MacNeill would attend more frequently so as to counteract the influence of a small section that had the definite purpose of rushing a rising, which he felt militarily could have no success. He was afraid that their mystical view of the need for a blood sacrifice would bring about a premature clash with the English, which would be futile and disastrous, as it would waste this opportunity for advancing the cause of Irish freedom while England was at war and would cause the Volunteers to be disbanded, the leaders to be executed and would put a premature end to the military movement for resistance in that generation. His was essentially a military mind. He was a convinced revolutionary, but he thought always on technical lines, and militarily speaking he could only sympathise with a policy that offered a reasonable prospect of success. 'Ginger' with MacNeill, The O'Rahilly, Hobson and others were opposed to the idea of a blood sacrifice as such. They were of the opinion that the Volunteer movement was growing stronger every day and that they should continue to build it up and let circumstances develop before adopting an aggressive policy. 'Ginger' used to talk of that section half banteringly and half ruefully as the 'Army of Destiny'.

P. S. O'Hegarty, IRB Supreme Council, England

In May 1915 Seán MacDermott came to see me in Welshpool, on his way back from London . . . I asked him whether my place in the [Supreme] Council had been filled, and he said no. Well, then, said I, I want to be recorded as against the Rising. I think the Volunteers should be well intact against the possibility of conscription. I am still of that opinion. The risk of the operation was so great that it should not have been undertaken, and it was only the stupidity of the British that saved us.

W. T. Cosgrave, B Company, 4th Battalion

I met Thomas MacDonagh early in the spring of 1916 when he spoke of a rising within the next month or two, and went on to express a desire to hear my views. I told him it would be little short of madness – as we lacked men and munitions. While there had been some expansion in Volunteer recruiting throughout the country – Dublin did not share in the increase to any great extent. MacDonagh enquired as to whether my opinion would be affected by such developments as a German naval fleet . . . I agreed that developments such as these would completely alter the situation – that the Volunteers alone were not capable of a sustained conflict. I was not impressed with gaining a moral victory; that while there was a certain glamour in maintaining a succession of risings against British domination, our policy should be directed towards leaving things better than we found them.

Although the Rising was planned with the utmost secrecy, many Volunteers, particularly in Dublin, were aware that action was imminent. Some Volunteer leaders spoke openly about the likelihood of violence as a means of preparing their men for the rebellion. IRB membership became increasingly important during this period as a means of ensuring the secrecy of the Military Council's preparations within the wider Volunteer movement.

Jim O'Shea, Irish Citizen Army, Dublin

James Connolly's lectures were great and he stressed the point always that cover was the most essential point. I remember he pointed out in his abrupt way that if you shot a soldier you were not to get up and cheer but keep pegging away and always make sure that officers and NCOs got special attention from riflemen. He pointed out that a man properly covered and sniping would upset a battalion or company advancing against us in the street . . . He lectured us on house-fighting, saying he was going to fight his way and not the way the British wanted. He also stated that it would be a new way and that the ordinary soldier was not trained for this particular style of scrap.

Helena Molony, Irish Citizen Army, Dublin

Connolly's military tactics were unique. There was a certain amount of bluff in them. There was a huge blackboard outside the door of Liberty Hall, and each Saturday there were flamboyant notices on it, such as 'Citizen Army, Attack on Howth tomorrow. Such and such a company to assemble here. Arms to be carried.' I remember saying to him, 'Why put up a thing like that and bring the police on us?' He said, 'You know the story of Wolf!', so naturally I saw the wisdom of it.

Donal O'Hannigan, B Company, 4th Battalion, and IRB

I remember after one of these lectures a debate or discussion between Connolly and Clarke. Connolly held that in the event of a rebellion and if the English used artillery against the rebels, it would be equivalent to recognition that they were fighting the armed forces of another country and that other nations would recognise us as such accordingly. On the other hand, if they only used rifles and other small arms, they could claim they were only dealing with a riot. Clarke maintained that no matter what they used – even poison gas – it would make no difference, as all the nations at that time were too interested in looking after their own affairs and skins to take any interest in us.

Michael Lynch, Volunteers and IRB, Dublin

. . . one day he [Éamonn Ceannt] approached me and asked me was I willing to join what he called the inner organisation which was behind the Volunteers. He told me that, sooner or later, it meant a fight against the British, but he did not divulge to me the impending proclamation of a republic. He gave me a few days to think it over. I agreed, and he administered the oath to me, one day very early in 1916, at the junction of Grantham Street and Heytesbury Street. He said: 'You needn't raise your right hand. Just remove it from the handlebars of your bicycle.'

Thomas Byrne, IRB and B Company, 1st Battalion

A few months before Easter 1916, it was generally understood that there would be a fight.

Simon Donnelly, C Company, 3rd Battalion

As the weeks advanced, feeling was growing more tense, and for the first time grants of money were made to each unit to speed up the purchase of arms and other equipment.

Jim O'Shea, Irish Citizen Army, Dublin

Now things were getting busy and everything seemed to move towards a certain object. This was not hidden or spoken of with bated breath. We all knew and discussed openly our aims and objects, and we told everyone what we were drilling for.

John MacDonagh, 2nd Battalion

It had been arranged some weeks before the Rising that Tom would occupy Jacob's [biscuit factory] with his battalion and he and Connolly had met to discuss the matter at the underground lavatory in Kevin Street.

Joseph O'Connor, A Company, 3rd Battalion

As to how much our officers and men knew, I cannot say . . . at no time was it stated, at any of our important meetings, that we were starting an insurrection, with or without assistance, but very definitely an atmosphere was cultivated leading to the uprising, and I think it was this that kept the British guessing, and the fact . . . that our movement was sober, both officers and men.

Áine Heron, Cumann na mBan, Dublin

Although I never got any definite information about the Rising, I felt in my heart that it was coming and it was what I had been looking forward to always and I wanted to be in it, though the time was not really opportune for me, as I expected a baby – my third – in August.

Marie Perolz, Cumann na mBan and Irish Citizen Army, Dublin

The Countess told me about a fortnight before the Rising that the scrap was definitely fixed for Easter.

Oscar Traynor, F Company, 2nd Battalion

In a further lecture in Dawson Street, which proved to be the final one, all the officers of the Dublin Brigade were mobilised to attend. During the course of the evening a number of officers spoke, including Thomas MacDonagh, Éamonn Ceannt and Éamon de Valera. Each of these officers spoke on his own particular subject, all giving the impression that in a very short time the Volunteers would be going into action . . . It became obvious after a time that the speakers were holding the meeting for the attendance of someone of greater importance. This eventually proved to be so, as later in the evening Patrick Pearse, accompanied by his brother Willie, entered the room. Patrick Pearse was wearing his greatcoat, a Volunteer green, and a slouch hat, when he entered the room. His brother Willie helped him to take these off. Pearse then approached the head of the table and, after a short time, was introduced to the Volunteers by one of the officers who had already spoken. Patrick Pearse rose amidst dead silence, stared over the heads of the Volunteers assembled in the room and paused for almost one minute before he spoke. The first words he uttered sent a thrill through the persons present. The words were somewhat as follows: 'I know that you have been preparing your bodies for the great struggle that lies before us, but have you also been preparing your souls?' These words made such a deep impression on all present that there was dead silence for a considerable period. Following this, Pearse went on to urge the Volunteers to do everything possible to prepare themselves for the great struggle that lay ahead . . . Most of us left the meeting, which was held on the Saturday week preceding the Rising, with the impression that in a short time we would find ourselves in action in the field.

Min Ryan, Cumann na mBan, Dublin

For little more than a week before the Rising there was tremendous excitement – a sort of seething undercurrent. You felt that something was going to happen, but what it was you did not know.

Jerry Golden, B Company, 1st Battalion

[Edward Daly] told me that if I was engaged in any area outside the 1st Battalion area he was sure I would do my duty as a soldier of the Republic. This was the first mention I had heard from anyone about a republic, and when I asked him what he meant by it, he replied that when the day and hour had been settled on which to strike the blow for Irish freedom, the Irish Republic would be proclaimed by the provisional government of the Republic. Every Volunteer in arms would be expected to defend the Republic with his life if necessary and some of the leaders would fall in the fight, but the others would carry on even in face of overwhelming odds. While he was speaking to me I noticed his eyes. They appeared to shine, and I saw he was in earnest in every word he spoke.

Diarmuid Lynch, IRB Supreme Council and Volunteers

The first meeting of what I may term the 'Committee on Manholes', summoned by Seán MacDermott, was held in the office of the Gaelic League, 25 Parnell Square, early in April . . . My report was handed to Seán MacDermott on Monday of Holy Week (to the best of my recollection) – a separate sheet for each battalion area, accompanied by sketches showing the exact locations. We also had duplication 'keys' made with which the manhole covers could be lifted, and provided for each battalion a set of demolition tools.

The days before the Rising witnessed a series of dramatic events which destroyed the possibility of a mass insurrection. Acting with ruthlessness and duplicity, the Military Council forged 'the Castle Document' to persuade the Volunteers' indecisive president, Eoin MacNeill, to back the rebellion. They also misled leading Volunteers and kidnapped their most outspoken opponent, Bulmer Hobson. After learning of the interception of the Aud's cargo of rifles, MacNeill issued a countermanding order which foiled the nationwide mobilisation planned for Easter Sunday. With little left to lose, the Military Council resolved to rise on the following day.

Bulmer Hobson, IRB centre and general secretary, Volunteers, Dublin

In the early months of 1916 there was a feeling of growing tension, and, as far as I was concerned, of growing disbelief in the protestations of Pearse and MacDermott. This was greatly heightened when, about a week before the insurrection, MacNeill brought me in a [Dublin Castle] document, which purported to be secret orders issued by the British authorities for the suppression of the Volunteers, and desired me to have it circulated throughout the movement. I read this document with considerable doubt and asked MacNeill where he got it. He said that he was not at liberty to tell me. The document did not appear to be authentic on the face of it, and, unable to get any information as to where it came from, I finally said to MacNeill, 'Are you completely and absolutely satisfied as to its authenticity?' 'I am,' he said, and on that assurance I circulated it all over the country.

Desmond Ryan, E Company, 4th Battalion

Some of us were very sceptical of it. Peter Slattery asked Willie Pearse jocosely, 'Whoever forged that?'

Bulmer Hobson, IRB centre and general secretary, Volunteers, Dublin

There was a concert organised by Cumann na mBan and held at 41 Parnell Square on Palm Sunday, 16 April. On the spur of the moment I made a speech in very guarded language, so as not to excite the suspicions of the authorities, and yet sufficiently definite to be intelligible to the many Volunteers who were in the hall. I warned them of the extreme danger of being drawn into precipitate action, which could only have the effect of bringing the movement to an end, and I said that no man had a right to risk the fortunes of the country in order to create for himself a niche in history. The majority of the audience seemed to be in agreement with what I said.

Denis McCullough, IRB president and Volunteers leader, Belfast

I arrived just as Hobson was speaking and to my amazement I heard him advocating a policy of waiting; 'that this was not Ireland's opportunity and that a more favourable time would come later'. I forget the reasons he gave us for this policy, but no doubt he thought that they were sound ones. To me it sounded like bedlam. I had just left Tom Clarke, who told me the Rising was fixed for the following Sunday, and here was the secretary of the Irish Volunteers advocating, publicly, a policy of delay. I feared that divided councils would be fatal to any attempt at an armed rising, and, only partially informed as I was, I was very distressed. I left the hall and on my way out met Seán MacDermott limping in. I told him what Hobson was saying inside and with a good, round oath Seán said that we would 'damned soon deal with that fellow'.

Leslie Price, Cumann na mBan, Dublin

On the Thursday night I attended the Cumann na mBan meeting. We were making bandages and packing first-aid materials. I have an idea we had been told at the meeting that we were to be at the Black Church, or rather along Mountjoy Street, at twelve o'clock on Sunday and that we were not to congregate in groups . . . Just before we parted, she [Kitty O'Doherty] said to me, 'You know the Rising is to take place on Sunday?' I was very young compared with her – I was only about 21 – and it made a shocking impression on me. Immediately I went kind of cold. I thought of all the men I knew, and I could not visualise success when I realised the strength of the British Empire. It terrified me. I said to her, 'Don't you think you are terribly indiscreet to say that to me? And to think that so many men's lives could be jeopardised by telling me, a real raw recruit!' I don't know how I got the courage to say it to her. I think she was taken aback by my attitude . . . I did not sleep that night. I intensified my prayers.

Liam O'Brien, F Company, 1st Battalion, and IRB

On Holy Thursday night, 1916, I had no suspicion whatever that anything abnormal was afoot. I knew, as everyone knew, that at the 'manoeuvres' ordered for the following Easter Sunday, a prize would be given for the best-equipped company, and I was a bit worried as my equipment was not complete. On my way to the drill hall, I went into the large D.B.C. restaurant situated at that time in Lower O'Connell Street, went up to the top floor and sat down opposite two men very well known to me, Séamus O'Connor, solicitor, and Piaras Béaslaí, vice-commandant of the 1st Battalion. They were talking earnestly together in Irish, and in a very low tone so that I could not follow their conversation. After a while Piaras Béaslaí went away and Séamus O'Connor turned to me and said in English: 'I have just had the life frightened out of me by Béaslaí.' 'How is that?' I said. 'He has just told me that the Rising is to come off on Sunday.' I said, 'Would you mind passing that tea?' The statement had seemed to me just a pointless absurdity. O'Connor went on to express indignation at being left in ignorance, pushed aside, treated like this when he was a member of the Volunteer Executive and entitled to know everything that was going on.

Bulmer Hobson, IRB centre and general secretary, Volunteers, Dublin

The first definite information I had that an insurrection was to occur in the immediate future was late in the evening of Holy Thursday, when J. J. O'Connell and Eimar O'Duffy came into my office and told me that an insurrection had been planned for the following Sunday. With them I went immediately to MacNeill's house at Rathfarnham, arriving a considerable time after he had gone to bed. We got MacNeill up and hastened then to St Enda's to see P. H. Pearse, arriving about 2 a.m., knocking Pearse up. MacNeill, O'Connell and I went in to see Pearse, leaving O'Duffy, who was not a member of the [Volunteers] Executive, outside. Pearse then admitted that an insurrection was to take place, and told us that nothing we could do could prevent it. This was in striking contrast to the assurances which he had so recently and so frequently given, that he was acting loyally with his colleagues on the Executive Committee.

MacNeill, O'Connell and I then returned to MacNeill's house, where MacNeill, as chief of staff, wrote an order authorising me to take complete charge in Dublin, and to take all necessary steps to prevent the Volunteers being drawn into taking the initiative in an offensive action against the government.

. . . Apparently after we had left him, Pearse communicated with some of his friends, because, quite early on Good Friday morning, MacDermott and MacDonagh went to MacNeill's house. They appear to have told him that the Rising was inevitable, and to have convinced him that he could do nothing. It was often easier to convince MacNeill that nothing could be done than it was to spur him into positive action. MacNeill thereupon sent me an order countermanding the order which he had given me a few hours before . . . That afternoon I was asked by Seán Tobin . . . to attend a meeting of the Leinster Executive of the IRB at Martin Conlon's house in Phibsboro. I was reluctant to go, and did not see any purpose to be served, and at the same time I had a suspicion that this was a ruse to get me out of the way . . . I was, therefore, not surprised when, as I entered the house, some members, who were armed with revolvers, told me that I was a prisoner, and could not leave the house.

Martin Conlon, IRB centre, Dublin

On and off in the course of his confinement in my premises, Mr Hobson was inclined to be obstreperous, protesting against his arrest and so on, all of which was quite natural in the circumstances. I did what I could to calm him down, making clear my position in the matter as being that of merely carrying out orders. I also had occasion to calm down the Volunteers in charge of the prisoner . . . they had begun to bemoan the fact that they were engaged on this job of prisoner-guarding and so would be out of things now that the fight was on . . . They were even suggesting he should be executed and dumped on the railway line which runs at the back of my place, but possibly they were not really in earnest about this. In any case, I made it clear to the Volunteer guards that I would not countenance any unauthorised action . . .

Fionan Lynch, F Company, 1st Battalion

About 5 a.m. on Easter Saturday morning there was a terrific rat-a-tat-tat at our door in Mountjoy Street and we all drew our guns in expectation of a raid. The man at the door, however, was Seán Connolly . . . and he brought a despatch to Seán MacDermott with regard to Casement's arrest. On Seán's orders, Gearóid [O'Sullivan] and myself at once foraged a taxi and drove out to St Enda's with orders to inform Pearse that he should come at once in the taxi with us to Liberty Hall. We reached St Enda's about 6 a.m. and, when Pearse had dressed, we brought him to Liberty Hall, where conferences went on throughout the day.

Liam O'Brien, F Company, 1st Battalion

With all hopes dashed, Pearse and MacDermott visited MacNeill early on Saturday morning. And for the first time this patriot-scholar learned of the *Aud* débacle. This altered MacNeill's views. Protesting that he had been unfairly dealt with, he now feared the British would come down on us with all their might. Therefore, we might as well stand together and meet the coming storm as best we could. The others said, 'Thank God!' At least there was to be unity of action. As the day wore on and nothing happened, Dr MacNeill changed his mind. He thought the situation might be saved if a clash with the British could be averted, but, knowing it useless to put this view to the others, he decided to issue the order cancelling operations on the following day on his own responsibility.

Colm O'Lochlainn, Executive Committee, Volunteers

I travelled back to Dublin on Easter Saturday morning by train from Killarney and when the train arrived at Mallow Junction I saw Seán Fitzgibbon, Dr Jim Ryan, Ginger O'Connell and Liam Lynch there. Ginger O'Connell was on his way to Waterford. Liam Lynch had been in Kerry and was on his way back to Cork to take charge there. It was from him I learned for the first time that the arms ship had been seized and Casement (of whose coming no one was aware) had been captured. Seán Fitzgibbon had been in Tralee for some days on a mission solely connected with the distribution of arms when landed. He also had been kept in ignorance of the intended rising . . . When we got to Dublin, we first called to Volunteer HQ at 2 Dawson Street, and saw Thomas MacDonagh. He was very curt with us and gave us no information whatever. We were looking for Bulmer Hobson but could not find him there. MacDonagh was engaged in burning a lot of papers . . . Fitzgibbon and I then went to O'Rahilly's house at 40 Herbert Park and met The O'Rahilly there . . . The O'Rahilly immediately drove us out to Eoin MacNeill's house at Woodtown Park, Rathfarnham. We told MacNeill what had happened and what news we had. MacNeill immediately came out with us and drove to Scoil Éanna to see Pearse. After some conversation with Pearse in the hall of St Enda's, MacNeill and Pearse came out to the steps of the house, and it was there I heard Pearse say to MacNeill, 'We have used you and your name and influence for what it was worth. You can issue what orders you like now, our men won't obey you.' MacNeill said he would do as his conscience and common sense bade him, and if Pearse had any more to say he could meet him at 9 p.m. that evening at Dr Séamus Ó Ceallaigh's house at 53 [54] Rathgar Road.

Liam Tannam, E Company, 3rd Battalion

Holy Saturday evening came. The air was rather electric; almost all officers suspected that the Easter manoeuvres arranged for [the next day] were really 'the day', but no positive orders had been issued to company commanders.

Joseph Connolly, Volunteers leader, Belfast

I do not remember precisely what he [MacNeill] said [at 54 Rathgar Road on Saturday night] but the general trend was that things were in a very unsatisfactory state, that things had gone all wrong, arrangements had been badly handled and had already broken down. He proposed accordingly to call off the 'mobilisation' that had been arranged for Easter Sunday. While we were talking Tomás MacDonagh arrived and was shown in direct to MacNeill . . . MacDonagh was extremely solemn, almost tense as he was told this and said to MacNeill – 'You realise of course that you are issuing an order which may not be obeyed.' MacNeill's reply was equally tense: 'Well, the responsibility for disobedience will be on those who disobey.' MacDonagh then said, 'I will have to consult my friends about it.'

Liam O'Brien, F Company, 1st Battalion, and IRB

I hurried to Nelson's Pillar and caught what must have been the last Terenure tram. I got off and looked for the address given me. I saw a car standing at the kerb-stone and just getting into it recognised Thomas MacDonagh. I said: 'Hello, Tomás, where is No. 54?' He said: 'In there, Dr Séamus O'Kelly's' . . . MacDonagh said nothing more and went off. It was the last time I spoke to him . . . The atmosphere was very tense. MacNeill seemed strangely unlike his usual self . . . All looked oppressed, almost frightened, shall I say, by the seriousness of the situation; all except Arthur Griffith, who seemed almost as usual, certainly far cooler and more 'normal' than anyone else . . . MacNeill told how he had been left completely in the dark, only found out things gradually and by accident and realised that Sunday's all-Ireland manoeuvres were to be turned into an offensive action, an insurrection; how he had expostulated with the leaders; how . . . he had agreed with them that if the British attacked he would stand in with them, of course, such having always been his position, but that in the course of the day (that Saturday) hearing of the disaster off Kerry, and especially in view of the utter unpreparedness of the country as reported to him by [Seán] Fitzgibbon, confirming what information he had himself, he had come to the conclusion that the enterprise was madness, would mean a slaughter of unarmed men and that he felt it to be his bounden duty to try and stop it . . . I remember finally Arthur Griffith remarking that it was very late and that he would be off; that I would be going the same way home; 'Give Mr O'Brien his orders and we will be going,' he said. Then I noticed a little pile of sheets . . . These were copies of the 'cancelling order', as it was called, the same [as the one that] appeared next day in the *Sunday Independent* . . . I took the three copies of the order. I stopped to talk to Seán T. O'Kelly – who was sitting near the door. 'What is all this about, Seán?' I said. 'You see for yourself and you know as much as I do now. You see there has been a split,' he answered. 'What have I got to do with a split?' I said. 'I am only a private soldier.' 'I am in the same boat,' he replied, 'only when I came to MacNeill this evening and found that this order had already gone out to some places it seemed to me that it would only be right that every place should get it, to prevent people in one place going out thinking that the place beside them would be going out, when they wouldn't be.' 'Then you think I ought to travel with this order,' I said. 'Yes, I think you ought,' replied Seán. 'All right,' I said.

Nora Connolly, Cumann na mBan, Belfast, and daughter of James Connolly

When we got in to Dublin, it was before six o'clock in the morning. I went round to Liberty Hall, and knocked at the door . . . The officer of the guard came . . . and he brought me up, and along the corridor to where Daddy was . . . I said: 'What is happening? . . . Is the fight really off? There is fighting to be here, and not in the north? What does it mean? Why are we not going to fight?' He sat up in the bed. The tears ran down his face. Evidently they had a meeting before that, and he was very upset . . . I remember saying: 'Are we not going to fight now?' He said, 'The only thing we can do is to pray for an earthquake to come and swallow us up, and our shame.'

Fionan Lynch, F Company, 1st Battalion

On Easter Sunday morning the Sunday paper carried Eoin MacNeill's cancellation of the 'manoeuvres' for that day. Gearóid [O'Sullivan] and myself were at early Mass and we brought back the paper with us to Seán MacDermott. It was the first and only time that I saw Seán really angry and upset.

Seán McGarry, IRB and Volunteers, Dublin

I walked home in a daze to find Mick Collins, who had been staying with [Joseph] Plunkett and who came after Mass to breakfast in my house. I showed him the paper. He became dumb. We breakfasted in silence and left for Liberty Hall, where we found the Military Council was in session.

Oscar Traynor, F Company, 2nd Battalion

On our way down we purchased a *Sunday Independent* and were astonished to find what appeared to be a countermanding order for the Easter manoeuvres . . . we reached Father Matthew Park, and found a state bordering on chaos there.

Cornelius O'Donovan, 1st Battalion

In Liberty Hall, quite a crowd of Volunteers and Citizen Army men had gathered, and the figure of the Countess Markievicz moving among us was, to me, unique and impressive. She was very angry with MacNeill . . . the opinion was freely expressed that Volunteers, Citizen Army and every Irishman worthy of the name would be arrested before a shot was fired . . . One thing that stands out in my mind is the feeling of relief some men showed that day, as a result of the 'manoeuvres' being called off . . . while others were thoroughly disgusted. I couldn't explain these two diametrically opposed attitudes. And yet, a day later, both groups were in the thick of the fight.

Séamus O'Sullivan, B Company, 1st Battalion

While we were waiting, Madame Markievicz came into the room, with a small automatic in her hand, and asked in a peremptory tone if anyone there knew where Hobson was, or his woman (meaning his secretary) – 'I want to shoot him.'

Marie Perolz, Irish Citizen Army, Dublin

Don't talk to me about Sunday morning at Liberty Hall. The first who came to me was Tom Hunter. He threw his arms around me and said, 'We are fooled again.' That day I didn't want to live any longer. We were all in a state. Tom cried like a baby.

Helena Molony, Irish Citizen Army, Dublin

Connolly was there. They were all heartbroken, and when they were not crying they were cursing. I kept thinking, 'Does this mean that we are not going out?'. . . It was foolish of MacNeill and those to think they could call it off. They could not. Many of us thought we would go out single-handed, if necessary.

Desmond Ryan, E Company, 4th Battalion

I never saw Pearse so silent and disturbed. He simply could not speak to anyone. Then the two brothers went off quietly. We all felt it was a crisis; that the whole movement was in the balance; that everything might now collapse.

Seán McGarry, IRB and Volunteers, Dublin

I found Tom Clarke afterwards and for the first time since I knew him he seemed crushed. He was very weary and seemed crestfallen. The shock of the morning's blow had been terrific. I accompanied him that evening. He was very silent. He regarded MacNeill's action [as] the blackest and greatest treachery.

Marie Perolz, Irish Citizen Army, Dublin

That night they had a meeting at Liberty Hall – the last . . . If ever I saw a heartbroken man I saw him that night, Patrick Pearse. He nodded at me. They struck me like men going out into a losing cause.

Maeve Cavanagh, Irish Citizen Army, Dublin

That night [at Liberty Hall] he [Connolly] said to me with a grim and determined air, 'We fight at noon and they [Irish Volunteers] can do as they like.' . . . I asked him, 'What time will I come down in the morning?' 'Come down at eight o'clock,' said he. 'As early as that?' said I. He turned and looked at me and said, 'Do you think that too early for a revolution?' We both laughed.

Jim O'Shea, Irish Citizen Army, Dublin

I was doing guard over the last meeting of the republican government before the fight . . . Commandant Mallin came down from No. 7 and spoke to me on top of the stairs. I sprang to attention and saluted him. He told me to 'stand at ease'. He said, 'Jim, we will be fighting in a short time and we may have to fight alone as MacNeill has finished the Volunteers by calling it off this morning. It will be short and sharp.' These are the exact words he used – 'We will be all dead in a short time.' I asked him if none of the Volunteers would fight. He said there was no knowing. He asked me how the lads were taking it and I told him that the Irish Citizen Army would give a good account of themselves before they went down. He seemed delighted at this and he asked me how I felt and I told him I was willing to go down as long as I could bring a good crowd with me.

6

A Place in History: The Rising in Dublin

Was the Rising an attempt to seize power, a spectacular political gesture or an act of blood sacrifice? The strategy of the Military Council (now the 'provisional government') was defensive – a little over a thousand rebels fortified a ring of buildings in the centre of Dublin and awaited the arrival of British forces – and they attached much importance to symbolic actions such as proclaiming the existence of the Irish Republic. Rank-and-file rebels were less aware of the propagandistic purpose of the Rising and generally more optimistic about its military potential.

*

The rebellion that began on Easter Monday was not the rebellion that the Military Council had planned. The postponement of Sunday's general mobilisation resulted in a poor turnout the following day, forcing the Military Council to curtail its plans, although its basic strategy remained intact. The following accounts convey the excitement and confusion of the mobilisation, and the attitudes of the rebels' families.

Annie Cooney, Cumann na mBan, Dublin

Some time about 7 [a.m.] Seán O'Brien, who was also a member of C Company, brought the actual mobilisation order . . . He would not give it to me but insisted on giving it himself to Con [Colbert]. He went into the room, woke him up and gave him the despatch. Con got up at once and then the hurry and bustle started. He got into his navy-blue suit and went off on his bicycle to eight o'clock Mass and Holy Communion. He told me to have his breakfast ready when he came back. I did so. He was not back for a while because he went to give a few mobilisation orders. When he came back he sent my brother, who was very young but a member of the Fianna, to Éamonn Ceannt to offer his services as despatch carrier . . . My sister Lily was sent to Larry Murtagh to mobilise the Chapelizod section of F Company. She went on her bicycle before we got our own mobilisation orders, which came exactly at nine o'clock . . . Lily, when she came back, and myself were feverishly busy filling Christy Byrne's and Con Colbert's haversacks and our own with any food we could find. They were both now in uniform. We helped them to buckle on the haversacks and Sam Browne belts and they were all excited to get out. During the time I was buckling him up, Con – who had not a note in his head – was singing 'For Tone is Coming Back Again', he was so excited and charmed that at last the fight was coming off. He thought of nothing else. The pair went off, wheeling their bicycles which were loaded up with pikes, their rifles and small arms. We saw them off at the door and waited till they were out of sight.

James Foran, A Company, 4th Battalion

I said to the brother-in-law, 'Goodbye, and if anything happens to me will you look after the wife and kids?' 'Right,' said he. I went home and got ready and I let on I had to go on a parade. I took the brother-in-law's bicycle, he was after paying ten shillings for it. All the kids were there and asked me, 'Where are you going?' 'I am going off to the war,' I said.

Patrick Kelly, G Company, 1st Battalion

I was in bed at 11.15 a.m. when L. McEvatt came into my room and kept pulling my big toe till I woke up . . . I dressed hurriedly while my father and mother got out my rifle and some sandwiches. I will always remember my father as I saw him that morning. He worked the bolt of the rifle, sighted it and fired imaginary shots. As he handed me the rifle he remarked, 'If I was a few years younger I would go with you.' Mother and Father wished God's blessing on me as I hurried away.

John Kenny, F Company, 4th Battalion

My father showed emotion, but my mother was calm and controlled. She gave us her blessing, told us to fight well, and added: 'Remember that your deaths are ordained by God and not by the English.'

Joseph Byrne, A Company, 3rd Battalion, and British Army

On Easter Monday morning a knock came to my door. When I answered it there was a DMP man outside who informed me I was to report back to my regiment immediately as there was trouble in the city . . . I then left my home and made my way to my mother's house, where I knew I would find my brothers . . . My mother put her arms around me, and when she saw me she said, 'God bless you, I knew you would do it,' and she burned my British uniform.

Jim O'Shea, Irish Citizen Army, Dublin

I spent what I believed was my last time at home in a strange manner. My people thought we were mad to try anything and were not as sympathetic as I would wish. Therefore, I was very distant . . . I was sorry I parted with my people as I did but I considered I had done my best and I felt a savage exultation thinking of what we were about to do.

Gerard Doyle, B Company, 4th Battalion

My father had joined the British Army about seven or eight days before the Rising. He had been a member of Redmond's Volunteers, and the first time I ever saw him in uniform was on the Easter Monday morning as I myself was leaving the house to report at Larkfield, Kimmage. He had come from Wellington barracks, South Circular Road, and we just met and passed each other with a casual 'Good morning'!

Cornelius O'Donovan, 1st Battalion

On Monday morning, I got word to mobilise a portion of the company, about half my own section, and, on my way, I was to notify some members of Cumann na mBan to get to their posts. I can never forget the way in which the news was received in different houses. But what disappointed me most was the number of Volunteers on my list that I found had gone off to Fairyhouse races or somewhere else for the bank holiday.

Liam Archer, F Company, 1st Battalion

At 10 a.m. on Easter Monday, D[iarmuid] O'Hegarty delivered to me an order to have my section mobilised at Columcille Hall, Blackhall Place, at 10 a.m. The members were scattered over a wide area as far apart as Oxmantown Road, and Vernon Avenue, Clontarf. I enlisted the aid of my brother, who had a motorcycle combination. My first two calls at Jones Road and Clonliffe Road drew blanks; both members had gone out for the day. At this point the motorcycle combination broke down for the second time and, telling my brother to go home, I set off on foot for Blackhall Place, giving up the idea of mobilising my section.

Peadar Doyle, F Company, 4th Battalion

I was reading the *Daily Independent* at five minutes past nine precisely, when Captain Con Colbert knocked at my door and enquired for me ... I immediately dressed and bade what at the time I thought was a last farewell to my wife and family. I walked by Golden Bridge [on the] Grand Canal and arrived at Emerald Square at 10 a.m. precisely to find that I was the first to arrive excepting a policeman on duty. I will leave it to your imagination as to how one could or should feel under the circumstances, parading for about half an hour attired in a semi-military uniform, fully armed and 500 rounds of ammunition, etc., and your only companion a policeman.

Liam Tobin, C Company, 1st Battalion

I was struck by the small numbers who turned up ... I had often seen our company, C Company of the 1st Battalion, muster a bigger number than the whole battalion did on that morning.

Fionan Lynch, F Company, 1st Battalion

All the company officers were present and, with the exception of one officer, carried out the orders of the Commandant [Ned Daly].

This officer [Captain Alright] said that the whole thing was lunacy, and he left the hall and went home.

Séamus Kavanagh, C Company, 3rd Battalion

The company was about ninety strong, only about one third turned out. The battalion quartermaster, James Byrne, failed to turn out. The company captain, Eddie Byrne, also did not turn out, and Lieutenant Simon Donnelly took charge of the company.

Joseph O'Connor, A Company, 3rd Battalion

When I saw the Commandant [de Valera] he told me we were going into action at twelve o'clock. I asked him were they mad. His reply was: 'I am a soldier and I know you are a soldier also.' I saluted and retired. Before leaving the room he shook hands with me and said: 'We may never meet again.'

Patrick Egan, C Company, 4th Battalion

It was about 11 a.m. when the Volunteers started to assemble at Emerald Square, Cork Street. While waiting for the line-up, the men stood in groups, chatting quietly. In a conversation with Captain McCarthy, he told me that a split had occurred in the Executive body, that MacNeill and Hobson were against us turning out, and spoiled our chances of success. I replied that we 'have to see it through', or words to that effect. Just then, some girls came into the square in a hysterical state; they apparently heard that the fight was about to commence.

Oscar Traynor, F Company, 2nd Battalion

I was greatly concerned, as the general impression created was that the Volunteers were divided in their decisions as to the action to be taken, and that some were out and some were not taking any action at all.

Jerry Golden, B Company, 1st Battalion

On my arrival in 5 Blackhall Street I found about 250 men gathered in the hall and rooms on the ground floor . . . The commandant then said that if any man present did not agree with the opinions of the Supreme Council of the Irish Republic he was at liberty to return home, but if anyone did so, he would ask him to leave his arms, ammo and equipment behind, as some of the men present were not fully armed. No man left the rank . . .

Nicholas Laffan, G Company, 1st Battalion

This announcement was greeted with a great cheer. The four companies, A, C, F and G, marched out of the hall together. The men were all in good spirits and joked about who would fire the first shot.

Dan McCarthy, D Company, 4th Battalion

While a number of us felt that we were marching out that day to take part in a rising, I believe that quite a number of Volunteers who paraded had no idea where they were going and what was to take place.

John Shouldice, F Company, 1st Battalion

I would say that perhaps one third of those who mobilised on Easter Sunday and the majority of those who mobilised on Easter Monday were aware that they were going into action.

Seán Prendergast, C Company, 1st Battalion

We didn't even give a thought where and how the fight was to be waged. Our loyalty and trust were reposed in our commanders, whom we idolised and respected.

Liam O'Brien, F Company, 1st Battalion, and IRB

The mobilisation that morning was very poor – little more than a third of the possible muster. There were barely 800 Volunteers – most of them members of the IRB – and less than 200 of the Citizen Army. So the occupation of the city was incomplete from the start. Trinity College and the Provost's House should not have been neglected. Shortage of men forbade the occupation of the commanding Shelbourne Hotel in the Stephen's Green area. With more men, de Valera could have occupied the stretch of the canal on either side of the Mount Street Bridge instead of only a house or two, and so on.

Jim O'Shea, Irish Citizen Army, Dublin

In a conversation I had with him [Michael Mallin] afterwards he told me his reason and Connolly's for [occupying] Stephen's Green. This was his plan. It was intended that at least 500 men would take over this area. It would be barricaded at different entrances, such as Merrion Street and the street at the Shelbourne Hotel and all streets leading to the Green. It was to be a base, as it had all the necessaries for a base . . . Now this is a rough plan of the 'scrap'. When the fight was on for a day or two it was assumed that most of the barracks would fall, as they would be attacked from two sides. The men in the city would move out and the men in Wicklow and Kildare move in. Of course this was fixed on the assumption that there would be about 5,000 men in Dublin. It was the published number in Volunteer papers at the time and the rough plans were made on that number.

Bulmer Hobson, IRB centre and general secretary, Volunteers, Dublin

There were no plans, and there could not have been plans which could seriously be called military. The tactic of locking a body of men up in two or three buildings to stay there until they were shot or burned out of them was nothing but a demonstration, and one which would have been completely disastrous to this country had it not been saved by the consequent mishandling of the situation by the English government.

Joseph O'Connor, A Company, 3rd Battalion

. . . a minimum garrison of 500 was in his [de Valera's] mind and in ours [for Boland's bakery] . . . when the time to strike came he found himself entirely without his battalion staff. He had no vice-commandant, no adjutant and no quartermaster; the captain of B Company had only been appointed; no captain in C Company and no captain in D Company and with scarce one hundred men.

William O'Brien, Irish Transport and General Workers' Union leader

Connolly told me that the question of the occupation of the Castle was very carefully considered and rejected because it was a big straggling building requiring a large number of men to hold it and commanded in some places by higher buildings which overlooked it . . . He emphasised it was very easy to take but difficult to hold.

Thomas Slater, C Company, 2nd Battalion

I was definitely told on Easter Monday . . . by Thomas MacDonagh at Jacob's that the Bank of Ireland [on College Green] was not to be entered on account of its sentimental associations.

Thomas Doyle, F Company, 4th Battalion

Éamonn Ceannt said there were two reasons against taking Guinness's brewery: one was the vastness of the place, it would be nearly impossible to garrison it, and the other reason was that there was no food in it . . . Hugh Byrne said to the group around, 'Is the man mad? The most magnificent food in Ireland is in Guinness's.'

The rebels struck at midday. The first clashes occurred at the Phoenix Park, where an attempt was made to blow up the Magazine Fort armoury, and Dublin Castle, whose surprisingly vulnerable defences were breached by an audacious Citizen Army raiding party. On the south side of the city, the South Dublin Union, Stephen's Green and Jacob's biscuit factory were occupied, while, across the Liffey, the rebels seized the Four Courts and the General Post Office on Sackville Street.

Frank Burke, E Company, 4th Battalion

We boarded a '17' tram – one of those open-top vehicles which are not to be seen nowadays – and the driver got orders 'full steam ahead to O'Connell Street'. Our destination was Liberty Hall. The first sign that there was anything unusual in the air was at Jacob's biscuit factory. When passing there we noticed a large crowd of civilians – men and women – being ordered back by Volunteers with fixed bayonets. Jacob's factory was in the hands of the insurgents! The excitement was commencing. On down George's Street our tram rattled its way. Near the junction of George's and Dame streets we heard a burst of rifle fire – the attack evidently on Dublin Castle. Our tram stopped right opposite the Bank of Ireland.

Evidently the situation had become too hot and dangerous for the driver. He just left the tram there.

Arthur Agnew, 'Kimmage Garrison'

On Easter Monday morning we marched out of camp at 10.30 hours under [George] Plunkett, carrying all arms, rifles, shotguns, pikes and small arms. We also carried some crowbars and pickaxes. Nearly everyone had a pike, the staffs of which were of various lengths, some of them six feet . . . We marched to Harold's Cross, where we boarded a tram. Plunkett insisted on paying the conductor for our tickets. We got off at O'Connell Bridge and formed up and marched to Liberty Hall.

Joe Good, 'Kimmage Garrison'

I remember seeing Joe Plunkett with plans in his hand outside Liberty Hall. He was beautifully dressed, having high tan leather boots, spurs, pince-nez and looked like any British brass-hat staff officer. Connolly looked drab beside him in a bottle-green thin serge uniform. The form of dress of the two men impressed me as representing two different ideas of freedom.

Helena Molony, Irish Citizen Army, Dublin

The [Citizen Army] women had no uniform, in the ordinary sense – nor the men either. Some of the men had green coats. They wore an ordinary slouch hat, like the Boer hat, and mostly a belt. They insisted they were citizen soldiers, not military soldiers – at the same time regimented and disciplined. I had an Irish tweed costume, with a Sam Browne. I had my own revolver and ammunition.

Jim O'Shea, Irish Citizen Army, Dublin

It was moving to 11.30 a.m. and we each had our own thoughts and little things that never mattered before came up in our minds. Home, people, friends and the chances of the fight, what it would be like being killed, what of the next world. Those remote things that never gave you a thought before seemed important at the moment. It did not fill you with sorrow or foreboding, only a kind of abstract removal from realities . . . I was standing at ease in the rank next to the path, and an old man, tall and stout, black soft hat and flowing beard, looked at me and spoke. I immediately summed him up as a Fenian. He wished us luck and God's help in our terrible task. He gripped my hand and I noticed his palm was terribly callused and dry. Its feel was peculiar when he gripped my hand and tears fell down his face as he walked away. I often thought of the old man whoever he was. He knew all that was to be known, as I suppose he had been through it before I was born.

Séamus Robinson, 'Kimmage Garrison'

Beresford Place was full of Citizen Army men and women. Everything was bustle and excitement. We formed up in front of, and [with] our backs to, Liberty Hall, and Margaret Skinnider, whom I knew, rushed over to me and said, 'It's on.' I asked, 'What's on?' She said, 'The rebellion, of course.' This was the first positive information I had that action was to be taken that morning . . . we formed up in a procession and moved along the quays, feeling as if I were walking on air.

Jack Plunkett, Volunteers staff officer

When in front of the GPO, Seóirse [George Plunkett] gave his company the order to left turn, charge, and, as some of the men could not believe their ears, he had to say, 'Take the GPO.' One of them gave such a whoop of delight, [because] something was actually going to happen, that [it] threatened to disorganise the whole plan. Some thought it was a joke.

Charles Donnelly, E Company, 4th Battalion

When crossing O'Connell Street from Abbey Street on our way to the GPO, we saw the Lancers charging down O'Connell Street. Lieutenant [Michael] Boland was leading our party and, when he saw the Lancers, he gave the order 'right and left form'. On this order we extended along O'Connell Street with our backs to Prince's Street and our rifles at the 'ready' with bayonets fixed, ready to meet the Lancers. Fortunately, or unfortunately, shots rang out from the Henry Street corner of the GPO. I saw horses falling and the Lancers retiring. The doors of the GPO were barricaded and we could not get in. We went to Prince's Street, and smashed the windows there to make an entry. My brother-in-law, John Kiely, was killed when getting through the window by a shot which was alleged to have been fired by a British officer from a window in the Metropole Hotel. We had to move from room to room to get to the main hall. The first thing I saw was a DMP man lying downwards on the floor, resting on his arms and moving his head from side to side. I think he was suffering from fright. The first incident I can remember was seeing Paddy Sweeney with a tin grenade in his hand, with the fuse burning, which he had picked off the floor. He tried to throw it out of the window but the street outside was crowded. He dropped it and kicked it into a corner. Liam Clarke, who came along just then, picked it up and it exploded in his hands. When I saw him he was bleeding freely from the face and knees.

Father Michael Curran, secretary to Archbishop William Walsh, Dublin

The first person I saw in the portico outside the GPO was James Connolly in uniform with a huge Colt revolver, shouting out orders. Volunteers were battering out windowpanes. When James Connolly saw me, he called, 'All priests may pass!', as the Volunteers were keeping the inquisitive on-lookers at some distance. The crowd then showed comparatively little excitement. I passed in to the building. The newly arranged central hall was a scene of immense activity but nobody was unduly excited. It must have been shortly after half past twelve.

Fintan Murphy, GPO

Inside the building there was feverish activity fortifying it and getting in stores as well as establishing communication with the other garrisons in the city. Headquarters staff was established in the central hall on the ground floor and the sorting room was made into a hospital.

Kevin McCabe, Imperial Hotel outpost, GPO

We started breaking all the windows and barricading them and the doors . . . Then we occupied the rooms upstairs and we started breaking open the walls towards the Imperial Hotel, which was over Clery's. We were at this work for a couple of days and then joined up with Volunteers who were working on the walls coming towards us. Some of these walls at Clery's were three feet thick. Some others of us broke through the walls up Earl Street as far as Lloyd's public house. Other fellows built a barricade of furniture across the street where Hickey's shop was . . . All the furniture in these houses had been thrown out into Earl Street to make the barricade. I remember the sickening thud of a piano as it fell on the street pavement.

Frank Burke, GPO

Shortly after our arrival the tricolour was hoisted on the flagstaff at the left-hand corner facing Prince's Street. Commandant Pearse read aloud to the public on the street the Proclamation of the Irish Republic and copies of the Proclamation were posted on the walls and pillars of the building.

Jeremiah O'Leary, GPO

We took copies of them and helped to post them up in various parts of the city.

Min Ryan, Cumann na mBan, GPO

I remember the flag interested me because I had never seen our tricolour flying like that before.

Michael Cremen, GPO

I saw Connolly and Pearse together in the street just as the tricolour was being hoisted on the GPO. As Connolly shook hands with Pearse, I heard him say, 'Thank God, Pearse, we . . . have lived to see this day!'

Gary Holohan, Magazine Fort raiding party

When I reached Rutland Cottages the house was packed with men and they were still arriving on foot and on bicycles. We distributed automatic pistols to the men who had no small arms and made everyone leave his rifle in the house and remove his equipment. Then we sent them to the Phoenix Park in batches, some on bicycles and some on the Ballybough tram. Paddy Daly and I went on bicycles and called at Whelan's on Ormond Quay, where we bought a football . . . After a few minutes' chat together, as if we were a football team with followers, we moved around to the front of the [Magazine] Fort in a casual way, some of the lads kicking the ball from one to the other. When we got near the gate they rushed the sentry who was standing outside, and then another party rushed in and took the guard room completely by surprise. I was detailed off with Barney Mellows to take the sentry on the parapet. I rushed straight through the fort, which is a rather large place, and I had some difficulty in locating him. I eventually saw him looking at me over a roof. I rushed towards him, calling on him to surrender. He came towards me with his bayonet pointed towards me. I fired a shot and he fell, and at that moment Barney came along the parapet. The poor sentry was crying, 'Oh, sir, sir, don't shoot me. I'm an Irishman and the father of seven children.' . . . When I met Paddy Daly he told me he could not find the key of the high-explosives store and he had set the charges in the small-arms ammunition store. Eamon and I lit the charges and my brother Pat gave us a hand. While we were placing the charges, most of the attacking party were clearing away. We informed the prisoners that one of their men was injured and told them to give him attention. We also ordered them not to go down the Park in the direction of the city. We took the guards' rifles and went to the waiting hackney car . . . I followed behind the car on my bicycle. As the car turned towards the gate leading to the Chapelizod Road we noticed a youth [Gerald Playfair] of about 17 [14] years of age running towards the gate. He stopped and spoke to the policeman who was in the middle of the road directing the traffic, and then ran away in the middle of the road towards Islandbridge. I left the hack and followed him, and when he got to the corner of Islandbridge Road he ran towards one of the big houses, evidently with the intention of giving the alarm. I jumped off my bicycle, and just as the door opened I shot him from the gate. At that moment the car arrived at the junction of the road and two large explosions took place in the Fort. The lads on the car started to cheer, and then they thought it wiser to put the rifles that were in their hands into the well of the car.

Helena Molony, Dublin Castle raiding party

We went right up to the Castle gate, up the narrow street. Just then, a police sergeant came out and, seeing our determination, he thought it was a parade, and that it probably would be going up Ship Street. When [Seán] Connolly went to go past him, the sergeant put out his arm; and Connolly shot him dead . . . it appeared that the men behind Connolly did not really know they were to go through. Connolly said: 'Get in, get in' – as if they already did not know they were to go in . . . there was hesitation on the part of the followers. Seán Connolly shouted: 'Get in, get in.' On the flash, the gates were closed . . . It breaks my heart – and all our hearts – that we did not get in. We would have captured the under-secretary [Matthew Nathan], who was having lunch in the Castle. We went into the City Hall and at once manned it.

Constable Peter Folan, Royal Irish Constabulary

The second shot of the Rising was fired at me . . . when the Citizen Army marched up to the Upper Castle Gate, I happened to be standing at a ground-floor window at the left-hand side of the gate as you go in, preparing to go home, as Sir Matthew Nathan had informed me there was no more to be done for the day. I saw the first shot being fired and Constable O'Brien, who was standing at the left-hand side of the gate as you go in, fall. When the Citizen Army approached, the constable made a sign to them with his left hand, to pass on up Castle Street. The gate was open all the time, as usual. I think it was a man in the first or second line of marchers that raised his gun and shot the policeman. Another took aim and fired at me, but I threw myself to the ground . . . The two soldiers who were on sentry duty at the gate had fled into the guard room when they saw the policeman shot. The Volunteers emptied their shotguns through the windows on the soldiers inside the guard room . . . The Volunteers could have easily taken the Castle, there was not a gun in it, and any ammunition to be found was blank. The fact of MacNeill countermanding the parade had lulled the Castle authorities into a sense of security.

Jim O'Shea, Irish Citizen Army, Stephen's Green

When we came to the head of Grafton Street, a policeman passed a remark about playing soldiers. He got an awful shock when he saw us marching straight into St Stephen's Green Park. He had thought we were manoeuvring until we fanned out and ordered people out of the Green. The poor gardener on duty thought the end of the world had come when we demanded the keys. I got busy getting the people out of the garden. My first person was an old priest – a canon – who was sitting on a seat. I told him what I wanted and he asked me the reason. When I told him the fight for the Republic had started, he shook. I was terribly sorry for him as I escorted him to the gate. By this time there were about a hundred persons outside wanting to know what was up.

John MacDonagh, Jacob's biscuit factory

At twelve exactly, we set out to take up position in Jacob's biscuit factory in Peter Street. Tom [MacDonagh] asked me to march in front with him and, on the other side of him, marched an alert man, well dressed in a blue suit, carrying a cane and smoking a cigar. I whispered to Tom, asking who he was, and he told me, 'That is Major John MacBride.' We were followed by a lot of well-known G-men . . . As we marched through Cuffe Street and Mercer Street, the separation women of the Irish soldiers in the British Army became hysterical in their abuse of us. The mildest of their remarks was 'Go out and fight the Germans!' There was some difficulty about the keys which were to admit us to the factory, so a window about six feet from the ground had to be broken, through which we climbed in. One Volunteer, in scrambling through the window, let off his shotgun and bored a large hole in the ceiling. John MacBride . . . picked some of the powder from his moustache and casually warned the boys to be more careful.

Peadar Doyle, South Dublin Union

On entering the convent one of the nuns who opened the door enquired from me if we had come to read the gas meters.

Dick Balfe, Mendicity Institution outpost

When we reached the Mendicity Institution we broke one small door and entered . . . On the stroke of twelve o'clock a small party of sappers came along unarmed. We allowed these to pass knowing what was coming along. In a few minutes the main body of troops in column of route came into view. We had sixteen men altogether including officers. All had Lee-Enfield rifles. Every man had at least 100 rounds of ammunition. Myself and some others had 500 rounds each. Two shots were fired rapidly and the commanding officer dropped. I heard afterwards that he was shot between the eyes and in the heart. The column halted right opposite to us after the two shots and it was a case of fire and one could not miss. The column were four deep. There were from 200 to 250 at least in the column. At the time we had been putting out a tricolour flag and we saw the officer in front drawing his sword and pointing towards it. This was the officer who was immediately shot dead. The firing became continuous and rapid and it eased off. Some of the British soldiers tried to protect themselves against the quay wall and eventually ran up side streets and in through houses. The casualties were numerous and the ambulance was a considerable time removing the wounded. At four o'clock p.m. they came down eight deep. They must not have known where the first attack had come from, as the officer who first saw us was immediately shot dead. We altered our tactics then and we concentrated firing on the rear of the column. As they were nearly at Queen Street Bridge we suddenly concentrated the firing on the head of the column. The column stopped. It was just a matter of firing as rapidly as possible into a solid body. This column also broke up and ran in all directions. No man got past Queen Street Bridge.

The unarmed Dublin Metropolitan Police offered little resistance to the rebels. Nonetheless, by early afternoon six policemen had been shot, two fatally. The Irish Citizen Army – perhaps motivated by memories of police brutality during the 1913 Lockout – accounted for both fatalities.

Michael Soughley, Dublin Metropolitan Police sergeant

On the 24th April when the rebellion started we were withdrawn from the streets by order of Colonel E[dgeworth-]Johnstone, chief commissioner, Dublin Metropolitan Police. We had to report to our barracks in the normal way as if reporting for duty during that week. No one interfered with us.

James Burke, South Dublin Union

We went down Cork Street and had not proceeded very far when we saw a crowd at the corner of Jameson's distillery and a policeman outside the gate of the distillery. The policeman stepped out and asked us where we were going. I took a small .32, which I had carried since the time of the camps, and told him that was our business. He quietly moved back and we proceeded on our way.

Charles Saurin, GPO

. . . a poor scared DMP man in uniform hurriedly passed us, muttering 'Good lads' to us as he went by, perhaps more for self-protection than out of sympathy. We did not molest him in any way.

Father Michael Curran, secretary to Archbishop William Walsh, Dublin

It was after my return from the Rotunda that I noticed that the ten or twelve policemen with their inspector, whom I had seen at the foot of Nelson's Pillar some hours previously, had now moved right under and against the wall of the GPO, near the corner of Henry Street. They were very tense. I spoke very strongly to the DMP inspector, saying it was a scandal to leave the police there with the firing going on. There they were almost under the fire. I think I added that the situation was one for the military and not for the police. Two or three minutes afterwards they moved off. Quite unhindered they went off towards Store Street. That was sometime coming on to three o'clock. Not a hair of these ten or twelve policemen was touched while they stood at the Pillar or while the firing went on.

Séamus Robinson, Hopkins and Hopkins outpost, GPO

We walked over quietly, I wondering how long we would be bursting into a burglar-proof jeweller's shop – steel shutters all round.

The section scattered to find a ladder, and in the meantime I held up a mountain of a DMP man. With my little shotgun I must have looked like a Lilliputian threatening Gulliver with a peashooter. I had to break into something bordering on blasphemy before I could get that good-natured, and only mildly scared, bobby to stand until we could get inside the building. He kept backing away and repeating that he had nothing to do with us, that the military would deal with us. I told him, as seriously as I could, that if he didn't stand his wife would be a widow and his children orphans. No good. I was getting worried. He kept backing away. I did not want to shoot the man, but also I didn't want him to go away too soon to tell his precious military that we were out – until I was in. Again, no good. At last I yelled, as savagely as I could: 'Stand or' – and I took aim – 'by God or the devil, or both, I'll let you have two ounces of indigestible buckshot in your stomach.' He stood.

John MacDonagh, Jacob's biscuit factory

As we were entering the building, a very officious DMP man refused to leave the street when ordered by Tom [MacDonagh], who warned him that he would be shot if he persisted. I whispered to Tom, advising patience, but he answered that it might be necessary to shoot some of these policemen and detectives to show our own men that we were at war.

Seán Prendergast, Four Courts

We weren't long in position [on Hammond Lane] when a deal of excitement arose due to a big burly policeman endeavouring to pass through our lines. A scuffle ensued and the brave bobby was overpowered, but not before he had received a slight revolver shot in his elbow. In the midst of the mêlée he could be heard to say, 'I'm as good an Irishman as any of ye.' We admired his pluck but not his indiscretion . . .

William Stapleton, Jacob's biscuit factory

In the evening [on Monday] at Crosskevin Street end a man, who appeared to be a plain-clothes policeman, was ordered to move on. He had been observing our positions and taking notes. He refused to do so, and instructions were given that he was to be fired on. It so happened that one of our best shots was at the barricade and he opened fire and shot the man dead.

Frank Robbins, Irish Citizen Army, Stephen's Green

[James] Connolly, having been satisfied that each man thoroughly understood his instructions, then gave a general direction in the following strain: that we were, if such chance came our way, to encourage Irishmen in the British Army to come over to our side. Regarding the RIC and DMP, he left that question to our discretion with the words: 'Remember how they treated you in 1913.' For some years many of the DMP had been carrying small arms, and the RIC were a semi-military police force, well trained in the use of arms, and, therefore, in our opinion, placed themselves in the category of an armed force, to be dealt with as we thought fit.

Patrick Kelly, Church Street, Four Courts

I was detailed to take up duty on the barricade at Upper Church Street, facing Constitution Hill and the main approach from Broadstone Station. After some time I saw a policeman in uniform coming from the direction of the station. I took steady aim at him and was about to press the trigger when Captain Laffan knocked up my rifle and asked what I was doing. I pointed to the policeman and said I was going to shoot him. He said, 'You can't do a thing like that, the man is unarmed.' I remarked that I was unarmed in 1913 . . . I afterwards felt that Captain Laffan was due my thanks for staying my hand.

Charles Donnelly, GPO

On Tuesday or Wednesday a person whom I recognised as a member of the detective division came to one of the barricades and casually enquired how long we thought we could hold out. I told [Patrick] Pearse about this and asked if we could shoot him. He said: 'No, let him go.'

The Easter Rising was a remarkably public affair. The General Post Office, the rebel headquarters, was located at the centre of the widest and busiest street in Dublin. Undeterred by the sporadic shooting between rebels and soldiers, vast crowds turned out to observe the rebellion.

Father Michael Curran, secretary to Archbishop William Walsh, Dublin

There were several hundred people, perhaps over a thousand, between Abbey Street and Henry Street [on Monday] . . . As time went on, the crowds grew more reckless, passing under the line of fire of the soldiers [at the Rotunda] and Volunteers.

Laurence Nugent, K Company, 3rd Battalion

There was no use in warning these people about their danger. They were curious and did not understand what was the cause of all the trouble. Bullets were whining but they did not seem to mind.

Charles Saurin, GPO

. . . the scene was just like a bank holiday, which, of course, it was. There were big crowds all over the street, a great deal of attention being devoted to dead horses down near the Pillar . . . There was no fighting of any kind taking place here. All the noise there was was shouting and cheering from the people who swarmed around, some of whom were indicating their patriotism by tearing down British Army recruiting posters from the pillars of the GPO portico.

Ernest Jordison, general manager, British Petroleum Company (Ireland)

There was a great lot of people about, from the entrance into O'Connell Street near Parnell Street, and onwards, mainly on the footpaths. I actually saw boys with cricket bats and balls, playing in the middle of the road, before reaching Nelson's Pillar, where I saw two dead horses lying in the road, on the left-hand side of the Pillar, and an immense lot of blood all over that part of the road.

Charles Donnelly, GPO

Later in the day [Tuesday] a big burly man of the dock-labourer type came to the window and said he wanted to fight with Mr Connolly. I told James Connolly about him and he said: 'Let him in.' I brought him to James Connolly, who gave him a Martini rifle and a bandolier of ammunition. He told me to instruct him in the use of the weapon.

After trying for a long time to teach him to load and use the rifle, I realised that he would never learn. I went and told Connolly this and asked him to take back the rifle. He told me to send the man to him. When the man reported, Connolly told him he wanted a strong man who could use a pike. The man accepted gratefully and was put on guard at the main door of the GPO. I saw him there for a couple of days. On Wednesday morning I saw him coming down Henry Street in the direction of O'Connell Street, in the middle of the road. He seemed to have lost his head, as he was unarmed and was moving along in a pugilistic attitude. He was riddled with bullets.

Oscar Traynor, GPO

Whilst I was talking to [James] Connolly he was approached by a man who was somewhat under the influence of drink. This man said that he wanted to join the garrison, and Connolly asked him why . . . 'Because,' the man said, 'I want to fight for Ireland.' 'Are you sure you want to fight for Ireland?' Connolly asked him. 'I am certain,' said the man. 'Well, then,' said Connolly, 'will you go home now, have a good sleep, and when you are sober come back and tell me that you still want to fight for Ireland and I'll give you a rifle.'

Jimmy Kenny, GPO

Sometime afterwards two foreign seamen came to one of the windows and offered their services.

Liam Tannam, GPO

So I said: 'Tell me why you want to come in here and fight against England.' He said: 'Finland, a small country, Russia eat her up.' Then he said: 'Sweden, another small country, Russia eat her up too. Russia with the British, therefore we against.' I said, 'Can you fight? Do you know how to use a weapon?' He said: 'I can use a rifle. My friend – no. He can use what you shoot the fowl with.' I said: 'A shotgun.' I decided to admit them. I took them in and got the Swede a rifle, the Finn a shotgun. I put them at my own windows. There was another alarm and again we manned the windows but it was a false alarm. Everyone cocked his piece, including the Finn, who cocked his shotgun. When the alarm passed he stepped down off the barricade, banged the shotgun against the terrazzo floor and off it went and down came a shower of plaster over six or seven of us. Joe Plunkett ran up on hearing the explosion and started to abuse the Finn. The Finn looked at him, looked at me, at everyone. Joe said: 'Can you not talk, man?' The Swede spoke up and said: 'No. He has no English.' 'Who are you?' Joe said. I intervened then and explained to Joe. Joe looked at me and said: 'Amazing, but obviously that man there is a danger,' pointing to the Finn . . . Some of our men were filling fruit tins with explosives and bits of metal, and Joe thought it would keep him out of danger at the time. I was transferring the Finn when the Swede spoke up: 'Where he go, I go; we together.' I had to take the two of them. They were there to the end and were captured.

The rebels were shocked by the ferocity of public opposition to the Rising. Women from the slums were most vocal: many had husbands or sons serving in the British Army, but their anger also reflected the danger to which their families, homes and livelihoods had been exposed. Over half of the 450 people killed during Easter Week were civilians, and this was another factor in the unpopularity of the rebellion. However, some rebels detected a shift in attitudes over the course of the week as they held out against the odds.

Thomas Young, Marrowbone Lane distillery, South Dublin Union

I met a party of unarmed British troops headed by some members of their families who caused some commotion amongst us. It was only the soldiers' wives that attacked us. We were on bicycles. The ladies pulled us off the bicycles and we had to use the butts of our rifles to defend ourselves.

Thomas MacCarthy, Roe's distillery, South Dublin Union

During the time we were trying to knock down the gate we were practically attacked by the rabble in Bow Lane, and I will never forget it as long as I live. 'Leave down your [fucking] rifles,' they shouted, 'and we'll beat the [shit] out of you.' They were most menacing to our lads.

Liam Archer, Mary's Lane outpost, Four Courts

The people were very hostile and there was some excitement. [Piaras] Béaslaí ordered me to fix my bayonet. This I did and immediately a very fat dame in spotless white apron and voluminous shawl leapt in front of us and, beating her ample bosom with clenched fists, called on me to 'put it through me now for me son who's out in France'.

Patrick Kelly, Church Street outpost, Four Courts

I was approached by a British soldier who was apparently on leave from France. He asked me what we were about. I told him it would be better if he left the neighbourhood and asked no questions. He attempted to pass into North Brunswick Street and I stopped him. He became very abusive and used some bad language, saying it was a nice state of affairs that a man who had fought for the country could not walk the streets. At this stage we were approached by a number of women of the dealer type (wearing shawls). They urged the soldier to take the rifle from me. It was my intention, if he tried to take my rifle, to shoot him with my revolver. I loosed the flap of the holster to facilitate a quick draw. The latter action seemed to decide him against taking the chance.

William Stapleton, Jacob's biscuit factory

We were booed and frequently pelted with various articles throughout the day. We were openly insulted, particularly by the wives of British soldiers who were drawing separation allowance and who referred to their sons and husbands fighting for freedom in France. As dusk was falling, about seven or eight o'clock, we retreated from the barricades to our headquarters at Jacob's, at the Bishop Street entrance, and while waiting to be admitted at one of the large gates we were submitted to all sorts of indignities by some of the local people. It was difficult to preserve control due to the treatment we suffered from these people. We were actually struck, and those in uniforms had their uniform caps knocked off . . . No sooner had we barricaded the entrance when the mob tried to burst the gate in. They kicked and barged it with some heavy implements, but seeing that that was of little effect they tried to set fire to it with old sacking which had been soaked in paraffin and pushed under the door and ignited.

Vinny Byrne, Jacob's biscuit factory

When we came out on [Malpas] street, a lot of soldiers' wives and, I expect, imperialistic people – men and women – came around us. They jeered and shouted at us. One man in the crowd was very aggressive. He tried to take the rifle off one of our party. Lieutenant Billy Byrne told him to keep off or he would be sorry. The man, however, made a grab at the rifle. I heard a shot ring out and saw him falling at the wall.

Thomas Pugh, Jacob's biscuit factory

The women around the Coombe were in a terrible state, they were like French Revolution furies and were throwing their arms round the police [prisoners], hugging and kissing them, much to the disgust of the police.

Frank Robbins, Irish Citizen Army, Stephen's Green

. . . [On Tuesday] Commandant Mallin issued orders for a general evacuation of the Green to the College of Surgeons . . . On the way they were attacked by a number of civilians. In this number was a young woman who had been extremely obnoxious not only then, but on the day before. This woman was the most daring of her kind. She followed our three men down the street and was using very offensive language. Being a woman our men on every occasion were endeavouring to ignore her. My patience was exhausted from the previous day's experience when watching her continual interference with our outposts. One thing stopped me from endeavouring to quieten her, and that was the fear of hitting one of our men. There was no danger of doing so on this occasion. With my mind firmly made up I ran into the centre of the roadway, dropped on one knee with the feeling that this woman would be a good riddance. Captain McCormack was the last of the three, and he was still on the roadway. I remember waving my right arm and shouting, 'Get out of the way, Mac.' Captain McCormack, seeing my motion, though I can't say if he knew my intention, was moving away. Lieutenant Kelly, who was now almost at the door, guessed my intention, and shouted, 'Frank, don't shoot,' while at the same time he ran out into the roadway and grasped my arm. I felt sore over it and wondered would the [same] consideration have been shown by the opposing forces if they were to be obstructed in the same way.

Jim O'Shea, Irish Citizen Army, Stephen's Green

When we were near the path, one of the soldiers' women, who had been screaming most of the morning, rushed at Mallin with the intention of tearing at him. I had my bayonet fixed and nearly got her, but Mallin knocked it up and we ran to the side door and hammered with the butts of our rifles.

Laurence Nugent, K Company, 3rd Battalion

As I arrived at the church at Leeson Park [on Wednesday] a party of British soldiers came up along Leeson Street from Donnybrook. They were a machine-gun corps with fourteen machine-guns and ammunition carts. They had marched all the way from Dún Laoghaire in the heat, pushing or driving their guns and carts. They were mostly lads, territorials and poorly trained. Before they arrived at the church they were halted by their officer, and in a moment every man was lying on the ground. I never knew tea to be made in such a short space of time, for within a few minutes every man had a cup of tea. Upper Leeson Street was loyal to the empire.

Eileen Costello, Gaelic League

There were many guests in the [Gresham] hotel from the north of Ireland who had come for the races. They were saying that the rebels should all be shot . . . one of the guests – a man from the midlands – was collecting money for the purpose of making a presentation to the two [British Army] snipers on the roof for 'saving the lives of the guests'. I met him. He had a pencil and paper and was writing the names of the subscribers to the presentation. When he approached me for a subscription I said, 'Are you asking me to reward these Englishmen who are shooting our own men down? Have some sense of proportion. I won't give you a penny. You should be ashamed for asking it.' He turned to the other residents and induced them to jeer at my attitude . . . A correspondent from the *Manchester Guardian* spoke kindly to me. When he saw the other guests were avoiding me he said: 'Don't mind them, Mrs Costello, I'll stand by you.'

Maire O'Brolchain, Cumann na mBan, Dublin

The householders, rushing round for food and fuel and light – gas cut off – were very bitter against the fools who incommoded them . . . But when the guns of the [British patrol boat] *Helga* were heard pounding on Liberty Hall, only the English and a few pro-English welcomed the sound. The fighters were our countrymen fighting for Ireland and must be helped.

John Shouldice, Church Street, Four Courts

On Monday and Tuesday a good number of the local residents, especially those who had relatives fighting for England in the European War, were very antagonistic and their womenfolk especially made our fight none the easier. However, we gradually got the sympathy or, if not, the respect of the great majority of the people when they saw for themselves that we were conducting the Rising in a fair and clean manner and with such small numbers against the might of England.

Conscious of the importance of presenting the Rising as an honourable assertion of the right to national sovereignty, the provisional government was disgusted by the widespread looting that occurred. Many looters were clearly indifferent or hostile to the rebels. Their actions presented more of a challenge to some rebel garrisons than the military during the first days of Easter Week.

William O'Brien, Irish Transport and General Workers' Union leader

. . . prior to Easter Week I had mentioned to James Connolly that as soon as the insurrection started I thought there would be widespread looting and his reply was merely, 'That will be one more problem for the British.'

Jeremiah O'Leary, GPO

In the late afternoon, I observed big crowds in Earl Street and Abbey Street, breaking shop windows and beginning to loot the contents . . . I reported to Pearse and Connolly that disorders were breaking out. Connolly was rather abrupt and probably resentful of my butting in, but Pearse said that there was a shortage of men, that he had none available to take up police duties, and he asked me to try and organise a volunteer force to take up the task. He indicated a box of wooden batons which lay in a corner of the main hall and said I might arm the men with these. I went out to the front of the GPO, stood up on one of the stones that front the pillars and made a short speech, denouncing the looting and calling for volunteers to help to suppress it . . . We moved over towards Earl Street, but there was such a dense, milling crowd there that we became broken up and submerged by the crowd immediately.

Father Michael Curran, secretary to Archbishop William Walsh, Dublin

. . . the first victim was Noblett's sweetshop. It soon spread to the neighbouring shops. I was much disgusted and I did my best to try to stop the looting. Except for two or three minutes it had no effect. I went over and informed the Volunteers about the GPO. Five or six Volunteers did their best and cleared the looters for some five or ten minutes, but it began again. At first all the ringleaders were women; then the boys came along. Later, about 3.30 p.m., when the military were withdrawn from the Rotunda, young men arrived and the looting became systematic and general . . . I am sure that eyewitnesses that late afternoon and next day would say that what most impressed them, and impressed them most unfavourably, was the frivolity and recklessness of the crowd, most of all, of the women and children.

Eamon Bulfin, GPO

I remember we were still on the roof when Lawrence's went on fire. It was a sports shop, and all the kids brought out a lot of fireworks, made a huge pile of them in the middle of O'Connell Street and set fire to them. That is one thing that will stick in my mind forever. We had our bombs on top of the Post Office, and these fireworks were shooting up in the sky. We were very nervous. There were Catherine wheels going up O'Connell Street and Catherine wheels coming down O'Connell Street.

Kevin McCabe, Imperial Hotel outpost, GPO

There was a boot shop at the corner – Tyler's – now Burton's the tailor's, and the crowd of looters rushed in there and took every pair of boots and shoes in the shop. I actually saw a boy and girl in the office lighting a bundle of papers to set fire to the place. I closed the door and threatened to keep them there unless they put out the fire. They beat it out quickly then.

Arthur Agnew, GPO

Our orders were that the looters were to be stopped and made to drop their loot on the street. If they failed to do this they were to be shot.

Patrick Kelly, Church Street outpost, Four Courts

During the afternoon a woman came to the barricade. She was heavily laden. The load she carried was covered by a shawl. I challenged her and asked what she had. She replied bread for the children. I insisted that she should show me what she had. She threw open her shawl and exposed a vast array of silverware, trays, teapots, coffee sets, etc. I was at a loss what to do, so I allowed her to enter a tenement house in Lisburn Street.

Michael O'Flanagan, Four Courts

On Wednesday afternoon we noticed four or five men and women coming from the direction of Mary's Lane. Between them they were carrying a piano . . . We fired a few shots over their heads as a warning and they dropped the piano and made off.

Helena Molony, Irish Citizen Army, City Hall outpost

On my way to the GPO [on Monday afternoon], I met [Francis] Sheehy-Skeffington in Dame Street, looking very white and dispirited. His job was to mobilise a police force, and stop the looting . . .

He was standing in the midst of the bullets, as if they were raindrops. He was a fighting pacifist.

Denis Daly, GPO

Men, women and even children seemed to have gone mad. In the cellars of one house in Henry Street I saw them wading in wine more than a foot deep.

Áine Heron, Cumann na mBan, GPO

When we emerged from the GPO [on Tuesday morning] I felt scared for the first time. There was a crowd of drunken women who had been looting public houses and other shops. They had their arms full of the loot. They were at the other side of the road and they called out all sorts of names at us, but they were too drunk to attack us.

Thomas Leahy, GPO

The whole populace was very much dumbfounded and their long suffering under the economic conditions and low wages for their labour made them more determined to grab all they could. It was a pity to see them, especially able-bodied men doing this kind of thing, instead of being in the firing line with us.

Bulmer Hobson, (anti-insurrectionary) IRB leader, Dublin

His [James Connolly's] conversation was full of clichés derived from the earlier days of the socialist movement in Europe. He told me that the working class was always revolutionary, that Ireland was a powder magazine and that what was necessary was for someone to apply the match. I replied that if he must talk in metaphors, Ireland was a wet bog and that the match would fall into a puddle. I thought of this later as I watched the Dublin mob, not joining Connolly in the Post Office but looting the shops in O'Connell Street, and I thought of this again when I read in the press how the British soldiers after the surrender had to protect their prisoners from the violence of the Dublin mob.

Robert Barton, Royal Dublin Fusiliers

. . . the War Office was greatly concerned because the troops in Dublin had been looting, an offence for which they would be shot if they were in France . . . There were a great many charges of looting against the British troops, and the War Office had instructed the authorities in Dublin to stop the looting and to collect what had been looted and return it.

Little fighting occurred in Dublin until the arrival of overwhelming British Army reinforcements on Wednesday.

Thomas Dowling, Mary Street, Four Courts

From Monday to Wednesday we had very little action . . . The only casualty in my section occurred on Wednesday morning, when one of our men accidentally shot himself in the foot and was removed to the Richmond Hospital.

Kevin McCabe, GPO

The rest of the week was spent consolidating our position and waiting for something to happen. We did practically no shooting as there was no target.

Christopher Byrne, Marrowbone Lane distillery, South Dublin Union

We were so free from fighting that Séamus Murphy, the O/C, suggested that we should have a sing-song – to keep the fellows' hearts up.

Padraig Ó Ceallaigh, Jacob's biscuit factory

There was little military activity in Jacob's – just occasional sniping by the British and ourselves.

Thomas Pugh, Jacob's biscuit factory

The only time I was in the firing was when I was on the top floor of Jacob's, where they had a rest room and library, with a glass roof and glass windows. A bullet came through . . . I was mostly on the ground floor and only went up to the library to look for a book.

Cornelius O'Donovan, Four Courts

We were really suffering from the strain of looking for a soldier to fire at, and I remember well the callous and, shall I say, brutal pleasure I felt when I 'picked off' one who was crossing Grattan Bridge, although he dodged from side to side, and kept his head low most of the time. Another who fell to one of our group was too easy a mark. He walked out of Chancery Street, in full kit. Our man at a loophole saw him, and asked me what would he do. Well, what could we do? Here was a soldier, armed and probably looking for a chance to fire on us. One bullet did it, and then the marksman raised his hat, and said, 'He's dead, or dying now, anyhow. May the Lord have mercy on him!'

The tension and boredom arising from inactivity provided an unexpected threat to morale during the first half of the week. Isolated from the outside world, and subject to fantastic rumours, the rebels sought to occupy themselves while preparing for the inevitable onslaught.

Desmond Ryan, GPO

We sat behind our loopholes. Time dragged. We even wrote letters. We watched the bleak and deserted street tumble into ashes. We watched the smouldering ruins rise. We watched for the soldiers who never came.

Diarmuid Lynch, GPO

When quiet again reigned inside the building I suggested to Tom Clarke that we take a look through the letters which had been sorted into a pigeon-hole marked 'RIC Headquarters'. Tom smilingly agreed. They afforded interesting reading . . . We chuckled at the fact that all their spying was now in vain, and that neither they nor their superiors [had] realised the imminence of the climax.

Fintan Murphy, GPO

In the telegraph room, efforts were being made to despatch and tap messages; and across the road in the Marconi Wireless School over the D[ublin] B[read] C[ompany] attempts were made to broadcast the news of the insurrection to the world.

Luke Kennedy, GPO

Later on that [Monday] evening when it was dark I was instructed ... to go across to Reis's wireless station at the corner of Abbey Street to see if I could do anything with the wireless as the people there could not get the plant to work. At this time, the wireless mast and aerial were in position on the roof. I went across and succeeded in getting the plant to work. As soon as the plant was fixed the Easter Week Proclamation was sent out on air in Morse.

Liam Tannam, GPO

Blimey [Johnny O'Connor] was engaged on the job of climbing up the wireless mast to fix some wires and he was being sniped at all the time, but he fixed it. How he had the pluck to carry on and how he was not riddled beats me. I learned from Fergus Kelly that he could send out messages but that the instrument was unable to receive. He could not send them very far but perhaps ships could pick them up and relay them.

Patrick Colgan, GPO

Sometime during Wednesday we were ordered to break open the safes [in the living quarters of Post Office secretary Arthur Hamilton Norway] to search for arms ... In one press we found the blood-stained second lieutenant's British Army uniform of a son of the secretary. He had been killed in France some short time earlier. In an envelope we found a lock of his fair hair, marked by the boy's mother. I forget the name of the boy [Fred]. There were a number of letters from the boy to his mother. With the uniform was a .45 revolver in a holster.

James Kavanagh, GPO

There was a good deal of fun during the week. In close proximity to the Post Office in Henry Street there was an institution called the Wax Works ... it was not long till a number of our troops were arrayed in various uniforms and costumes from the wax figures, and musical instruments were also acquired, such as mouth organs, melodeons and fiddles, the playing of which and the singing which accompanied them made a good deal of the time pass very pleasantly.

William Daly, GPO

Some genius put the figures at the windows and immediately a fusillade of bullets came through and we had to duck for a few minutes until the firing died down. The idea of the wax figures of Wolfe Tone and King Edward being riddled by bullets amused us a great deal.

Séamus Pounch, Fianna Éireann, Jacob's biscuit factory

During a lull in the fighting in Jacob's we held a miniature ceilidh – Volunteers and Fianna, Cumann na mBan, Clan na Gael Girl Scouts . . . a real welcome break in the serious business we had in hand.

John MacDonagh, Jacob's biscuit factory

Some of the Volunteers discovered an old-fashioned gramophone, in a corner downstairs in Jacob's, that played 'God Save the King', and one day when Tom [MacDonagh] and [John] MacBride were making their tour of inspection it was put on to take a rise out of them.

Seosamh de Brún, Jacob's biscuit factory

After nights lying on tiled or metal floors, the strenuous exertion erecting defences, exciting rushes to attention, the men reclined, smoked, read and chatted, some wrote diaries of events to date . . . A piano was strummed occasionally in an upper portion of the building in contrast with the rifle fire. The bookcase in the library was broken open and pillaged. I can distinctly remember the interest evoked by quotations from Julius Caesar . . . [we] made a study circle during fatigue hours. It reminded one of school rather than a war camp.

William Oman, Irish Citizen Army, Stephen's Green

I found things very different in the College of Surgeons to what they were in Jacob's. Commandant Mallin had a very, very strict code of discipline . . . Any man who was available had to assemble at a given time for the rosary. We had to make down our beds and, in the morning reveille, which was not sounded, of course, we had to make up our beds and fold them up, etc. Due to the fact that there were so many injured in the college . . . no noise or hilarity was allowed.

Desmond Ryan, GPO

Rumours of Ireland ablaze are as common as rosary beads round the necks of the watchers at the front windows. Cork and Kerry and Limerick are up and the Curragh line is held on both sides. Soldiers are attacking the Archbishop's Palace in Drumcondra. Forces are marching to our relief. Jim Larkin is fighting his way across from Sligo with 50,000 men. Submarines had sunk a transport in the Irish Sea.

Fintan Murphy, GPO

Stories of the progress of events in other centres came up to us from below of the most varied and sometimes fantastic nature – some said the Germans had landed here, there and everywhere – a German submarine was coming up the Liffey – the Volunteers were marching in from the country – the whole of the country was up in arms . . . The German fleet was in the Bay!

Liam Archer, Church Street, Four Courts

On Wednesday evening an official statement was circulated that help was at hand as two German warships had arrived in Dublin Bay. We were all enthused . . . It was questionable if the circulation of this rumour served any useful purpose.

The members of the provisional government sought to project a sense of composure and purpose throughout the Rising. Despite previous tensions between the Citizen Army and the Volunteers, it was James Connolly – 'commandant-general' of the 'Dublin Division' – who directed the fighting. Patrick Pearse also impressed many Volunteers by his charismatic presence and inspiring rhetoric rather than by his military abilities. His appointment as president of the Irish Republic – rather than the more senior Fenian Tom Clarke – may have been due to his exceptional abilities as a communicator.

Desmond Ryan, GPO

Behind the central counter mattresses had been placed. Here Pearse, Connolly, Plunkett, MacDermott and Tom Clarke slept in turns. They all had to be given opium, according to a Red Cross worker, before they could sleep. Beds were brought in later for them. On the Tuesday morning, they were all seated together on boxes and barrels, pale and tired. But they were very calm and humorous ... MacDermott was as gentle and as fiery as he always was. Tom Clarke seemed quite at home.

Seán McGarry, GPO

I never knew him [Tom Clarke] to be cooler. His normal air of business seemed to have been accentuated and he gave his orders decisively and as calmly as if he were in his own shop.

Patrick Rankin, GPO

He [Clarke] looked about thirty years younger and seemed so happy you could imagine you were talking to him in his old shop in Parnell Street. He thanked me for getting through to the GPO but he would have been delighted and happy to have had some hundreds of his own people from the northern counties present.

Charles J. MacAuley, Joseph Plunkett's surgeon

In a tiny room there was a group of people whom I remember very distinctly. Stretched on a pallet on the floor was Joseph Plunkett in riding breeches and wearing a green Volunteer uniform shirt. In the room also seated there was Tom Clarke in civilian clothes with a bandolier across his shoulders and a rifle between his knees. He was silent and had a look of grim determination on his face. I was greatly impressed by him. It was as if he thought his day had come. He never spoke ... The last thing I remember about the Post Office in the early hours of Easter Tuesday morning was being escorted to the top of the stairs leading down to the ground floor by Seán MacDermott. He shook hands with me at the top of the stairs. He had a charming personality and appeared calm and gracious as usual, but I felt an element of sadness in his farewell.

Ignatius Callender, GPO

I had never met [James] Connolly before and he impressed me very much by his remarkable coolness.

William Whelan, GPO

I remember a panic when we arrived at the Post Office from Fairview. Crowds of people were looting the shops and I can't say what caused the panic, but a lot of us dropped on our knees with our rifles 'at the ready' – some fired, at what, I do not know. The panic was spreading and Connolly came out of the Post Office and marched up and down the road in front of it. He said, 'Steady, we are going to have a good fight.' He quelled the panic.

Oscar Traynor, GPO

We reached Eason's in Abbey Street and, although at this time [Wednesday afternoon] heavy firing was taking place, Connolly insisted on walking out into Abbey Street and giving me instructions as to where I should place a barricade. While he was giving these instructions, he was standing at the edge of the path and the bullets were actually striking the pavements around us. I pointed this out to him and said that I thought it was a grave risk to be taking and that these instructions could be given inside.

James Kavanagh, GPO

Not alone was he continually planning raids, but he took part in most, and it was in one of those outside raids he received the wound which kept him inactive for the last couple of days of the fight. I noticed a thing about Connolly that I thought peculiar. He seemed to take no notice of rank. He would call out a number of men and then say to one of them 'Tom' or 'Pat' or whoever it might be, 'Take these men and go to such a place and do so and so and report back to me.' Very often the man in charge would be a full private.

Oscar Traynor, GPO

Pearse assured [the rebels who arrived at the GPO on Tuesday] that they had done a great and noble work for their country, and said that if they did not do anything else they at least had redeemed the fair name of Dublin city, which was dishonoured when [Robert] Emmet was allowed to die before a large crowd of its people. He said: 'Be assured that you will find victory, even though that victory may be found in death.' That was another terribly thrilling moment.

Patrick Colgan, GPO

He [Pearse] told us how glad he was to have us with them in the fight; that our action in marching in from Kildare, even if we did no more in the rebellion, would gain us a place in history . . . With the knowledge that my name would live in history and that I had made a great contribution . . . I felt elated.

Catherine Byrne, Cumann na mBan, GPO

Pearse gave me a blessing in Irish . . .

Claire Gregan, fiancée of Bulmer Hobson

I said goodnight to Pearse, who stood there very solemn in a Napoleonic attitude with his right hand on his breast.

Eily O'Hanrahan, Cumann na mBan

I came back again to Pearse and asked him whether he remembered my message. He said 'yes' in a vague tone, as if he were up in the clouds, so I went to [Michael] O'Rahilly and repeated the message to him, so as to be sure the grenades would be sent.

Louise Gavan Duffy, Cumann na mBan, GPO

I was brought into the Post Office and I saw Mr Pearse. He was as calm and courteous as ever. I now think it was very insolent of me because I said to him that I wanted to be in the field but that I felt the rebellion was a frightful mistake, that it could not possibly succeed, and it was, therefore, wrong . . . I suppose what I meant was that I would not like to be sent with despatches or anything like that, because I felt that could not be justified. He asked me would I like to go to the kitchen.

Michael Knightly, GPO

Seán MacDermott came to the door, shook hands and introduced me to The O'Rahilly. 'Have you got any news?' he asked eagerly. 'The only news I have,' I replied, 'is that artillery are on their way from Athlone.' 'Damn it,' he said, 'only for MacNeill yesterday we would have the whole country with us. As it is we might get some terms.' To this I did not reply. I had heard the matter discussed by my colleagues [at the *Irish Independent*] during the day and one conclusion come to was that every man who signed the Proclamation would be shot.

Min Ryan, Cumann na mBan, GPO

Then I had a talk with Tom Clarke in the kitchen that Tuesday night . . . The gist of it was – that people naturally now would be against them for rising and coming out like this; that one of the reasons for being against them would be because of the countermanding order, but that they had come to this conclusion that it was absolutely necessary that they should have the Rising now, because if they did not have it now, they might never have it; that when the men had been brought to a certain point they had to go forward; that, in any case, a rebellion was necessary to make Ireland's position felt at the Peace Conference so that its relation to the British Empire would strike the world. I asked him: 'Why a republic?' He replied: 'You must have something striking in order to appeal to the imagination of the world.' He also said that at all periods in the history of Ireland the shedding of blood had always succeeded in raising the spirit and morale of the people. He said that our only chance was to make ourselves felt by an armed rebellion. 'Of course,' he added, 'we shall be all wiped out.' He said this almost with gaiety. He had got into the one thing he had wanted to do during his whole lifetime.

Eamon Dore, GPO

I had travelled from west Limerick on Monday and Tuesday and knew the failure in the country and had been warned, when I got to the General Post Office, not to tell anyone of the conditions in the country.

Tom Harris, GPO

We got into the Post Office [on Tuesday afternoon] . . . Connolly paraded us and said, 'it didn't matter a damn if we were wiped out now as we had justified ourselves'. I thought this was a bit rugged.

Robert Holland, Marrowbone Lane distillery, South Dublin Union

We got word that the city was on fire but that we had only few casualties whilst the British were suffering heavy losses. We certainly believed this, as this was our own case. We had no one killed and only two wounded and these were back in the fight again. If all the garrisons were like ours, and we had no doubt that they were, we were doing very well indeed. We had only to bide our time. We must win and none of us thought otherwise. Failure was the last thing that I or the rest of us thought of . . . We were more than two days and a half fighting and that was longer than four previous rebellions put together. A trickle of reinforcements kept coming in and we were all in high spirits, all young men determined to win, and this was our only object. I and the rest of us had made our Easter duty and God would see us on the winning side. I was thinking all about my school days, the lectures that the Christian Brothers gave us each Friday from twelve o'clock to one about the Mass Rock and the Famine, of Blessed Oliver Plunkett and of Emmet and Tone, McCracken and the Sheares. All these came back to my mind in the dark of the night . . .

Michael Knightly, GPO

I had concealed my pessimism from those with whom I had been on duty, for they were burning with enthusiasm and convinced that we were going to win. I envied their optimism and felt it would be cruel to say anything that might discourage them.

Michael Hayes, Jacob's biscuit factory

My immediate inclination was to side with MacNeill . . . I entered Jacob's very early in the morning, having made up my mind that this was the only course but that the venture was a hopeless one. There must have been a number of people in the Rising who, if they had been given an opportunity of coming to a conclusion, would not have taken part at all.

Padraig Ó Ceallaigh, Jacob's biscuit factory

That the Rising was a gallant but hopeless venture which could not end but in early defeat seemed the general feeling amongst the Jacob's garrison.

Of the practical issues with which the rebels had to contend, the supply of food gradually became the most pressing. Some rebels who, decades later, could remember little else about the Rising vividly recalled what they ate, or went without, that week.

William Daly, Reis's outpost, GPO

A pint jug of steaming hot tea was handed to me while sitting upon the mattress and in another minute a plate with three fried eggs and sausages with plenty of bread and butter was placed before me. I had had only two packages of biscuits since 9.30 a.m. the previous day. That early morning breakfast was one of the most glorious meals I have ever had, the memory of it lingered with me for many a day as I was young and healthy and had not a care in the world even in the midst of the events taking place around me.

Mary McLoughlin, Clan na Gael, GPO

This was the first time I saw a whole salmon cooked laid on a dish.

Bridget Foley, Cumann na mBan, GPO

I can still see the vision of the big sides of beef going into the ovens for their lunches.

Pauline Keating, Cumann na mBan, Four Courts

We had plenty of food in the Four Courts. A man used to go out early every morning, bring in bread, meat and other food for the day. We knew him as 'Looter' Flood.

Nicholas Laffan, Church Street, Four Courts

The food supplies included tinned milk, coffee and milk, tinned meat, Oxo cubes and cheese . . . Each night we received a ten-gallon can of hot soup from the Master of the North Dublin Union.

John Shouldice, Church Street, Four Courts

Monk's bakery, part in Church Street and part in North King Street, was held by G Company under Captain N. Laffan. Commandant Daly put some Volunteers in charge and compelled the bakers to continue at their work as long as the supply of flour lasted . . . In addition to the rations brought by some of the men we obtained our supplies of bread, meat, etc., by requisitioning them in the name of the Republic from local grocery and provision shops . . . The meals generally consisted of rashers and eggs and tea and stew.

Thomas Pugh, Jacob's biscuit factory

We explored the different places and found a lot of crystallised fruit and tons of chocolate at the top of the house and we gorged ourselves. We were well off as regards that kind of food, but we would have given a lot for an ordinary piece of bread.

Thomas Meldon, Jacob's biscuit factory

A Fianna boy, who was attached to HQ as orderly, discovered in a display case an extra-rich cake which he disposed of with remarkable speed and with dire results, but although very ill, he refused to go home.

Thomas Doyle, Marrowbone Lane distillery, South Dublin Union

There was very little food there, and part of the time they were trying to prevent the men from using the roasted malt that was there.

Thomas Young, Marrowbone Lane distillery, South Dublin Union

I signalled that there were three cattle being driven along Marrowbone Lane towards Cork Street. Ned Neill opened the gates and drove the cattle through them. He closed the gates. In a few moments the owner of the cattle came along and stood in consternation. I asked him what his trouble was, and he replied by asking me had I seen three heifers. I, of course, assured him that no cattle had passed that way . . . Another incident was when I saw a messenger boy peering through the closed gates. I noticed a basket on his bicycle containing trussed chickens, and frantically signalled Ned Neill, who opened the small wicket gate and asked the boy what he was doing . . . The boy replied that he was delivering these chickens to the Viceregal Lodge. Ned Neill took the basket of chickens off the bicycle and told the boy to give the Lord Lieutenant Ned Neill's compliments. The boy's reply was: 'For [fuck's] sake, mister, take the [fucking] bicycle as well.'

Robert Holland, Marrowbone Lane distillery, South Dublin Union

I was told to kill one of the cattle, as I was then an apprentice butcher. I got a jack-knife and a few penknives and sharpened them in the yard on a sandstone. When I had them ready I tied up one of the cattle to a winch and killed it with a sledge hammer . . . [Con] Colbert was very anxious about the hide and he asked me a lot about curing it to make moccasins. I knew nothing about this and he went and started to cure it himself.

Patrick Colgan, GPO

The last time we got food was on Tuesday night. Later on Thursday afternoon I called to the kitchen. I saw Desmond FitzGerald, who told me there was no food available then. He gave me a bucket filled with tea and two or three old empty salmon tins to drink from . . . the nice strong tea had been given us in a bucket which had contained Jeyes Fluid.

Liam Tannam, GPO

The men were supplied rather sparingly with the food and Desmond FitzGerald, who was in charge of the catering, was heartily cursed in every jail in England where men were confined when, starving with hunger, they thought of the food they had left behind them in the GPO. I myself even dreamt of it.

Eamon Dore, GPO

On Friday, Seán Mac Diarmada called me and said he and Tom Clarke and a few others were going to have something to eat. It was about three o'clock. I went with him upstairs and seated at that table were Tom Clarke, Seán Mac Diarmada, Diarmuid Lynch, Seán McGarry and myself. We had a fried mutton chop each – where they came from I do not know – but I was hungry, it was the first real meal in days. While we were eating Father [John] Flanagan, Pro-Cathedral, who had come in earlier to attend the wounded, came into the room and Seán McGarry said, 'Hello, Father, would a fellow go to hell for eating meat on this Friday?' 'Why, Seán?' said he. 'Because, Father, I am going to chance it.' It was the last joke for a good while.

Liam Tannam, GPO

[By Friday] I was rather exhausted and hungry and the only thing I could get to eat was a raw egg and a square of Chivers jelly.

Séamus Kavanagh, College of Surgeons outpost

. . . we lived mostly on bread and tea. I think we got soup on one or two occasions. On the Saturday prior to the surrender, we were contemplating the execution of a horse, which was in a stable at the rear of the College of Surgeons, in order to provide food for us.

Despite clerical condemnation of the IRB, many Volunteers (and some Fenians) were devout Catholics. The powerful impact of Pearse's writings ensured that the Rising would come to be seen as an event steeped in Catholicism, and the form of republicanism that triumphed in Ireland after 1916 was influenced by the piety of such figures as Éamon de Valera rather than by the Fenian secular tradition.

Ignatius Callender, GPO

The scenes in almost every chapel on Saturday night were amazing – the chapels were crowded with men and boys for confession. Similar scenes were witnessed on the Sunday morning, thousands of men and boys receiving Holy Communion.

Charles Saurin, GPO

On arrival at Father Matthew Park I found a big number of Volunteers there . . . a young priest, a curate in Fairview parish, appeared. We all knelt down and were given conditional absolution. He held up a crucifix before us all and spoke directly on the sacrifice we might have to make before long and the need to be prepared for it. He also heard confessions of men who wished to make their confession direct to him in the hall. It was while he was speaking to us all as we knelt each on one knee before him clasping our rifles in both hands that Peter Traynor came round the corner and halted suddenly at the scene before him . . . I caught the look in his eyes and could see that he was struck by the drama and by something deeper than just drama in the young priest holding up the crucifix and exhorting the kneeling armed men before him to think on what it represented and of our brief mortal life.

Father Michael Curran, secretary to Archbishop William Walsh, Dublin

At five minutes past twelve [Easter Monday] I interviewed Count Plunkett. He said he had come to see the archbishop. I informed him that the archbishop was ill in bed . . . Count Plunkett then told me that there was going to be a rising, that he had been to see the Pope and that he had informed Benedict XV . . . making it plain that it was the wish of the leaders of the movement to act entirely with the good-will or approval – I forget which now – of the Pope and to give an assurance that they wished to act as Catholics . . . All the Pope could do was to express his profound anxiety and how much the news disturbed him, and asked could their object not be achieved in any other way, and counselled him to see the archbishop as soon as he arrived home.

Thomas Doyle, South Dublin Union

One of the interesting things that [Éamonn] Ceannt said was that we had the papal benediction, that we had the Pope's blessing.

Maeve Cavanagh, Irish Citizen Army, Dublin

While they were being bombarded from Beggars Bush, Father O'Reilly from Westland Row went to hear the confession of the boys who were fighting, and one of them sent the priest up to Cathal [MacDowell], who told him he wanted to go to confession. The priest, finding out he was not a Catholic, said he would try to get one of his own clergymen for him. Cathal said he would rather not have one as he might give them away. He laid down his Howth rifle and the priest baptised him.

Frank Burke, GPO

Each night we said the rosary and indeed at frequent intervals during the day. 'Twas not an unusual sight to see a Volunteer with his rifle grasped firmly in his hands and his rosary beads hanging from his fingers.

Áine Ní Riain, Cumann na mBan, GPO

I don't know where all the religious objects that all the people in the GPO were wearing came from.

Min Ryan, Cumann na mBan, GPO

Desmond FitzGerald was there . . . the first thing he asked was: 'Now listen, girls. Have you been to confession?' He asked every girl who came into the place the same question.

Michael Knightly, GPO

Amongst my companions were Noel Lemass and . . . a bread-van driver who had no previous connection with the Volunteers . . . I asked the latter if he had been to confession. He replied: 'No, I do not think it matters as I believe I would go straight to heaven if killed here.'

Liam Tannam, GPO

The Finn[ish volunteer] was not a Catholic. He had no English but before he left he was saying the rosary in Irish.

John MacDonagh, Jacob's biscuit factory

I remember John MacBride telling me what satisfaction he derived from confession, as he had been away from the sacraments for some years. 'Just kept putting it off,' he explained.

Séamus Kenny, Marrowbone Lane distillery, South Dublin Union

During the week some of the fellows began to cry when they heard shots, because they were a long time from confession, and we sent word to Mount Argus for a priest to come and hear their confessions. Father Ciaran and another priest came down from Mount Argus, and they gave us all Agnus Deis.

Joseph Dolan, South Dublin Union

Each night of the week Ceannt and Brugha called all the men together, gave a short account of what had happened during the day, rosary was recited and prayers said, and all retired for the night . . . After the fight on Thursday it was observed that a picture of the Crucifixion hanging on the wall opposite the windows was left untouched although the wall all round was torn with bullet marks.

Joseph Dolan, South Dublin Union

About three o'clock [on Friday] I had occasion to see Commandant Ceannt and found him in a room at the head of the stairs. I knocked, opened the door and saw him kneeling in the room, his rosary beads in his hand, and the tears running down his cheeks. Without disturbing him I retired.

Many priests were active during the insurrection, ministering to combatants and civilians, liaising between rebels and the authorities, and seeking to minimise the violence and suffering of the week. Most opposed the Rising.

Seán O'Shea, Fianna Éireann, Boland's bakery

Father Union, CC, Ringsend, and [the] parish priest of Star of the Sea, Sandymount . . . upbraided us for our foolhardiness and urged that we go home and stop our madness. William Byrne took them to task and ordered them out of the garrison.

Séamus Kavanagh, Boland's bakery

Some of the men complained to Captain Simon Donnelly that the priest [Father McMahon] was advising them to give up and go home, but on Captain Donnelly speaking to him and threatening to withdraw permission for him to enter the position, he refrained from making any more remarks to the men.

Patrick Kelly, Church Street, Four Courts

After hearing my confession Father Albert addressed me as follows: 'Go forth now, my child, and if necessary die for Ireland as Christ died for mankind.' I felt exalted and could have faced the entire British Army single-handed.

Leslie Price, Cumann na mBan, GPO

I got safely to the door of the [Pro-Cathedral] Presbytery [on Thursday] . . . I kicked and kicked, and pressed all the bells . . . The door was opened a little bit and I was let in by a priest, Father Michael O'Flanagan [John Flanagan]. I said to him, 'I have been sent over by Tom Clarke for the priest.' He said, 'You are not going to the Post Office. Let these people be burned to death. They are murderers.' Mrs Wyse Power was the only one to whom I ever told this. I knew then, by some other remark Father O'Flanagan made, that it was the linking up with the Citizen Army he did not like. It took a certain amount of courage to fight a priest. I said, 'If no priest is going to the Post Office, I am going back alone. I feel sure that every man in the Post Office is prepared to die, to meet his God, but it is a great consolation to a dying man to have a priest near him.' Whatever effect I had on him, he said, 'Very well. I will go.' . . . We passed a man in Moore Street who had been shot and was dying on the road, but he had drink taken. The priest did not stop for him. I was horrified. Further down Moore Street on the left we came to Henry Place, I think. At that place, a white-haired man was shot but not dead. He was lying, bleeding, on the kerb . . . I remember the priest knelt down to give him absolution. You see the difference. Here he knew a man who was respectable . . . We got to the Post Office and I brought Father O'Flanagan to Tom Clarke. I remember Tom Clarke took Mick Staines aside, and he said on no account was he (the priest) to be let out of the Post Office.

Joseph Furlong, Jacob's biscuit factory

When the mob outside were loudest in their abuse of us, an old priest came along, and before them all made the sign of the cross at all parts of the building. This acted like magic on the mob, and they melted away.

Thomas Leahy, GPO

When they were being surrounded a priest came out of the building and started to paint a Red Cross sign on the wall of a chemist's shop our forces were in. We marvelled at him, for the bullets were falling all around the place he was painting the sign.

Father James Doyle, curate, St Mary's Church, Haddington Road

At about 1.30 [p.m. on Wednesday] a message was received at the Presbytery saying that a badly wounded [British Army] officer was at No. 75 Haddington Road . . . and would a priest come down and attend to him before he died. I went immediately and attended to him. He died a few minutes afterwards; he was a convert, having been a Baptist. I went to leave by the front door and when coming out I heard the whiz of bullets. I said, 'Is there any back way out?' and was told I could get out by Percy Lane. I went out by Percy Lane. There were some soldiers of the Staffordshire Regiment with fixed bayonets guarding the Percy Place entrance to the lane. They appeared to be rather astonished when they saw me coming out of the lane and they shouted, 'Halt.' . . . I still went on; then they dropped on their knees and levelled their rifles at me . . . That was the first time I looked down a rifle barrel and I did not like it. I went on towards Baggot Street, by the canal, and at the little bridge at Mount Street Crescent there was another platoon of the Staffords. I said to them, 'Are there any Catholics among you? If there are I am going to give general absolution now.' One of the soldiers spat on the ground and said, 'Naw-a-o, Church of England.' I said, 'How dare you? I will report you to your superior officer.' They all stood to attention. I again told them I was going to give absolution. I then gave the field absolution. I saw one man at the back bless himself. Some of these fellows were killed about ten minutes afterwards when attacking a nearby house.

Eilis Ní Riain, Cumann na mBan, Church Street, Four Courts

Rosary after rosary was recited during the last twenty-four hours as the British military were closing in on the area. The firing was intense on Saturday. The noise of rifle firing was deafening. Soon we learned that the military were closing in on the outskirts of our area and that our dear comrades were vacating their outposts and retreating to their headquarters in the Four Courts. Father Augustine was still on his knees; he consoled the wounded and staff alike and prayed for the success of the men in action.

Pauline Keating, Four Courts

A Franciscan priest came [on Saturday] and said: 'Girls, girls, you don't know what you have done; you have blown up the whole of Dublin.' . . . We thought we were heroines, but when he had finished with us, we thought we were all criminals.

Despite the Proclamation's commitment to universal suffrage and equal rights, de Valera refused to allow women into Boland's bakery, and they were generally confined to traditional roles such as cooking, nursing and carrying despatches. Nonetheless, the contribution made by republican women – often in the face of opposition from their male comrades – was a significant one.

Min Ryan, Cumann na mBan, GPO

We were there at the assembly point at twelve o'clock on Monday. We spent the day there . . . At five o'clock she [Sorcha McMahon] got a notice from Ned Daly to say they did not think our services would be further required.

Leslie Price, Cumann na mBan, GPO

You know the Volunteers, the kind of men they were; they thought that we should be away from all that danger. However, this was where I showed lack of discipline. Bríd Dixon and I decided that we were not going home. Here was something that would never happen in our lives again. We decided to go down to the centre of the city, see what was going on, and get into any building that was available.

Bridget Lyons, Cumann na mBan, Four Courts

I was dying to get in somewhere . . .

Catherine Byrne, Cumann na mBan, GPO

I went over to the footpath opposite the Post Office to speak to Michael Staines. I asked him to let me in but he said no, I was to go home. He added: 'I'll tell Paddy on you' (that was my brother) . . . The Volunteers had broken in the front window of the office, but the side windows had not yet been broken . . . I kicked in the glass of the window. I jumped in and landed on Joe Gahan, who was stooping down inside performing some task. He started swearing at me, asking: 'What the bloody hell are you doing there?' I cut my leg and arm with the glass as I jumped and he drew my attention to the bleeding, which I had not noticed. While we were talking and laughing, an explosion occurred. Joe looked behind him towards the front of the Post Office and the remark he passed to me was: 'Here is your first case.'

Pauline Keating, Cumann na mBan, Four Courts

We busied ourselves mainly with the washing-up and the cooking.

Bridget Lyons, Cumann na mBan, Four Courts

We spent a lot of time making tea and sandwiches . . . Barney Mellows came in and woke us – this is my most vivid recollection – and said that Lieutenant Clancy had taken over a post . . . and two girls were required to go over to him and his men. Somebody said, 'Call that fat girl that came up from the country.' I resented the slight, but my patriotism asserted itself . . . It was a hazardous expedition over broken glass and with bullets flying . . . We cooked joints of meat, tea and fried potatoes for constant relays of men.

Catherine Byrne, Hibernian Bank outpost, GPO

In the early morning Captain Weafer said he wanted one of us to volunteer to go across to the GPO for rations for the men . . . I asked a Volunteer for rations, saying I had been sent for them by Captain Weafer. It was then Desmond FitzGerald spoke, saying: 'I'll give no rations until I know how many men he has.' I said, 'There are a few women there too and am I to go back under fire and give that message to Captain Weafer?' He said: 'Yes, and tell him Desmond FitzGerald sent that message.'

Eilis Ní Riain, Cumann na mBan, Church Street, Four Courts

I remember taking off his [Ned Daly's] boots and socks on Wednesday, bathing his feet and giving him fresh socks with plenty of boric powder.

Bridget Foley, Cumann na mBan, GPO

Captain Weafer sent the two of us and Máire Lawless to open a first-aid station at Skelton's . . . First of all we went into Clery's shop on the instructions of Captain Weafer. We got aprons, sheets and towels, soaps and dishcloths and anything that would be useful to tear up into bandages. We must have been very simple, because in the middle of our activities we started trying on fur coats . . . I remember the next day a civilian was brought in terribly badly wounded on a stretcher . . . Dr Tuohy came in. I can't say whether we sent for him or whether he came with the stretcher. He asked me to hold a bowl of water while he was washing the wounded man. He was an awful sight as he was frightfully badly wounded in the stomach. I stuck it out as long as the doctor was doing his part, but when I took away the bowl of water I got well and truly sick. I think he died soon after.

Mrs Martin Colon, Cumann na mBan, Church Street, Four Courts

One fellow – [Jack] Hurley from Cork – who had come over from London to be in the fight, was brought in dying from a bullet in the head. I had to sit by him till he died.

Ignatius Callender, GPO

Before leaving [Ned] Daly on the Tuesday I told him that I had 110 rounds of .303 at home. He said it would possibly be required and if at all possible to get it to Church Street area. On the following morning my mother came into my bedroom and saw me with the ammunition . . . She put it inside her blouse and taking 2*s*.6*d*. and a milk jug went off on the pretence that she was going to Stoneybatter to get milk, eggs and rashers for breakfast for Lieutenant Anderson and Captain Connolly (of the 'Pals' Royal Dublin Fusiliers) . . . she got the 'stuff' safely delivered at Mrs Murnane's house in Blackhall Place. One of Mrs Murnane's daughters got it safely over the barricades in King Street.

Máire Smart, Cumann na mBan, Dublin

In the course of the week – Wednesday or Thursday – an old friend of my father's called Cox . . . came to the house with a parcel and asked me would I be afraid to go as far as Boland's mill with it. I was terrified but I went and succeeded in getting there. When I reached the bridge at Barrow Street, I saw a woman lying dead on the bridge. A woman ran out of a neighbouring house and told me that the dead woman had been lying there since the day before and warned me not to go any further. But I had to go and reached the gate of the mill in Barrow Street.

Bridget Foley, Cumann na mBan, GPO

We had no difficulty in getting through as we made up all sorts of pitiful stories about sick relatives, etc.

Thomas Young, Marrowbone Lane distillery, South Dublin Union

At about three o'clock on Wednesday morning the expected party [of Volunteers] arrived, headed by my mother. She had been out from midnight, going around the whole neighbourhood and making sure there were no soldiers in any groups or formations in any place. She reported then to Con Colbert that the area was perfectly clear and said she would lead them in to Marrowbone Lane, which she did.

Marie Perolz, Irish Citizen Army, Dublin

. . . [Michael] Mallin came to me and told me what my position was to be in the Citizen Army . . . Any message that was to be delivered would be given to me. Said Mallin with his heavenly smile, 'Is it dangerous enough for you?' I felt very proud. But afterwards I had a bitter feeling of frustration, as I did not take part in the fighting.

Min Ryan, Cumann na mBan, GPO

We went with letters to the wives of three [captured] British officers . . . I always remember the look on the women's faces when they read the messages. We asked: 'Is there any message?' They looked at us as if we were awful women.

Maeve Cavanagh, Irish Citizen Army, Dublin

On Wednesday they told me there was a train to Kilkenny and they asked would I go there with a message to [J. J.] O'Connell. I said I would and they gave me a written message, which I concealed on my person. I understood that it was to the effect that the Kilkenny and Waterford Volunteers should take combined action for a rising . . . I gave him the message. 'They should have awaited till there was conscription,' O'Connell said. 'Look at that, it is all over already,' showing me an English paper. I said, 'Sure an old woman could take Kilkenny today. If you are afraid to give the message, let me see the men and I'll give them the message and take the responsibility.' He replied, 'You shall certainly not see any man under my command.' To my consternation he broke down and cried, and said, 'I deserve that, I'll be called a traitor.' I was very sorry for him, as I saw he was under a terrible strain, but not of indecision . . . someone who was in gaol with O'Connell told me that he – O'Connell – wondered why they kept sending these hysterical women after him. I was amazed because if anyone was hysterical it certainly was not I. I had formed the conviction that day that he was not a revolutionary.

Leslie Price, Cumann na mBan, GPO

I remember about four o'clock on the Thursday evening when Tom Clarke called for me. Being a despatch carrier was a most miserable job. It turned out to be very sad, for my courage . . . I suppose, from the military point of view, he knew the GPO was practically surrounded then. I remember I had seen Connolly brought in when he had gone out under the arches in the front of the Post Office and had been wounded. I remember saying to myself, 'Here's goodbye to you.' Tom Clarke looked at me. He had sort of steely eyes. He said, 'You are to cross O'Connell Street.' I could have cried but, when I looked at his courageous old face, I said, 'All right.' I did not cry.

Min Ryan, Cumann na mBan, GPO

It was late on Wednesday evening when we were coming back [after delivering despatches] . . . we were determined to get back. It would be absolutely idiotic not to; if the men were to die, we would too; that is the way we felt.

Mairead O'Kelly, Cumann na mBan, Church Street, Four Courts

As it came towards the Friday I was getting restless, especially as I did not appear to be doing work of great value. There was plenty of girls and I began to worry about mother . . . I decided to go home on Friday afternoon.

7
Circle of Fire: The Battle for Dublin

Believing that the interception of the *Aud* and Eoin MacNeill's countermanding order had ended any possibility of a rebellion, the British authorities were unprepared for the events of Easter Monday. Despite this humiliation, the military response to the insurrection was prompt and effective. Dublin Castle was quickly secured, as were other strategic locations, and the army moved to cordon off the principal rebel garrisons. The Irish Command awaited the arrival of reinforcements from Britain before moving decisively against the rebels on Wednesday.

*

The army encountered its first and only major setback when two battalions of the 178th Infantry Brigade, marching from Kingstown towards the city centre, was halted at Mount Street Bridge by a small but determined group of outposts. Despite the availability of alternative routes into the city, and a lack of heavy machine-guns, the army launched a frontal assault on the well-fortified rebel positions. The ferocious battle that ensued, which accounted for almost half the British Army's total casualties during the rebellion, was not characteristic of the more methodical fighting that followed.

Joseph O'Connor, Boland's bakery

C Company occupied 25 Northumberland Road, the schoolhouse on Northumberland Road and the parochial hall [St Stephen's] opposite the schoolhouse, [and] Clanwilliam House at the corner of Lower Mount Street immediately in front of the canal bridge with a clear line of fire to Haddington Road. The value of 25 Northumberland Road was that it also overlooked the exit from Beggars

Bush barracks. In addition C Company had men in a builder's yard alongside Clanwilliam House. They were on a pedestal, which enabled them to fire over the wall, which was strongly built.

Thomas Walsh, Clanwilliam House outpost

On arrival at Clanwilliam House . . . we knocked at the front door and were admitted by George Reynolds, who was in charge of this position. The following were also there when we arrived: Paddy Doyle, Dick Murphy, Jimmie Doyle and Willie Ronan. We, with the rest of the garrison, now barricaded the hall door from inside with heavy furniture from an adjoining room. We were now brought upstairs to a room overlooking a considerable amount of Mount Street. We placed a couch and some chairs and cushions in one of the windows of this room. We lifted up the bottom sash of this window and made ourselves as comfortable as possible, with our guns pointing towards Mount Street. We now remembered B Company lectures on street-fighting and the first thing to do (we were told) on entering a house was to break all window glass and to sandbag the windows with whatever we could get in the way of coal, etc. We told Reynolds this and asked him if we could go ahead and strengthen our position. But he said no, we could not do that, as he had promised to hand back the house the way he had got it.

Jimmy Doyle, Clanwilliam House outpost

At about twelve o'clock midnight [on Monday], a lot of damn cats started to fight outside in the garden and this seemed to get on my nerves. I had noticed a candle on the shelf when I first took up the post. I struck a match, found the candle and lighted up. I placed a towel over the window. Shortly afterwards Reynolds came down. He started at the candle and then said, 'Good God, are you afraid to be in the dark?' He blew the candle out and went back up . . . Shortly after he returned again and said, 'It must be lonely down here. We'll barricade this place and you can come upstairs.'

Jimmy Grace, 25 Northumberland Road outpost

About twelve o'clock on Tuesday night the Lieutenant [Michael Malone] called me aside and told me we could not hope to win owing to the confusion caused by the GHQ countermanding order, and also the overwhelming odds against us, and the failure of the expected German aid to arrive. He asked me did I agree that Paddy Rowe and Michael Byrne, who were mere boys (both were under 16), should be sent away, that in his opinion they would only be killed if kept on in the house . . . Micheál said gently but firmly, 'It's orders, boys, you must go.' So at about 2.30 a.m., they crept out through the skylight and over the roofs, gloomy enough, because they had been told that under no circumstances were they to come back to No. 25.

Thomas Walsh, Clanwilliam House outpost

The stillness of Mount Street was weird. Not a soul passed, but in the distance there was considerable rifle fire. Dawn came and was followed by a lovely sunny morning.

William Christian, St Stephen's Hall outpost

About [1]2 p.m. on Wednesday, my father came to see me. He confirmed what we had already heard – that there were thousands of troops landing at Kingstown (now Dún Laoghaire) and they were on their way to the city. He also had the disheartening news that the Volunteers were being shot down everywhere and he felt our chances were poor. With a father's natural anxiety for the safety of his son, he begged me to come home with him, but having taken up my post nothing but death would make me desert it. While this grieved him, I think he also admired my spirit and, wishing me God's blessing and promising to pray for me, we parted.

Jimmy Grace, 25 Northumberland Road outpost

Next day, Wednesday, about noon, two girls, my sister and a Miss May Cullen . . . arrived after an adventurous journey with food and a despatch. We could not admit them but took the despatch through the letter box. It said that English troops had landed at Kingstown and that 500 of them were advancing on the city from Williamstown. 'This is it, Michael,' I said . . . Micheál went into the bathroom, the windows of which were on the side of the house looking towards Ballsbridge. He said, 'Look, Seumas.' One glance was sufficient. We would have to make our stand where we stood, for the khaki-clad figures were approaching. Micheál opened fire from the bathroom window, which was on the third floor . . . I followed suit from another window on the second floor.

Thomas Walsh, Clanwilliam House outpost

I fired for the first time from my Howth gun, and for that matter from any other rifle. I do not know what happened to me, or how long I was unconscious. In the excitement I did not heed the lectures and did not hold the weapon correctly. The result was, the butt hit me under the chin and knocked me out . . . for the remainder of the scrap I remembered it was a Howth gun I had to deal with.

William Christian, St Stephen's Hall outpost

The sound of machine-guns reached us from a distance and then gradually grew louder and louder until we ourselves were in the thick of it . . . As the British troops drew nearer, the bullets fell on the roof of the school opposite like a shower of hail. Excitement gripped us and we braced ourselves for the encounter. Because of our position we had to wait until the British troops actually passed us before we could fire on them; and then they came – hundreds and hundreds of them – stretching right across the road – and so intent were they in gaining their objective – the capture of Clanwilliam House – they completely overlooked our post. We opened fire and men fell like ninnypins. Those who got past us had scarcely reached the bridge before they had to face a battery of fire from Clanwilliam House. We emptied our guns on those who thought to turn back . . .

Jimmy Doyle, Clanwilliam House outpost

Reynolds shouted, 'Open fire.' With our first volley they scattered for cover and some fell. We could see the flashes of Malone's and Grace's rifles coming from the windows [of 25 Northumberland Road], and Reynolds said, 'Good old Mick.'

Thomas Walsh, Clanwilliam House outpost

I fired again and again until the rifle heated so much it was impossible to hold it.

Áine O'Rahilly, Cumann na mBan, Dublin

From our house in Northumberland Road we saw everything that happened . . . the garrison in 25 held their fire until they were level with the house. Fire was opened on them and they fell like flies. The soldiers were bewildered and began to fire at the houses on our side of the road, not knowing where the firing was coming from.

Thomas Walsh, Clanwilliam House outpost

From here we could see terrible confusion among the enemy. They were being attacked from 25 Northumberland Road, held by Mick Malone and Jimmy Grace. Those who managed to get by 25 ran towards the bridge and took cover anywhere they could find it, on house steps, behind trees, and even in the channels of the roadway. We kept on blazing in the channels, and after a time, as they were killed, the next fellow moved up and passed the man killed in front of him. This gave one the impression of a giant human khaki-coloured caterpillar. Those that managed to get under cover of the bridge, both from Northumberland Road and Percy Place, now attempted to cross the bridge, led by an officer. They charged in small groups of about eight to twelve, but they did not succeed. They went down on the bridge again, and again they made the attempt, but did not survive. By now there was a great pile of dead and dying on the bridge.

William Christian, St Stephen's Hall outpost

. . . pictures of those thrilling moments of life and death flash through my mind. The frustrated expression on John McGrath's face at one stage when his shotgun jammed and left him temporarily out of action . . . Joe Clarke hunched behind one of the windows, tugging at his Martini rifle and murmuring, 'O my God, oh my God.' . . . his ammunition was a dud. Pat Doyle, who was in charge, had a Mauser rifle with about 100 rounds of ammunition. His was the only reliable gun in the house and I do not doubt but that he made that gun do the work of six.

Captain E. Gerrard, British Army officer, Beggars Bush barracks

. . . Major Harriss organised a continuous barrage of rifle fire against the windows of the houses in Northumberland Road. About three rifles were laid on each window and at a signal by whistle at least ten rounds from each rifle were directed at each window. Our men were in the windows of Beggars Bush barracks. They had sandbags. I often thought there must have been a terrible lot of people killed, but what could they do! They were being sniped at at the time.

Jimmy Grace, 25 Northumberland Road outpost

The Tommies were bewildered not being able to locate the source of the volleys, and their casualties grew. Soon, however, they had possession of almost every house within point-blank range. With the help of hand grenades they came even nearer, and I was forced from window to window seeking a spot to return their fire.

Séamus Kavanagh, Roberts' builders' yard outpost

Nobody succeeded in crossing the bridge, although some went down Percy Place and others turned right along the canal bank. Some of those who went down Percy Place succeeded in getting into some of the houses and some were shot. Those who turned to the right came under fire from Roberts' yard and they were wiped out before they were able to take cover.

Jimmy Doyle, Clanwilliam House outpost

It was easy to see the officers with revolvers leading them on. When they came to the Parochial Hall the garrison there opened up on them also. A small number reached the bridge and Reynolds shouted, 'Pick up your revolvers and let them have it.'

Áine O'Rahilly, Cumann na mBan, Dublin

In the middle of the fighting when the bullets were flying and the road was strewn with the dead or dying, Father Wall of Haddington Road came along on his bicycle. He was visibly frightened, but he left his bicycle against a railing and went from one body to another administering the Last Sacraments.

Thomas Walsh, Clanwilliam House outpost

There was some commotion in Lower Mount Street and quite a crowd of onlookers rushed on to the bridge, led by a clergyman, and cleared it of both dead and dying . . . when the last civilian was out of sight the firing started again, and the bridge was rushed before but with the same result. Again the bridge was filled with dead and dying, and again cleared by the civilians, who now had white sheets to carry the wounded on.

Jimmy Doyle, Clanwilliam House outpost

While the removal of the dead and wounded was in progress I heard another blast of a whistle and the enemy made another charge from Haddington Road cross. Reynolds shouted, 'Stop, the nurses,' but the charge came on and Reynolds shouted, 'Fire, but for God's sake be careful of the nurses.'

Joseph O'Connor, Boland's bakery garrison outpost

The enemy had succeeded in clearing the schools and the Parochial Hall but they were met with point-blank fire from Clanwilliam House, from Roberts' yard, from the railway line at Alexandra Basin and from the [water] tanks on top of the workshops.

Séamus Kavanagh, Roberts' builders' yard outpost

Later on a still more determined onslaught than the previous one was made to gain the bridge. This time the enemy succeeded in crossing the bridge and having done so they did not seem to know what their objective was or where they were going. Some turned left towards Warrington Place and others turned right running down towards Clanwilliam Place. Those who came in our direction were completely wiped out.

Jimmy Grace, 25 Northumberland Road outpost

Do not believe any person who tells you he does not know what fear is, because there were moments from about 5.30 onwards when the fire was so intense that I could not reply, that I trembled from hand to foot in a panic of fear . . .

Thomas Walsh, Clanwilliam House outpost

During the . . . fight Paddy Doyle would say, 'Boys, isn't this a great day for Ireland,' and little sentences like this. He was very proud to live to see such a day. After some time Paddy was not saying anything. Jim spoke to him and got no reply. He pulled him by the coat and he fell over into his arms. He was shot through the head. We told Dick Murphy about him and we three said a prayer for his soul . . . Dick Murphy was now very silent, and I turned to him and touched him but he was gone to meet his maker.

Jimmy Doyle, Clanwilliam House outpost

Most of the houses in Percy Place were now occupied by the enemy and they had started to fire on us from the windows . . . Fire was now directed on us from all directions. The wall of the room facing the windows was cut to pieces and the plaster on the ceiling was falling. We could now hear explosions on the ground floor . . . I think I was knocked unconscious. The next thing I recall was that poor Reynolds was bending over me; he was wiping blood from my nose and face. He said, 'You are all right, Jimmy, but the rifle is finished.' I noticed it on the floor with the stock split.

Thomas Walsh, Clanwilliam House outpost

Our Mauser ammunition was now exhausted. I had about twelve rounds of .45 revolver ammunition, and Jim had about ten rounds for his .32 revolver. The house was smouldering in several places, the smoke and fumes were shocking. It was now about one hour before dark. We realised we could stay no longer, and prepared to leave. While doing so, poor Reynolds stood up on the drawing-room landing to fire the last shot. Whether he got his man or not we did not know, but he fell dead in our midst.

Jimmy Doyle, Clanwilliam House outpost

I heard a terrible explosion and almost the whole ceiling in the room fell down and I could see very little with dust and smoke. I heard Ronan calling again from the other room. I went to him. He said, 'I think the roof is on fire, Jim.' We had to rely on our revolvers now, as all the rifle ammunition was used. Somebody called from downstairs. I think it was Tom Walsh. We went down the stairs, keeping close to the wall for cover, and, on going into the drawing room, I saw Paddy Doyle and Dick Murphy lying dead. Murphy was still holding his rifle. Poor Reynolds was on the floor, in a pool of blood . . . I could never recall what happened after this, nor do I know how I got out of the house . . . I recall that I was stretched out on the ground close to a wall, and that my nose was still bleeding. The whole area was lighted up, I suppose by the flames from Clanwilliam House. My rifle was underneath me.

Thomas Walsh, Clanwilliam House outpost

We went to the basement and there was a door leading into a yard. This we had barricaded with kitchen furniture. In the door was a small window about a foot square. We burst out the glass, and I lifted Jimmy Doyle out first, then Jim and Ronan, and I next crawled out myself.

Joseph O'Connor, Boland's bakery

We lost, all told, six men killed and many wounded . . .

Padraig O'Connor, Volunteers, Dublin

The place was literally swimming with blood.

Thomas Walsh, Clanwilliam House outpost

They suffered shocking losses. Their official figure for killed and wounded was something over 200, but I am sure there was much more than this lying along the Northumberland Road, on the house steps, in the channels, along the canal banks, etc., and in Warrington Place, and there were several high-rank officers among them. The casualties were so great that I, at one time, thought we had accounted for the whole British Army in Ireland. What a thought! What a day! But a lot of their losses were their own fault. They made sitting ducks for amateur riflemen. But they were brave men and, I must say, clean fighters.

The rebels were handicapped by the inadequacy of their arms and ammunition, and were often forced to rely on shotguns and home-made bombs. But the British Army also faced difficulties, given the inexperience of many of its soldiers and the unfamiliar challenges of street-fighting.

Joseph Kinsella, pre-split Inchicore Company

On Easter Monday I remember coming up Harold's Cross and seeing a platoon of London or Liverpool Irish from Larkfield going towards the city. What struck me most about those men was the way that they were armed: most of them were carrying twelve-foot pikes, and that, to my mind, was very ridiculous.

Joseph O'Connor, Boland's bakery

In the whole garrison of, we'll say, one hundred men, to the best of my belief there were not more than fifty rifles. A number of the rifles were Martini-Henry, Mark 6 and Mark 7. They, with the ordinary Lee-Enfield, used .303 ammunition, but in the case of the Mark 6 and Mark 7 Martini they fired a different .303 type of cartridge. This caused us great confusion, and we frequently had to stop to change the ammunition supplied to the men even in the hottest of corners. In addition we had the Howth rifles, which fire an altogether different ammunition, and then we had the shotguns, the cartridges of which had been loaded with heavier shot. Just prior to the outbreak a quantity of shotguns of an inferior quality was distributed among the companies. With this extra-loaded shotgun ammunition used in these inferior shotguns they were positively dangerous. During the course of the fight someone contrived a means of inserting a couple of these inferior shotguns into a metal rain-pipe and firing the triggers by the means of a string. This was, I would say, not very deadly, but the roar and the splatter of the shot was very demoralising on enemy approaches.

Nicholas Laffan, Four Courts

Sixty-nine members of my company [G Company, 1st Battalion] of about 200 paraded. There were about fifteen in uniform. We had forty service and other rifles firing .303 ammunition, twenty Howth rifles, seven rifles of other calibres, and two shotguns . . . and about thirty revolvers and automatic pistols.

John Shouldice, Church Street, Four Courts

The total garrison of my post in Reilly's and at the crossing was about twenty men, about ten in uniform . . . We had about ten or twelve service and carbine rifles suitable for .303 ammunition, about six Howth rifles for which the supply of ammunition was limited; and about six bayonets. There were about three or four revolvers. We had no explosives or grenades.

Frank Burke, GPO

We were able after some time to distinguish the different sounds of the guns. The Howth rifles sounded like small cannon compared with the modern rifle. It was easy to recognise the report of the shotguns and the rat-a-tat-tat of the machine-guns.

John Kenny, GPO

The Howth gun . . . was a very accurate and deadly weapon, although it was very heavy, it had a kick like a mule and only fired one bullet before having to be reloaded.

Robert Holland, Marrowbone Lane distillery, South Dublin Union

. . . it was a bad weapon for street-fighting. Flame about three feet long came out through the top of the barrel when it was fired, and a shower of soot and smoke came back in one's face. After three shots were fired from it, it would have to be thrown away to let it cool and the concussion of it was so severe it drove me back along the floor several feet.

Seán Kennedy, Four Courts

. . . the Howth rifle, not being furnished with wooden casing, would be very hot after use and in grabbing it with my hands I got severely burned from the red-hot barrel.

Joseph O'Connor, Boland's bakery

. . . whilst I was talking to one of the men, the rifle which he had been using stuck to his hand and we had to pull his hand from the rifle, leaving the skin thereon.

Oscar Traynor, GPO

So continuous was their fire at this time that the barrels of the rifles became overheated. It was then that Captain Poole, who had served in the British Army and in the South African campaign, proposed that, in the absence of any suitable oil for cooling the rifles, we should open some sardine tins and use this oil. This was done, with the result that the men were able to continue in action.

Captain E. Gerrard, British Army officer, Beggars Bush barracks

At about four o'clock on Wednesday afternoon some of the Sherwood Foresters arrived in Beggars Bush barracks – twenty-five – as far as I remember, untrained, undersized products of the English slums . . . The young Sherwoods that I had with me had never fired a service rifle before. They were not even able to load them. We had to show them how to load them.

The Easter Rising is widely viewed as a chivalrous affair, particularly compared to the guerrilla war that followed, and the rebels depicted themselves as a conventional military force engaged in a clean fight. The following accounts outline acts of gallantry, as well as more questionable behaviour, by both sides. Some British soldiers deliberately killed innocent civilians, notably at Portobello barracks and North King Street. However, by turning the centre of Dublin into a war zone and (in many cases) fighting without uniforms, the rebels bear much of the responsibility for the civilian casualties that occurred.

William Christian, Boland's bakery

As I was having my tea in the house that evening my attention was drawn to a young man in khaki uniform who was entering a house on the opposite side of the road. While waiting to be admitted, he stood facing us with his arms well away from his body, indicating that he was not armed. This put Pat Doyle into a bit of a fix, as he had him covered from the time he came into view, and of course, he could not fire on an unarmed man.

Eamon Bulfin, GPO

There was a tram upturned at Earl Street and in the middle of all this shooting, scurrying and general tumult, we heard a voice shouting: 'I'm a bloody Dublin Fusilier. I don't give a damn about anyone.' He staggered out to the middle of O'Connell Street, where he was riddled with machine-gun fire. One of our men, with a white flag, went over to where he lay, knelt down, said a prayer over his body and dragged him in to the side.

Seán Nunan, GPO

On the far side of Moore Street, a British soldier was lying, badly wounded in the stomach and calling for help. Despite the fact that the street was swept by machine-gun fire from the Parnell Street end, George Plunkett took a water-bottle from the man alongside me, crossed Moore Street, gave the soldier a drink and then carried him back to our headquarters.

Jim O'Shea, Irish Citizen Army, Stephen's Green

At about 8.30 [p.m. on Monday] an incident occurred which nearly caused a lot of trouble. A British soldier in khaki came along the path and stopped inside the railings at our gun pit. He pretended to be drunk . . . He called me a b[astard] and a lot of other names. He was using very filthy language. At that moment Miss Gifford and an old lady were at the trench with milk and bread. I asked him to stop cursing. He passed a remark about prostitutes fighting with us. I told him I would give him a chance if he went away. He became worse, so I picked up a shotgun and shot him at close quarters.

Dick Balfe, Mendicity Institution

I had lost complete use of my arms and legs but was fully conscious . . . I was left behind when the company surrendered, as I was thought to be dead. I am not familiar with what subsequently happened outside the Institution [on Wednesday]. Sometime late in the evening I heard the British breaking in and then after an interval a British officer appeared armed with two automatics; also a Dublin Fusilier arrived with fixed bayonet. I was at this time able to sit up but had no use of my legs. While they were deciding whether to use a bayonet or a bullet on me, an officer of the RAMC [Royal Army Medical Corps] came in and claimed me as his prisoner, saying that there had been enough of this dirty work.

Jimmy Grace, 25 Northumberland Road outpost

On Saturday morning about 8.30 I was lying under cover in a shed at the rear of 60 Haddington Road. A servant girl came out into the garden and I opened the door of the shed a little way and I asked her for a little bread and a drink of water . . . The servant girl did not betray me. I learned afterwards that [the] Davises, who occupied No. 60 Haddington Road, sent for the English . . . I left the pistol on the ground and stood up and had just taken a few mouthfuls of water when the glass of the window of the woodshed was smashed open and three or four rifles levelled in my direction. At the same time the door was pulled open and I was covered by the English troops with rifles. I did not get even time to stoop to pick up the pistol. They shouted, 'Hands up.' I was then ordered out of the shed and a soldier sprang forward and drove his bayonet against my chest, but an English officer in plain clothes dashed the rifle on one side and said, 'We want this man a prisoner as we want to keep him for questioning.'

Albert Mitchell, Red Cross ambulance driver

Shortly after 9 a.m. a British staff officer came out and ordered me to start the engine, as he wished to be taken to Portobello barracks. I told him I had no instructions to carry any but wounded or hospital cases, and he replied that he was giving me my instructions. To argue seemed useless . . . I thought it better to comply.

Laurence Nugent, K Company, 3rd Battalion

These ambulances did military work under cover of the Red Cross, and the military in Upper Baggot Street used Baggot Street Hospital as their headquarters and used the tower of the church in Haddington Road for sniping.

Jerry Golden, North Circular Road Bridge outpost, Four Courts

I looked towards the [Phoenix] Park and saw an ambulance, called the Canadian Women's Motor Ambulance, which at that time was to be seen around Dublin, turning . . . I noticed soldiers, three or four of them, sitting on the floor of the ambulance, and the next instant a machine-gun in it had started to fire and sprayed the barricade with a shower of bullets. Fortunately, none of us were hit, but not so the soldiers in the ambulance . . . before the ambulance reached Upper Grangegorman we saw the soldier who was working the gun slump over it and it ceased to fire.

Albert Mitchell, Red Cross ambulance driver

While driving through Moore Street to Jervis Street Hospital one afternoon towards the end of the week the sergeant drew my attention to the body of a man lying in the gutter in Moore Lane. He was dressed in a green uniform, and I took the sergeant and two men with a stretcher and approached the body, which appeared to be still alive. We were about to lift it up when a young English officer stepped out of a doorway and refused to allow us to touch it . . . When back in the lorry I asked the sergeant what was the idea? His answer was – 'He must be someone of importance and the bastards are leaving him there to die of his wounds – it is the easiest way to get rid of him.'

Nicholas Laffan, Church Street, Four Courts

During the day we captured a G-man who was going round our posts dressed in woman's clothes, spying out our position and getting information as to the strength and actual positions of our forces.

Robert Holland, Marrowbone Lane distillery, South Dublin Union

I noticed a woman that I had seen the day before leaning out of a window just opposite me. She had a hat, blouse and apron on her and I got suspicious. I told Mick O'Callaghan that I was going to have a shot at her. He said, 'No.' I said it was a queer place for a woman to be and that it was queer she should have a hat on her, as she must have seen the bullets flying around but took no notice of them. I made up my mind. She was only about thirty-five or forty yards away from me and I fired at her. She sagged halfway out of the window. The hat and small little shawl fell off her and I saw [that] what I took to be a woman was a man in his shirtsleeves.

Constable Patrick Bermingham, Dublin Metropolitan Police

One rather amusing incident I remember towards the end of Easter Week is seeing a British soldier who was on duty as sentry at Patrick's Close near Kevin Street barracks, and who was very much intoxicated, firing indiscriminately in the air and at windows and doors. Then he would lay down his rifle and light his cigarette and then carry on firing as before . . . we arrested him and brought him to the police barracks.

Áine O'Rahilly, Cumann na mBan, Dublin

A little girl called [Margaret] Veale aged about 12 or 13 [13] years to whom I used to teach Irish, was killed during Easter Week by a soldier, who aimed at her as she stood at her window in [103] Haddington Road, looking out through binoculars.

Captain E. Gerrard, British Army officer, Beggars Bush barracks

One of my sentries in Beggars Bush barracks, about Tuesday evening, said to me, 'I beg your pardon, sir, I have just shot two girls.' I said, 'What on earth did you do that for?' He said, 'I thought they were rebels. I was told they were dressed in all classes of attire.' At a range of about 200 yards I saw two girls – about 20 [years old] – lying dead.

George Chester Duggan, civil servant

My father, George Duggan, was manager of the Provincial Bank of Ireland's head office at 5 College Street . . . On Wednesday afternoon, there was a ring at the bank house door in College Street. My father opened it, and a very young subaltern, a sergeant (the worse for drink) and a number of British soldiers entered and began to search the house, insisting that sniping was going on from the building. My father denied that any such thing was happening. When they reached the top floor and noticed the skylight open, their suspicions, despite my father's explanation, seemed to be confirmed. The sergeant became truculent, threatened that he would shoot my father out of hand as being in league with the rebels, and ordered him down to the basement . . . where he proposed that the shooting would take place. On the way down, my father appealed to the subaltern to exercise his authority and not allow an innocent person to be shot. The subaltern at last began to realise that he and not the sergeant was in charge of the party. When they reached the second floor, my father took him into the drawing room and showed him the photographs of my two brothers in uniform, one a captain in the Royal Irish Fusiliers, the other a lieutenant in the Royal Irish Regiment, who were killed in August 1915, at Suvla Bay in Gallipoli, fighting with the 10th (Irish) Division. This convinced the subaltern of the truth of my father's assertions and he ordered the party to leave the bank.

Seán O'Duffy, Church Street outpost, Four Courts

. . . I saw a man named Peadar Lawless crossing [North] King Street from a house on one side of the street to a house on the other side of it. I had a short conversation with him. I asked him, 'Are you not in it?' He said, 'No.' Later on his body and those of others were found in a cellar.

Father James Doyle, St Mary's Church, Haddington Road

Just as I got to the gate of the Nurses' Home there was a bang, what must have been a bullet hit the wall beside me about waist high. At first I thought it was a nervous sentry. I heard the scurrying of feet down Baggot Lane the minute the shot went off . . . Next day Father Felix Waters, SM, Leeson Street, came to sympathise with us on the death of Father McKee . . . Afterwards Father Wall told me just as he closed the door he thought he heard a shot. When Father Waters was near the gate of the Nurses' Home he felt a pain. He put his hand to his side and saw blood on his hand. He walked to the City of Dublin Hospital, where they detained him. He died the following day as a result of the wound. There was no inquest.

James Kavanagh, GPO

On one of my journeys when returning to the Post Office I was halfway across the Metal [Ha'penny] Bridge when I saw two people, a man and woman, fall, shot dead at the corner of Liffey Street and Bachelor's Walk. I don't know where the shots came from.

Seán Cody, Church Street, Four Courts

I had the misfortune to become detached from my comrades and remember meeting a lady in a side street who invited me to come up to her room, which was in the top flat, where she said I could get a good view of the British occupying the Broadstone. I followed the lady, and, seeing British soldiers in the railway sheds and behind piles of sleepers, I opened fire and used up all my ammunition. There was no replying fire until I was back on the street below again, when the whole house was peppered with rifle fire.

Peter Clifford, GPO

I was stopped by Irish Volunteers, and while I was speaking to them a boy was shot alongside us. He was shot accidentally by a young fellow in the Irish Volunteers.

Due to shortages of food and other essentials, conditions in the inner-city areas within the military cordon grew desperate. Many civilians were killed as they attempted to find food or flee the fighting. Despite the efforts of firemen, ambulance drivers and civilian volunteers, decomposing corpses lay scattered throughout the city by the end of the week.

Father James Doyle, St Mary's Church, Haddington Road

The moment the trouble started all differences in social standing disappeared. I saw one man, a K[ing's] C[ounsel], walking along the road with a salmon or a cod in his hand. I saw another rather prominent man wheeling a perambulator full of groceries; all the artificialities of life suddenly disappeared, only to return of course.

Patrick Kelly, Church Street outpost, Four Courts

The staff of Monk's bakery in our area worked continuously baking bread, and we formed queues of people from the neighbourhood and rationed the bread . . . One of the men who had worked all the week in Monk's bakery opened the shop door to see if it was safe to leave for home. He was shot dead.

Mairead O'Kelly, Cumann na mBan, Church Street, Four Courts

We saw various civilians being killed. They would not stay indoors. We had instructions from the Volunteers to see that all civilians got food. This we gave them – mostly uncooked.

Joseph Byrne, Boland's bakery

. . . a poor woman (a Mrs Naylor from Ringsend) carrying some bread, ventured across the bridge to be shot through the head by an enemy sniper from the direction of Sir Patrick Dun's Hospital in Grand Canal Street.

Anonymous nun, Mater Misericordiae Hospital

During Easter Week Mr Alexander Blayney (surgeon) was on duty in the hospital. He never left it that whole week. He was operating day and night. There was neither gas nor electricity and he had to operate by the light of candles brought from the sacristy. There was no sterilisation of instruments or dressings as there was no boiling water at hand . . . Tuesday was the first day that any wounded were brought. Nine of these were detained, and the rest were treated and discharged. One of the badly wounded, Margaret Nolan, who was a forewoman in Jacob's factory, died that day, as did also James Kelly – a schoolboy who was shot through the skull. Another schoolboy, John Healy, aged 14, a member of the Fianna whose brain was hanging all over his forehead when he was brought in, died after two days. Another man, Patrick Harris, died also on Tuesday of laceration of the brain . . . On Wednesday the numbers of wounded increased, twenty-one being detained. Two of them were already dead when brought in and six died in the course of the day. Twenty-one wounded were detained for treatment on Thursday. Seven of them died within a week and another on the 14th

May. Eight of the nine wounded brought in on the Friday and who were detained for treatment died in the hospital. Only eight were detained on the Saturday. One of these was already dead and another insane.

Annie Mannion, assistant matron, South Dublin Union

On Tuesday we were in a state of panic. We did not really know what we were doing. Our stores were at the front of the houses, and our ambition was to get food up to the mental cases at the far end of the house. There was a great deal of dodging about to get to and from the stores . . . Patients who died during that week were buried in a temporary grave in the grounds . . . The military demanded food from the storekeeper and he supplied it to them as well as to the Volunteers.

Mairead O'Kelly, Cumann na mBan, Four Courts

It was a deserted city as I sneaked along from door to door, sitting down sometimes in tenement hallways. I saw several dead bodies lying in the streets in the broiling sun. Two of them had sacks over them.

Thomas Peppard, Mendicity Institution outpost

While we were in Arbour Hill we could see soldiers digging graves in a corner of the yard and also a lorry arriving with a man's leg sticking up over the side, apparently dead.

Albert Mitchell, Red Cross ambulance driver

My instructions were to visit all hospitals and morgues, collect all dead, search them to try to identify them, and then take them to Deans Grange Cemetery for burial. For this I was given the assistance of a sergeant and four orderlies . . . I reckoned we buried over 200 bodies of civilians and Irish soldiers, also some English soldiers in Deans Grange . . . I left my job of burying the dead on 6 May.

Large numbers of prisoners – mostly policemen and soldiers captured during the occupation of the garrisons – were held by the rebels during Easter Week. Despite subsequent press claims to the contrary, they appear to have been generally well treated. Some appeared surprisingly sympathetic towards the rebels, given the circumstances.

Min Ryan, Cumann na mBan, GPO

[Michael] O'Rahilly was in charge of the prisoners . . . He said to his men: 'Now, these prisoners are in our charge and we are in honour bound to see that they are treated as prisoners of war. If it's the last bit of food in the place, it must be shared with the prisoners, and if any man does not follow my instructions he will get this' – and he pulled out a gun.

Catherine Byrne, Cumann na mBan, GPO

My sister was upstairs still and somebody sent up for a drink for the DMP man who was on duty when the Volunteers had entered the building and taken him prisoner. One Corkman – Tom Walsh – had taken off the policeman's helmet and filled it with .303 bullets, saying he would like to put one of them through his head.

Liam Tannam, GPO

In the Post Office at several times I saw an Indian Army officer, an Irishman I believe, assisting Dr James Ryan. He had his tunic off. I also saw a Dublin Fusilier and a Connaught Ranger assisting in washing and peeling potatoes. The Dublin Fusilier volunteered to go into action with us but this was the job allotted to him.

Michael Staines, GPO

The Connaught Rangers asked me to give them back their rifles, as they wanted to fight . . . They said they were willing to do anything for us, stressed the fact they were Connaught Rangers and would rather fight. I put them to work in the kitchen.

Áine Ní Riain, Cumann na mBan, GPO

I remember the British Tommy – a Dublin man – who was cooking all the time and joking with the girls. He was in great humour and he had rosary beads round his neck.

Michael Knightly, GPO

The soldiers were preparing tea and were as cheerful as if nothing out of the ordinary had taken place. I asked one of them if he thought the place would be stormed. 'No,' he said, 'I think it will be shelled.'

Seosamh de Brún, Jacob's biscuit factory

. . . every day a diminutive soldier of the Fianna Éireann both in stature and years – the youngest recruit I believe of the heroic boys who fought with us – armed with double-barrelled shotgun slung over his shoulder, escorted two stalwart six-foot-odd policemen prisoners to the helpful task of peeling potatoes for the troops. This daily parade as it passed brought smiles to the faces of many, if not to the prisoners.

Nicholas Laffan, Church Street, Four Courts

About 8 p.m. [on Thursday] Commandant Daly brought up about thirty DMP men and let them go free through the Richmond Asylum grounds. They were very grateful. I remember his last words to them were 'Forget all you have seen', and this met with a chorus of 'Yes, sir, we will.' Apparently, they thought at first he was going to shoot them and were surprised to get away so easily.

By the end of the week the rebels were under enormous physical and mental stress due to hunger, sleep deprivation and the effects of shelling. Combatants on both sides succumbed to paranoia, resulting in several fatal shootings. Although the untested rebel leaders appeared to have coped well with the pressures of combat, Éamon de Valera was one of several whose behaviour was questioned by subordinates.

Mrs Martin Conlon, Cumann na mBan, GPO

The heavy gun from the *Helga* had begun on Wednesday morning and made us frightened and heartsick.

Oscar Traynor, GPO

As far as I can remember, the shells started late on Wednesday. They were shrapnel shells, and the amazing thing was that instead of bullets coming in it was molten lead, actually molten, which streamed about on the ground when it fell. I was told that the shrapnel was filled with molten wax, the bullets were embedded in wax, and the velocity of the shell through the barrel and through the air caused the mould to melt. As the first of these shells hit the house, the Volunteers rushed and told me about them. I rushed up and found an old fellow crawling about on his hands and knees gathering the stuff up as it hardened. I asked him what he was doing and what he intended to do with the stuff. He said, 'Souvenirs.'

Cornelius O'Donovan, Four Courts

I think it was on Thursday we were shelled. One man was with me at the loophole, on the lower of the two floors we occupied, while two others were similarly posted on the floor above. The big gun appeared on the south side of the Liffey, in that inset on the quay, close to SS Michael and John's Church. We kept peppering away at the gunners whenever one of them showed himself, but, as we did not get much chance of taking deliberate aim, I cannot say that we hurt any of them. Perhaps we did. Then came a shattering explosion, and the room trembled. Their first shell hit rather low, between the two windows of the room I was in. We had not enough sense, or military training, to then retreat, but kept on having a shot at the gunners. Soon, the second shell entered our room, through the window at which we were not . . . For more than a minute after the shell burst in the room, I think we did not realise whether we were dead or alive. I remember distinctly, while the room was full of dust, smoke and falling ceiling, hearing the voice of a comrade from the floor above, calling my name and asking were we dead or alive down there. The humour of that question aroused me, and I then realised that my comrade and myself were uninjured . . . We made our way to the ground floor, where we found our comrades praying for us, as dead.

Liam Tannam, GPO

[Mick] Boland and I had just emerged on to the [GPO] roof when a shell burst beside us. The spot seemed to be suddenly deprived of air and we were left gasping. I saw two spots of blood on Boland's face and ran to catch him as I believed he might be dangerously wounded but he pushed me off, wiped the blood off his face with the back of his hand and said, 'Don't mind that, it's only b[loody] shrapnel.' Boland had been in the South African War.

Molly Reynolds, Cumann na mBan, GPO

. . . that Thursday night is beyond description. It was the night the *Helga* shelled us from the Liffey.

Bridget Foley, Cumann na mBan, GPO

I don't know what the others felt but I was terrified.

Thomas Doyle, South Dublin Union

I never slept one single hour of that whole week. Once the first two days passed I never thought of sleep, just lived without sleep and never thought of it.

Patrick Egan, Roe's distillery, South Dublin Union

The dawn was breaking when I visited Seán Nugent's post. He had made a comfortable bed with the sacks behind his barricade. Seán was lying down with his shotgun and improvised bayonet (a blade of a garden shears) nursing in his arms. He was fast asleep, and the hammer of his gun was cocked. I remember standing over him, afraid to disturb him, fearing the gun might go off and blow his head off. I gently grabbed the hammer with one hand and woke him up.

Séamus Robinson, GPO

I had nothing to eat since Tuesday and had no sleep since Monday. It was now fairly late on Thursday evening . . . When I found myself for the first time among a crowd without any personal responsibility a sleep reaction set in. I felt overpowered from want of it. I had almost to implore a Volunteer officer who seemed to be in charge of the beds on the ground floor. He pointed to a bed under a counter. I crept into it . . . I had only five hours' sleep followed by five hours' lone sentry duty . . . I had to keep knocking my knuckles against a granite stone windowsill to keep awake . . . my head was swimming.

James Crenegan, Mendicity Institution outpost

There was no relief – you just slept at your post when you got a chance, and food was usually brought to us at the windows.

Peadar O'Mara, Boland's bakery

[By Thursday] Volunteers were beginning to feel the strain of constant firing and loss of sleep and were observed dozing in their positions.

Frank Robbins, Irish Citizen Army, Stephen's Green

I fell fast asleep, lying face down with my rifle pointing to the Shelbourne Hotel. I had only two hours' sleep out of a period of sixty hours' duty, and that was on the roof of the College of Surgeons on Monday night.

Nicholas Laffan, Church Street outpost, Four Courts

On Friday the British military kept up a constant attack on our position from an armoured car in which they rushed up reinforcements, keeping our barricades at Red Cow Lane and Church Street continuously under fire. Our men were beginning to feel the effects of the week's strain . . . This was the worst night we had. With the glare of the fires it was hard to detect their movements, as they could attack, retire and then come in stronger numbers. I remember standing in a corner of Moore's factory on Friday night and the rifle and machine-gun fire from the enemy was so intense that to cross the room was certain death. The windows were so low and afforded so little protection from crossfire that I had to crawl across the floor. The fires were still blazing and were very severe on the men's eyes. They had been without sleep for days, could only with difficulty keep their eyes open, and they dropped off to sleep through sheer exhaustion, and could not be easily wakened.

James Coughlan, South Dublin Union

Fogarty, I was told, lighted his pipe when near a window. F. Burke leaned across from the other side of the window to light his cigarette from Fogarty's lighted match, and presented an easy target to a British soldier in the hospital across the roadway. As F. Burke fell, with a bullet through the left side of his neck, an officer, Lieutenant 'Willie' Byrne, I think, entered the room and, sizing up the situation, exclaimed to Fogarty: 'You are responsible for that man's death.' Shortly after this incident – when I was told of it – I visited the room and saw F. Burke's body lying in the pool of blood where he died. From the instant of F. Burke's death until some weeks later Fogarty was mentally deranged, and during the remainder of Easter Week with us he was kept disarmed, and a Volunteer – Jim Kenny – was detailed to keep him company and out of harm's way.

Joseph O'Connor, O/C, A Company, Boland's bakery

I have seen statements made by privates in our garrison, men who could not possibly have known anything of the amount of work the officers had to perform (and they were very free in the expression of their personal opinions of the officers) – that was very unfair. At no time up to Thursday did I receive any order or hold any discussion with the commandant [de Valera] that was not in perfect order and clear with precise instructions as to what he required to be done.

Séamus Kavanagh, Boland's bakery

[On Wednesday] Commandant de Valera arrived on the scene and wanted twenty men to carry out a bayonet charge . . . the charge was cancelled as there were not sufficient men to take part in it . . . The following morning Captain Donnelly brought Séamus Doyle, Bob Cooper and I to Commandant de Valera, who instructed us to report back to Roberts' yard to the position we had occupied the previous day. I think it was Captain Donnelly who pointed out to the commandant that to get into the yard we had to cross a twelve-foot wall, as we had not removed the barricade on the gate and cottage. He then cancelled the instruction.

Joseph O'Connor, O/C, A Company, Boland's bakery

On Thursday night we were expecting an enemy approach along the railway line but it did not occur. Later the commandant decided that the men should get some means of resting and withdrew them into the malt stores of Messrs Guinness & Co. situated on Grand

Canal Quay. Personally I did not like the change. I felt that we were confining the men into a comparatively small space and that it would be an easy task for the British to isolate us . . . After a couple of hours the commandant did order the men back to their positions and that each company was to occupy its former position as nearly as possible.

On Thursday night Sackville Street was set alight by incendiary shells as the British Army attacked the rebel positions in and around the GPO. The overnight destruction of the finest street in Ireland resulted in a beautiful and terrifying spectacle that could be seen from beyond Dublin. The awesome scale of the destruction reinforced the gravity of the rebels' actions, heartening some and unnerving others.

Oscar Traynor, Metropole Hotel outpost, GPO

Some time on Thursday a barricade, which stretched from the Royal Hibernian Academy to a cycle shop [J. J. Keating's] . . . on the opposite side of the street, took fire as a result of a direct shell hit. It was the firing of this barricade that caused the fire which wiped out the east side of O'Connell Street. I saw that happen myself. I saw the barricade being hit; I saw the fire consuming it and I saw Keating's going up. Then Hoyte's caught fire, and when Hoyte's caught fire the whole block up to Earl Street became involved. Hoyte's had a lot of turpentine and other inflammable stuff, and I saw the fire spread from there to Clery's. Clery's and the Imperial Hotel were one and the same building, and this building was ignited from the fire which consumed Hoyte's . . . I had the extraordinary experience of seeing the huge plate-glass windows of Clery's stores run molten into the channel from the terrific heat.

Patrick Colgan, GPO

Hoyte's chemist shop was a most attractive sight with globular fire balls rising into the skies and dying out. The glass tower of the D.B.C. restaurant was also an attractive fire. The flames licking up the glass tower, dying out, the tower twisting and bending and finally collapsing.

Fintan Murphy, GPO

The old Metropole was blazing furiously just across the narrow width of Prince's Street, as well as the *Freeman's Journal* office and that whole block . . . Some of our men went out across to the stables at the back of the *Freeman's Journal* office and released the horses.

Oscar Traynor, Metropole Hotel outpost, GPO

. . . we heard a tremendous noise caused by the galloping of horses . . . we presumed that this was the beginning of an attack, and that the attack was being led by cavalry. Our men manned the windows and a number of them were in possession of our home-made bombs. As these horses approached, fire was opened on them. One of our men was swinging a home-made bomb, which was, in fact a billycan packed with bolts, nuts and, I believe, gelignite as the explosives. He was swinging this bomb round his head in order to gain impetus for his throw, when, to our horror, the handle parted company with the can and the can flew into the room instead of being thrown at the horses. Luckily for us it did not explode.

James Kavanagh, GPO

The noise of the explosions, the bursting glass of the big windows, the falling walls, etc., was terrific, and the heat was appalling . . . the heat from the burning buildings on the opposite side of the street was so intense that in spite of playing hoses on the barricades of [coal-filled] mail bags they were continually bursting into flames.

Kevin McCabe, Imperial Hotel outpost, GPO

In my simplicity I took up the phone to speak to the Fire Brigade. I was answered, rather to my surprise, and was asked where I was speaking from. I said: 'You must not ask too many questions' and was then told that they intended to let us burn out.

Frank Thornton, Imperial Hotel outpost, GPO

Very heavy shellfire continued all day Thursday and Friday, and shells which missed the Post Office from either the Park or the river end invariably hit the buildings either to our right or left of our own building. Notwithstanding this heavy shellfire and machine-gun fire from all around, I believe that we could have successfully held these buildings for an indefinite period, but what beat us in the finish was the rain of incendiary bombs which kept falling all around and our inability to deal with this particular type of fire . . . The fire continued to approach on us and we were virtually beaten out of the upper portion of Clery's and the Imperial Hotel, and, acting under very specific instructions from the commander-in-chief, orders were given that every floor must be defended and the building must not be evacuated until it was impossible for any enemy to occupy it and thereby create considerable damage to our headquarters across the road in the GPO . . . We remained until the ceiling of the first floor was falling all around us in flames and then retreated through Allen's, which was now one huge well of flames. We had to come down a ladder about fifteen feet which was on fire, and gradually worked our way out, having received severe burns . . .

Eamon Bulfin, GPO

The Imperial Hotel then went on fire and the men had to evacuate. The method they adopted was that they wrapped themselves round with big mattresses and ran across the street.

Frank Burke, GPO

The fires had now extended from Clery's right down to Hopkins' corner and from the Metropole Hotel, the next building on our right, down to O'Connell's Bridge. In fact, the whole area was one mass of flames but the GPO had not yet caught fire . . . What a change had come over the scene since Monday and Tuesday! Not a soul was now to be seen, only a huge wall of flames towering to the sky and great billows of smoke. The noise of bursting shells and tumbling walls and roofs was indescribable.

John MacDonagh, Jacob's biscuit factory

We could see, towards the end of the week, the glare in the sky from the fires which were raging in O'Connell Street. This heartened us, for it showed the magnitude of the Rising, which we knew would change the whole position of Ireland.

Desmond Ryan, GPO

I stood beside him [Patrick Pearse] as he sat on a barrel looking intently at the flames, his slightly flushed face crowned with his turned-up hat. He suddenly turned to me with the question: 'It was the right thing to do, wasn't it?' 'Yes,' I replied in astonishment. He looked at me again more keenly. 'If we fail, it means the end of everything, Volunteers and all.' 'Yes,' I answered. He looked back at the fantastic and leaping blaze. He spoke again: 'When we are all wiped out, people will blame us for everything. But for this, the war would have ended and nothing would have been done. After a few years, they will see the meaning of what we tried to do.' He rose and we walked a few paces ahead. 'Dublin's name will be glorious forever,' he said with deep passion and enthusiasm. 'Men will speak of her as one of the splendid cities, as they speak now of Paris! Dublin!' 'Ireland is a splendid nation,' I answered. 'They can never despise us again . . .'

The GPO caught fire on Friday, dashing the rebels' hopes for a glorious last stand. Floor by floor, the flames engulfed the building, forcing its evacuation at around 8 p.m. A desperate retreat to the shelter of a row of tenement houses in nearby Moore Street ensued. Conscious of the horrors that they had inflicted on Dublin's civilian population, and with few remaining military options, the leaders persuaded their reluctant followers that the fight was over. At 3.30 p.m. on Saturday, General Lowe met Patrick Pearse at the top of Moore Street to accept his surrender.

James Kavanagh

Some time during the early part of that day [Friday] I was playing a game of whist with a young chap named Christy Byrne and two others . . . when O'Rahilly came to me and said, 'Séamus, come here.' . . . He then told me that an incendiary bomb had struck the roof and set it on fire. I went with him to the top of the building . . . When we got to the roof the wooden framework was on fire. It didn't look much of a fire. There was no blaze and the wisp of white smoke coming from it was not much more than you'd see coming from a cigarette. We got a hose out through the skylight and played water on it. There was not much water, the pressure was very bad.

After a while the wisp of smoke appeared to be getting bigger instead of smaller . . . 'I don't think that's smoke,' said O'Rahilly, 'I think it's steam.' 'No,' said I, 'it's too dark for steam.' We then got all the fire extinguishers in the place and tried them but it was no use. The smoke got greater and after a while there was a tiny blaze.

Tom Harris

I remember being in the instrument room where it was first noticed that the Post Office was on fire. The ceilings were arched. You could hear the guns going and I saw a little hole, just a circle, which came in the plaster, about the circumference of a teacup, and I could see this growing larger. It was evidently caused by an incendiary bomb.

Eamon Bulfin

I remember distinctly the Post Office being hit by shells. We were informed that the floor above us was made of ferro concrete and that there was absolutely no danger of the floor coming down.

Fintan Murphy

By Friday morning we were well ablaze and strenuous efforts were made to extinguish it in the upper storeys but to no avail and bit by bit we were driven down till the roof finally collapsed.

James Kavanagh

All the home-made grenades and bombs . . . were on the top floor . . . I got a few fellows together, about half a dozen Citizen Army men, and they, with the assistance of some of the prisoners . . . got them all down to the basement. It was a long carry from the top of the building down to the ground floor, then across a courtyard, in through a door and down again, until the bottom was reached. The prisoners were mostly the guard who had been placed on the Post Office by the British military authorities but some of them were officers and men in uniform who had only been in the Post Office on ordinary Post Office business. I can remember two of them. One appeared to be a decent type of lad who told me he came from Tallaght, Co. Dublin. The other was a member of the RIC who had joined up. He was a dark-visaged, vicious-looking, cowardly fellow, who, I was afterwards told, said a lot of vile things about us and our treatment of the prisoners . . . But about the bombs! Our fellows did not carry any of them. The prisoners did that; our fellows only told them what to do and saw that they did it. Before half the bombs were down the fire had a terrible grip of the top of the building and pieces of flaming material were flying about, particularly down into the courtyard across which the bombs were being carried. The look of the RIC man was terrible at this time. His eyes were starting from his head, he was pale and terror-stricken. He was afraid of the bombs he was carrying. He was afraid to cross the courtyard with its rain of fire, but he was more afraid of the young Citizen Army man who was urging him on with a forty-five stuck in his back.

Louise Gavan Duffy

I thought we were going to stay in the building until we died.

Joe Good

Our military prisoners whom we had captured during the week appeared terrified, as was only natural in the confusion. I suggested to O'Rahilly that they be let go and take their chance of escaping. It looked to me as if we were trapped. O'Rahilly misunderstood me at first, thinking I wanted to exploit the prisoners in some way, and he almost struck me. Then he saw my point and apologised.

Liam Tannam

Finally, pieces of burning timber began to fall from the ceiling over us . . . I heard Tom Clarke declare that he would never leave the GPO alive. He said: 'You can all go and leave me here. I'll go down with the building.' He had an automatic pistol and was finally prevailed upon to go with the others. I think it was MacDermott who finally persuaded him . . .

Seán McGarry

[Tom Clarke] deplored the fact that the burning of the buildings had deprived us of a glorious fight, in which he felt that even with our limited resources we could give as good as we got.

Liam Tannam

Although there was no sign of panic I felt that panic might set in. I had a supply of cigars which I had taken from the Metropole. I lit one of these and walked up and down trying to appear as nonchalant as possible. I did this because I was an officer and felt that the eyes of the men were on me as they would be on all officers, but inwardly I was very far from feeling as nonchalant as I [was] assumed to be. There was grave danger that the ceiling would now collapse, bringing a burning mass down on top of us. Although I did not see what was going on at the Henry Street side door at that time, I learned that O'Rahilly had left the building with about thirty-five men in an effort to open the way of retreat through Moore Street. At this point I thought a song would be a good thing and I sang the 'Soldiers' Song', accompanied by a Cumann na mBan girl named Madge Fagan.

Frank Burke

The place was now an inferno. Some of our men were hosing the flames that had spread along the roof, and between the flames, the smoke and the water dripping down on us, we didn't feel very comfortable. Still, we made the welkin ring with rousing song and chorus, just to keep our spirits up.

Joe Good

I heard O'Rahilly calling for twenty men with bayonets to make a charge. There was not a very prompt response to his call, which seemed reasonable to me, because what or whom he was going to charge was not clear . . . O'Rahilly shouted, 'Are you Irishmen that you won't charge?' and the men stepped forward more promptly.

Eamon Dore

When the bombs were put out of danger I was put in charge of the Henry Street entrance to the Post Office – it was the only exit not on fire. After some time O'Rahilly and a group of men filed out and I asked one, John R. Reynolds, R.I.P., where they were going. In a most cynical voice he said, 'We are going to clear the British out of Moore Street, fight our way to Williams & Woods jam factory in

Parnell Street and then try to connect up with Ned Daly in the Four Courts.' . . . Pearse addressed us and told us our objective and said a few parting words while the British were firing from the ruins on the other side of O'Connell Street.

James Kavanagh

He [O'Rahilly] shook hands with me and bid me goodbye and then he said, 'I wonder do those fellows still think we're afraid of them,' meaning, of course, the British.

John Kenny

The O'Rahilly drew his heavy automatic pistol and, pointing towards Moore Street, gave the order to 'charge, for the glory of God and the honour of Ireland'. We were met by a heavy barrage of rifle and machine-gun bullets, and I only got about thirty yards when I was hit and I fell.

Eamon Dore

I saw O'Rahilly fall wounded and my nearest comrade, Pat O'Connor, was killed just in front of me and falling on me pinned me under him.

Liam Tannam

P.H. Pearse called me. He informed me that O'Rahilly had not returned and he asked me would I take some Volunteers and see what I could do in the way of securing a place to which the garrison could be evacuated in the direction of Moore Street . . . We rushed across the road into Henry Place and at the end of Henry Place turned the corner left and when we showed up opposite Moore Lane we came under fire from troops apparently in Parnell Street or some little distance up Moore Lane . . . The corner house of Moore Street . . . seemed the best place that could be got, especially as my mind was then running on the imminent danger of the collapse of the ceiling in the GPO. I instructed the men to enter at once and dashed back . . . The side door seemed rather crowded and I shouted at once, 'Come on,' and the garrison poured out into Henry Place with no semblance of order.

Joe Good

Pearse stood at the Henry Street exit with what appeared to be plans in his hand. There was some delay and there was something of a press behind him. The building was now well alight down to the ground floor. There was something of a crush, but no panic.

Jimmy Kenny

As each man left he was given provisions to carry. I saw some carrying hams and others cases of eggs . . .

Frank Burke

There was no panic whatsoever. We marched out in two deep, each man holding his rifle pointing upwards lest, in the closely packed formation, a rifle might go off accidentally . . . When we reached the side door leading into Henry Street, Commandant Pearse was standing in the small hallway watching and waiting until the last man had passed out of the building. As the street was being swept by machine-gun fire from the Mary Street direction, we had to make a dash across in ones and twos into Henry Place . . . I thought my overcoat, to which I had [a piece of] gammon fastened in front, might be an unnecessary burden and might possibly trip me as I ran, so I discarded both and threw them in a corner. I could see the bullets like hailstones hopping on the street and I thought that 'twould be a miracle to get to the other side scatheless. With head down as if running against heavy rain, I ran as I never ran before or since and got into Henry Place without a scratch.

James Carrigan

I took two loaves and when I got to Henry Place some Volunteer was trying to burst in a gate at O'Brien's mineral-water stores. Evidently his shotgun must have been at full cock at the time, because when he hit the butt of the gun against the gate the charge exploded into his throat and killed him instantly.

Oscar Traynor

When we entered Henry Place there seemed to me to be a state bordering on chaos. Men were trying to get shelter in doorways and against walls from the fire, which no one seemed to know whence it was coming.

Seán McLoughlin

There was terrible confusion – almost panic. No one seemed to have any idea what to do.

Eamon Bulfin

Volunteers, with bayonets, were called on to charge this [white] house and occupy it. It was very duskish, and we could not see very well. There was no cohesion. Nobody seemed to be in charge once we left the Post Office; it was every man for himself. After waiting for a couple of minutes, the general consensus was that there was no one in the house. We crossed at the end of Moore Lane and, having proceeded down Henry Place, we found that junction also under fire. We broke into a store, which was quite convenient to the entrance of Moore Lane, and brought out a vehicle – I think it was an old float – on which we piled all kinds of stuff. We moved the dray across the street to block the fire and, having formed some kind of an obstruction there, we crossed the lane safely.

Arthur Agnew

We crossed the lane by rushes – three at a time – between bursts of heavy fire.

Fintan Murphy

As each man rushed across and received his burst of fire, the next man would pause before making his dash. As there were some hundreds of us to get through, it became a very tedious job, as well as nerve-racking, wondering who would be the first to be hit.

Joe Good

The garrison crossed Henry Street into Henry Place. There was now considerable firing down Henry Street. I helped carry a wounded man and entered Henry Place at the rear of the main part. About halfway up Henry Place, which is L-shaped, there was a small whitewashed house. As our men were passing this house there was fire from five to ten rifles, some of them Howth rifles, I assumed, because the explosions were very loud. This house was held by our own men, but they did not know who were approaching and thought we were the British. There were shouts of 'You are firing on your own men' from our party, but the firing persisted. I saw one or two men fall while trying to pass the house. Our advance was halted . . . Some Volunteers attempted to break down a large door with their rifle butts, but in doing so shot three or four men who were behind them . . . I thought perhaps I could find a hand grenade to throw into the white house, although there was little doubt in my mind as to who occupied it.

Patrick Rankin

I was passed by a young Volunteer named Lieutenant F[rancis] Macken just before I came to Moore Lane. As he moved past me he shouted, 'Oh, my God,' and fell in my path. I caught him in my arms, but he was dead in a minute, shot in the centre of the forehead. I laid him down on the path and said a short prayer.

Joe Good

Most of the doors in Moore Lane were shut and the Volunteers attempted to break in. In doing so, they fired through the lock of one door, killing a girl and wounding her father in the chest.

Oscar Traynor

We reached the corner of Moore Street and Clarke called upon me to occupy these buildings, and to dig from one building to another in order to extend our position. We smashed our way into this building and progressed, as instructed, from house to house . . . We continued to extend our line until we reached the lane which intersects Moore Street about fifty yards from Parnell Street. I, at this stage, reported back to say that the line had now been extended as far as it was possible to go.

Séamus Robinson

We were using a very large crowbar, and each man would take his turn at the bar for a few minutes and then stop to rest, a fresh man taking his place. During one of my spells of rest I lay flat down on the floor awaiting my turn to work the crowbar and fell fast asleep.

Diarmuid Lynch

In one small room (basement) I came across two of our men lying fast asleep, their heads near the fender (a good fire was in the grate) and feet almost touching the wall opposite. They were so exhausted that they had to be lifted bodily through the bored walls.

Eamon Bulfin

We reached as far as Price's, or O'Hanlon's, which was a fish shop. I remember the smells there. We spent Friday night barricading all the houses that we occupied by throwing down all the furniture from the rooms – clearing all the rooms – down the stairways into the bottom halls, blocking up the doorways. One shell hit a house which we had evacuated, down at the lower part of Moore Street, and flattened it out absolutely. It went down like a house of cards. We had to evacuate the civilians from the houses, of course – under great pressure too.

Oscar Traynor

On entering one of the buildings in the middle of Moore Street we were met by a little family, an old man, a young woman and her children, cowering into the corner of a room, apparently terrified. I tried to reassure these people that they were safe. The old man stated that he was very anxious to secure the safety of his daughter and his grandchildren, and that, for that reason, he intended to make an effort to secure other accommodation . . . when we were forming up in Moore Street preparatory to the surrender I saw the old man's body lying on the side of the street almost wrapped in a white sheet, which he was apparently using as a flag of truce.

James Kavanagh

I felt very sorry for the people who lived in these houses. By going into them we were bringing death and destruction to the inhabitants, though we tried to make things as easy as we could. The floors in those houses were not at the same level, so that when we broke through the wall on a landing of one house we often found ourselves a good distance above the floor of the next, and mostly we would find we had burst from a hall or landing into a living or bedroom where frightened people were huddled together wondering what would happen to them. In one of these rooms there was an elderly woman and her son, a chap in his early twenties, huddled over a tiny fire. When we burst in she started abusing the son. 'It's out helping these men you should be,' she said, 'instead of sitting here as you are.' The firing was going on all the time and a number of our men were wounded, as well as some of the inhabitants of the houses. Séamus Donegan, an ambulance man and one of the Liverpool crowd, told me that a girl in a room that he was in was struck by a bullet. In the dark he was groping about to find out what was wrong with her. He thought he put his fingers into her mouth, as he thought he felt her teeth, but when he struck a match he found that it was through a hole in her skull he had put his fingers and, of course, she was then quite dead. John King, another of the Liverpool contingent, got a bullet through his hip and was lying on the floor bleeding and, I suppose, partly unconscious, being kicked and trampled on by men passing to and fro.

Frank Burke

We were completely surrounded. The military were entrenched behind a high barricade at the end of Moore Street. We could see from our windows dead bodies of civilians lying out on the path opposite. I took particular notice of one poor man with a white flag grasped in his hand, lying dead on the door-step of his house. He had evidently been shot while evacuating his home for a safer place. We had a very patchy sleep that night as we suffered from the hunger and the thirst.

James Kavanagh

Before it was quite dark I saw an old man come out of a shop on the opposite side of the street. No sooner did he appear than a bullet from one of the 18th Royal Irish, who were manning a barricade at the end of the street, struck him and he fell to the ground. It was evident that he was mortally wounded but he was not dead. He remained there all night and for hours it was terrible to hear his cries of 'Water, water, give me a drink of water.' It went on for hours until his voice got weaker and finally died away. Later when daylight came a little girl, about 4 or 5 years, came out of the shop and started bawling, 'Mammy, Mammy, my granddad is dead.' She kept repeating this over and over again. Her mother was inside the door calling her in and afraid to go out herself. She expected to see the child shot at any moment and could do nothing to prevent it. The 18th Royal Irish, a regiment of Irishmen in the British Army, had shot at everything that moved in the street, and at such short range their shooting was deadly. I saw three men attempting to cross the street killed by three shots, 1, 2, 3, like that.

Thomas Leahy

I remember P. H. Pearse coming into this room and seeing for himself what was taking place as regards the fate of those people. He instructed us to stop and have a rest till we got further orders.

Frank Burke

All our men had got safely from the GPO and were in silent occupation of the row of houses on this side of Moore Street.

Michael Cremen

My comrade at the other window soon complained that he could not stand the strain any longer and soon after this he collapsed, falling into a deep sleep from which several efforts on my part to arouse him were unsuccessful.

Frank Burke

'Twas impossible to keep awake. As soon as one sat down, one's head began to nod over one's rifle.

Joe Good

As far as possible, no lights, or very few, were lighted. Fires for cooking were used with great discretion, because the heavy smoke from them drew snipers' fire. Headquarters staff, consisting of Pádraig Pearse, Plunkett, James Connolly, but not Tom Clarke, passed the night in one room. James Connolly lay on a bed and was conscious the whole time . . . Most of the men by this time were utterly tired, exhausted and apparently despondent. A large number in the more or less darkened rooms were saying their Rosaries. During this period I noticed one other small party of young men. I had heard some talk of their being part of a bayonet charge that was impending. These young men I found discussing the hereafter somewhat academically . . . During this time in Moore Street Michael Collins was very aggressive and ill-humoured. Some men had built a barricade at the top of Moore Lane, and when they looked for his approval he said, 'So-and-so your barricade.' I was resting on the stairs at one period with my head in my hands and Mick said angrily to me: 'Are you [fucking] praying too.'

Frank Burke

I don't remember what time we awoke but I well remember the gnawing feeling of hunger and how I longed for a good strong cup of tea but there was nothing to be had up at our end of the line anyhow. I thought what a fool I was to have parted with that gammon. I would have eaten it raw . . . The Post Office was now a huge mass of flames and the roof was falling in. Explosions were frequent, as the flames came in contact with the bombs which we were unable to retrieve from the building. Sometime after midday an order came along for 'all men with bayonets to proceed to the front'. I prayed God that I'd get my blow in first if I should succeed in coming into close quarters with the enemy. On my way to the yard, I had the awful temptation of getting rid of my bayonet as no one was looking, but thank God I overcame such a cowardly action and proceeded to join the men out in the yard . . . We were told to keep very, very quiet. There was only a wide door separating the yard from the lane into which we were to go. We were then supposed to proceed into Moore Street and charge the big barricade about fifty yards away at the end of Moore Street. I could see none of us reaching that far.

Liam Tannam

It was proposed that eighteen men with fixed bayonets under the command of Captain George Plunkett should assemble in the yard of Kelly's [O'Hanlon's] fish shop . . . and charge the barricade held by the British at the Parnell Street end of Moore Street. There was no proper way of covering this charge and I personally thought it was doomed to failure . . . The barricade at the Parnell Street end of Moore Street was simply crammed with British soldiers bending over it and more standing behind them again and on it were two machine-guns. Facing up Cole's Lane – it runs parallel with Moore Street – was a piece of artillery, probably a 4.7. Every house in Parnell Street was crammed with British soldiers and an overflow of the troops were lying down on the paths.

Oscar Traynor

A man was actually moving the bolt of the gate in order to allow us to make our exit on a given signal. Almost on time for this charge to take place a Volunteer rushed into this yard and said that the bayonet charge was to be cancelled. We did not know the reason for the cancellation, but, apparently, negotiations with the enemy were being considered.

Frank Burke

The relief to me anyhow was like an answer to a prayer.

James Kavanagh

I was one of those selected to take part in the charge . . . we had little or nothing to eat during the week and were being kept up only by excitement, but on Saturday morning those selected for the bayonet charge were each to be given two raw eggs to sustain us in the effort. Before the eggs reached me the charge was called off. This was lucky for us. We would all have been shot down and killed long before we reached the barricade and, in any case, none of us knew anything about bayonet fighting . . . I was glad to get out of that bayonet charge and I was glad I did not get the two raw eggs. They would only have made me sick.

Fintan Murphy

I remember that morning going forward through the rooms from house to house and talking to each little group, trying to find out our position and what was happening. None knew much except that activities were at a standstill and we just waited. Later in the morning, officers came through and told us the dread news that negotiations were proceeding with the British. Firing had ceased some time now except for the crack now and again of a sniper's rifle. The hours passed slowly enough. Speculating of what was to come next, some of us managed to collect some food of sorts from the shops, others were unconcernedly shaving themselves and smartening up their appearances; some lay round asleep, exhausted.

Joe Good

I was sent from the room to get Tom Clarke. He was standing alone at a window some few houses away. He came into the headquarters staff room. I did not hear the conversation which followed, but I knew they were discussing the surrender as I heard sufficient of the letter, which was read out openly, to know what terms were being sought.

Seán McGarry

They were both together. Tom was very quiet – MacDermott on the verge of tears. MacDermott said: 'We have to ask the lads to give up themselves and their guns – to surrender.' There was anguish and bitterness in that speech.

James Kavanagh

We knew something was going on, but until we were called together by Seán MacDermott and told by him about the surrender we had nothing definite. He told us of the negotiations and that terms had been agreed upon. 'And', said he, with tears in his eyes, 'the terms are unconditional surrender.' He had a word of praise for all who had taken part in the fight and gave us all he had to give, a spoonful of syrup each out of the fruit tins in one of the shops we were occupying.

Joseph O'Rourke

MacDermott came in and said the game was up and that the soldiers were going wild and killing civilians in all directions and, as a result, we would have to surrender.

Arthur Agnew

The men kicked against surrendering but MacDermott said he looked to the men to accept it in the proper spirit. He said he was sure the men would be treated as prisoners of war, but as for Pearse and himself and the other men who had signed the Proclamation, they knew what to expect. 'We are', he said, 'accepting it on behalf of the people to save further bloodshed,' and finally he said, 'We have now surrendered.' All the men who were capable of thought and not dazed from want of sleep and fatigue were very down-hearted now.

Michael Cremen

When I awoke I noticed the fellows were all round me wearing most woebegone expressions and showing signs of deep depression . . . It transpired that, while I was asleep, Seán MacDermott came around and gave the word that the surrender had been offered.

John McGallogly

When I awoke the Rising was over and I hadn't fired a shot.

Frank Burke

To say that I was glad and thankful to God would be putting it mildly . . .

Charles Saurin

All I really felt at the time was that I was hungry.

Oscar Traynor

I remember, as we were going out into Moore Street and crossing through the ruins of one of the houses, meeting Seán MacDermott, who was marshalling the men into the street, and I said to him: 'Is this what we were brought out for? To go into English dungeons for the rest of our lives?' Seán immediately waved a piece of paper which he held in his hand, and said: 'No. We are surrendering as prisoners of war.'

Thomas Leahy

It was a bitter blow to us all at Moore Street. We were so confident that at least the fight could have lasted a while longer to give time for the country at large to reach Dublin to carry on . . . when we did finally reach the street it was then we realised the result and cause of the words of P. H. Pearse and Seán MacDermott to surrender, for all about the street were the bodies of the poor people who had left their houses willingly to help us and Ireland, in my opinion.

8

Left in a Fog: The Rising in the Provinces

Why did the Volunteer movement fail to rise throughout most of rural Ireland? The collapse of the nationwide insurrection is usually attributed to the interception of the *Aud*, the secrecy of the Military Council's plans and the impact of Eoin MacNeill's countermanding order. Devastating as these were, the witness statements of provincial Volunteers suggest that the inadequacies of the Military Council's strategy and deep-rooted differences between it and the separatist leadership outside Dublin also played a major role.

*

The strategic importance of a nationwide insurrection in the Military Council's thinking remains uncertain. The Ireland Report, submitted by Joseph Plunkett to the German authorities in 1915, outlined an ambitious role for the provincial Volunteers, but others argued that the idea of a nationwide insurrection came as an afterthought.

P. S. O'Hegarty, IRB Supreme Council, Wales

In May 1915 Seán MacDermott came to see me . . . There was then in contemplation only a Dublin insurrection, as a forlorn hope to awaken the people, and I do not know what changed it to an all-Ireland plan.

Diarmuid Lynch, IRB Supreme Council, Dublin

These [orders] Pearse gave to me early in January 1916, at St Enda's; I was to convey them orally to the Cork, Kerry, Limerick and Galway commandants. He outlined the positions which these brigades were to occupy on the Volunteer manoeuvres which had been decided on for the Easter weekend, viz.: Cork to hold the county to the south of the Boggeragh Mountains – left flank contacting the Kerry Brigade, which was to extend eastwards from Tralee; Limerick was to contact the Kerry men on the south and those of Limerick – Clare – Galway to the north. Limerick, Clare and Galway were 'to hold the line of the Shannon to Athlone'.

Liam O'Brien, F Company, 1st Battalion, and IRB

There were two vital areas, one Dublin city for political reasons, the other Kerry for strictly military reasons . . . A landing of arms at Fenit in Kerry from Germany to be followed by a seizure of Tralee, the despatch of arms northward to Limerick, the holding of the British forces in Limerick while arms were to be got across Shannon, sent along by rail with distributions on the way to Athenry . . . Arms also to be sent eastward from Tralee to West Cork for distribution among Cork Brigade. The midland areas in Leinster move generally westwards across the Shannon. Ulster to be abandoned and forces in Ulster to move to north Connaught and try and hold the northern end of Shannon . . . This may all seem pitiful, when one thinks of the relative strength of the parties engaged . . . Was there more in the plan? If asked what was to happen after these first movements of brigades and companies, I would be inclined to say that probably the leaders had no further plans; that subsequent movements would be dictated by circumstances.

The failure of the Rising in the north of Ireland was due mainly to tensions between the local Volunteer leadership and the Military Council. The separatist leadership in Ulster believed that the Volunteer movement was not sufficiently organised to rise, and that the Military Council's plans for Ulster were not achievable.

Denis McCullough, Supreme Council president and Volunteers leader, Belfast

When the date for the Rising was decided, we were to receive a coded message, the date given in which was to be read as seven days earlier, as the date set for the Rising. I was to mobilise my men, with all arms and ammunition and equipment available, to convey them to Tyrone, join the Tyrone men mobilised there and 'proceed with all possible haste, to join Mellows in Connaught and act under his command there' . . . I pointed out [to Pearse] the length of the journey we had to take, the type of country and population we had to pass through and how sparsely armed my men were for such an undertaking. I suggested that we would have to attack the RIC barracks on our way through, to secure the arms we required. Connolly got quite cross at this suggestion and almost shouted at me, 'You will fire no shot in Ulster: you will proceed with all possible speed to join Mellows in Connaught.' 'And,' he added, 'if we win through, we will then deal with Ulster.' . . . I looked at Pearse, to ascertain if he agreed with this, and he nodded assent, with some remark like, 'Yes, that's an order.'

Father Eugene Coyle, Volunteers leader, Co. Tyrone

He [Patrick McCartan] told me that at the meeting where he got this information of the date of the Rising there was a difference of opinion. A small minority of the delegates expressed the opinion that the Rising should be postponed until the country was better organised, as in many counties there did not exist any organisation whatever. The date was, however, fixed. Dr McCartan, on his return home from the meeting in Dublin at which the proposal to postpone the Rising was raised, told me that the leaders in Dublin seemed to imagine that 'Dublin was Ireland' – that if Dublin was well organised, their opinion was that all Ireland was likewise. The position in the North then was that in all areas except east and south Tyrone and Belfast city there was no organisation.

Seán Cusack, IRB and Volunteers, Belfast

My own impression of Mr McCullough's reactions to the orders for a rising on Easter Sunday 1916 was his perplexity at the orders he had received and his feeling of inability to carry out those orders.

Frank de Burca, O/C, 'Ulster Forces of the Irish Republic'

I took the orders from Pearse to the Ulster Council on the Wednesday of Holy Week . . . There were no orders for the Rising for an

Ulster county except Belfast and Tyrone. The organisation elsewhere was scrappy.

Father James O'Daly, Volunteers leader, Co. Tyrone

The plan of campaign ordered from headquarters was that the northern Volunteers – including Belfast – would concentrate somewhere in Tyrone, march across the Shannon and form up with the Connaught forces and await the arrival of the Germans. Without casting any reflection on headquarters, this seemed impossible. That a few hundred volunteers, poorly armed and without any means of transport, could pass the British garrison at Enniskillen and reach the western seaboard was truly heroic.

Father Eugene Coyle, Volunteers leader, Co. Tyrone

All the leaders there were strongly in opposition to this plan, as it was considered not practicable or possible to carry out those plans. The country over which the Volunteers were ordered to march was not organised and was strongly held by hostile forces.

Denis McCullough, Supreme Council president and Volunteers leader, Belfast

I found gathered in the McCartan home [on Good Friday], Dr Patrick McCartan, Father Daly, CC, Father Coyle, CC, and [Frank] Burke the organiser. Word had reached them somehow – I don't remember how, probably through Dr McCartan – of the arrangements for Easter Sunday in Dublin. They expressed the opinion – particularly the priests and also Burke – that the whole thing was engineered and inspired by Connolly; that it was not a Volunteer, but a socialist rising; that it had no sanction etc. from MacNeill . . . I stated specifically that my allegiance was to the IRB first and last; that I was satisfied that the proposed Rising was inspired and would be directed by the IRB through its leaders in the Volunteers, with Connolly and the Irish Citizen Army an integral part of any fighting force that would turn out; that I was taking my orders from the IRB through its Military Committee and that accordingly I was in Tyrone and was bringing my men to Tyrone, to carry out the orders I had received from Pearse and Connolly. I urged them to mobilise the men in the various districts where we had Volunteer units, and get them prepared to march on Sunday morning. They ridiculed the idea of a march to Connaught, pointing out the difficulties, almost the impossibility of such a march, mostly through very hostile territory. I agreed that I was aware of these difficulties, but orders were orders, and that perhaps the whole plan depended on our carrying out our share of them. McCartan agreed generally with me, but he was greatly swayed by the arguments of the priests, who were both sincere and loyal men. The argument went on through the evening without any definite conclusion as to action being arrived at.

Ina Connolly, Cumann na mBan, Belfast

We bought the [train] tickets in batches of a dozen and half a dozen so the authorities might not notice that all the travellers were nationalists and males. We arrived in Coalisland, Easter Saturday, with the first contingent from the North and started to fix up the Volunteer Hall for the convenience of the latecomers. The second batch would leave Belfast at 3 p.m. and then the last lot in the evening, about 7 p.m. Somewhat disappointed at the absence of the local people expecting our arrival, we were busy as best we could. A young man arrived with a despatch for Nora [Connolly], telling her of the order cancelling the manoeuvres all over the country . . .

Elizabeth Corr, Cumann na mBan, Belfast

Nora refused to credit this statement and said she was quite sure Dublin would fight.

Ina Connolly, Cumann na mBan, Belfast

By this time the second contingent had arrived and the third was on their way. Nora, I and four other Belfast girls decided that we would go to Dublin and offer our services there.

Denis McCullough, Supreme Council president and Volunteers leader, Belfast

I returned to Carrickmore with [Hugh] Rodgers. He left me off at the end of the road leading up to McCartan's house. On the way up, I took out the small automatic to examine it. I was fool enough to press the trigger to ascertain if it was loaded – it was, and the bullet went though my left hand, breaking no bones, but leaving a large gap where it passed out. I don't remember what happened then. I suppose I must have passed out, because I came to, sometime later, lying on the side of the ditch. I made my way somehow to Dr McCartan's house . . . The priests returned later and again the discussions and arguments were resumed, with no better results, despite Dr McCartan's report of his interview with Tom Clarke, in which he was informed that the Rising was to take place on Sunday. By this time I was worn out and getting into despair. Word had reached me that most of my men had arrived at Coalisland . . . I issued an ultimatum to the three Tyrone leaders present, viz. Dr McCartan, Fathers Daly and Coyle. I stated that I had made up my mind that if they would not undertake to get their men moving and ready to start with mine for Connaught in the morning, I would order my men back to Belfast and disband them there . . . the responsibility for the lives of those I had with me weighed heavily on me. A number of them were married men with families and the greater number were young men and boys, for whose lives and liberty I would be held responsible. I can say truthfully that I felt that my own life was only of secondary consideration, though I had real fear of a long term of imprisonment. When we reached Coalisland, I had a conference with the section leaders and explained the position, as I saw it, to them and my decision to get the men back to Belfast. Some of them demurred, but I insisted on my authority and ordered them to get their men on the road to Cookstown, the only station in Tyrone from which a train left for Belfast on that day.

Cathal McDowell, A Company, Belfast

When Denis McCullough arrived [at Coalisland on Sunday morning] he informed me he was taking this step as a result of cancellation orders he received from Eoin MacNeill. I reminded him of my interview with Pearse in Dublin and Pearse's instructions to me that any cancelling of orders should not be obeyed except they came direct from Pearse himself. Denis McCullough informed me that he was in supreme command of the Belfast men and that he was obeying the countermanding orders, and that I must obey his orders, as he was my superior officer.

Henry Corr, B Company, Belfast

None of us knew where we were bound for, nor what was happening. We were under the impression that we were bound for Dublin, but no one told us anything. On boarding the train at Cookstown we were handed our railway tickets and found they were for Belfast . . . We had no choice in the matter, as we were not asked either to fight or go home.

Frank de Burca, O/C, 'Ulster Forces of the Irish Republic'

During Easter Week 1916, I tried to get the Monaghan men out in the Rising. The men obeyed MacNeill's orders and refused to participate. I had to go 'on the run' from my own men, who resented my efforts to get them to do something.

James Tomney, IRB county centre and Volunteers leader, Co. Tyrone

When I got Pearse's order to remobilise on Monday, I mobilised about fourteen men of the Coalisland Volunteers . . . On Monday evening I met Dr McCartan in his home. A short time previous to my arrival the military had been there, raided the house, and, on leaving, set fire to his motorcar. When I met him he seemed to have had a bad time and showed the effects of it. Dr McCartan told me that things looked bad. The military were in the area . . . He said that he was not in favour of doing anything further, that military action under the circumstances in Co. Tyrone would be madness, and that I was to take my men home.

Ina Connolly, Cumann na mBan, Belfast

I travelled to Coalisland [from Dublin on Monday night] and found that the Volunteers had returned to Belfast. From there I went to Sixmilecross to Hugh Rodgers, as I was told he could put me in touch with Dr Pat McCartan to whom my despatch was to be delivered . . . It was an instruction from Pearse to mobilise all men in the county, seize all police barracks and hold up all trains with military supplies going south.

Nora Connolly, Cumann na mBan, Belfast, and daughter of James Connolly

It was fairly dark when I arrived there. McCartan was not there at the time, but they got in touch with him, and brought him along. I asked McCartan why he had got nothing done; did he not know the men in Dublin were fighting? He said they were all demobilised. It was much more difficult in the country to get the men together, once they had dispersed. There was no use waiting – waiting for what? We had a very bitter discussion. It was quite definite that nothing was going to happen – that they were not going to fight in the North at all.

Father Eugene Coyle, Volunteers leader, Co. Tyrone

Why specially condemn him [McCartan] for inactivity when in areas like Cork and Kerry with friendly populations, with better organisation, more men, more arms and better equipment, no action took place?

Rory Haskin, IRB and Volunteers, Belfast

On Tuesday or Wednesday [Seán] Cusack told me to travel to Carrickmore and to call on Dr McCartan and find out from the doctor his plans, the feeling of the men in Tyrone on the question of participating in the Rising and the possibility of the Belfast men coordinating with the Tyrone men in an effort to link up with some of the areas where military activities were taking place . . . It was around 9 p.m. when Dr McCartan arrived in the house. I gave him my message and in discussing the matter I learned from him that the Tyrone men were so disappointed with the mix-up in the plans that they would not be willing to take the field. He also stated that the men were not properly armed and equipped.

Thomas Wilson, IRB and Executive Committee, Volunteers, Belfast

Mr McCullough was not moving about [Belfast] at the time, and his absence seemed to leave the Volunteers in a confused position . . . There was no possibility of doing anything.

Seán Cusack, IRB and Volunteers, Belfast

There was an intense feeling of dissatisfaction amongst the men in Belfast who had travelled to Tyrone on the Saturday of Holy Week, 1916, against the leadership displayed on that occasion. Denis McCullough's prominence in the republican organisation pre-1916, his undoubted control in Belfast and the feeling of confidence the Volunteers in Belfast had in his leadership pre-1916 [were] shaken when the time for action came . . . I was instructed [after the Rising] to inform him that the rank and file in the Volunteers would be relieved to know that he would not attempt to again assume leadership.

The failure to rise in Cork, where the provincial Volunteers were strongest, was largely due to the confusion that paralysed the local leadership over Easter weekend. The reservations of Tomás MacCurtain and his deputy, Terence MacSwiney, about the viability of an insurrection were compounded by their knowledge of the split within the Dublin leadership and the string of contradictory despatches that reached Cork in the days leading up to the rebellion.

Patrick Higgins, Cork Brigade officer

Tomás [MacCurtain] and Terry [MacSwiney] were agreed that the people in Dublin were being fooled by the Germans, and they were disturbed because they believed the Germans were just using the Irish Volunteers in their own interests. Neither Tomás nor Terry had any faith in the Germans, and both of them disapproved of the policy of seeking aid from them . . . I think both of them were greatly influenced by MacNeill, but had lost almost all faith in some of the Dublin men . . . I got the impression that Tomás and Terry believed the Dublin men were going to fight whether anybody else did or not. They did not approve of that. Tomás was a very practical man, and he would not undertake a thing that he believed had not a reasonable chance of success. In plain language, the two of them thought the Dublin crowd were daft. Tomás always dominated Terry, though Terry did more talking. The plan on which the brigade was to be mobilised on Easter Sunday was not a Cork plan – it was what he had been ordered to do by Dublin.

Denis Lordan, Kilbrittain Company, Co. Cork

On Sunday, 16 April 1916, notification was given the men for the parade on the following Sunday (Easter Sunday). They were to have all arms and full equipment. Most of the men thought it was only a test mobilisation, with perhaps two days' marching for training purposes.

Liam Murphy, D Company, Cork City Battalion

There was no definite information in the [IRB] circle about the Rising until about a week before Easter at a meeting MacCurtain told us it was to be on Easter Sunday.

Tom Hales, Ballinadee Company, Co. Cork

On Wednesday, 19 April 1916, I was with Tomás MacCurtain in his own house at Blackpool. He instructed me to take charge of the [West Cork] battalion . . . He made it plain that this march had a serious purpose. He said we were going to get arms, but did not say at what point. An attempt may be made to prevent our movements, and we may have to fight. But we were to get to the place where we were to meet him at all costs and not to fight unless attacked.

Cornelius Murphy, B Company, Cork City Battalion

On Holy Thursday we knew that something more than an ordinary parade was on – at least the IRB men knew. We were told to go to confession. Our family had no doubt but that we were going into something from which none of us may return. We made our arrangements accordingly. We held a discussion as to whether we would take [my brother] Tadhg or not. He was very young. We decided finally, thinking of the aftermath of previous risings, that he had a better chance armed with us than unarmed at home.

Seán O'Hegarty, IRB and O/C, Bandon and Ballingeary companies

During the week before Easter I saw individually all the men of the company in and west of the village of Ballingeary, as well as the captain. Without being specific I made it clear that we were out for more than a route march on Easter Sunday. Let it be placed on record that every man who turned out on Easter Sunday was prepared to fight.

Even now I can recall clearly that on the Saturday Tadhg and Liam Ó Tuama, [from] Tuirmdubh, told their father that they were going out in the morning, that serious business was intended and that they might not return and asked his approval. I can recall how he closed his lips tightly and then said. 'Well, if it be God's will. Let ye go. Ye have my blessing.'

Annie MacSwiney, sister of Terence MacSwiney

I always see, most vividly, the scene as I opened the door on that Good Friday night. Terry stood on one side of the fireplace, his elbow on the mantelpiece, his head resting on his hand. Tomás stood in a similar attitude on the other side. Facing him, Seán O'Sullivan sat on a sofa near the window, elbows on his knees, his head bowed between his hands. [J. J.] O'Connell [who had been sent by MacNeill to Cork to prevent the Volunteers from rising] sat on an armchair, looking as if he had been defending himself; the rather odd look on his face suggested that he was at variance with his three companions; it was a rather smug 'take-it-or-leave-it' expression . . . it was clear to me that something was very seriously wrong.

Fred Murray, D Company, Cork City Battalion

On arrival in Cork I went at once to the Volunteer Hall in Sheares Street. It was sometime in the early hours of Saturday morning. I had difficulty in getting admittance, Langford was captain of the guard. Tomás MacCurtain was in bed but got up. He was in his pyjamas. He then asked me why I had come at that hour and I said 'Bad news; the arms ship has been captured.' It was a great shock to him. I said, 'There was a man captured also.' 'Casement?' he asked. I said, 'Yes.' He said, sadly, 'Things had been going too well.'

Jim Ryan, Volunteers and IRB, Dublin

On Good Friday 1916, at lunch in the Red Bank restaurant, Seán MacDermott asked me if I would take a despatch to Cork that evening . . . When I arrived at his office Seán MacDermott asked me if I was armed. I said yes. I had a revolver. He then handed me a despatch which was to be delivered to Tomás MacCurtain in Cork.

He said it was a very important message and that I should prevent it falling into hostile hands, even if I had to use the revolver to do so. He told me to destroy the message if necessary ... I gave MacCurtain the despatch from Seán MacDermott. The pith of the message was that agreement had been reached in Dublin and that the Rising was going ahead ... The reply I got for Seán MacDermott verbally from MacCurtain was: 'Tell Seán we will blaze away as long as the stuff lasts.'

Annie MacSwiney, sister of Terence MacSwiney

Later in the morning [on Easter Saturday] – I was still in bed – Terry came back in a much happier mood ... we learnt that a despatch had now come from Dublin saying all despatches thenceforth would be that of a unified command and signed by MacNeill and Seán MacDermott or Pearse.

Cornelius Murphy, B Company, Cork City Battalion

The countermanding order from MacNeill brought by Jim Ryan [subsequent to his first despatch] came when the parade was moving off from the hall in Sheares Street on Easter Sunday morning. The brigade officers took the decision to let the parade go on ... I think all the officers knew, before we were into the train at Capwell Station, that we were returning to Cork again that night. The IRB men knew anyway and that included practically all the officers.

Fred Murray, D Company, Cork City Battalion

Tomás had the countermanding order from MacNeill in his hand. He passed it to me and I read it. There was some short discussion in which Tomás asked what would happen in Dublin, and one of the two men said that a few of the hotheads may make trouble.

The poor turnout in Co. Cork, where only 60 per cent of the Volunteers mobilised on Sunday, raises questions about the local movement's commitment to an insurrection. A considerable proportion (although less than in Dublin) of those who turned out were aware that some form of conflict was likely.

Riobard Langford, C Company, Cork City Battalion

All the Cork Volunteers went to confession on Easter Saturday night. There was tension and everyone felt the day had come. There was no definite information about what was intended but the feeling was general that something more than an ordinary parade was due on Sunday.

Con Collins, D Company, Cork City Battalion

. . . an indefinite rumour got round on Saturday night that something serious was contemplated and this resulted in many not turning up.

Jeremiah O'Carroll, Farnanes Company

Why only four of our section turned out I cannot remember except maybe they were lackadaisical, or maybe it was some other reason that nobody would care to remember now.

Liam Murphy, D Company, Cork City Battalion, and IRB

On Easter Sunday 1916, 154 officers and men from the four city companies paraded ... every man on the rolls was mobilised. Thirty-eight officers and men of D Company turned out, out of about 120 on the rolls . . . The instructions that had been received were for an ordinary two-day exercise, but rumours were going about towards the end of the week that it was 'Der Tag'. When most of the men were advised to go to confession on Saturday, colour was given to the rumours and many did not parade because of the possible consequences.

Patrick Harris, B Company, Cork City Battalion

At the hall in Sheares Street on Sunday morning, scapulars and medals, which had been sent by some convent, were distributed, and it was evident that there was going to be a fight, but we did not know where we were going or what plans had been made.

Eamon Ahern, Dungourney Company

It was only when they saw so many of the Cork Volunteers going to Holy Communion on Sunday morning that they [the RIC] began to suspect something unusual was on.

James Crowley, Timothy Riordan and Maurice Healy, Ballinhassig Company

Our appearance [at Mass] aroused the interest of the priests there [Upton] and they commented on our foolishness in going out, poorly armed as we were, against immense and powerful forces.

Patrick O'Sullivan, Kilnamartyra Company

On the way my uncle, Dan Harrington, asked me, 'Do you expect to come back today?' I said I supposed we would go out some day and not come back. He said, 'We will be fighting.'

Séamus Fitzgerald, Cobh Company

None of us had any knowledge that an insurrection had been planned.

Cornelius Murphy, B Company, Cork City Battalion

All the rifles were collected and every man who paraded in B Company had a rifle. There was a considerable quantity of .303 ammunition. I know, I carried nearly a hundredweight on my back that day – including a spare pair of heavy boots.

Liam Murphy, D Company, Cork City Battalion

Most of D Company had rifles, some Mausers, some Italian. A few men were armed with revolvers. The result of collecting the arms of the men who did not parade was that almost everyone had arms of some kind. I had about 100 rounds of .303.

Cornelius Murphy, B Company, Cork City Battalion

Most of the county companies were badly armed, shotguns and pikes being the main weapons, and I think we were all more or less influenced by the tactics of the Wexford men of '98.

James Walsh, Lyre Company

Our arms consisted of a dozen shotguns, a dozen pikes and a couple of small rifles. We had about twenty rounds for each shotgun and about 100 rounds for the two small rifles.

Cornelius O'Mahony, Ahiohill Company

We had no rifles in the company. We had three air guns and ten or twelve shotguns, either belonging to the men themselves or on loan from local farmers.

Patrick Higgins, Cork Brigade officer

An old Fenian – Bill Connors from Crookstown – came along and joined us near Coolcower. He marched to Macroom, and was the oldest man in the whole parade. I said to him, 'You have no gun,' and he answered, 'Well, I'll stop a bullet anyhow.'

Tom Hales, Ballinadee Company

Discussing the possibility of a fight with Seán O'Sullivan on the road to Macroom, he said, 'The most we could do was to create a moral effect.'

Patrick Looney, Donoughmore Company

Later in the evening, Tomás MacCurtain and Terence MacSwiney arrived in Beeing in a car driven by Dave O'Callaghan. Tomás spoke to me and said, 'All is over, Casement is arrested and the guns are probably lost.'

Denis Lordan, Kilbrittain Company

Tomás MacCurtain and Terence MacSwiney arrived in a motorcar. They conveyed the news to Tom Hales that Eoin MacNeill had ordered off the intended operations. There was a short discussion, during which Tom Hales questioned MacNeill's authority to issue such a counter-order. It was decided that the whole force assembled at Kilmurray would march to Macroom and return home from there.

Charles Cullinane, Lyre Company

It was a beautiful morning but the day changed and turned out to be one of the wettest we could remember. All the men were saturated to the skin. Most of them had no overcoats.

David O'Callaghan, Castletownroche Company

Everybody was then drenched to the skin, as it had been raining heavily all evening. Nevertheless, all were in good spirits and many national songs were sung. There was an old Fenian in the shop at Ahadillane . . . He was inclined to be critical of the rising generation – he thought they were only 'playacting' with guns, but when he looked at our saturated clothes, he said that 'The weather was always on the side of England.'

Michael O'Sullivan, Castletownroche Company

Faces were coloured green where the dye from the hats had run on to them.

Christopher O'Connelly, Eyeries Company

We had brought no food, and there was very little to be had locally, with the result that most of the men had nothing to eat. The people of the locality were quite indifferent. Early next day we straggled back home.

Cornelius Murphy, B Company, Cork City Battalion

When we returned to Cork on Monday night we were wet, sore and sorry.

In Cork, as elsewhere, the failure to rise during Easter Week would haunt many. Unaware of the significance, scale and purpose of the fighting in Dublin, the Cork leadership was unwilling to join a rebellion that appeared little more than a futile gesture. Its decision to surrender arms to avoid conflict, in a deal brokered by the local bishop and lord mayor, represented a further humiliation.

Seán O'Hegarty, IRB and O/C, Bandon and Ballingeary companies

I gathered from their talk [on Easter Monday] that they [MacCurtain and MacSwiney] had been frequently in Dublin of late and that they had all along foreseen what actually happened, viz., a conflict of orders from the two sides there – the IRB and the Irish Volunteers. They told me how they had conflicting orders during the week and a final note on Friday from Seán MacDermott that all were now agreed to go ahead on Sunday; and then MacNeill's Sunday morning cancellation. They told me the arms ship was sunk and Casement captured; but it was mainly of the evil of 'dual control' that they spoke, and that seemed to exclude everything else from their minds.

Marie Perolz, Irish Citizen Army, and Military Council despatch carrier

When I got to Cork about 10.30 [on Monday], I went to MacCurtain's shop at Capwell. I saw Mrs MacCurtain and Tomás's foxy brother and, while Mrs MacCurtain was nice to me, I knew she did not want me. 'Where is Tomás?' 'I don't know.' . . . I did not see Terence MacSwiney. My impression was they did not want to find him. They said Cork will do its duty.

Riobard Langford, C Company, Cork City Battalion

A Miss Perolz arrived from Dublin on a motorbike on Monday with Pearse's message 'We start here at noon today.' She went to the hall but there were no senior officers there. It was late on Monday evening when MacCurtain and MacSwiney arrived in Cork and saw this message for the first time . . . There was some question of the authenticity of the message and Tomás said he had never known Pearse to sign in that way before. Mary MacSwiney was in the hall and she took part in the discussion about what action was to be taken. She said in effect: 'Was a fine body of men like the Irish Volunteers to be dragged at the tail of a rabble like the Citizen Army?' . . . I was in the hall all day on Monday. The atmosphere was very tense and strained. The younger officers particularly wanted to fight, and were resentful of the waiting policy adopted by the leaders. They expressed their views, but the weight of the influence and authority of the older men – as they regarded the brigade officers – was against them. A lead from them would have taken the majority of the Cork men into the fight in some way. Action in the city may have been inadvisable, but there was nothing to prevent the Volunteers mobilising outside the city on Monday or Tuesday.

Patrick Higgins, Cork Brigade officer

They were in a terrible mood, frustrated, puzzled and anxious. Two messages had come to Cork from Dublin that day . . . it was clear they were aware of the position in Dublin . . . I felt they had made up their minds not to call out the men again, and that they were justifying that decision by a recapitulation of all the arguments against such a course. They felt that the men would not turn out again if called upon. They seemed to have sensed the position in Cork, and to be to some extent influenced by consideration for the men, and the weakness of the arms position. There was the further difficulty that the county companies had all been demobilised, and no speedy means existed of remobilising them. They felt their own responsibility very keenly. The whole thing looked odd and mad at that moment. We discussed what would be done if they decided on mobilisation. There never had been any plan for Cork except the concentration on the previous day, and they did not know what to do. Terry said something to the effect that he could not stand for the city being bombarded and people being shot down.

Fred Murray, D Company, Cork City Battalion

My opinion is that if the arms ship had not been captured, the Rising would have taken place in Cork in spite of the countermanding orders.

Cork City and County Brigade officers

In view of the fact that nine separate despatches arrived in Cork during those fateful days, some contradicting or countermanding, others affirming previous orders, it can be well understood how bewildering the confusion was, and how unenviable the position of the Cork command.

Michael Ó Cuill, Volunteers, Cork

On Tuesday or Wednesday I met Tomás MacCurtain. He was very disappointed and seemed to blame the Dublin men. They did not seem to have acted in accordance with the arrangement made with Cork as he understood it . . . Tomás referred to the confusion that had arisen over the orders they had received from Dublin and said that he had told Pearse that they in Cork would obey any order issued by MacNeill as chief of staff . . .

I went to the hall. There I saw Tomás, Terry and Seán O'Sullivan . . . I said I was going to Dublin if there was to be no fight in Cork. They said everyone had the right to do what he thought best. They had decided to stand to arms and defend the hall if it was attacked.

Nora Daly, Cumann na mBan and Military Council despatch carrier

I told them what had been done in Dublin and Seán MacDermott sent me to deliver a verbal message: 'Tell Terry MacSwiney we are in action and I know he will follow us.' They both seemed to think Dublin was wrong and they were right . . . I told them I did not know why Dublin decided to go out on Monday but whatever Tom Clarke and Seán McDermott did was right in my eyes. They said they would wait until they were attacked as they were not in a position to attack . . . the only decision I could get out of Terry MacSwiney and Tomás MacCurtain was that they would not give up their arms.

James Crowley, Timothy Riordan and Maurice Healy, Ballinhassig Company

There were a lot of wild rumours. We were waiting for definite orders . . . We continued to stand to until the end of the week, but got no orders from anywhere.

Patrick Houlihan, Annascaul Company

We heard that the boys in Dublin were out and we were all anxious to do something, but no orders came.

Felix O'Doherty, Blarney Company

Thus a week of agony passed . . . here were we standing idle while our comrades were being surrounded in Dublin.

Annie MacSwiney, Cumann na mBan, and sister of Terence MacSwiney

. . . [Donal Óg O'Callaghan] spoke very critically of the Volunteer leadership in Cork, said that the Volunteers could have been got out of the city very easily during the week . . . He thought the Volunteer leaders were 'three incompetent men in a state of blue funk'. Seán O'Sullivan sat through this tirade with a quiet smile on his face but said nothing at all . . . On that Saturday the surrender took place in Dublin and, of course, changed the whole situation. On the following Monday night a meeting was held in the Volunteer Hall, which decided, by a large majority, to give some arms into the custody of the Lord Mayor 'until the crisis was over'.

Cornelius Murphy, B Company, Cork City Battalion

On the Monday after Easter Monday the meeting was held in the hall in connection with the proposal to surrender the arms to the bishop. The bishop and the lord mayor addressed the men. The fight was over in Dublin, the leaders were being executed, and their advice carried weight with the Volunteers. We were all young and inexperienced. It was no longer a case of being arrested – it was a case of being shot. The decision was that two thirds of the meeting or more voted in favour of surrender.

Fred Murray, D Company, Cork City Battalion

Tomás and Terry were in favour of it and Terry came to me and asked me to help in getting it carried.

Tom Hales, Ballinadee Company

I think it was on Friday that Pat Higgins came from Cork with news of the agreement to surrender arms. I was entirely against it; I would not countenance it and I refused to carry it out in this area.

Liam Murphy, D Company, Cork City Battalion, and IRB

I did not attend the meeting called to discuss the question of arms. I had heard what was to be proposed and refused to attend.

Tom Hales, Ballinadee Company, Co. Cork

Early in 1917 an enquiry was held in Cork into the action of the brigade officers at Easter 1916. I was there, so was Mick Hyde, and most of the units of the brigade were represented by one of their officers. My accusation against the brigade officers at the time was that we had been left in a fog, that arms had been lost unnecessarily and that the loss of arms all over the south was due to the action of Cork. I felt that the same situation could arise again and that something should be done to ensure that the same confusion would not arise. I was hard on the brigade officers and both of them felt very keenly about it. There was no mention of the effect of the loss of the arms ship at this enquiry. Tomás MacCurtain said to me later, 'If I live I will redeem 1916.'

Patrick Higgins, Cork Brigade officer

I thought they were concerned to advertise the fact that they (the Ballinadee men) wanted to fight and others did not. That point of view got little support, and the general feeling was in favour of reorganising and carrying on the movement under the same leaders.

Although over a thousand Volunteers rose throughout rural Ireland – mainly in Louth, Enniscorthy and east Galway – the only successful military engagement occurred in Ashbourne, Co. Meath, where sixty Volunteers from Dublin's 5th (Fingal) Battalion inflicted a decisive defeat on the Royal Irish Constabulary. The mobility and firepower of the rebel column, and its willingness to adapt to circumstances on the ground, anticipated the tactics of the guerrilla war that would follow, but the rebels also benefited from the tactical errors of the police and the striking reluctance of many individual policemen to engage the Volunteers.

Christopher Moran, Swords Company, 5th Battalion

On Easter Sunday, the battalion was ordered to mobilise at Saucerstown, the residence of Frank Lawless. About 200 men mobilised, all armed with rifles or shotguns, and carrying rations for two days. The quartermaster, Frank Lawless, distributed a lot of brand-new shotguns to Volunteers there. We were kept hanging around Saucerstown until 12 p.m. that night. Meanwhile, there was great coming and going of our senior officers, and it was quite apparent that something had gone wrong with the plans for the day. The Sunday papers had carried the notice from MacNeill, calling off the mobilisation and movement of all Volunteer units for that day, and this left us all in a great state of confusion. At 12 p.m. we were disbanded and told to proceed to our homes, and to hold ourselves in readiness to mobilise again at a moment's notice.

Charlie Weston, Lusk Company, 5th Battalion

There was great disappointment amongst the men but they took it quietly as just another of the many disappointments they had become used to.

Joseph Lawless, C Company, 1st Battalion

When my father came into my room [on Monday morning] holding a piece of paper in his hand, his eyes were alight with the excitement of joyful news, and with the announcement 'the day has come at last' he handed me the note to read. Pearse's peculiar backhand writing was unmistakable, and as I read the one-line message – 'Strike at one o'clock today. P. H. Pearse' – I knew the reason for his feeling of excitement which had now caught me up, and had me frantically dressing as I tried to think what had to be done.

Richard Hayes, vice-commandant, 5th Battalion

[Thomas] Ashe and Coleman returned with me to my house at Lusk, and about 7 a.m. we were roused from sleep by Joe Lawless, who handed Ashe a despatch from P. H. Pearse to his father (Frank Lawless) with (as well as I can remember) the words – 'Strike at one o'clock today.'

Joseph Lawless, C Company, 1st Battalion

Of course, everyone kept talking to everyone else, and I was questioned for further details, which I could not give, but I have a remembrance of Ashe shaking me by the hand, and saying something to the effect that 'This would be a day to be remembered in Ireland for evermore,' while his eyes shone with the light of excitement.

Richard Hayes, vice-commandant, 5th Battalion

Orders were at once issued to the four companies to mobilise at twelve o'clock midday at Knocksedan, a few miles from Swords.

The companies arrived fairly to time but in lesser strength than on the previous day – I should say approximately sixty.

Joseph Lawless, C Company, 1st Battalion

Tom Duke was getting ready to open drills for potatoes when I called and told me he was not going to be fooled by such false alarms again . . . after some words on the matter, he assured me that the St Margaret's men would be there when they heard the first shots fired and I had to be satisfied with this.

Charlie Weston, Lusk Company, 5th Battalion

There were very few there, only Swords men. There were only about sixty-five all present now.

Charlie Weston, Lusk Company, 5th Battalion

. . . we climbed the poles and cut the telephone wires. The local people who knew me well were shouting, 'Charlie Weston, are you gone mad?' . . . There were no barricades on the road and no holding up of traffic. We could hear the firing in the city quite plainly.

Michael McAllister, Swords Company, 5th Battalion

We remained in Finglas on that Easter Monday night, which turned out very wet, and, as we had no tents or shelters, we all got a good soaking.

Charlie Weston, Lusk Company, 5th Battalion

On Tuesday morning a sheep was killed by Joe Taylor, who acted as butcher. We had rashers, eggs, tea and bread for breakfast . . . Miss [Mollie] Adrian returned about 11 a.m. with instructions to send forty men into the city to the GPO. Twenty men were detailed by Ashe and under Dick Coleman proceeded to the city . . . Dick Mulcahy joined us at Finglas that day, also some men from the city who could not contact their own units.

Christopher Moran, Swords Company, 5th Battalion

Dick Mulcahy seemed to be more or less in charge now.

Charlie Weston, Lusk Company, 5th Battalion

On Wednesday morning we were organised into four sections. I was given command of No. 1 Section . . . At about 8.30 a.m. we moved on Swords with the object of capturing Swords police barracks and Donabate police barracks and destroying communications generally.

Bernard McAllister, Donabate Company, 5th Battalion

We cycled up to the barracks [in Swords], jumped off and rushed in. The sergeant and another constable were present. We told them we had come for the rifles. They offered no resistance. We took possession of the rifles and ammunition, about six rifles and fifty rounds of .303 for each.

Christopher Moran, Swords Company, 5th Battalion

The police [in Swords] were allowed to remain in the barracks and go free, on giving an undertaking that they would take no part in the fighting which we expected was yet to come, or assist the British Army, in any way.

Charlie Weston, Lusk Company, 5th Battalion

We were ordered to take a pickaxe, sledge and crowbar and burst in the door. Six of us rushed up to the door [of Donabate RIC barracks] and shouted at the police to surrender or we would break in the door. The answer was a revolver shot fired out of the top window. Immediately the window was riddled by bullets from our men. We proceeded to break in the door . . . When the door went in they immediately shouted that they would surrender . . . We went into the barracks and Ashe took the day book and looked up the entries . . . We had a chat with the police, who had now got over their nervousness.

Jerry Golden, B Company, 1st Battalion

We advanced up the road towards Garristown [in the early hours of Thursday] and on arrival outside the RIC barracks the commandant called on the occupants to surrender their arms to him in the name of the Irish Republic . . . As the RIC sergeant had refused to obey the commandant's order to hand over their arms, the commandant ordered us to fire a volley into the building. As we did so the police shouted that they would surrender if we spared their lives. The commandant replied that if they came out unarmed none of them would be injured. After a few minutes' delay the sergeant and three men opened the front door and came out unarmed . . . During this time Dick Mulcahy and his men had entered the Post Office and severed the telephonic and telegraphic lines, smashed the instruments and taken away all the stamps and post orders and money-order books, together with all cash in the office, giving a receipt for same in the name of the Irish Republic. When the commandant had ascertained that all arms and equipment had been removed from the barracks, he ordered some of the men to remove the imperial coat-of-arms plaque from the front of the building. While the men were doing this, one of them hoisted the tricolour on a brush handle to one of the high chimney pots.

Charlie Weston, Lusk Company, 5th Battalion

On Thursday morning some of the men were grousing that the Volunteers in the country had not risen. Ashe paraded the battalion in a field and spoke to us. He told us the facts as far as he knew them. He said the rest of the country outside Dublin had not risen, as far as he knew, but that they would rise. He said he was not going to keep any man against his will and that anyone who wished to go home was perfectly free to do so. He reminded us that we had sent twenty men to Dublin city, where he was sure they were in the thick of the fight. He called up No. 1 Section first and said, 'Are you willing to go on? Any man that is not let him step out.' Every man of the section shouted, 'Fight on.' . . . A couple of men from St Margaret's and Duke and O'Reilly, however, decided to go. I think Ashe was glad to be rid of them, as they were potential troublemakers from the start.

Bernard McAllister, Donabate Company, 5th Battalion

. . . while we were billeted at Baldwinstown on Easter Thursday morning a Father Kevelehan came into the camp. Ashe told us that he was the son of a Fenian and that he wanted to bless us. We all knelt down and he gave us conditional absolution and his blessing. A good number of the men went to confession in the chapel at Garristown that morning.

Charlie Weston, Lusk Company, 5th Battalion

Friday morning I was told by Ashe that we were going to cut the railway line at the Black Bull and at Batterstown and to take the police barracks at Ashbourne en route.

Jerry Golden, B Company, 1st Battalion

While we were waiting for the men to get into position, we saw three RIC men cycling round a curve in the road from Ratoath. The commandant ordered us to take them prisoner and disarm them; four or five of us rushed across the road and called on them to halt. The two constables jumped from their bikes, threw their arms and ammunition pouches on the side of the road, raised their hands over their heads and shouted 'we surrender', but the sergeant, whom I knew personally (Sergeant Brady of Dunshaughlin), fell against the ditch and tried to draw his revolver and shoot me, crying out at the same time, 'Golden, I'll get you before I die.' I was armed with a Martini rifle with a long French bayonet loosely attached and when I raised the rifle to fire and wound him, the cartridge jammed in the breech, so I made a lunge at him with the bayonet, but he avoided my thrust and when I withdrew the rifle the bayonet remained struck in the ground and the sergeant had grasped the muzzle of my rifle and pulled me down on top of him. I dropped the rifle and caught him by the throat and tried to strangle him. He had just drawn his revolver from his holster when Bartle Weston came to my assistance and struck him on the head with the butt of his rifle. The sergeant dropped his revolver and shouted out, 'Don't kill me'; he was then taken prisoner and disarmed.

Charlie Weston, Lusk Company, 5th Battalion

Ashe now had a conversation with the police prisoners. The police agreed to go into the barracks and ask their comrades to surrender. He put white handkerchiefs around their caps to indicate they were under a flag of truce. They went into the barracks but did not return . . . We got in front of the barracks and opened fire. Our fire was heavy and the windows were quickly shattered. Behind us were a couple of men with canister grenades. One of these grenades was thrown at the barracks and exploded with a terrific bang, but it did not go near the barracks. Immediately the garrison shouted that they would surrender and firing ceased. We all stood up and shouted at them to open the door. As they were trying to open the door, I heard Ashe shout, 'Stop them cars.' The garrison did not open the door and, on looking up the road towards Slane, I saw a number of cars coming down the hill from that direction.

Constable Eugene Bratton, Royal Irish Constabulary

On Friday morning a force of police were assembled in Slane under the command of County Inspector Gray and District Inspector Smyth . . . The county inspector was in the front car. I was driving the district inspector in my car, which was the last of the convoy. On reaching a point above Kilmoon we pulled up and the DI spoke to a man on the road. This man pointed with his hand and said: 'They' (meaning the rebels) 'are all along that road.' We started again immediately and did our best to get up to the county inspector to warn him, but the other drivers in front would not give way to us.

Charlie Weston, Lusk Company, 5th Battalion

The first cars pulled up short of the crossroads and I saw police jump from them with helmets and rifles. We jumped across the ditch into the field in front of the barracks, and in a few seconds Mulcahy came to me and ordered me to go up to the cross and see how many police were in it and where they were. I got to the cross and had a quick look up the road. I estimated there were a hundred police there and I returned to Mulcahy and reported this to him. He said, 'It does not matter if there is a thousand, we will deal with those fellows. Get your men along the road to the cross and hold the police from the cross. Keep them under fire and don't waste ammunition.'

Bernard McAllister, Donabate Company, 5th Battalion

Two civilians arrived on the scene in a small two-seater car during the fight. Apparently the police thought those were Ashe and Dr Hayes, as their car was similar to the one used by them, and they shot both of them.

Joseph Lawless, C Company, 1st Battalion

Ashe now appeared on the road and, after a hurried consultation with him, Mulcahy informed us in a very assured tone that the police had not a chance of success. They had walked into a trap, he said, and we were going to rout or capture the entire force when our attack was launched ... Mulcahy's words and confident manner completely restored our morale, and we again felt slightly ashamed of our needless feeling of panic before his appearance on the scene.

Jerry Golden, B Company, 1st Battalion

We were about two minutes firing at the motorcars when we saw one of the police – a Sergeant Shanaher – step out of the front one and attempt to cross the road to a cutting in the bank which would give him cover to fire on us. He was just in the middle of the road when I saw Mick McAllister step out on the footpath, raise his rifle and fire at the man, who staggered into the cutting and fell against the side of it with his rifle pointed down the road at us who were at the crossroads and only about sixty yards from us.

Constable Eugene Bratton, Royal Irish Constabulary

Sergeant Shanaher was the first man to fall; he was shot through the heart. He had taken cover at this time. There was a feeling afterwards that this sergeant was shot by one of his own men. He was a bad one and very tough on the men ... Firing was continuous and general by now. I was not armed and in civilian clothes. After some time I moved back towards Kilmoon and after travelling about 200 yards I was held up by a party of rebels who were behind the road ditch in our rear. Just at this moment a volley was fired in our direction. The rebels ducked for cover and I ducked too and out of that position, showing them a clean pair of heels ... I secured a bicycle from a house there and cycled to Balrath barracks and from there I phoned Navan and Drogheda RIC barracks and told them what had happened. I then made my way towards Ashbourne again, but not in too much of a hurry.

Bernard McAllister, Donabate Company, 5th Battalion

We fired on them and actually our fellows were making bets as to who would shoot the most. I noticed several fall and in one case I saw four out of a party of five get hit and fall.

Michael McAllister, Swords Company, 5th Battalion

We opened up with rapid fire on them and soon my rifle was burning my hands. This pinned the police to the ground and what fire was coming from them now became very erratic . . . our men were good natural shots and at this short range I knew we were decimating the enemy in their positions. After the initial burst of fire by us, our men settled down very calmly, and although this was our first experience of being under fire, they were behaving as veterans. They were not firing wildly or wasting their ammunition but deliberately picking their targets and dealing with them very coolly in their own time.

Bernard McAllister, Donabate Company, 5th Battalion

At this stage we could hear Dick Mulcahy, who was apparently in command of a party who was advancing on the police from the Slane direction in the fields on both sides of the road, shouting: 'Drive them out of it.' The police were acting like rabbits being driven from a ditch before a shooting party. We had a clear view and decimated them with our fire. Some took cover under the cars but were visible to us there.

Michael McAllister, Swords Company, 5th Battalion

They were, apparently, hugging mother earth for dear life. Some of them had realised their mistake in getting under the cars and tried to get out of that position but were promptly dealt with by us . . .

James O'Connor, St Margaret's Company, 5th Battalion

Dick Mulcahy then came along and he brought us across the fields, keeping under cover of the hedges and ditches on the main road, on the north or Slane side of the places where the cars were halted. We moved up along the road, firing at any RIC man we could see . . . I thought Dick Mulcahy was a very brave man, as he went up the middle of the road disregarding any cover and firing at the RIC as he went. He had a big pistol.

Charlie Weston, Lusk Company, 5th Battalion

I could hear Mulcahy's voice in the intermittent fire. He was shouting, 'Will you surrender? By [God] if you don't, we will give you a dog's death.'

Michael McAllister, Swords Company, 5th Battalion

All this time they were presenting beautiful targets to us and were crowding in on their comrades who were nearest to us and who were not in any happy position. It was soon apparent that the police were in a state of confusion, and some of them had already discarded their rifles.

Joseph Lawless, C Company, 1st Battalion

. . . as they pushed toward the police position, [John] Crinnigan was following closely behind my father. A few yards away, but concealed from them by the overhanging bushes of the hedge, they could hear a voice loudly berating the police for skulking in the ditch and calling on them to get up and fight like men. Moving out to get a view of the speaker, [my father] saw a police officer (whom we subsequently were told was District Inspector H. Smyth) standing on top of the bank and waving his revolver towards them, as he reviled the police for their cowardice in his efforts to get them to stand up and fight the closing enemy. Smyth was undoubtedly a brave man who stood there exposed, to show the police that they need not fear to get up there also. Hearing the movement of my father towards him, he fired at him on the instant, and his bullet, missing my father, penetrated Crinnigan's heart, killing him instantly. My father's shot at the same time hit Smyth on the forehead and smashed his skull. He still lay as he fell – as I came along – feet on bank and head near the edge of the roadside, and, although his brain matter spattered the grass beside him, he yet lived, his breath coming in great gasps at long intervals, and the muscles of his face relaxed . . . I neither lamented nor rejoiced in the passing.

Charlie Weston, Lusk Company, 5th Battalion

I should add here that there was no fire from the barracks during the fight with the main police force. Some of my men were covering it off to prevent the police from leaving.

Jerry Golden, B Company, 1st Battalion

The police party had a head constable in charge and he told Commandant Ashe that he was the only senior officer left, as the DI was dead and the county inspector seriously wounded. Some of the wounded police were crying out for help and the commandant detailed some of us to attend the wounded while others were detailed to collect all arms, ammunition and equipment . . . There were ten police dead, including DI Smyth, and about fourteen seriously wounded, including County Inspector Gray, who died the next day, and four of the rank and file of the police died before their wounds could be dressed . . .

Joseph Lawless, C Company, 1st Battalion

Some of them were young fellows of twenty-six or seven or thereabouts, and some were middle-aged men of over forty . . . One man, a youngish fellow, had a rather bad scalp wound where a bullet had made a perfectly straight furrow, laying bare his skull from forehead to crown and right in the centre . . . Another oldish man looked sick and frightened-looking, and, noticing that one of his cartridge pouches seemed to have been struck by a bullet, I asked him if he was wounded, but he only shook his head sadly and made no reply . . . The one who had the bad scalp wound was without his helmet, which, no doubt, had been badly damaged by the same bullet. He was probably suffering some pain and was hysterically walking from one to the other asking how bad his wound was.

Bernard McAllister, Donabate Company, 5th Battalion

The police in the barracks surrendered also on seeing their comrades on the road doing so.

Joseph Lawless, C Company, 1st Battalion

Here they were addressed by Ashe from the top of the roadside bank north of the crossroads. Ashe's speech was short and to the point. We knew, and they knew, that there was nothing we could do with such a number of prisoners (about seventy-five, not counting casualties), but, nonetheless, Ashe managed to be impressive and convey a hint of magnanimous forbearance in dismissing them to their homes with the warning that should any of them again be found in arms against the Republic they would be shot out of hand.

Constable Eugene Bratton, Royal Irish Constabulary

When I arrived back at the scene of the fighting, the first thing I saw was the DI's whistle on the road. I knew then that all was up with him. The next thing I saw was the dead bodies of seven of our men on the side of the road. I went further down and I saw Tom Ashe. He had a revolver in his hand and had his men under control. The wounded constables, who numbered, I think, about thirteen, were being attended to by Dr Hayes . . . I got the DI's body into the car and travelled back to his house outside Navan with it, where I handed it over to his unfortunate wife.

James O'Connor, St Margaret's Company, 5th Battalion

Two priests arrived after the RIC surrendered and attended to the dead and wounded. They were very hostile to us and called us 'murderers' . . . We were all in good humour and spirits after our victory at Ashbourne. We now had plenty of rifles and ammunition and plenty of good food.

John Austin, Post Office messenger

Tom Ashe and his men were at the crossroads. They were very excited after the victory and were cheering, as men would after a football match . . . The road that evening was a terrible sight with blood and bandages strewn on it.

Michael McAllister, Swords Company, 5th Battalion

Everyone was in good spirits and our morale had rocketed upwards. This was our first engagement and we had come out of it with flying colours. We now felt that we were a match for any force the British might send against us, even if we were reasonably outnumbered.

Jerry Golden, B Company, 1st Battalion

I am sure if any person could have taken a photo of the column on the march it would have been a unique one, as most of the cyclists had three rifles or carbines slung across their shoulders or strapped to their bikes, and nearly all had not shaved since the previous Monday. We certainly looked like some of the brigands or pirates you would read about in some adventure story.

Charlie Weston, Lusk Company, 5th Battalion

Sunday about 11 a.m. Head Constable Keely of Balbriggan and Sergeant Reilly of Swords of the RIC were held up by our guards and brought into camp. Ashe sent Mulcahy into the city with the head constable to see Pearse. Ashe told me they had surrendered in the city and the police wanted us to surrender also.

Joseph Lawless, C Company, 1st Battalion

Gradually a spirit of utter dejection settled over the camp and men spoke hardly at all . . . by the time he did return, the camp had settled down into a dull apathy that covered, if it did not conceal, the tortured thoughts of its occupants. These thoughts were less concerned with our personal and material well-being than what we imagined to be the shame of our defeat . . . We were naturally apprehensive of our fate and particularly the fate of our leaders, but I think I can truthfully say we were less concerned about this than about the apparent ruin of all our hopes and dreams of a free nation. Walking aimlessly up the avenue with such thoughts running in a never-ending circle through my head, I saw Sergeant O'Reilly sitting by himself on the bank while his guard stood dejectedly by. What did he think about it? He did not look much like a victorious enemy as he gazed sadly about him . . . O'Reilly was one of those, I think, who, finding himself at middle age in the service of the enemy now at war with his countrymen, was seriously disturbed by his latent sympathy with their efforts, but yet felt bound by his contract of service as well as his dependence on it for the welfare of his family.

Bernard McAllister, Donabate Company, 5th Battalion

While Mulcahy was away there was a lot of talk amongst the fellows about not surrendering even if the city had done so. When Mulcahy returned he said to us, 'It is all up, boys.' On hearing this, some of the men broke down and cried bitterly and some of them wanted to fight on . . . Mulcahy now said a few words to us about being soldiers and finished by saying: 'Are you going to desert your officers now?'

Michael McAllister, Swords Company, 5th Battalion

There were groans and catcalls and some of them shouted that it was a trick and that even if the Dublin men had surrendered why should they do so? Mulcahy reminded them that they had come out as soldiers, had behaved as well-disciplined soldiers of Ireland, and that Pearse, who he had seen, was proud of them. It was his orders that they should now surrender as soldiers. This had a quietening effect on the men and you could feel their pride returning.

John Austin, Post Office messenger

When things had quietened down, the surviving police came down to the village and bought themselves some drink and food. They had money, as the rebels had not interfered with any of their personal belongings. They were very shaken and were shivering. One of them remarked to me that the rebels were great men, and I replied, 'If you had won, I know what you would do.'

Nora Ashe, sister of Thomas Ashe

Tomás [Ashe] said the police who took part in the fight at Ashbourne were not a bad lot at all. One of them asked permission to go home to his sick wife and Tomás gave it. They would do anything for him afterwards. While he was in prison in England the police kept his gun and sword polished and in good order for him until he came home.

Constable Eugene Bratton, Royal Irish Constabulary

Subsequent to the battle of Ashbourne I was brought to Buckingham Palace and decorated by the King for my actions. I resented this, but I had no alternative.

9
The Saddest Parting: Surrender

The Rising ended in as chaotic a fashion as it had begun. Although Patrick Pearse signed a general order of surrender at the headquarters of the Irish Command at 3.45 p.m., the only other garrison to surrender on Saturday was the 1st Battalion at the Four Courts. During the next day, the garrisons at Boland's bakery, the Royal College of Surgeons, Jacob's biscuit factory and the South Dublin Union capitulated. The decision to surrender provoked dismay among the rank and file, who had little awareness of the military position beyond their own garrisons and had, in many cases, resolved to fight to the death. Few chose to escape despite plentiful opportunities.

*

The Four Courts garrison surrendered on Saturday evening, except for around sixty rebels in North Brunswick Street who had lost contact with the rest of the 1st Battalion. The latter eventually agreed to an uneasy truce until Pearse's general surrender was confirmed the following morning.

Michael O'Flanagan

I do not know how long I slept but sometime round four o'clock Lieutenant McGuinness wakened me and told me that an order had come through from Commandant-General Pearse to the effect that a surrender had been decided on, and that we were to take steps to give over the position to the enemy forces. In addition, he told me that any men who could manage it should avail of any and every opportunity to escape if it were at all possible. I then went to the toilet for a wash and while there I met the vice-commandant of the battalion, Piaras Béaslaí, and informed him of the position. He knew nothing about the order to surrender and scoffed at the idea, pointing out that the position was 'impregnable and could be held for a month' . . . Some short time afterwards, when all the rifles had been surrendered, Commandant Daly fell-in the battalion in the courtyard of the Four Courts and addressed the men. He told us of the order received, which he had no alternative but to obey, and that as far as he understood the ordinary rank and file would, after interrogation, be set free; but that as far as the officers were concerned he did not know what would become of them. He emphasised the fact that, while we were beaten by a superior military force, we were not, however, cowed, and that we should carry ourselves with pride and conduct ourselves as true soldiers of the Republic.

Eamon Morkan

[The surrender order] was received with grave disappointment, as the great body of the Volunteers had made up their minds to fight to a finish. Speaking for myself I realise now that I was most unreasonable, and at first refused to hand up arms and ammunition. I think this feeling can be explained by . . . the belief that we must not under any circumstances surrender the arms and equipment which we had made so much effort to obtain.

John Shouldice

It was then ascertained that the surrender was unconditional, which put us all in a very depressed state – knowing that we would meet with very little mercy from our old enemy. Nevertheless there was a feeling of pride amongst us that we defied the might of England for a whole week.

Bridget Lyons, Cumann na mBan

A Volunteer rushed in and asked me for a hatchet – we had been using it for chopping wood – and he started to hack the butt of his rifle rather than surrender it. Some others of the Volunteers tried to cut a hole through the wall of the backyard, though I don't know where that would have brought them to. Tom Walsh was among them and he and others cried bitterly. Three fellows came to me and gave me their revolvers to keep for them, thinking that I would get away. Eventually, quite suddenly, I found myself alone.

Seán O'Duffy

Somewhere around three o'clock on Saturday when I was in Moore's factory I met Father Albert. He placed his hands on my shoulder and said, 'My poor fellow, it is all over. Pearse has surrendered.' This shook us very much. I told Father Albert that I could only accept the information from my captain and he immediately went in search of him and soon we all knew the worst. There were between twenty and thirty of us then in Moore's factory. Father Albert hastily heard our confessions. Although we mostly voted 'Aye', it was agreed that if our leader wished to continue the fight we would also do so. He told us that the fight would be continued . . . We barricaded the windows with the material available, mostly portions of cart-wheels. We had nothing else available. A British soldier made his appearance at Lisburn Street when we were barricading a window facing that direction and he was shot by Peadar Breslin . . . About 10 p.m. I heard a voice shouting, 'For God's sake and for the sake of the wounded and dying and for the rest of the people listening to me, the British commandant has agreed to a truce.' Running to a window I beheld, standing on the street with outstretched arms, our good friend Father Augustine. Firing ceased and we made our way to the ground floor, where stretcher parties were organised to bring in the dead and wounded in the vicinity . . . The next thing was a rather pathetic scene in which one of the Cumann na mBan girls wept and she was sought to be consoled by one of the Volunteers, who said there would be plenty of good men left in Ireland; the assumption was, of course, what we all thought – that we were going to be shot.

When Elizabeth O'Farrell, the Cumann na mBan nurse who conveyed Pearse's surrender order to the rebel garrisons, arrived at Boland's bakery on Sunday morning, Éamon de Valera, the 3rd Battalion commandant, did not accept the authenticity of the order, demanding that it be countersigned by his immediate superior, Thomas MacDonagh. De Valera, whose authority had been undermined by his erratic behaviour during the latter part of Easter Week, struggled to persuade his men to surrender.

Joseph Byrne

The whole situation was extremely bewildering owing to lack of any news; and the lull in firing across the city seemed to suggest that some unexpected change had taken place ... we could not conceive a collapse so quickly, believing that the rest of the country had risen. The local sniping still continued throughout the whole of Saturday night.

Joseph O'Connor

... when I saw the commandant, I asked him if he had any orders in case we were forced out of our positions. I meant what direction we were to take, as needless to say surrender never crossed my mind. I knew perfectly well that surrender would mean hanging and the only thing I dreaded was to be hanged. I wondered if they had any plan thought out of a concentration on the Dublin Mountains. The commandant told me that no such plan had been made but that he personally would like to try it when he found that he could be of no further assistance to his comrades in the centre of the city ... When Miss Farrell saw Commandant de Valera the order was not countersigned by the brigade commandant of the Dublin Brigade, and Miss Farrell took the order back, but she returned very soon and satisfied the commandant that it was his duty to surrender. He sent for me and showed me the order. He asked me what my reactions were, and I told him that we came out as soldiers under orders and that we would continue to carry on as such. He then instructed me to mobilise the men and be prepared to march down from the positions to the point of surrender, stating that he himself would, under cover of a white flag, inform the British that we had been ordered to surrender.

Patrick Ward

He [de Valera] made it plain that this was an order he had received himself and which he was passing on as an order. It was possible in the position we had held, not being by any means surrounded on all sides, for the whole garrison to leave by the railway and proceed home quietly, but this would not fulfil the terms of the surrender, and Commandant de Valera stated, as we had gone into battle on an order, the order to surrender was equally binding.

Peadar O'Mara

We could not understand why this should happen . . . The excitement in Boland's was terrible. What did we want to surrender for? This was the main topic. Volunteers were shouting themselves hoarse, denouncing everyone who had surrendered; others were singing songs and some were openly crying.

The Royal College of Surgeons was primarily occupied by the Irish Citizen Army. Shortly after noon on Sunday a white flag was raised over the college as the garrison of 121 rebels (including eleven women) surrendered.

Frank Robbins, Irish Citizen Army

The whole St Stephen's Green division was paraded into the Long Room, when Mallin read out the news . . . Mallin in the course of his address said that it was quite possible for a number of the men and women then present to get back to their own homes, should they desire to avail of the opportunity, and nothing the worse would be thought of them for doing so. The most that could befall himself was to be shot by the British. This was only to be expected, and he hoped to meet it as an Irishman should. A small number of those present took the opportunity of getting away. Any who did this had a definite motive for their action. A few were given instructions to leave for different reasons, though much against their own will. When Mallin made the suggestion that anyone who desired could leave, some of my comrades shouted, 'No! We have worked together, we have fought together, and, if necessary, we will die together!' This statement got the general approval of all.

The next unpleasant task for Commandant Mallin to perform was hauling down the tricolour and putting up the white flag to replace it. While carrying out this act, he and those with him were sniped at from the British posts. The scenes that were occurring inside the college were of a heart-rending nature. Strong, brave, upstanding men and women, all of whom had taken risks of one kind or another during that week, not knowing and not caring if they would forfeit their lives, were broken-hearted. The act of surrender was to each a greater calamity than death itself at that moment ... A British soldier appeared in the building to make arrangements for the surrender with Commandant Mallin. This visit changed the whole atmosphere immediately. Instead of a continuation of the prevailing depression a new spirit of independence, hope and exaltation took its place. We were satisfied that all things that were possible had been done. There was nothing to be ashamed of. A manly part had been taken for the vindication of our principles. We had failed in our object; others had failed before, and they had not been ashamed or afraid of the consequences. Why should we?

Jacob's biscuit factory, which saw less action than any other garrison, had the most disorderly surrender. Its distraught commandant, Thomas MacDonagh, appeared overwhelmed after O'Farrell's arrival on Sunday morning. Declaring that he would never surrender, MacDonagh relented at around three in the afternoon after General Lowe personally made clear the consequences – for his men and the local residents – of a refusal to surrender. MacDonagh came close to provoking a mutiny when he disowned responsibility for the surrender, telling his men that he did not believe the assurances (offered by a priest) that none who surrendered would be shot.

Peadar MacMahon

On arrival, I was shown into the room occupied by Commandant MacDonagh and by Major MacBride. I told Commandant MacDonagh what had happened in the Green and gave him the despatch from General Connolly to Commandant Mallin. Commandant MacDonagh said that he would never surrender; that General Connolly was a prisoner and that he would not take orders from a prisoner.

Father Aloysius, Capuchin friar

He said they had ample provisions and could hold out for some weeks. MacDonagh believed that a peace conference in Europe was on the point of being summoned and was convinced that Ireland would command attention and a right to participate if it were a belligerent.

John MacDonagh

Tom [MacDonagh] said as Pearse was a prisoner he was not a free agent to give orders. Finally the instruction from Pearse was brought by the priests and Tom, after consultation with the other officers, consented to go out to meet the British general [Lowe] . . . Father Monaghan begged the men to go home for God's sake, but they remained till Tom came back and lined us all up outside to surrender.

Louise Gavan Duffy, Cumann na mBan leader

When Thomas MacDonagh came back I said to him that it was all over, that it should not have taken place, that it was wrong and could not have succeeded. He said to me, 'Don't talk to my men if that is the way you are feeling. I don't want anything to be putting their spirits down.'

Eamon Price

On his return he summoned all officers to the staff room. A silent company awaited his report. Major MacBride sat calmly beside him at a table. Tomás announced that Pearse had surrendered and had issued an order to all units to do likewise. He read the order, pointing out that we were not bound to obey orders from a prisoner. He solicited the views of those present as to the most desirable course to be pursued. Each officer spoke up in turn, and though some were in favour of fighting it out the majority counselled obedience to the order. Outstanding amongst the former was, I remember, Séamus Hughes. He delivered a fiery speech, pointing out that by surrender we would, in fact, be offering our leaders as a sacrifice and that it were better to die with guns in our hands than to face the firing squad. On the other hand Micheál O'Hanrahan in his slow, calm and reasoned tone advised surrender. Personally I supported Micheál. By holding out in Jacob's we were inviting the destruction of the factory by incendiary shells and not merely the factory but the surrounding thickly populated areas. If we left

Jacob's we could only reach the country in twos and threes and our prospects of getting together again were well-nigh hopeless. MacDonagh listened carefully and then summed up. His voice shook as he spoke and finally with tears in his eyes broke down, crying, 'Boys, we must give in. We must leave some to carry on the struggle.' It was a poignant moment and one to remain indelibly in the memories of those present. We were ordered to convey the decision to our men and to make the necessary arrangements for evacuation. When the garrison was assembled on the ground floor, there was a scene of incredible pandemonium and confusion. Men, old in the movement, seeing their dearest hopes dashed to the ground, became hysterical, weeping openly, breaking their rifles against the walls. Others took things quietly but grimly prepared for the inevitable. I advised the very young lads and the older married men with dependent children who were not in uniform to try to get away. I must say that not all took that course but stuck manfully to their officers.

Thomas Slater

There was a good deal of confusion and a lot of recrimination that we were surrendering without having been in action at all . . . a good lot of us cleared out and got away.

Thomas Meldon

I came across a young Volunteer (later Commandant Thomas Burke of 2nd Battalion, Dublin Brigade) leaning on a shotgun and in floods of tears. Feeling that he required some heartening, I spoke to him, and, much to my surprise, was turned on with the bitter retort: 'I came out to fight, not to surrender.'

Padraig Ó Ceallaigh

I saw a few Volunteers hurling their guns away in disappointed rage. For some others there was, I think, a feeling of relief that the strain of the week was over; the strain on us was probably more intense because of our comparative inactivity. There was also the uncertainty . . . we rank and file had only a dim idea as to what was happening elsewhere in Dublin and none at all of the position outside it.

Maire O'Brolchain, Cumann na mBan

I fainted at the news, it nearly broke my heart. After a week in which Tom MacDonagh kept us up by telling us 'We are a great success' – even after going up on the roof to look across at the GPO – such flames! I cannot forget it – Poor Tom, he was so full of hope.

Séamus Pounch, Fianna Éireann

I dumped my gun with the rest and it was the saddest parting I can remember.

Michael McDonnell

I said to him [John MacBride]: 'Commandant, you had better get out here.' He replied by saying: 'Mac, every G-man in Dublin knows me.' And I said I had been upstairs looking out the window and there was not a G-man in sight . . . He slightly bowed his head as if in deep emotion and replied: 'Oh, Mac! I wouldn't leave the boys.'

Until the arrival of Thomas MacDonagh, who conveyed the news of Pearse's surrender order, morale had remained high at the South Dublin Union, whose small garrison had successfully resisted British attacks throughout the week. Éamonn Ceannt's 4th Battalion surrendered at 6.30 p.m. on Sunday.

Michael Lynch

On Sunday morning I was on duty on the front building, when a Franciscan priest from Church Street came into view. He was carrying a white flag and was accompanied by two British officers, one an immaculately dressed fellow of about 5'2", and the other an old veteran of about 5'6". They stopped in front of the side gate. We pulled down the barricade and admitted the priest. He asked for Commandant Ceannt. What took place, I do not know. Shortly after the priest's departure, Commandant Ceannt summoned us all down to one of the dormitories on the ground floor. He told us that arrangements for a surrender had been made, and that he was handing up his post and surrendering to the British. He said that if any of us wished to break away, we could do so, but suggested that, as we had fought as an army for the week, we should surrender as an army. Not a single man left.

James Coughlan

'As for us,' he [Ceannt] said, referring to the signatories of the Proclamation, 'we know what will happen to us.'

Séamus Kenny

A British officer and Éamonn Ceannt came along [to Marrowbone Lane] and they had the white flag. I think there was a priest with them. One of our fellows got on his knees to shoot the British officer but another of our men took the rifle from him . . . We did not wait to see who else came with them, we hopped it.

Annie Cooney

There was dreadful grousing [at Marrowbone Lane distillery]; they were saying, 'Was this what we were preparing for and living for all this time? Is this the end of all our hopes?' . . . He [Ceannt] was like a wild man; his tunic was open, his hair was standing on end and he looked awful. He evidently hated the task of asking the garrison to surrender. He put his two hands on the barricade, with his head bent, and presented a miserable appearance.

Robert Holland

Colbert saluted Ceannt and walked back towards me in the yard. I asked him what was the news and he said that all was over. When I heard this I felt kind of sick in my stomach, putting it mildly, and everybody else felt the same, I'm sure. It came as a great shock. Colbert could hardly speak as he stood in the yard for a moment or two. He was completely stunned. The tears rolled down his cheeks. I glanced at Captain Murphy and he had turned a sickly yellow. Harry Murray bowed his head . . . Ceannt, the British Army officer and the clergyman had withdrawn to the front gate. Colbert then announced that we were surrendering unconditionally and that anyone wishing to go or escape could do so. We were all in a state of bewilderment but I have a distinct recollection of Joe McGrath (of Hospitals Trust) saying: 'Toor-a-loo, boys, I'm off.' He crossed the wall. Some others broke also.

The rebels experienced mixed emotions during the surrender. Some were relieved to have survived, but many (particularly those in garrisons that saw little action) felt humiliated. The rebel leaders emphasised the importance of an orderly surrender. Given the public hostility at the time, few rebels could have anticipated that their dignified surrender and subsequent punishment would engender more sympathy than the six days of scrappy fighting which preceded it.

Michael Knightly, GPO

I was worked up at the time as I thought of what was likely to happen, especially the shooting of our leaders and the humiliation of the rank and file. I burst into tears. A Church Street priest, who was standing close by, said: 'Ah, be a man.' I felt very hurt but made no reply.

John Kenny, GPO

The ambulance men hurried me away at the order of an officer and I was taken to Jervis Street Hospital, where I was left in the basement with many other casualties. The place was like a charnel-house, but one Volunteer in uniform was trying to prop himself up on his arm and sing 'God Save Ireland' when a rush of blood from his mouth ended the song and, falling back, he feebly waved to me and expired. My next recollection was of lying in a nice clean bed, with a crucifix in my hands and the voice of Reverend Father Flanagan, administrator of the Pro-Cathedral, intoning the prayers for the dying.

Padraig Ó Ceallaigh, Jacob's biscuit factory

Before we reached the British, some of the boys just walked out in the crowd, which almost lined the way to the point of surrender, and escaped. The leaders . . . could easily have escaped. However, they presumably thought they were in honour bound by the agreement to surrender, and the 'hit-and-run' technique of the Black-and-Tan days had not been developed. But, it was the gallant hopelessness of the fight, the executions and the subsequent jailings and repression, that brought about a revulsion of feeling in favour of the Volunteers and indeed largely led to the more successful fight of 1919 to 1921.

Patrick Kelly, G Company, 1st Battalion, Church Street outpost, Four Courts

The colonel swore and asked if this bunch of men and boys had held his battalion for three days. [Gary] Holohan replied that if he (the colonel) thought there were any more men he would have to find them himself . . . We were next told to dump our arms and equipment on the roadway. After parting with my rifle I felt sad, as if I had lost a very dear comrade.

Patrick Smyth, wardmaster, South Dublin Union

He [Ceannt] came out to the British officer and on meeting him the British officer put out his hand to shake hands with him but Ceannt remained rigid and did not shake hands. The British officer said, 'You had a fine position here'; Commandant Ceannt replied, 'Yes, and made full use of it. Not alone did we hold your army for six days but shook it to its foundation.' The British officer then asked him, 'How many men had you here?' and he answered, 'Forty-one, all told.'

Séamus Kavanagh, Boland's bakery

The commandant was ahead of us with a strong guard. One of the British soldiers, pointing to the commandant, asked me, 'Is he your colonel?' I replied, 'Yes, but we do not call him colonel – we call him commandant.' He then asked me his name. I told him it was de Valera, and he said, 'He was a Devilero, all right.'

Joseph Byrne, Boland's bakery

We proceeded in file up Grattan Street, the white flag borne in front. The commandant then gave the order 'Halt! Right turn! Ground arms!' and we cast down our arms and equipment with resounding crashes on the road in futile anger and disappointment at the unfortunate end of our bid for freedom and at the thought of having to deliver ourselves as prisoners to an enemy who, we knew, would not acknowledge us as combatants in war, but as outlaws without any of the rights of enemy prisoners.

James O'Shea, Irish Citizen Army, College of Surgeons

Major [de Courcy] Wheeler asked Mallin were all his men here. When Mallin replied that they were all here, Major Wheeler was surprised, as he thought there would be about 200. He then addressed us and told us to get blankets as we might need them. We were then formed in twos and marched out of the college. We were all right until we got to Grafton Street, when the guards got tough. Smoking or talking was forbidden. We were marched to the Castle and got a good idea of what we would have to go through from the Dublin Fusiliers, who cursed and jeered us in Dame Street. We were marched into the Castle yard and into a yard on the left, where we saw a big pit. We were told that in an hour's time we would be in it. They made a jeer and joke of Madame Markievicz . . . After a time we were marched down to Kingsbridge, through Thomas Street, where there was a great display of soldiers' women shouting, 'Bayonet them,' etc., and then on to Richmond barracks.

Frank Robbins, Irish Citizen Army, College of Surgeons

At the head of the column was Commandant Michael Mallin and Madame Markievicz, who looked very picturesque in that strange and rare scene by the fact of her attire. She was dressed in an Irish Citizen Army tunic, a pair of riding breeches and puttees and a lady's hat with an ostrich feather around the band, part of which showed slightly over the top. Hundreds of people from around the vicinity were standing about, some out of curiosity, a small number sympathetic towards us, but the vast majority openly hostile.

Liam Tobin, Four Courts

. . . we were feeling rather disheartened as we were marching from the Four Courts, and a number of fellows started shouting that we should whistle or sing something to raise our spirits. As well as I can remember we did whistle 'The Boys of Wexford' or some such marching song, and we felt a little better.

Eamon Morkan, Four Courts

In spite of the seriousness of the situation the Volunteers generally were in very good spirits and insisted on singing and uttering cries like 'We'll rise again.'

Joe Good, Four Courts

There were repeated orders by the British to cease smoking, but apparently at that stage the Volunteers would take orders only from their own officers.

Mortimer O'Connell, Four Courts

We then marched down the quays, turned up to the left into one of the streets and eventually went down Henry Street to the Pillar, where we were searched by soldiers. They had two baskets or crates into which they threw all sorts of things they found in the search. However, when they found money they put it into their pockets instead of into the baskets. At the head of the column was Ned Daly, and forming up the rear was [Piaras] Béaslaí with the men of the No. 1 Dublin Brigade. When Béaslaí was being disarmed they tried to take his sword from him but he refused to hand it over. Breaking it on his knees, he shouted, 'Long live the Irish Republic.'

Eamon Price, Jacob's biscuit factory

In these chaotic conditions Tomás [MacDonagh] instructed me to take charge in marshalling the garrison and advancing it to the place of surrender . . . Here we lined up between cordons of British soldiers blocking each end of the street . . . By a series of parade-ground manoeuvres, the arms were laid down and the men formed up in column of route. I was really proud of my Volunteers then.

Thomas Doyle, South Dublin Union

Éamonn Ceannt and General Lowe marched at the head of the men. Éamonn looked great: he had his shirt thrown open, his tunic thrown open and was swinging along at the head of his men. He looked a real soldier.

Eamon Dore, GPO

One outstanding memory remains of that Easter Saturday evening while we still stood prisoners in O'Connell Street – it was the sound of marching men. Into the street from Abbey Street came the old 1st Battalion with their loved commandant, Ned Daly, leading. Still the same quiet, calm, self-possessed Ned, unconquered and unconquerable as his men marching four deep behind him. He brought them up O'Connell Street, dropped out when he came to his allotted position and then drilled his men, leaving them two deep 'standing easy'. He and they had fought the good fight, held their positions intact and could have held out much longer, but, against his better judgement, he accepted the order of surrender. I heard a British sergeant say to another, 'That's an officer and those fellows know their stuff.'

Thomas Leahy, GPO

Covered by their machine-guns, we formed up as best we could after leaving our wounded sitting up at the side of the wall to be removed by Red Cross ambulance afterwards. We then turned in to Henry Street . . . under their orders and when we reached Nelson's Pillar and halted for a moment, we saw for the first time the state of the late HQ of the Republic – in ruins and still smouldering – and the remainder of that side all in the same condition. Again we got another reminder from the British to get moving and I need not here mention their typical language to us to do so. Both sides of the streets were lined with troops, five or six, with fixed bayonets, machine-guns, artillery and all forces at their command to receive our surrender. One of our group fixed a tricolour to his rifle and gave us the command 'Eyes right to the GPO' before passing it. I learned afterwards his name was Seán McLoughlin, mattress-maker by trade. He formed us up in ranks four deep and gave us the order to march towards [the] Parnell monument, where the British field staff were standing. After being halted by them we got orders to advance in fours and lay down our arms and everything in our possession. Again our comrades gave these people a lesson. Before finally parting with their guns, etc., some of them smashed and left them useless before their very eyes. We were there ordered to line up along the edge of the footpath, the bayonets of the troops in some cases touching our backs, they were so close to us.

John Shouldice, Four Courts

The appearance of O'Connell Street and the GPO – what was left of it – was an unforgettable sight. From the GPO to O'Connell Bridge on both sides of the street the buildings were mostly burned out; a number of them were still smouldering, also a good portion of Lower and Middle Abbey Street. The bodies of some civilians shot during the week were lying about, also a few horses about O'Connell Bridge. The heart of the city presented a picture of utter desolation.

Seán Kennedy, Four Courts

Our first sight of O'Connell Street in ruins made such an impression on us that anything could have been happening in our immediate vicinity without our knowledge. The flames of the burning buildings and the crackling of the burning timbers had such an effect on us that we were dumbfounded. It is a memory that I will never forget.

Fintan Murphy, GPO

It was a sad moment for all of us, whether we felt defiant as some did or just dejected at our failure . . . We marched over opposite towards the Gresham and got the order to 'left turn' facing across the street. The British still kept at a respectful distance till we got the order 'two paces forward – lay down arms – two paces retire'. This done – we were now defenceless and with a rush the British came forward and surrounded our column. They were evidently surprised at the fewness of us and kept enquiring whether there were not more of us to come. The British officers now began to pass down the ranks and with abusive remarks and sneers asked each his name and address, and searched our pockets for bombs and ammunition.

Patrick Rankin, Newry Company, Co. Down

We were marched out to O'Connell Street and halted between the Parnell statue and Nelson Pillar facing the Gresham Hotel, where each Volunteer laid down his arms and ammunition in front of them. We were then eased off from our original positions to make room for further Volunteers and inspected by an enemy officer who was accompanied by about twelve aides-de-camp. When the officer came to me he stopped and discovered at my feet several rounds of dum-dum bullets, called me a dog and several choice names. I stared at him but never answered for fear he would call me a coward. None of my comrades spoke up on my behalf, as they were aware that we had moved from our original position. The officer eventually moved on while his aides were filling their pockets with small arms, etc., for souvenirs. I was saying my prayers as never before as he moved away.

Patrick Caldwell, 'Kimmage Garrison'

A British officer who had been examining the ammunition that we had deposited in O'Connell Street opened a shotgun cartridge and shouted to Captain Lee-Wilson, 'Look at this bally cartridge: it has five bullets, each of which would kill a bally elephant.'

James Kavanagh, GPO

There was a formidable array of British 'brass hats'. You'd think it was the end of the Great War and the Germans were surrendering. They had nearly as many generals as we had men. At least, they looked like generals to me, but then I'm not very well up in military affairs.

Some Volunteers felt that public opinion had shifted during the course of Easter Week. Some of those gathered outside Boland's bakery, the South Dublin Union and the College of Surgeons expressed support for the rebels, while others would have felt it prudent to remain silent. But public opinion remained deeply – and often violently – hostile.

Michael Lynch, B Company, 4th Battalion

At the beginning of the week, the civilian population, particularly the women, were very antagonistic. Some of our men were actually beaten on the face with shawls and hats, and every kind of insult was heaped on us. It was quite different at the end of the week, however, when we marched out [of the South Dublin Union] to surrender. Although a proportion of the people still seemed dazed and almost afraid to voice their feelings, a small group of men and women cheered us to the echo.

Peadar Doyle, F Company, 4th Battalion

All along the route to St Patrick's place we were greeted with great jubilation, particularly in the poorer areas . . . The journey from St Patrick's place to Richmond barracks was not so free and easy as the journey from the [South Dublin] Union.

Robert Holland, F Company, 4th Battalion

On our route we were subjected to very ugly remarks and catcalls from the poorer classes . . . When we were almost at the Coombe maternity hospital, two drunken men insisted on falling in with us. They were ejected from our ranks several times on the route but eventually must have got into the ranks in my rear, for about two months later I saw these two men taking their exercise in Knutsford Prison . . . At Kilmainham we were jeered at and as we passed by Murray's Lane both men, women and children used filthy expressions at us. F Company, which was mainly made up from Inchicore, heard all their names called out at intervals by the bystanders. They were shouting, 'Shoot the Sinn Féin [bastard]s.' My name was called out by some boys and girls I had gone to school with and Peadar Doyle was subjected to some very rude remarks. The British troops saved us from manhandling.

Joseph Byrne, O/C, D Company, 3rd Battalion

We marched out through the Clarence (now Macken) Street gate of Boland's bakery and into Grand Canal Street. Here our spirits were considerably lightened, for a great crowd of the residents in the vicinity, men and women, were out in the street, many weeping and expressing sympathy and sorry, all of them friendly and kind.

Louise Gavan Duffy, Cumann na mBan leader

We saw a large crowd of loafers gazing at the people out of [the College of] Surgeons; they were murmuring against them, but when the order was given to set off a cheer was raised.

Annie Cooney, Cumann na mBan, Dublin

There were two lines of armed soldiers marching at each side of us, for which we were presently thankful, as we would have been torn to pieces by the 'separation' women who followed us shouting out abuse and obscene language at us. They were kept at bay by the soldiers.

John McGallogly, 'Kimmage Garrison'

The civilians (mostly women in shawls) hooted at us as we passed by.

Michael Staines, 1st Battalion

All down Great Britain Street to Capel Street we were booed by the crowd and would have been attacked in some places, only the Notts and Derbys, who lined the street, kept them back. The only place we got a cheer was passing Great Strand Street, where there was quite a crowd of people. I recognised one man in the crowd. When I met him about twelve months afterwards I asked why they cheered while the others jeered. His answer was: 'We were prisoners.'

Frank Burke, E Company, 4th Battalion

Whilst standing here [Sackville Street], looking around at a city in ruins and thinking that by our action we had earned the hatred and contempt of the populace, a fine big member of the Fire Brigade passed along and in a low voice said, 'Ye have my sympathy, boys.' What a consolation it was to us to hear that simple expression.

Mortimer O'Connell, F Company, 1st Battalion

While we waited we saw a big woman of the nocturnal pavement walk down O'Connell Street and outside Gill's she took a slug from a bottle she carried and shouted, 'Up the Bloody Republic.' Immediately an officer and soldiers began to run towards her. We expected she would be bayoneted but that did not happen.

John O'Reilly, Enniscorthy Company, Co. Wexford

At about six o'clock that evening [*c.* 2 May] we were marched – twenty-eight altogether – from the military station to the quay, where we were put aboard the trawler HMS *Aurania*. A considerable number of Arklow people, men, women and children, lined the route and cheered us loudly. This surprised us, as most of the men in Arklow had then been working in Kynoch's munitions factory and some in the British Army. The British officer was very vexed at them cheering us and threatened them with a revolver, and his men put back the crowds with bayonets.

The rebels and British soldiers now came into close contact for the first time. While some soldiers were outraged by the actions of the rebels, many behaved in a professional, curious or even friendly manner.

Joseph Lawless, Swords Company, 5th Battalion

The soldier on my right was a rather beefy red-faced sergeant, and his indignation at our preposterous attack on the Empire knew no bounds. Almost the whole way along [to Swords] he cursed us fervently and went into all the gory details of what he would like to do to us if he had his way. 'Here I am,' said he, 'having come safely through two blankety years in the blankety trenches in France, come here for a blankety rest, and then run the chances of getting a blankety bullet from a lot of blank-blank-blanks like you,' and so on, ad nauseam. I could understand how he felt even then.

Seán Kennedy, C Company, 1st Battalion

After some time there [Sackville Street] we were approached by a British officer who was apparently going round taking the names of the men in the ranks. He was, apparently, a very decent type, and he told us if we had anything on us which we should not have, we were to drop it on the ground at our feet.

Diarmuid Lynch, 'Headquarters Battalion'

At the request of the British major in command of the escort I walked in front with him. He was much interested in the stubborn resistance made by the GPO garrison, and was curious about events therein during the week.

Michael O'Flanagan, C Company, 1st Battalion

We were then interrogated by a British officer whom I later learned was an Irishman named Captain de Courcy Wheeler, who subsequently rose to the rank of major in the British Army. Wheeler, in the course of the interrogation when he came to where I was standing between my brothers George and Frank, all of us being in uniform, said, 'This seems to be a family affair.' He was particularly interested in our cap badge and anxious to know what regiment we belonged to, seemingly regarding the cap badge as a symbol of regimental identification.

Alfred Bucknill, deputy judge advocate general, British Forces in Ireland

I was very surprised to hear two of them, [Piaras] Béaslaí and [Éamonn] Duggan, say they were solicitors.

Josephine MacNeill, Volunteers sympathiser

After some efforts on my part and the cooperation of a decent English officer, whose name I can't remember, I was allowed to see 'Ginger' O'Connell separately in some sort of barrack room. The officer sat there the whole time. When 'Ginger' had gone, the officer, in showing me out, spoke with the greatest respect of the men of Easter Week. He understood from the quality of the prisoners that they were men of high character and motive and many of them of superior education and not the riff-raff they were represented [to be] by the English and Irish press.

Joe Good, 'Kimmage Garrison'

The Volunteers were covered by men with fixed bayonets, and each Volunteer was covered from the rear. Some of the British officers stepped forward and began to meddle with and inspect the arms we had deposited. I considered them rather undisciplined to behave like this in the presence of senior officers and to have much more freedom than I thought proper. Major General Lowe was present. He passed along the ranks of the Volunteers and addressed me, saying, 'What is your name?' I answered somewhat flippantly: 'Good.' He apparently thought this was a joke. I noticed his indignation and said, 'G-o-o-d, Good,' whereupon he said: 'Come on, you're not dead yet.' I answered this by saying: 'No b[loody] fear, I'm not.' He attempted to strike me with his riding cane across the legs and I jumped in the air, missing the cane, whereupon there was a scream of laughter from some British officers who were standing at the entrance to the Gresham Hotel. Lowe then completely lost his head and shouted: 'Go in, the whole b[loody] lot of you,' whereupon they fled like sheep.

. . . To go back to O'Connell Street after the surrender, it would only be fair to say how harsh treatment arose. The bearing and behaviour of the Volunteers was that of men who had done something laudable and, as their behaviour had been chivalrous, they expected that military etiquette would be observed by the enemy. The British soldiers – officers and men – were obviously irritated and puzzled by the Volunteers. They were shocked at the small numbers that surrendered and at the variety and crudity of their arms. They regarded the Volunteers as shameless, impertinent traitors, and said so. The following incident illustrates this: a British sergeant said to one of the Fianna boys: 'Look at this that you fired' and held up for inspection a Howth rifle bullet. It was soft-nosed, fully half an inch in diameter, and was wedged in the cartridge case with paper. 'A dum-dum,' the sergeant said. 'Well, you wouldn't let us get the right stuff,' the Fianna boy answered reproachfully and some of the Volunteers laughed aloud.

John Kenny, F Company, 1st Battalion

We had to go through the ranks of the British at the top of Moore Street and I was foolish enough to ask a soldier for a drink. He raised his rifle with its fixed bayonet in a threatening manner above the stretcher on which I was lying, but another soldier angrily intervened between us and threatened his comrade in turn, telling him he should be ashamed of himself.

Ignatius Callender, D Company, 1st Battalion

Generally speaking the Tommy was not a bad fellow. Personally I found him a decent fellow, even if at times his language was not all that could be desired. Often I heard him speak of the officers in terms not very complimentary.

Many of the soldiers who suppressed the rebels were Irish. Some were even familiar with them: Captain de Courcy Wheeler, for example, arrested his wife's cousin, Countess Markievicz. Some rebels were treated badly but others encountered ambivalence, sympathy and even support from Irish soldiers, many of whom had enlisted in support of Home Rule rather than Britain. These accounts highlight an underlying weakness of British authority in Ireland: its reliance on the pragmatic acquiescence – rather than affection or loyalty – of the population.

Seosamh de Brún, B Company, 2nd Battalion

The factory [Jacob's] was then taken over by a detachment of the Dublin Fusiliers and by a curious coincidence as one brother left the factory in the republican ranks, another marched into it in the uniform of the British Army.

Eamon Price, C Company, 2nd Battalion

A British officer approached me [at New Bride Street] and requested me to arrange the men to lay down their arms. I recognised the officer. He was the son of a judge and a barrister in civil life and I had occasion to do business with him in my capacity as clerk in the High Courts. He recognised me likewise and to a certain extent our relations were friendly and courteous.

Charles Saurin, F Company, 2nd Battalion

. . . a British [Army] NCO picked up one of the revolvers off the ground and strolled over to us and addressing those opposite to him enquired what was the reason for going out with weapons such as these to shoot our own people, as he put it, and to think that we were doing something for Ireland. He added that his father had been a Fenian and that he himself was perfectly convinced that what he was doing now was the right thing for his native land. His eloquence was checked by a sharp-featured officer who came striding across the street to him and said: 'Now then, Saunders, you're always talking, talking; can't you keep quiet for once? What do you mean by talking to a lot of bloody rebels?' A hum went down our ranks as we realised the category in which we were being put and that perhaps there was not going to be so much of the prisoner-of-war business for us . . . The men of the Royal Irish Regiment, who were kneeling or crouching around guarding us [at the Rotunda], started an altercation with the alleged Shropshires through the railings and told them to shut up and clear off and so forth. One of them leaned across to near where I was on the edge of the grass and said: 'Do you know what them so-and-sos would do if they saw a so-and-so German? They'd run like so-and-so hell!'

William Daly, 'Kimmage Garrison'

The military doctor who dressed my wound [at Dublin Castle] was a gentleman who admonished me for being so foolish as to take up arms against the government and destroy the good work that J. E. Redmond was doing. I naturally disagreed with him and took it all in good part. When he finished he asked for a souvenir and I offered the penknife, which he refused, but asked me for any ammunition or anything that would incriminate me, as he would destroy any evidence on me . . . He wished me luck on leaving him.

Maeve Cavanagh, Cumann na mBan, Dublin

At various intermediate stations men were getting in to go back to the front, and the women seeing them off were screaming and wailing. I had the English paper in my hand and one of the soldiers asked to see it. He said to me, 'Isn't it terrible! Have you friends in it?', meaning the fighting in Dublin. I said, 'Yes.' He said, 'If it was conscription we would be all in it with them.' I said, 'What good would you be in that uniform?' . . . On the train there was a fine tall soldier in khaki in the corridor. He started to tear the coat off his back. His comrades tried to pacify him and push him into a carriage. He resented being in the British Army . . .

James Kavanagh, C Company, 3rd Battalion

The prisoners were standing in the channel facing the houses [on Sackville Street] and the guards were standing on the footpath facing the prisoners. Those in front of me were the 18th Royal Irish, and the one immediately in front of me told me he had been a Volunteer, I suppose a Redmond Volunteer, but I didn't ask him. He said we should have waited till they came back from France and they would have been in the fight.

Patrick Colgan, Maynooth Company, Co. Kildare

I was taken by a little brat of a second lieutenant of the Royal Irish Regiment who kept prodding me with his revolver and telling me what a pleasure he would have in killing me. Luckily for me his attention was attracted when the other boys came out. We were put up against the front of a house beside the barricade. The brat placed a soldier facing each of us. He ordered the soldiers to kneel on one knee; the soldiers had levelled their rifles on us. Then a voice above and behind us spoke and enquired what was happening. The brat said he was going to shoot us swine. The voice said he was an Irishman, he was against us, we had fought a clean fight and if the officer gave the order to fire he would fire on him. We thought it was a joke to prolong our agony. The brat was in a rage. He ordered the soldiers to stand up; the voice and the brat kept arguing. The voice reminded the brat that only for the rebellion they would be in France and he wouldn't like it if taken a prisoner to be shot out of hand. An escort shortly afterwards marched us to Mary's Abbey. On the way the soldier on my right said to me, 'That was a near thing, I was the fellow facing you.' I said he couldn't help it. He then asked me if I remembered him. I didn't. He told me he came from Edenderry, Offaly, and that he had travelled in the same carriage from Broadstone Station to Maynooth one Sunday evening some time before when we were returning from seeing a football game between Louth and Kerry.

. . . On Sunday morning we had a new guard. The corporal was a decent poor fellow. When he learned I was from Kildare he became quite friendly. He told me he was from Carlow; his name was Boland. As the day wore on he became inebriated. He couldn't understand why we should start a rebellion until the lads returned from the Dardanelles . . . He brought in porter in his water-bottle. Only Mangan and Seán Milroy drank porter. We collected amongst us and asked Boland to bring us in some bread; in all we collected three shillings. I gave up my remaining 7*d*. He brought us a big loaf, some cheese and another bottle full of porter. Mangan and Milroy had an unexpected feast. By this time he was very tight. He was sitting on the counter drinking with us when a sergeant came along and placed him under arrest . . . The sergeant in charge of our guard (a Dublin man) was a vicious type. He was an ignorant thug. He instructed them to shoot at the least sign of movement. He searched us about twenty times during the night. He seemed very anxious to get possession of a gold watch and chain which Frank Sheridan wore.

James Burke, A Company, 4th Battalion

We were brought over to Kilmainham Jail, where some drunken soldiery of the Dublin Fusiliers immediately set upon us, kicking us, beating us and threatening us with bayonets. As a matter of fact my tunic was ripped off me with bayonets, and our shirts and other articles of clothing were saturated with blood. We looked at one another the next morning and we thought we were dead. The Dublin Fusiliers were the worst of the lot. The English soldiers were mostly decent. Most of them were young fellows who did not know one end of a rifle from the other as far as I could see.

Patrick Kelly, G Company, 1st Battalion

We next had a visit from a soldier who wore the badge of the Royal Irish Fusiliers [in Richmond barracks]. He was very friendly and said he was an Irishman and proud of it and that he admired the way we fought. (He was somewhat under the influence of drink.) He asked if he could do anything for us.

Vinny Byrne, E Company, 2nd Battalion

We were going over to the lavatory under military escort, which was across the square [at Richmond barracks] and I met a sergeant of the Royal Irish Regiment there one evening. He remarked to me that he did not mind fighting with genuine rifles, but firing these Mauser guns was not playing the game. He told me that his captain had been killed at the South Dublin Union, or wounded – I am not sure now – 'a very decent man'. He said: 'You know, I am a Dublin man, and it is hard luck to get shot down by your own.' He asked me did we get any bread and butter since we came in. I replied, no, that we were only getting war-ration biscuits. He said: 'If you can manage to come over in the morning' – that is, to the lavatory – about 10 a.m. – he would see me there and would have some bread and butter.

Seán O'Duffy, A Company, 1st Battalion

After some hours, we were left in a larger room [in Richmond barracks], and one of our number recited the rosary. The armed sentry at the door put in his head and said, 'I am glad to hear you at that, for I'm a Catholic myself.' In all probability, he was one of the Irishmen in the British Army Dublin Fusiliers.

William Christian, B Company, 3rd Battalion

On Saturday morning we were changed from the cattle pens to a long hall in the main [RDS] building. There were about twenty of us (prisoners) in all and the desire to make us comfortable was shown in the large bucket of tea which the English sent in to be shared out amongst us. Later that evening an Irishman, an officer, in the uniform of the RAMC, spoke to [Jimmy] Grace. He spoke in a low tone something to the effect that the Volunteers had surrendered and that their work seemed to have been in vain as the city was in the hands of the English. This was disheartening news indeed and who will blame Grace if he broke down under it. The officer rebuked him and told him not to let the British see how he felt. He could still serve his country by keeping a brave face.

Seán Byrne, C Company, 3rd Battalion

A British officer [at the RDS] asked me had we got anything to eat and I told him we had nothing except water and biscuits. He said to me, 'I'll get some tea, because the same blood is in my veins as is in yours.' One of the soldiers told us that this officer had paid for the tea out of his own pocket.

Some soldiers behaved as occupying armies do everywhere: Volunteers were humiliated, robbed, beaten, bayoneted, threatened with summary execution and murdered in cold blood. The demeaning treatment of the main body of rebels in the grounds of the Rotunda provoked outrage. Inevitably, it was these experiences, rather than the many acts of decency by individual soldiers, which came to shape the popular memory of the aftermath of the Rising.

Joe Good, 'Kimmage Garrison'

We were all marched then to the small green in front of the Rotunda Hospital and forced back until we were closely packed. Eventually we managed to squeeze down into a sitting posture. Those near the margin of the grass plot were threatened with rifle butts when they stretched their feet out on the pathway. An enemy officer, one of our previous prisoners whom we had allowed to depart, walked around the Volunteers, saying: 'I know this one and that one.' 'Monkey-face', 'Beast-face', 'Ape-face', were some of the expressions he used . . . It was impossible to relieve ourselves in any way until morning, we were so closely packed. When we did get to our feet in the morning, a cloud of steam arose in the air.

Michael O'Flanagan, C Company, 1st Battalion

. . . we got no food or water; nor were any arrangements made to segregate the sexes or provide sanitary facilities . . . We were not allowed to rise from the sitting or lying position which we had adopted during the night.

Charles Saurin, F Company, 2nd Battalion

Somewhere about seven o'clock, I should imagine, the military guard was replaced round us by a party of DMP men in full uniform, helmets and greatcoats and everyone armed with a revolver. It was a strong guard and they stood around us at ease or, perhaps I should say, ill at ease, for a more uncomfortable crowd of men I had never seen before. They could not or would not look straight at us, and I think I can give them the credit of stating that I felt they were ashamed of the part they had to play.

Liam Tobin, C Company, 1st Battalion

We thought, as well as I remember, that they [DMP] did not fancy that sort of job, and as a matter of fact we did not either as we thought it was rather lowering to our dignity as soldiers that we should be placed under a police guard. In charge of the enemy forces there was Captain Lee-Wilson, who was dressed in the usual military uniform, but wore a smoking cap with a fancy tassel hanging out of it. He kept walking round and round, stopping now and again to speak to his soldiers, saying, 'Whom do you consider worst, the Boches or the Sinn Féiners?' . . . I remember that evening that those of us who wanted to relieve ourselves had to do it lying on the grass alongside our own comrades; there was nowhere to go and we had to use the place where we lay.

Mortimer O'Connell, F Company, 1st Battalion

I remember, having dozed off for some time during the night, waking to hear a British sergeant shout, 'These are the b[astard]s who shot our men in North King Street.' . . . It became clear to me that we would be massacred by the South Staffordshires for the slightest provocation. However, fortunately for us, a high-ranking British officer who must have understood the position took it on himself, either to relieve that guard of South Staffordshires, or bring in the Dublin Fusiliers to stand between us and the Staffordshires.

Patrick Rankin, Newry Company, Co. Down

The officer in charge was a brute; he gave many orders to sentries, such as 'If any Volunteer stood up or went on his knee he was to be shot.' This officer was dressed in khaki and very drunk. We slept there the whole night; the weather was good, thank God. When morning came there were three or four of my companions lying on top of me and others likewise. The church bells were ringing calling the faithful. An old woman passed by saying, 'God bless you, boys.' I thanked God for one kind person that morning. The enemy officer in charge came along, drunk as usual; he took the rifle with bayonet from the sentry and went over to Willie Pearse, who was close to the path, and cut the epaulette from his tunic with the bayonet.

Thomas Leahy, E Company, 2nd Battalion

During the first stroke of daylight on Sunday morning, 30 April 1916, several of the British officers walked through the crowd of us, jeering and insulting any of our officers they happened to see in uniform and using the usual English foul language. One very small prig made Tom Clarke stand up to be searched or something else, for he seemed to know him from the rest of us. Whatever Tom said to the officer, he just smacked him across the face with his gloves. It nearly caused a riot or bloodshed, for some of the lads jumped up to resent it, only for the intervention of Commandant Ned Daly to ignore the whole thing.

Eamon Dore, Volunteers, Limerick

[Tom] Clarke had an old pre-Rising bullet wound in the elbow which healed partly, making it difficult to flex the elbow. [Captain Lee-]Wilson, finding it difficult to take off Clarke's coat because of the stiffness, just forcibly straightened the arm and so reopened the wound, causing terrible pain. Not satisfied with this he stripped all three to the skin in the presence of us and, being broad daylight, in the presence of those nuns, etc., looking out windows. A comrade of mine who is still alive and who was lying beside me on the grass swore out, 'If that fellow lives through the war – meaning the 1914–18 war – I will search for him and kill him for this.' He and four others kept that promise.

John MacDonagh, C Company, 2nd Battalion

Finally [on Sunday morning], we were all lined up and began the long march to Richmond barracks in Inchicore. Again, as we passed, the British soldiers' separation women screamed and swore at us, imagining that we had perhaps stopped the money they were getting on account of their men fighting in France. On this long march over stony streets, I was struck by the sight of a wife keeping step with her husband, Seumas Murphy, both prisoners. I knew both of them, and knew they had left their young children at home. On the barrack square we were halted, and at once were surrounded by another contingent of soldiers' wives, who picturesquely bally-ragged us. One 'lady' called us 'grocers' curates', meaning grocers' assistants. 'They're not even grocers' curates,' screamed another.

Charles Saurin, F Company, 2nd Battalion

We were sick and exhausted but we tried to carry ourselves well and march like soldiers between the Staffords lads . . . An old woman with a shawl round her standing on the pathway in front of the GPO called out as we went by: 'Look at what was trying to keep out the government. You might as well try and keep out the ocean with a fork.' We crossed O'Connell Bridge, where on the path against the parapet lay a dead man face downwards . . . At the corner of Francis Street . . . was a mass of howling, shrieking women from the back streets who called us filthy names and hurled curses at us. The sentry on duty there kept pushing them back with the butt of his rifle. They kept up their screeching till our column had passed them by. The mounted officer in charge of us showed faint amusement at all these women's hatred and excitement; the Staffords marched stolidly on.

Mortimer O'Connell, F Company, 1st Battalion

On the way to the Richmond a few of us helped Seán MacDermott, whose stick was taken from him. The sergeant bayoneted one or two men on the way up. Going up High Street we were stormed and pelted with refuse of all types and sorts by what we called the 'separation women'.

Eamon Dore, Volunteers, Limerick

Beside me was a comrade called Fitzsimons who turned to me and said, 'Are you down-hearted?', to which I replied, 'Are you?' He said out loud, 'I'm not down-hearted.' The soldier walking beside him lunged his bayoneted rifle at his, Fitzsimons's, 'seat', giving him a nasty wound. We arrived, a rather dishevelled lot, at the Richmond barracks, and it was an all too common sight to see prisoners falling in a faint from loss of food and being prevented for over twenty-four hours from performing the ordinary calls of nature.

Frank Robbins, Irish Citizen Army

On being detained in the Castle for a while a fresh order was given to march, and we then proceeded out by the Ship Street gate to Christchurch Place, High Street, Thomas Street, James's Street, when we reached Richmond barracks in Inchicore. Throughout this journey we were left in no doubt as to the opinions of the vast majority of the citizens, which were expressed in no uncertain language, and the British military were given every encouragement to play havoc with us. Little did we think that the Dublin citizens would ever go so far as to cheer British regiments because they had as prisoners their own fellow citizens – Irishmen and Irishwomen – just as they were. Looking back and remembering these scenes along the route, particularly at Inchicore, the cheering and waving of hats and Union Jacks for the Staffordshire Regiment as they marched us into Richmond barracks, the cries of encouragement to the young Englishmen in that 'regiment' to 'shoot the traitors' and 'bayonet the bastards', seem to be incredible and just one bad dream . . . were the British Army to have withdrawn at that moment, there would have been no need for court martials or prisons as the mob would have relieved them of such necessities. A very small section of those assembled did spread a ray of hope amongst us by raising their voices in our support.

Joe Good, 'Kimmage Garrison'

From the Rotunda we marched along O'Connell Street. A solitary fireman was working near Kelly's Corner and he said out loud: 'I'm with you, boys.' That was the first word of approval I had heard from Dubliners that week.

Frank Burke, E Company, 4th Battalion

As we were passing the vicinity of the Castle, the wives and dependants of the soldiers were lined along the street and they certainly made no secret of their antipathy towards us. The soldiers were encouraged by words and gestures 'to give us the bayonet and finish us off'. Their language, I must say, was most choice.

Frank Thornton, 'Kimmage Garrison' (GPO area)

. . . on our way up along Patrick Street, if it weren't for the fact that we were so strongly guarded by British troops, we would have been torn asunder by the ex-soldiers' wives in that area.

Oscar Traynor, F Company, 2nd Battalion

In the course of our march through the city we passed through a number of hostile groups of people who shouted all sorts of things at us, including calling us 'murderers' and 'starvers of the people'.

Outside the gates of Richmond barracks I saw a Capuchin priest who, as we were entering the gates, kept saying, with tears in his eyes, 'Misneach' [courage], which was completely unintelligible to the enemy forces.

Gerard Doyle, B Company, 4th Battalion

The crowd followed us up to the gate of the [Richmond] barracks, where a woman rushed up with an uplifted jug and hit one of us. The [British Army] officer knocked her back into the mob shouting at them that they should be ashamed of themselves.

Patrick Rankin, Newry Company, Co. Down

As we arrived near the barracks things began to get a little bit more sharper as Dublin's worst was let loose from their stockades, the women being the worst. They looked like a few who were around during the French Revolution. One of my companions answered one of the women and a sergeant broke through our ranks and struck him on the breast with his rifle with full force saying, 'If you speak again I'll kill you.' The women were allowed to follow our men to barracks, shouting to the soldiers, 'Use your rifles on the German so-and-sos.'

George O'Flanagan, 1st Battalion

Men fell from exhaustion on the way. We stood for about two hours on the square in Richmond barracks, men continually falling down from exhaustion. We then got a drink of water, the first for twenty-four hours. The weather was very hot.

Thomas Dowling, C Company, 1st Battalion

On my arrival, and while standing on the square, I collapsed with hunger and was removed to the side of the parade ground for attention. While being attended to I heard some British soldiers endeavouring to get possession of a ring which Commandant Joseph Plunkett was wearing, but which he refused to give up.

Joe Good, 'Kimmage Garrison'

We were there about an hour and a half, I would say. Men began collapsing in the ranks. Had we been left there another half hour few of us, I think, would have been left standing. One of the first to collapse was Joe Plunkett. Two British soldiers lifted him by the shoulders and dragged him on to the footpath. A party of British soldiers – Irishmen of an Irish regiment – rushed towards us shouting, and would have attacked us only they were halted by our guards.

Patrick Kelly, G Company, 1st Battalion

The sun was strong and beamed down on us. We were both hungry and thirsty, and to make our lot worse a number of soldiers came to curse and jeer us. They demanded our watches and anything of value we had. I had a watch which was a present from my father. A soldier armed with rifle and fixed bayonet ordered me to hand it over. I refused to comply and he threatened me with the rifle.

Seán O'Duffy, A Company, 1st Battalion

All of those who were taken at the surrender paraded in the barrack square and were offered drinks of water by the soldiers of the British Army, some of whom were Irishmen. They expressed sympathy – or rather pity – for us. During this period the soldiers came along and asked us to give them any material we had – watches, medals, etc. – for safe custody or, if we so desired, it could be brought to our homes. Later it was learned that the articles were not delivered.

Frank Burke, E Company, 4th Battalion

On reaching the square in Richmond barracks, each man was searched and anything of value taken off him. I had only ten shillings in my pocket but that, of course, was taken. I remember afterwards when we were all making claims for property stolen from us, that for fun I filled in a form for my ten shillings. Over a year elapsed and I had forgotten all about the affair, but His Majesty had not. The money was even brought by hand to me when I lay sick with the 'flu in St Enda's at Easter 1917.

Robert Barton, Royal Dublin Fusiliers

I found things [at Richmond barracks] in a chaotic state. Prisoners' effects were in buckets and bags littered around the office, and I first tried to put them in order and to find out to whom the properties belonged. The bundles had been systematically pillaged.

Thomas Leahy, E Company, 2nd Battalion

We were all brought into a large room and again searched before passing into it and everything personal or otherwise taken from us by the soldiers, even money, watches, etc. They informed us that they would be of no further use to us, as we were likely to be shot and they hoped to be on the firing parties; most of these men were so-called Irish and in Irish regiments. We again gave our names. I observed, after we had sat down or lay on the floor, that we were thrown together, officers, men and leaders, without distinction. We were served out with three or four large pails or buckets of water placed in different parts of the room without any means of getting a drink from them, unless you put your head into them, as no cups, mugs, etc., were provided.

Michael Knightly, F Company, 1st Battalion

In Richmond barracks we were herded like cattle and as some unkindly acts of soldiers have been described by others, I should like to contrast the actions of a Sherwood Forester. His battalion had suffered severely at Mount Street Bridge, but he made no complaint. I discovered that in searching me at Ship Street the military failed to find *1s.6d.* which I had in a small vest pocket. I asked this soldier if he would get me some cigarettes. He said he would do his best and I gave him a shilling. After a few hours he returned with two packets of Woodbines. 'These were all I was able to get,' he said, 'and as I thought the change would be of no use to you I brought you chocolate for the balance.' . . . I must say that my experience of British Tommies . . . was that their conduct generally was considerate. I am aware that others had not the same experience.

10
Dying for Ireland: Punishment

Nothing did more to shift public opinion in favour of the rebellion than the actions of the British authorities in its aftermath. The execution of the rebel leaders and the arrest of over 3,500 nationalists (many of whom were innocent) provoked outrage. Although most were quickly released – as were 1,272 of the 1,836 prisoners interned in Britain – the arbitrary nature of the repression was much resented. In contrast to earlier Irish insurrections, the wartime context ensured that the normal processes of civil law were set aside in favour of a response driven by military, rather than by political, considerations, an approach which proved counter-productive.

*

Most prisoners were brought to Richmond barracks, where they were questioned, fingerprinted and repeatedly inspected as the authorities sought to separate the ringleaders from the rank and file. Despite their fearsome reputation, the DMP's G-men (who were responsible for political crime) had little intelligence on the identity of the separatists beyond the most prominent leaders. Although some G-men behaved in a malicious fashion, others merely did their job, while a surprising number of policemen – whether due to self-preservation or personal sympathies – were reluctant to identify separatists.

Robert Holland, F Company, 4th Battalion

Our names and occupations were taken. After this we were marched off into what was known as the gymnasium hall. It was a wooden structure with a galvanised and glass roof. The entrance was a wide door and inside was a half-wood partition and glass. When we were inside the hall an officer gave the command to keep to the right-hand side. He then gave us orders to sit down on the floor. We were in rows about ten deep. I was about three quarters of the way up the hall and could see the glass partitions down at the door which was on my left. At the entrance I could see Johnny Barton and Detective Officer Hoey, with whom I had personal acquaintance a few years later. There were Detective Officers Smith and Bruton, and Inspector Barrett and many others whom I did not know, all members of the detective force. In groups they came to the glass and scrutinised us. After about twenty minutes they came in, in groups of two. Barton and Hoey were together. They created an impression on me that will never leave my memory, as they cynically walked slowly down along the hall with a sneer on their faces. Barton had an ash-plant walking-stick and Hoey had an umbrella. As they scrutinised our faces slowly Barton now and again said, 'You, and you and you, get up and over to the other side of the hall.' Hoey took up where Barton left off. Anyone Barton missed, Hoey got, using the same tactics. The other detectives followed the same procedure. These called themselves Irishmen, the very scum that kept us in British bondage. That identity parade will never leave my memory, as I saw Con Colbert, Éamonn Ceannt, Willie and Phil Cosgrave, Major MacBride, Peadar Doyle, Gerald Doyle, Mick Hayes, Willie Corrigan and scores of others in derision being pointed out and shouted at 'Get up and over here.' This went on for the best part of two hours, and when they had completed their job to their satisfaction they then marched them out of the hall. Those of us who were left must have looked a very squalid sight, as now our leaders and intellectuals had been taken away from us.

Thomas Leahy, E Company, 2nd Battalion

At this stage we were surprised to see Dublin Metropolitan Police come into the room with CID officers and what were known at the time as G-men, some of whom were known to some of our lads, and who were considered friendly. However, they pointed out to the military officers all the prominent leaders and officers of those who had taken active part in the labour struggle in the past leading up to Easter Week.

Patrick Rankin, Volunteers, Newry, Co. Down

We were seated around the floor in the gymnasium when a party of G-men arrived each with a large flower in the buttonhole of his coat. One would imagine that they were going to a wedding as they were all smiles.

Frank Burke, E Company, 4th Battalion

The G-men now advanced rubbing their hands with glee at the prospect of being able to render such service to their King and country! What a degrading sight! Irishmen picking out their fellow countrymen for the firing squad and long terms of imprisonment.

Mortimer O'Connell, F Company, 1st Battalion

Mick Collins, being unknown at that time, was put on the other side of the line.

John MacDonagh, C Company, 2nd Battalion

The Volunteers who had put up such a magnificent stand in the Boland's mills area came in later, led by Éamon de Valera, who towered above his men, and got a cheer from us.

Patrick Colgan, Maynooth Company, Co. Kildare

At about 5.30 [p.m.] we were taken on to the square and formed into columns of fours. We were kept there for quite a while during which detectives roamed each rank and pulled out various Volunteers for court martial. Hoey was very active. He appeared to be relishing his job.

Eamon Dore, Volunteers, Limerick Company

He was the most dangerous and vindictive of the lot and it was he who persisted in the picking out of Seán Mac Diarmada and it was because of this act he was later executed. Many escaped that scrutiny because in the fighting they had become so dishevelled that even their comrades did not know them.

Seán Kennedy, C Company, 1st Battalion

Among the detective officers concerned I noticed Smyth, Hoey, Gaffney, Barton, all of whom, with the exception of Gaffney, were subsequently executed by our forces during the Tan War. Gaffney, as far as I can recollect, left the country and went to England.

Joe Good, 'Kimmage Garrison'

Later, these detectives walked amongst us as we sat on the gym floor and picked out the men they wanted, including Jack and George Plunkett. I was sharing Michael Collins's overcoat. The floor was hard. A British sergeant said to Michael Collins: 'What has you here, Collins?' and Mick replied: 'England's difficulty.' There was a long pause then.

Frank Robbins, Irish Citizen Army

Johnny Barton and a number of detectives were keeping themselves busy, particularly Barton. He did more than his duty when the official military inspection was finished. Even though he was present at the inspection, he came around to the room after it, and stood in front of each one in order to identify those whom he considered were officers or people of note . . . As Johnny Barton stopped in front of Joseph Connolly he opened his conversation by saying, 'What is your name?', though he knew perfectly well beforehand that he was a brother of Seán Connolly's. The next observation was: 'Seán is dead.' Joe replied, 'He died for his country,' to which Johnny retorted, 'He was a disgrace to his country.' For resenting this insult, Joe was separated from us.

William Stapleton, B Company, 2nd Battalion

Where there was a doubt about identification they seemed to select, as important, Volunteers who were in uniform. Dick McKee, who was sitting immediately behind me, was dressed in full uniform, minus a hat, but wearing a civilian overcoat, and was not identified.

John MacDonagh, C Company, 2nd Battalion

One man, Dick Davys, who looked very important in his uniform, was asked by the famous detective Johnny Barton (in later years shot in the streets), 'Don't I know you?' 'I know you,' roared back the Volunteer, which answer got him put among the leaders and a long sentence as well.

Patrick Colgan, Maynooth Company, Co. Kildare

Amongst the crowd brought in to identify us was a soldier who had been a prisoner in the GPO. I met him on Thursday. He was carrying out some job near our post. Some Volunteers were taunting him and I intervened on his behalf . . . When he was brought in to identify anyone he could he walked down the line and failed to recognise us. When passing me he winked and passed on. I believe he came from Rathfarnham and although he knew all the Rathfarnham Volunteers he did not identify one person for the British. I heard he called to the relatives of the Volunteers in Rathfarnham to inform them of the welfare of the Volunteers.

Jack Plunkett, Volunteers staff officer

At one of the interrogations the British Tommies were brought in and asked did they recognise me . . . One of them certainly had seen me but said he did not recognise me. He said the same of the others as far as I can make out. He was a Dublin lad who had been helping in the kitchen of the GPO, washing up, etc. I had provided him with an apron or something else for this work. One of the officers also failed to recognise me at least. I heard from others that he had done the same with everybody and that he had said he was a doctor, not a policeman.

Maurice Collins, F Company, 1st Battalion

I remember one incident of a detective whom we had taken prisoner while in Church Street named Heffernan. I told the boys that although he was a detective he was to be treated well. It so happened that while I was in Richmond barracks this same detective was brought along to identify any prisoners. Good enough of him, he passed me by although he knew me well.

Constable Patrick Bermingham, Dublin Metropolitan Police

We pretended we never saw the men before.

Patrick Kelly, G Company, 1st Battalion

Seated along the floor by the wall I noticed Commandant MacDonagh and Commandant E[dward] Daly. They looked tired and sad. As I looked at Commandant Daly he gave me a sad smile and that was the last I ever saw of him. After the police had looked us over we were moved towards the door, where we passed through a barrier. Each one of us had to leave our fingerprints as we moved out.

John MacDonagh, C Company, 2nd Battalion, and brother of Thomas MacDonagh

I escaped, though Pearse's brother Willie was executed. On my way out, I was stopped by a detective and brought before Quinn, a superintendent of the police. 'This is MacDonagh's brother.' The superintendent made little of this discovery of his subordinate, and I passed through. At the door, I turned and saw Tom for the last time. He waved his hand to me, in the old cheery manner.

Maurice Collins, F Company, 1st Battalion

On the morning that we had received orders from the British that we were to be deported I was standing beside Seán MacDermott in the barrack square and said to him, 'It looks, Seán, as if we will be all together wherever we are going this time.' He replied, 'No, Maurice, the next place you and I will meet will be in heaven.' Up to that he had not been court-martialled and I could not understand why he passed this remark.

Joseph O'Rourke, 2nd Battalion

On Sunday night we were told we were going away and that there was to be a boat in the middle of the night. We were about twenty-five in a room and I was in a room with [Seán] MacDermott. Men had been picked out but not MacDermott. We went out to 'fall in' in the barrack square, and as we went out there were three or four cases of army beef and biscuits, and as we marched out we were each handed a couple of biscuits and every second man got a tin of bully-beef. While I was accepting these I heard a voice, that of Johnny Barton, the G-man, saying: 'Ah, no, Johnny, you're not leaving us. You are to stay here.' So MacDermott just stepped out of the ranks and stood beside him, and the rest of us went on.

Seventy-nine female rebels were arrested in Dublin. Some were ridiculed and humiliated, but women were generally treated more leniently than men. Many of the rebels had assumed that women would not be arrested, and the military were often reluctant to arrest women. Some were only imprisoned after insisting – to both Volunteers and British officers – that it was their right. Just one woman – Countess Markievicz – was court-martialled, and only five were interned in Britain, but many endured harsh treatment (particularly in Ship Street barracks and Kilmainham Jail) before being transferred to the more comfortable Mountjoy Prison.

Helena Molony, Irish Citizen Army

A window was smashed at the back [of the City Hall on Easter Monday], and then we knew they were pouring in – and they did come in at the back. A voice said: 'Surrender, in the name of the King.' At this point I felt a pluck on my arm, and our youngest girl, Annie Norgrove – there are three or four sisters of them – said to me: 'Miss Molony, Miss Molony, we are not going to give in? Mr Connolly said we were not to surrender.' She was terrified, but there was no surrender about her. The call for surrender was repeated: 'How many are here? Surrender.' . . . the troops poured up the stairs and came in to where the girls were. It would never occur to them, of course, that they were women soldiers. Actually, the women in the Citizen Army were not first-aiders, but did military work, except where it suited them to be first-aiders. Even before the Russian Army had women soldiers, the Citizen Army had them. The British officers thought these girls had been taken prisoner by the rebels. They asked them: 'Did they do anything to you? Were they kind to you? How many are up there?' Jinny Shanahan – quick enough – answered: 'No, they did not do anything to us. There are hundreds upstairs – big guns and everything.' She invented such a story that they thought there was a garrison up on the roof, with the result that they did delay, and took precautions. It was not until the girls were brought out for safety and, apparently, when they were bringing down some of the men, that one of the lads said: 'Hullo, Jinny, are you all right?' The officer looked at her, angry at the way he was fooled by this girl.

Rose McNamara, Cumann na mBan

We all collected in front of the fort [in Marrowbone Lane] and shook the hands of all the men and gave them all 'God Speed', and told them to cheer up. Some were sad and some trying to be cheerful. After command from [the] captain to form fours all marched out the front gate through [the] city to St Patrick's Park (Ross Road), all the girls marching behind, singing; one of our girls picked up a rifle in the street, carried it on her shoulders. We all (twenty-two of us) gave ourselves up and marched down between two lines of our brave men. We waited until all the arms were taken away. The men gave each of us their small arms to do as we liked with, thinking we were going to go home, but we were not going to leave the men we were with all the week to their fate; we decided to go along with them and be with them to the end, whatever our fate might be. Some of the girls had as many as three revolvers; some had more. The sergeant in Richmond barracks told us we would be searched in Kilmainham, so after a while we reluctantly gave them up to him. After all the arms were taken from the men at Ross Road we were all marched under military escort to Richmond barracks, the girls singing all the time amidst the insults of the soldiers and the people along the route. We were then separated from the men and led away to the far side of the barracks for the night where we got tea . . . Our treatment here was not too bad.

Min Ryan, Cumann na mBan

When we came to the door, a high-ranking officer and a young officer were arriving [at Jacob's] to take the surrender. They came in a small two-seater car. I suppose the high-ranking officer was General Lowe. The young officer stood, and we stood too. Louise stood up with great dignity. One of the officers said: 'We are not taking women, are we?' The other said: 'No.' We went off. Louise said: 'The cheek of him anyway – not taking women.'

Bridget Martin, Cumann na mBan

While I was having my dinner, several soldiers and three detectives arrived and searched the house. Again they failed to find the [IRB's] money or anything incriminating; but they arrested me and told my sister that I might not be returning and that I should take an overcoat and a case. Six soldiers and three detectives brought me to the lorry, which they had left at the other side of the blown-up bridge. I refused to climb into the lorry unless they got a ladder or something. One of them went to a house and commandeered a chair and I had to get in. One of the soldiers asked me did I know where I was going. I said I didn't and didn't care. He told me that the soldiers were digging a trench in the yard of Richmond barracks and they were going to put 500 Sinn Féiners in it and bury them alive. I said if we couldn't live for Ireland we could die for it ... We were all taken to Ship Street barracks ... That was a terrible place; there were no sanitary arrangements. A sergeant came with a bucket which he placed behind the door. We became infested with fleas and lice.

Kathleen Lynn, Irish Citizen Army

We had dusty grey blankets which were all crawling with lice. I never slept during the time I was there. I could not. The scratching was not so bad in the daytime but in the night-time it was perfectly awful.

Helena Molony, Irish Citizen Army

We were kept for eight days in the dirty room in Ship Street barracks. It was a disused room at the back of the building, on the west side. There were old bits of mattresses in it, used by the soldiers. They were covered with vermin; and before a day had passed we were all covered with vermin too ... The soldiers were decent enough to us. The Dublin Fusiliers were there. They would bring us in a dish of fried bacon and bread. On Friday, we got nothing except hard biscuits and dry bread. We were glad when the sergeant said: 'It is bad stuff, but that is what we are getting ourselves.' We were delighted that they were cut off from supplies.

Annie Cooney, Cumann na mBan

We were all – twenty-two of us – brought into a large building [in Richmond barracks] up the stairs and we were first put into a rather small room, where we were divided up for the night, eleven of us in each of two rooms. A British military sergeant had charge of us and brought us tea in a bucket and some hard biscuits which we called dog biscuits. We ate and drank what we got, as we were hungry. The sergeant apologised for the sort of food he had to give us. We spent the night there – not sleeping, as we had no mattresses or any sort of sleeping accommodation. In any case we thought it safer to remain awake, as we did not know what the soldiers might be like. We spent the night saying the rosary and talking. We wondered what was happening to the men. There was a small, rather primitive lavatory attached to our room, for which we were thankful; we had not to go out at all to the corridors. I should mention that we still had the guns in our possession that were given to us by the Volunteers to keep. During the night the sergeant asked us if we had any guns on us, as we would be likely to be searched by the soldiers at some later stage. We foolishly said we hadn't, thinking we would be sent home and could hold on to them and not be searched. When he had gone out, Miss McNamara, who was in charge of us, became a bit worried about the position. Eventually she decided we should say the rosary for guidance as to what we should do. We noticed a fireplace in the room and somebody suggested that we should put them up the chimney . . . The next morning . . . we were brought out to the square again, lined up and marched off to Kilmainham.

Pauline Keating, Cumann na mBan

As we came out of the gates of Richmond barracks there was a hostile crowd – mostly women – awaiting us. They started shouting at us, but Madame [Markievicz] told us not to mind them, shouting, 'Keep your heads up, girls,' and a few other phrases like that. She was smoking cheroots. When we arrived at Kilmainham there was an old jailer waiting for us. He brought us to a doorway and pointed to an inscription above it: 'Sin no more, lest a worse thing come to thee'. There was a violent protest from us girls. We shouted at him that we had not sinned. He retorted that if we had not come out to kill, we certainly had not come out to cure.

Rose McNamara, Cumann na mBan

We were all lined up; names taken (which we gave in Irish, which the soldiers couldn't understand) . . . We were then divided up into threes and left in cells, carefully locked, bolted and barred.

Annie Cooney, Cumann na mBan

We were put three in a cell, the majority on the ground floor [in Kilmainham]. They were dreadful, filthy places, not having been used for years before that. We got two palliasses – which the soldiers called biscuits – between every three prisoners . . . We took turns at night on the palliasses, not sleeping very much, of course . . . All our food was dished up to us by soldiers, the same as they got themselves. We got no cutlery. It was all in mess tins, cocoa and skilly. The same tins were used all the time for all the meals. The taste of the skilly was in the cocoa . . . We got out for exercise for an hour every day and were locked up in our cells the rest of the time. The lavatory was outside and the wardresses accompanied us to and from it. We were allowed to wash at a pipe at the end of the corridor.

Kathleen Lynn, Irish Citizen Army

We were more comfortable than in the other place [Ship Street]. I was able by degrees to get rid of my intruders. I had to pick them out one by one. I suppose the lavatory accommodation was better there. I must have been able to undress because I remember picking my undergarments . . . I remember we were given one basin of water for the three of us to wash in. It was more than we had in the other place. I, being the doctor, used it first, Miss French-Mullen second and Miss Molony was last.

Bridget Martin, Cumann na mBan

We sang all the national songs through the night, although the soldiers tried to shut us up. The prison was filthy . . . We had to sit on the dirty floors with our backs against the dirty walls . . . When we wanted to go to the lavatory we had to knock at the door and two soldiers with fixed bayonets brought us to the lavatory, which was a dry closet that had no door. The soldiers stood jeering at whatever girl was in the closet, with the result that for the eleven days I was in Kilmainham I never went to the lavatory and on my transfer to Mountjoy I had to be treated at once and for a long time after by Dr Cook, the prison doctor. This horrible experience had a permanent effect on my constitution. After three or four days in Kilmainham, seventy-two out of seventy-three women prisoners were released, leaving me quite alone there . . . I spent that night by myself in Kilmainham – in a different cell – so terrified that I remained on my knees behind the cell door all night. I should mention that the soldiers often were drunk and two of the Church Street priests thought it advisable one night to stay in the prison all night for the protection of the girls.

Bridget Martin, Cumann na mBan

Countess Markievicz was brought in one day. She was in uniform and shouted to us, 'Penal servitude for me.' She seemed delighted with herself.

Rose McNamara, Cumann na mBan

Tuesday, 2 May: Awakened very early by sounds of shots outside our windows. Exercise for half an hour. Very cold. We then arranged a sixteen-hand reel which we danced and enjoyed much to the alarm of the five armed soldiers on guard of us and two wardresses.

Wednesday, 3 May: More shots during daybreak. Exercise as usual; not allowed to dance today. Singing in the cells since we came here. Some of the girls dancing in their cells.

Annie Cooney, Cumann na mBan

We all heard the volleys on that morning as on the previous mornings of the other executions. Myself and my cell mate [in Richmond barracks] knelt down and said the rosary for whoever had been executed. We did not then know who it was . . . Father Albert, who had attended the doomed men that morning before and during their execution, came to visit the women prisoners in the cells, which were opened to him by the wardresses. We were very glad to see him, especially because we immediately felt his sympathy for us, whereas the prison chaplain, Father Ryan, whom we knew, had quite disapproved of us, and showed it very definitely, refusing even to take a message to our mother. Father Albert showed his sympathy so plainly that we cried on his shoulders and he consoled us, gave us his blessing and heard our confessions.

Annie Cooney, Cumann na mBan

We had the same routine every day until the Sunday. On that day we were all brought to Mass in the prison church. We were on the gallery, from which we had only a view of the altar and the front seat. We were able to see Éamonn Ceannt, Michael Mallin, Con Colbert and Seán Heuston, who were kneeling in the front seat. They were the only ones to receive Holy Communion, which we thought significant. That affected us all and I began to cry. We craned our necks to try to see more, but the wardresses pulled us back.

Áine Ceannt, wife of Éamonn Ceannt

Next morning [8 May] the women were all interrogated, singly, and, although they had made no previous arrangements amongst themselves as to the attitude they would adopt, every one of them stated that she had gone out with the men and would have done anything that she was asked to do. The British military tried to get the girls to say that they were only doing first-aid.

Rose McNamara, Cumann na mBan

Monday, 8 May: Just after going to bed we heard great commotion outside our cell and heard that prisoners were going to be released. Our cells were then thrown open and we were told to get ready. We were going to be released. We danced with joy and put on our clothes; went downstairs, where were assembled a crowd of British officers and the governor of the jail, with candles lighting (having no gas), also Reverend Father McCarthy. Our names were called out and we were given a lecture, to be good in future or else.

Bridget Martin, Cumann na mBan

The following Saturday or Sunday, in the middle of the night, we were all brought in the Black Maria to Mountjoy Prison. We made some fun for ourselves on the journey. We remained there for about six weeks. After Kilmainham it was just like going into a hotel, even though we had only a plank bed. It was spotlessly clean and we had sheets and they did our laundry for us. We had a very decent woman – Miss O'Neill – as wardress. After the Bishop of Limerick's letter was published, we could do what we liked. She was very religious. At first we had only half an hour's exercise together, but after a short while our cell doors used to be left open. The governor and the assistant matron, Miss Armstrong, a Protestant, were very decent to us. After a while, with her connivance, we used to cook sausages, bacon and eggs, which we got from our friends for our tea.

Kathleen Lynn, Irish Citizen Army

We were hailed rather with joy by the wardresses because we were interesting prisoners. We were not like ordinary criminals. I got quite fond of the wardress who looked after us . . . After a while, we were allowed visitors and parcels, and then we were inundated with all sorts of presents and luxuries. The only thing we longed for was clean bread and butter. We had all sorts of cakes and fruits, etc., but we wanted something plain. We were allowed, after a little while, to have association. We would be walking in the grounds and talking to each other . . . We had not a bad time while in Mountjoy.

Like women prisoners, teenage boys received relatively sympathetic – or patronising – treatment. Despite the important role played by some of Na Fianna Éireann, they were quickly released.

Vinny Byrne, E Company, 2nd Battalion

I was home about a week when the house was raided by British military on a Saturday morning. I happened to be in the house at the time. An officer and a sergeant entered the house. One of them asked: 'Does Vincent Byrne live here?' I replied: 'Here I am.' He said: 'Come along with me, boy.' I was taken away in a military lorry to Ballsbridge Fire Brigade Station. The sergeant sat in the back of the lorry with me. He passed the remark: 'You little [bastard], you would shoot me!' I said: 'Yes, it was either you or me for it.' He was very friendly. When we arrived at Ballsbridge, I was brought before a council of officers. They asked me my name and address and where I was during the Rising. I told them: 'In Jacob's biscuit factory, fighting for Ireland.' I was told to leave the room. I went into another room where there were five or six other men. The sergeant came in, and called me out to the passage. 'You got no dinner, sonny,' he said. I replied, 'No.' He said: 'How would you like some steak and onions?' I said: 'I would like them very much, if I got them.' He took me into one of the stables and told me to wait for a few minutes as he would be back. He came in with a plateful of meat and potatoes. He divided the meal into a dixie-lid, gave me one half and he had the other. He told me then to go back to the room which I had left, wishing me luck and saying that he was finished with me now.

Seán McLoughlin, D Company, 1st Battalion

As I moved through [Richmond barracks] a captain caught me by the shoulder and pulled me out and said, 'How old are you?' I said, 'Why?' 'You are too young to be an officer,' he said. I made no reply. He thereupon tore the tabs from my coat. 'You are no longer an officer now,' he said.

William Stapleton, B Company, 2nd Battalion

A number of us were asked our ages, and those who were 16, 17 and 18 years of age were called out and, I understand, were sent home the following day. I was not yet 19 but, in spite of the advice of Dick McKee and others, I gave my age as 21 and I was not called out.

Vinny Byrne, E Company, 2nd Battalion

On Friday evening, we were told to 'come on, get ready', and we all thought we were going to be deported. We paraded on the square – about twelve or fourteen young lads. We were given the command: 'Right turn, quick march.' We kept marching until we came to a big gate; the gate was opened for us and closed behind us. Someone of the party remarked: 'Oh, God, lads, we are out.' . . . strangely enough, in later years I was officer commanding this same barracks where I was held prisoner.

Over 3,200 prisoners passed through Richmond barracks before being tried, deported or released. Mass imprisonment was a new experience for this generation of republicans, one which reinforced their ideological convictions and strengthened the bonds between those who would form the elite of the revolutionary movement during the guerrilla war that followed.

Daniel Hegarty, Mallow Company, Co. Cork

The conditions there were terrible. We were crowded into barrack rooms without a bit of furniture. Each man got two army blankets, one to put on the floor to lie on and one to put over him. We used our boots as pillows. We got only about an hour's exercise while we were there.

Charlie Weston, Lusk Company, 5th Battalion

We were together in one room, which was very overcrowded. That night Tom Ashe sang an old rebel song for us, 'The Cottage by the Lee'.

Michael Knightly, F Company, 1st Battalion

The prisoners, despite the revolting conditions under which we were kept – a large boiler in the room served as a latrine – were cheerful and uncomplaining. I was particularly impressed by a North Co. Dublin man . . . He had not been a Volunteer, but his brother not turning out, he procured his uniform and rifle and joined up. He was a real philosopher. As we watched the rain from our window one day he remarked: 'It is a grand thing to be in from the rain.'

Padraig Ó Ceallaigh, B Company, 2nd Battalion

Amongst the rank and file the tension of the previous week had ended and, while none of us knew his subsequent fate, there was in

Richmond barracks generally, in my experience, an air of devil-may-careness and good humour.

Patrick Kelly, G Company, 1st Battalion

We sat on the floor with our backs to the wall and tried to guess what would happen next. The sentry tried to cheer us up by opening the door and telling us we would shortly be taken away and anyone left behind would be shot.

Eamon Morkan, A Company, 1st Battalion

At this time we all had the feeling that we were going to pay the extreme penalty. Later those of us remaining in the barrack room were ordered out to the square, and at this stage I felt that instead of being executed we were going to be returned ignominiously to our homes.

Robert Holland, F Company, 4th Battalion

Inside Richmond barracks, we were packed chock-full into a billet and three or four buckets were left in to act as latrines. The door was locked and we had hardly room to sit down. We were in this room all night. Everyone seemed to be in serious thought and no one wanted to converse, as we were practically jammed tight together . . . I opened the conversation with 'What will be the next British move?' Tom Young answered – 'The Lord only knows.' Martin Kavanagh said, 'I would not be surprised if we were shipped to France.' Mick Liston was of the opinion that we would be shipped to some of the colonies, as they had previously done so with other insurgents, or if not that we would all be executed. After a pause Colbert spoke. He said that from his point of view he would prefer to be executed and said, 'We are all ready to meet our God. We had hopes of coming out alive. Now that we are defeated, outside that barrack wall the people whom we have tried to emancipate have demonstrated nothing but hate and contempt for us. We would be better off dead, as life would be a torture. We can thank the Mother of God for her kindness in her intercession for us that we have had the time to prepare ourselves to meet our Redeemer.' Colbert then called us all to recite the rosary for the spiritual and temporal welfare of those who fought and died in the cause of Irish freedom, past, present and future generations. We were in darkness and, remembering no more, I fell asleep.

Michael Knightly, F Company, 1st Battalion

We slept in our clothes on the floor of our room, huddled together for warmth. During the day we watched from a window some of our leaders being conducted to a room for court martial. I saw J. J. Walsh, head up, and apparently very proud of his part, being led in. Outside the room I noticed John MacBride standing with a raincoat across his arm, looking quite unconcerned. Captain Dick Stokes, who fought under him, told me that before the surrender at Jacob's factory, he called some of the officers together. Addressing them, he said: 'Some of you may live to fight again and, if you do, take the open country for it and avoid a death trap like this.'

W. T. Cosgrave, B Company, 4th Battalion

John MacBride told me on one of those nights that his life-long prayer had been answered. He said three Hail Marys every day that he should not die until he had fought the British in Ireland.

Hugh Hehir, C Company, 2nd Battalion

The general view [of the leaders], as far as I can recollect, was that Eoin MacNeill's countermanding order was all for the best, as the country was not sufficiently organised at that time to engage in an insurrection with any reasonable prospect of success and that the protest made in Dublin would have the effect of arousing the nationalist spirit.

Father Paddy Browne, friend of Seán MacDermott

He was rather severe against it [the countermand], in his condemnation of MacNeill, because, he said, that in his opinion it would have been a really formidable Rising with a much better chance of world reverberation than that week's fighting in Dublin. I think he felt very bitter . . . He said what a pity that it prevented the Rising being a respectable rising, that it would have been over a considerable part of the country, employing a lot of British troops, and that, as far as the Germans were concerned, it would have been a more valuable thing than the mere flash in the pan it was.

William O'Brien, Irish Transport and General Workers' Union leader

He [Éamon de Valera] said he was glad that he had no responsibility for deciding anything and that he simply obeyed orders given to him.

Joe Good, 'Kimmage Garrison'

Our company officers compared most favourably with any British officers I had seen. They were not at all disheartened. I made some cynical remark to Ned Morkan and he replied: 'If they let you live six months you will see the reaction.'

Jack Plunkett, Volunteers staff officer and brother of Joseph Plunkett

When I met Joe now at the time of the interrogation he said . . . that if we had not come out, Ireland might have been down 200 years, but that we had now started a new advance.

Michael Staines, GPO

He [Joseph Plunkett] said it was a glorious week and we had made our protest. He did not criticise anybody.

Jack Plunkett, Volunteers staff officer and brother of Joseph Plunkett

He [Joseph Plunkett] said to me afterwards, when we were sitting on the floor in that disgusting gymnasium in Richmond barracks, 'Do you know, I don't feel half as bad as I ought to!' His enthusiasm for the coming events made him forget his bodily sufferings . . . He said very definitely that they were going to shoot him but would not shoot us. He also said they would shoot the signatories to the Proclamation. He was worrying a lot about Tomás MacDonagh.

Peadar MacMahon, C Company, 2nd Battalion

He [Thomas MacDonagh] said that . . . we would live to see the fruits of that week but that he and a number of leaders would, he hoped, be in heaven at that time.

Liam O'Brien, F Company, 1st Battalion

'We hoped to push the ball up the hill high enough for others to push it up the whole way after us,' said Seán MacDermott to me during the long conversation I had with him and Tom Clarke while we were sitting on the floor of the gymnasium of Richmond barracks on the Sunday night of the surrender . . .

Joseph Gleeson, 'Kimmage Garrison'

Tom Clarke seemed pleased with the outcome of the Rising. I think he said, 'We have a minimum loss, which will result in a maximum gain.'

Liam O'Brien, F Company, 1st Battalion

Seán MacDermott . . . remarked to me: 'The only failure in Ireland is the failure to strike.'

Liam Tannam, E Company, 3rd Battalion

There was a huge number of prisoners in Richmond barracks. [Prime Minister H. H.] Asquith came along and interviewed quite a number of them and expressed the opinion that they were all very fine fellows, had fought a clean fight and acted like gentlemen, and ordered that they be treated of the best. His order was taken literally by the chief cook, who had been employed, I believe, in the Dolphin Hotel, and from the date of Asquith's visit [13 May] until I was shifted to Knutsford about 6 June, we had eggs and ham for breakfast, tins of jam, genuine butter and porridge (if anyone liked it). For dinner we had roast beef or perhaps mutton and plenty of vegetables (far more than we could eat), more bread, jam, butter and tea. Tea was on a similar lavish scale, while the soldiers garrisoning the place were on the roughest of rations, and in carrying the stuff from the cook-house to our quarters we were besieged by hungry soldiers, begging tins of jam, hunks of cheese or bread or anything that could be conveniently handled.

Due to a lack of evidence, most rebels were interned rather than prosecuted, although 171 of those deemed the worst offenders were court-martialled. Of these, 160 were found guilty, and ninety received death sentences, of which all but fifteen were commuted to lengthy terms of imprisonment. (In addition, Sir Roger Casement was subsequently hanged on 3 August 1916.) As the Defence of the Realm regulations did not proscribe insurrection, the rebels were accused of taking part 'in an armed rebellion . . . for the purpose of assisting the enemy', a charge that many rejected. The trials were rushed affairs, relying on inaccurate evidence, with few legal safeguards and often arbitrary outcomes. Some leaders fought to avoid a death sentence. Others demonstrated little interest in the proceedings other than to repudiate allegations of dishonourable behaviour or to exploit them for propagandistic purposes.

Alfred Bucknill, deputy judge advocate general, British Forces in Ireland

It was obvious from the commencement that there would be great difficulty in getting sufficient legal evidence to pin any particular offence against any particular person . . . The difficulty of collecting evidence in the cases was very considerable, as it was necessary in every case to prove that the accused had surrendered with arms from some place which had been held by the rebels and where fighting had taken place. In many cases lists of prisoners had been taken but no officer could identify the accused as the person who had actually surrendered and of course there was the risk of people giving false names and addresses, which in fact was done in several cases. Beyond the Proclamation of the Irish Republic, which contained the names of seven signatories, we knew very little of the prime movers in the rebellion.

W. T. Cosgrave, B Company, 4th Battalion

All Volunteer prisoners who had been engaged in Easter Week in the South Dublin Union and in Marrowbone Lane were charged with having been in Jacob's . . . Captain Rotheram, one of the best known and most popular sportsmen of the County Westmeath, the best polo player at No. 1 in Ireland, took the surrender of the Volunteers at South Dublin Union and Marrowbone Lane, and marched with the prisoners to Bride Road. He was called upon the following day to give evidence of the surrender in both places. His reply was that he had seen these men yesterday, that he did not know them, not having seen them before, that he would not know them again; that he would not feel justified in giving testimony.

Molly Reynolds, Cumann na mBan

On the Friday following my return home, Father was released from Kilmainham Jail. He told me that while he was in jail it was arranged that when he was being court-martialled he would say that I had gone into the GPO for stamps, that he came in to look for me and both of us were held there for the week.

Seán McGarry, 'Headquarters Battalion' and IRB leader

The last time I saw Tom Clarke he had received his court martial notice. He regarded it as a formality so far as he himself and the other signatories were concerned, but it contained a clause charging him with taking up arms, etc., for the purpose and with the intention of helping the enemy. He asked me to point out to everyone that this gave him a truthful plea of not guilty and to plead accordingly.

Peadar Doyle, F Company, 4th Battalion

Éamonn Ceannt came to us early one morning and gave instructions that each of us was to make the best defence possible.

Alfred Bucknill, deputy judge advocate general, British Forces in Ireland

I gathered from most of the statements made by the accused that they had no knowledge on the Monday morning that there was going to be a rebellion until they were suddenly rushed in to the South Union gate at the double and taken in to the huts where the fighting took place, where they were told to barricade themselves as they were about to be attacked by the military. This was their version.

Kathleen Boland, sister of Harry Boland

During the course of conversation [in Mountjoy Prison], my mother, who, in her simplicity, thought that she might be able to get Harry out of his difficulty, said, 'Wasn't it an extraordinary thing to arrest you, and you only coming from the races!' But Harry bluntly replied, 'Ah, no, Mother. I was not coming from the races. I went out to strike a blow against the bloody British Empire.' I can still remember the expression on my mother's face when she realised the hopelessness of her effort to save him.

Patrick Colgan, Maynooth Company, Co. Kildare

Harry Boland suggested to the others that they should go before the court as 'snappy' as possible. Jim Whelan had a cut-throat razor and they had a shave of sorts. The only water for them to use was contained in one of our drinking receptacles (salmon tins). I felt very sad at parting from Harry Boland.

Alfred Bucknill, deputy judge advocate general, British Forces in Ireland

I took the summary of evidence in her [Markievicz's] case, and from the statement of a page-boy at a hotel facing Stephen's Green it appeared that he saw her fire her revolver at a window in the hotel from which an officer in uniform was looking out. When I asked her whether she wished to say anything, she said, 'We dreamed of an Irish Republic and thought we had a fighting chance.' Then for a few moments she broke down and sobbed.

Jack Plunkett, Volunteers staff officer

The court martial was awfully funny. There were at least three British officers. One of them, a general, who was president of the court and wore as many ribbons as his coat would hold, was a regular buffoon, whatever his military achievements may have been. His ignorance of the job was ludicrous. He must never have conducted a court martial before. The charge included some reference to aiding the King's enemies and when I asked him to define the King's enemies, he could make no reply. He said nothing for a while and then said: 'Well, if you can't understand the King's English, there is no use talking. Do you plead guilty or not guilty?' I said, 'If you can't explain who the King's enemies are, I am going to explain my position. If the people of Ireland are the King's enemies, I am guilty.

If I fought, it was for the people of Ireland I fought.' . . . it was perfectly clear to me that anything I could say would not affect the issue in the slightest.

Liam Tobin, C Company, 1st Battalion

The prosecutor explained to the court that we were charged, under some act or other, with being taken in arms against the King and with helping the enemies of His Majesty the King and so on. He finished up by saying that the penalty for this was death, but the president of the court contradicted him on this point and said that the wording of the Act was 'maybe death'. I was hoping sincerely that the president was right but there appeared to be some doubt about it. They turned over the leaves of books and papers to see which was right, and I must say that while the trial went on it was not clear to me which way it had been decided.

John McGallogly, 'Kimmage Garrison'

On Wednesday [3 May] I was brought for court martial along with J. J. Walsh, William Pearse and Seán McGarry. The president of the court read the names of the members and I think he asked had we any objection to any of them. We hadn't. The charge was read and then the evidence of Lieutenant King of the Royal Irish Rifles [Fusiliers] was taken. He stated that, while a prisoner, he had seen the other three in the GPO. In my case he told how I had taken him prisoner and three times during his evidence he said, 'I will never forget his face until my dying day.' I grinned at him. We were then asked if we had anything to say. J. J. Walsh and Willie Pearse were in uniform. J. J. said he held no official position in the Volunteers . . . Willie Pearse said he was merely a personal attaché of his brother. Seán McGarry and I both stated that we had nothing to say. The president then told us that the sentence would be promulgated in due course, and the trial was over. It did not last fifteen minutes.

W. T. Cosgrave, B Company, 4th Battalion

I denied conspiracy with the Germans, saying there was not a word of truth in the charge, and I made no admissions . . . I was told sentence would be promulgated and the trial was over in ten or fifteen minutes.

Diarmuid Lynch, 'Headquarters Battalion'

. . . I despatched a note to the American consul requesting that he be present at my court martial to hear a statement which I intended to make respecting the assertion of our officer prisoner in the GPO, viz. that he and his fellow prisoners 'were left to die like rats in a trap' . . . Due to the fact that I was in charge of the squad that shifted the prisoners from the GPO basement on Friday of Easter Week, he was called on to testify to my presence in the GPO as a participant in the Rising – an unnecessary formality on the part of the court . . . neither his recognition of me nor the manner of it mattered a hoot. Here I was, one who participated in the Rising, and so proud of the fact – as well as of the pre-Easter 'character' which Lowe's subordinates gave me in the pre-court martial 'hearing' – that any man who should endeavour to prove the contrary I would deem my worst enemy.

Liam Tobin, C Company, 1st Battalion

Being very exhausted, I slept heavily [in Kilmainham Jail] and I can remember nothing except that during the night I was awakened by being shaken by a British officer and a couple of armed soldiers, who had a lantern. They got me off the floor and put me standing up. I was completely dazed with sleep. The officer asked me my name and I told him. He said: 'You have been sentenced to death,' reading from a document he held. With that he left, brought his soldiers with him, and closed the door. In a matter of minutes, as far as I can remember, he reopened the door and said, 'And the sentence of the court has been commuted to ten years' penal servitude.' He repeated this practice with the other prisoners . . . apparently considering this procedure a rather good joke.

John McGallogly, 'Kimmage Garrison'

Sometime later [in Kilmainham Jail] I was awakened by three redcaps opening the door to announce my sentence. One of them said, 'You have been tried and found guilty and sentenced to death. Do you understand?' I said, 'Yes.' He paused a second or two and then continued, 'Out of considerations of mercy the sentence has been commuted to penal servitude for ten years. Do you understand?' Again I said, 'Yes.' He told the others to give me a shake, and I was duly shaken. Then he asked did I want anything to eat, and in the same sullen tone as before I answered, 'Yes.' They gave me three biscuits. I wondered afterwards why he ordered the others to shake me. It may have been that my lack of reaction to the death sentence caused him to think I was half asleep. I was wide awake but actually I was always sceptical about anything they said and always on guard against any show of anything other than sullenness . . . When we were assembled next day, J. J. Walsh said, 'There are some missing.' The sergeant in charge replied, 'You may thank your stars you are not missing too.'

Joseph O'Connor, A Company, 3rd Battalion

With the dawn on Wednesday morning [3 May] I was awakened by volleys being fired. I instinctively knew what was happening . . . Each morning after, I awoke before the shots were fired and after a minute or two the volleys would go off.

Áine Ceannt, wife of Éamonn Ceannt

. . . they were awakened at dawn by a volley of shots, followed almost immediately by a revolver shot. Lily O'Brennan insisted that they were shooting the prisoners, but the other girls laughed her to scorn.

Patrick Colgan, Maynooth Company, Co. Kildare

We all knelt and recited the rosary.

Bridget Martin, Cumann na mBan

We had no appetite for our skilly that day as we heard the shots that killed our leaders. The military sergeant did not leave us in any doubt. He came in and told us with great satisfaction that 'four more were gone today'.

Liam Tannam, E Company, 3rd Battalion

When the executions began the volleys awakened us each morning and we were informed each morning by a red-haired Royal Irish

Regiment sergeant that our turn would come very soon, and he gloated over having been present at the executions, and in one instance described how he had seen the brains scattered over the wall.

Rose McNamara, Cumann na mBan

Monday, 8 May: Loud reports of shots at daybreak. We say prayers for whoever it was; heard terrible moans; then a small shot; then silence. We heard from one of our members that poor Con Colbert, É. Ceannt, Mallin and Seán Heuston had been shot.

Denis McCullough, IRB president and Volunteers leader, Belfast

I next met him [MacDermott] for a moment, in Richmond barracks [*c.* 10 May], on his way out to Kilmainham Jail, to be executed. He put his arms around me and bade me goodbye. I lay awake all night and heard the shots in the early morning.

Convicted or interned rebels were deported, a process that began only one day after the general surrender. Deportation was a dismal experience: hostile civilians lined the route between Richmond barracks and the North Wall, and conditions on the ships were grim. However, many of those deported after the executions began on 3 May detected a shift in the public mood.

Frank Robbins, Irish Citizen Army

The British officer in charge, riding on horseback, came down the ranks, impressing upon the soldiers to carry out instructions and not to waste time with any prisoner who stumbled or fell. It took very little reasoning on our part to understand the full meaning of this order . . . a group of us near the end of the column began humming some of our marching songs, then some became bolder and sang. The singing was spreading right through the whole body when a number of NCOs came hurrying along, speaking in the usual British Army fashion and threatening dire results. This dampened our ardour somewhat . . . On Sunday night, 30 April, we were put aboard one of the LNW boats. There were probably up to 300 or 400 prisoners all penned in the cargo hold of the ship. One bucket of water had been placed there, but before half of us had reached the cargo hold the supply of water was exhausted . . . Seeing my approach, one of the soldiers immediately halted me. I told him I was seeking water as there was none in the hold, and his reply came quick and sharp, leaving no doubt of his intention. 'You dirty Irish pig, get back into the hold or you won't require any water.' This was rather a shock to me because, generally speaking, the ordinary British soldiers had shown a different attitude during the day towards their prisoners. Most of us then endeavoured to settle down with the object of having some rest, but there was very little space for this purpose. We made all kinds of attempts to be as comfortable as possible under the circumstances. A group of us managed in this way; two sat back to back, one at each side, and across our legs lay the heads or legs of other colleagues. In that position I went to sleep and did not awaken until the ship arrived at Holyhead early next day, when I was stiff, cold and sore. On looking around before we were taken from the hold of the ship, some very revolting scenes met our eyes. During the trip some of the men had got sick, and, having no room, actually vomited on their nearest colleagues or on themselves.

Thomas Pugh, B Company, 2nd Battalion

We were marched off [on 2 May] to get the boat at the North Wall. We went past the Royal Hospital, Kilmainham, and we started singing marching songs, 'Eileen Óge' and others. One of the British officers came and told us that if we did not stop singing he would order his men to shoot. As we were going along Ormond Quay there was a little wizened man sitting on some steps and the officer gave orders to shove him into the crowd of Volunteers. This man turned out to be a Russian sailor off a Russian boat, and he was sent to Knutsford . . . At the top of the gangway was an English officer named Bruen whom I knew well. I often had a drink with him. He was in the Connaught Rangers. He said to me, 'I know you. Where did I meet you?' 'In Nagle's public house,' I told him, and he shoved me on.

Robert Holland, F Company, 4th Battalion

We all heard the orders being given to the escort that 'any of us who stumbled or faltered, to stick the bayonet in us.' We marched out the gate [of Richmond barracks on 2 May] and there met the mob of Sunday night. They had gathered more forces. They subjected us once more to catcalls and filthy expressions and followed us as far as Kilmainham cross, where a road block had been erected. We marched down John's Road, Kingsbridge, all of which were familiar to me. I wondered would I ever see these places again. But that mattered little to me as I was sick at heart. Along the north side of the quays down to the North Wall there were very few people on the streets. We could hear the advance guard of soldiers giving orders to clear off the streets – 'Get in and close those windows.' As we passed O'Connell Bridge I saw the O'Connell Street ruins smouldering and sections of the Fire Brigade still using hoses . . . We were put into the hold of a cattle-boat, as that was the kind of smell that was in it. As the last of us got in the lights were switched off and we found ourselves locked in. We got no rations leaving Richmond barracks, and the only thing we next knew was the boat moving and we were out to sea being tossed about. A lot of others and myself got sick with the heat and foul smell and a torpedo or mine would have been a happy release.

Gary Holohan, Fianna Éireann and IRB, Dublin

We got a rather coarse reception from the soldiers' wives and the lower classes. It was very depressing . . . We had no idea where we were going. We had an idea that they might press us into the navy.

Mortimer O'Connell, F Company, 1st Battalion

The general idea was that we were going to be interned. I thought that an attempt might be made to draft us into the British Army. This, we decided, we would not let happen.

Patrick Colgan, Maynooth Company, Co. Kildare

We hadn't heard that other men had been deported already. We hadn't a notion what was going to happen to us. All sorts of rumours spread through the ranks. The most persistent rumour was we were being taken to France to dig trenches . . . As we got to the northern quays there were many people about who acted very friendly.

Padraig Ó Ceallaigh, B Company, 2nd Battalion

I noticed some women and girls crying as we passed by – the first sign perhaps of change-over in feeling in our favour.

Liam Tobin, C Company, 1st Battalion

I remember that just at the end of the North Circular Road, a man, obviously he was a baker judging by the flour all over him, ran out of a shop and pushed his way through the surrounding guards. He loaded my hands up with packets of cigarettes, Woodbines, for which I was very grateful.

Michael O'Flanagan, C Company, 1st Battalion

On our way from Richmond barracks to the North Wall all our men were in great spirits and sang the marching songs of the Volunteers. On arrival at the North Wall we were marched directly on to the boat and we were left on deck surrounded by an armed escort. After about a half hour and as soon as the British military authorities had completed the ship's complement of prisoners, the sloop moved out en route for England. The night being calm and the weather good, we enjoyed the crossing. Some of the men slept. As we were on deck, the passage was easier for us, and during the night some of the sailors, who were sympathetic to us, handed us mugs of hot coffee or cocoa and bread which we greatly appreciated.

Jimmy Kenny, D Company, 4th Battalion

We boarded a cattle-boat and were treated like cattle too.

John O'Reilly, Enniscorthy Company, Co. Wexford

The party, which numbered 1,000 prisoners, were booed and cheered through the streets of Dublin [on *c.* 8 May] – different receptions in different places . . . but the big majority of the people of Dublin cheered us.

John MacDonagh, C Company, 2nd Battalion

We sang national songs until orders came that any man singing would be shot. In the temper our guards were in just then, we knew they would not hesitate to carry out their threat. We were amazed at the sight of O'Connell Street, smoking ruins and one half of the street practically demolished. On the boat, we were packed like cattle, and a drunken British officer called us all sorts of traitors and dirty dogs. 'And I am an Irishman!' he announced. At this, we jeered, which brought him somewhat to his senses. 'Why didn't you wait till the war was over, and we'd all be with you!' he shouted. Finally, he wept and passed round cigarettes. Lying on top of each other, we slept on the boat, and again in the train, not knowing or caring where we were brought.

Peadar Doyle, F Company, 4th Battalion

A military officer came to us in the hold of the boat and enquired as to what we wanted. Tom Hunter told him very quickly that we wanted tea, sugar and cigarettes. He left and returned with a good supply. He then asked several questions and summed up by saying that he was at the battle of Mons and that it was only 'so and so' to the battle in O'Connell Street, but that we the Volunteers must have known that he was an Irishman and although he had not even a stick of rhubarb with which to defend himself he did not even get hit. He further remarked that we had started the 'racket' too soon and he bid us goodnight and good luck and the boat steamed off. The port holes were our only means of observation and when passing Lambay Island and Ireland's Eye, Séamus Hughes gave us the 'Last Glimpse of Erin' in his usual great style.

Joe Good, 'Kimmage Garrison'

On our journey one Volunteer remarked: 'If they choose to have an accident now and say an enemy torpedo struck us, it will solve their problem.' Perhaps he was right, because the personnel of what was afterwards to become GHQ IRA were aboard that boat – that is to say, Michael Collins, Dick Mulcahy, Gearóid O'Sullivan, etc.

Liam Tannam, E Company, 3rd Battalion

On 6 June a party of us were paraded, marched down the quays to the North Wall. On the way down by Capel Street Bridge I heard some encouraging cries from some people. This came as a great surprise, for my last memory of people had been an unhappy one. I had experienced some of the spitting through the windows of the GPO. We were embarked on a cattle-boat in filthy surroundings and tightly crammed; almost everyone vomiting under these conditions.

Josephine MacNeill, Volunteers sympathiser

Somehow or other we got wind of the hour the prisoners were to be taken to the boat and groups of sympathisers, including myself, waited for ages on the quays. After some hours our patience was rewarded by seeing the prisoners march down – at least a few hundred of them – strongly guarded by soldiers with fixed bayonets in front, in the rear and at each side. We ran along beside the line of soldiers guarding them on the outside and kept up a continuous conversation with the prisoners in the ranks. All – both prisoners and their sympathisers – were in the highest spirits and only the soldiers looked a little nervous and depressed owing to the surge of popular sympathy. When the prisoners were embarked, we stood on the quayside and sang patriotic songs.

Condemned prisoners were transferred to Kilmainham Jail, whose prisoners were treated more harshly than those in Richmond barracks. Between 3 and 12 May fourteen of the leaders were executed in Dublin; Thomas Kent was executed in Cork on 9 May, while Roger Casement was hanged in Pentonville Prison on 3 August. Given the scale of the insurrection and its wartime context, this response was hardly draconian, but its impact was pivotal to the transformation of opinion. The rebels' willingness to die for their beliefs evoked widespread admiration, as did their success in presenting themselves as part of a tradition of martyrs dating back to Wolfe Tone. Perhaps the most powerful aspect of the executions, in terms of their public impact, was the piety of the condemned men. Patrick Pearse compared his fate to that of Christ, the Marxist James Connolly received Communion before his death, and Casement converted to Catholicism. Contrasting responses – such as Seán MacDermott's anti-clericalism and Michael Mallin's bitterness – were overlooked in the narrative of martyrdom that came to form a powerful foundation myth for the independent Irish state.

Diarmuid Lynch, 'Headquarters Battalion'

That Sunday afternoon the twenty-five or thirty of us in the guard room [Ship Street] were marched off to Kilmainham. On being escorted into the old-wing cells a warder unceremoniously cuffed and pushed a couple of our men through the doorway. My protest against such treatment of 'prisoners of war' was answered by a baton on the jaw . . . The whitewashed cell walls were much smeared with blood – evidence of brutal treatment . . . We soon learned that an inquisition was afoot in an adjoining room. British officers demanded the name of each prisoner called before them, his rank, position occupied during the fight, the name of his commanding officer, etc. Immediately I passed along word that none of their questions should be answered. The inquisition soon ceased; we were all marched off to the disused rooms of the old prison infirmary.

Gerard Doyle, B Company, 4th Battalion

When we had passed through the cordon of soldiers and down through the dark passages of the jail we were marched into the main hall – the scene beggars description. Some of the soldiers acted in a decent manner but others were brutal, and when a prisoner lifted his hands over his shoulders to be searched the soldier would bring up his knee into the pit of the prisoner's stomach while others hit [him] in the face . . . It was pitch dark in the cells and right through the prison we could hear the banging of doors. We could also hear the shouting and screaming of prisoners who were being beaten up in the cells through which the soldiers had run amok.

. . . I was asked when brought in [to Kilmainham Jail], my name and occupation. In reply I informed them that I was a plasterer by trade and when I was asked if I knew who was in command of the South Dublin Union, I said, 'No.' The officer then produced a paper stating that the man before me had said that I was well known to the police and that he had signed this statement. When I asked to see this statement, one of the military police hit me on the side of the head and knocked me against the side of a table. The second officer, who had not spoken to me up to this, said to the policeman, 'That will do,' and ordered that I be taken back to my cell. On my way back I met J. J. Burke but I failed to recognise him as his face was all swollen and black and blue – he had been given a terrible beating.

Father Aloysius, Capuchin friar

I spent some hours between the two cells [at Kilmainham, 2 May] and the preparations these two men made to meet death was simply inspiring and edifying. When I met [Patrick] Pearse I said, 'I am sure you will be glad to know that I gave Holy Communion to James Connolly this morning.' I can't forget the fervour with which, looking up to heaven, he said, 'Thank God. It is the one thing I was anxious about.' I heard the confessions of Pearse and MacDonagh and gave them both Holy Communion. They received the Most Blessed Sacrament with intense devotion and spent the time at their disposal in prayer. They were happy – no trace of fear or anxiety.

Alfred Bucknill, deputy judge advocate general, British Forces in Ireland

Pearse, MacDonagh and Clarke were tried on the first day that the court sat and were all condemned to death and executed on the following morning [3 May] at Kilmainham Jail . . . I believe, from what those who were present . . . told me, that these three men and indeed all who were executed died bravely. MacDonagh indeed came down the stairs whistling. They were blindfolded in a passage and had a piece of paper pinned on their coats over their heart and were then led out. They were shot at two different spots in the jail. I saw the places of execution. They could not be overlooked from any windows, but the noise must have been terrific. It frightened the people living near who thought it was artillery. Each firing party had twelve men, and the executions took place at 3.45 a.m. . . . Every arrangement was made to get the relatives to the jail on the night before the executions, and a priest was always in attendance at the execution and burial. A large grave was dug at Arbour Hill detention barracks and the bodies were removed there for burial.

Sergeant Michael Soughley, Dublin Metropolitan Police

On the morning of the first executions [3 May] there was only one firing party for the three men executed and I was told that the soldiers displayed considerable nervousness when the third man was brought out to be executed. On all subsequent mornings there was a different firing party for each man shot. There was great admiration amongst the staff of the jail for the manner in which the executed leaders met their fate, especially Tom Clarke, who, notwithstanding his age and frail constitution, expressed his willingness to go before his firing party without a blindfold. I was told that as far as the others were concerned they did not care whether they were blindfolded or not. Death did not seem to hold any terrors for them.

Captain E. Gerrard, British Army officer

. . . our medical officer was Colonel H. V. Stanley, RAMC. He said to me, 'I was the medical officer who attended the executions of the first nine Sinn Féiners to be shot. After that I got so sick of the slaughter that I asked to be changed. Three refused to have their eyes bandaged' – I can't remember who the three were – anyway, he said that there were three – 'they all died like lions. The rifles of the firing party were waving like a field of corn. All the men were cut to ribbons at a range of about ten yards.' That is what he said to me. He was an Irishman.

Geraldine Dillon, sister of Joseph Plunkett

During my first visit to Richmond barracks, my father told me that the day Joe [Plunkett] was court-martialled, he saw him standing in the rain below his window in the barrack square. He knew he was to be shot, and they gazed at each other for about half an hour before Joe was moved off. My father was weeping as he told me this.

Grace Plunkett, widow of Joseph Plunkett

He was so unselfish, he never thought of himself. He was not frightened – not at all, not the slightest . . . He was quite calm. I was never left alone with him, even after the marriage ceremony. I was brought in, and was put in front of the altar; and he was brought down the steps; and the cuffs were taken off him; and the chaplain went on with the ceremony; then the cuffs were put on him again. I was not alone with him – not for a minute. I had no private conversation with him at all. I just came away then ... I saw him again that night, to say goodbye ... I was allowed to stay only a short time with Joe, yet I believe that Min Ryan and Father Brown were allowed to stay a long time with Seán MacDermott. Min Ryan was there with Seán MacDermott for ages and ages. In fact, she said her conversation ran out altogether. She did not know what to say to him. There would be a guard there, and you could not talk. I can't understand how she managed to stay quite a while. I was just a few moments there to get married, and then again a few minutes to say goodbye that night; and a man stood there, with his watch in his hand, and said: 'Ten minutes.'

Sergeant Michael Soughley, Dublin Metropolitan Police

This NCO told me that when Commandant Daly arrived at Kilmainham with his escort, he was informed that as Tom Clarke was about to be executed he could not see him. Daly said he would like to see him dead or alive and he was allowed to remain. When the three men were executed their bodies lay in an old shed in which prisoners broke stones in bad weather. Daly went out to this shed – stood to attention and saluted the remains. He then took off his cap, knelt down and prayed for some time. He put on his cap again, saluted again and returned to his escort. Daly stood in the same spot the following morning for his own execution ... When I arrived at the home of Mrs Clarke on the first occasion that night, I knocked at the door and Mrs Clarke opened it. She was in her dressing gown and seemed to be very nervous and was shaking. I later discovered that this was not so, but that it was cold she was. I said I was very sorry to hear of her husband's death that morning, that I knew him well and never expected he would meet such an untimely end. She replied that there was nothing to be sorry about, that he had died as honourably as he had lived.

Eily O'Hanrahan, Cumann na mBan, and sister of Michael O'Hanrahan

On Wednesday night [3 May] sometime after we went to bed, probably between twelve and one, a lorry with military drove up to the door accompanied by a car with a policeman in it. They banged on the door, and at once the people opposite, Green was their name, put their heads out the window. The military told them that if they did not shut their windows and put out their lights they would do it for them. We opened the door and the policeman gave in a letter from the O/C of Kilmainham, to the effect that Micheál would like to see his mother and sisters before his deportation to England. We decided we would not let Mother come, as we thought it meant our arrest. The policeman said we would be sorry if we did not take her. We left Máire with Mother, and Cis and I went, under the impression that we were under arrest. All the streets had military on duty, who held us up frequently. We did not know where we were, as it was pitch dark. At last we arrived at Kilmainham. This was the first time we knew where we were. We were shown into a little whitewashed room off the hall, with two candles. We were sitting there for a while. I went to the door once or twice and asked the soldiers in the hall why we were not being brought to my brother. I heard a woman's voice in the hall. 'That seems to be Mrs Clarke,' I said to Cis. I went to her and she said, 'What brings you here, Eily?' 'I don't know except that we were told Micheál was being deported.' I said to Mrs Clarke, 'Is there anything you want to tell us?', as she seemed to hesitate. 'They are executing the men,' she said. I said, 'Could it be possible that Micheál would be executed?' She then told us that she had been there the night before to see her husband before his execution, and she had been called this night to see her brother, Ned Daly.

After a short time some soldiers came and brought us up the dark iron stairs and along the iron corridor to Micheál's cell. There was nothing in it, no light even, but an old bag thrown in the corner, and a bucket, no bed, no chair, no table, a place in which you would not put a dog. Micheál was standing in the cell. When we rushed forwards he caught us in his arms. He asked us did we know the circumstances that brought us, and where was Mother. We told him why we had not brought her and we said we knew now why we had been sent for. He said he would have loved to see Mother and Máire, but that it was better after all Mother had not come. He was not in any way agitated. The only thing that worried him was what was to become of my mother and us. He said he did not know where [his brother] Harry was. They were devoted to each other and did everything together. He told us not to fret, and we tried to reassure him that we would be all right and that the women of '98 had to endure that too. There were six soldiers and two officers and any time we said anything referring to the Volunteers and the movement, one of the officers came forward and said we must speak of nothing but personal matters. I mentioned that Tom Clarke and Pearse were gone and one of the officers interrupted me. Again in the course of conversation I mentioned that MacDonagh was gone and again I was stopped. We told him that Ned Daly and two others were going with himself. We rushed in all this information in a hurry and with the greatest difficulty. We were left there only a short time, although we had been told that the interview would be for twenty minutes. We asked to be permitted to stay to the end, but the officers said that would be out of the question. I asked Micheál if he had anything to eat. He said some bully-beef had been left in to him in a billycan, but he had not eaten it. I asked had he not had a bed. He said no. Then one of the officers said to Micheál if he had any affairs to settle he should do so without delay. I said, how can anyone situated as he is without a table or chair even settle anything? A table and chair and a candle in an old candlestick were brought. It was then we saw how bad the cell really was. Micheál wrote his will on paper headed with the Kilmainham stamp. He left all he had – which was only his books – to Mother and to his sisters after her death . . . When he had finished the will he said he would be seeing Father in a few hours. We asked him had he seen a priest. An officer said his clergy had been sent for and would be here presently. Micheál said he had asked for Father Augustine and Father Albert. These priests were marvellous. They saved the reason of many people whose sons and brothers were executed . . . The two officers witnessed the will. Although these men did their duty, they were not aggressive.

We said goodbye to Micheál. He did not weep, but kept up his courage. We did not give way either then. He kissed us several times and told us to give his love to Mother and Máire and to Harry when we found out where he was. I think he was afraid

Harry would be executed too. We came downstairs and I got weak, and when I got to the ground floor I fainted. A stretcher was brought and I was laid on it. One of the soldiers, an Irishman, made himself very objectionable and seemed to gloat over the executions. When I became conscious again I was brought back to the same room we had been in before. One soldier – an Englishman – was very kind, he brought water and tried to console us. He said, 'After all, ladies, your brother is getting the death he would have wished for.'

The same lorry and the same car brought us home, and the same soldier who had been so kind in the prison to us came forward and said he would like to shake hands with us, and that we had his deepest sympathy.

Áine Ceannt, wife of Éamonn Ceannt

Micheál O'Hanrahan was, I believe, the first sentenced man to be attended by Father Augustine. After Father Augustine gave the last rites of the Church to Micheál, the governor of Kilmainham said, 'You may go now, Father.' Father Augustine replied, 'No, my Church can give consolation to the end,' and so he accompanied Micheál from the cell to the yard, witnessed the execution and anointed him as he dropped. He did the same for each of the doomed men whom he attended, including Éamonn.

Father Augustine, Capuchin friar

. . . I [went] to Willie Pearse, whose hands were already tied behind his back. He was beautifully calm, made his confession as if he were doing it on an ordinary occasion, and received Holy Communion with great devotion. A few minutes later he stood before the firing squad, and with Our Lord in his heart, went to meet his noble brother in a better land . . . After I had left Willie Pearse I saw O'Hanrahan for a short while in his cell . . . He was one of the truest and noblest characters that it has ever been my privilege to meet. His last message to me before he went out into the dark corridor that led to the yard where he was shot was: 'Father, I'd like [it if] you saw my mother and sisters and consoled them.' I promised him I would, and, whispering something in his ear, I grasped the hands that were tied behind his back. In his right hand he pressed mine most warmly; we exchanged a look, and he went forth to die.

W. T. Cosgrave, B Company, 4th Battalion

At daybreak on Friday morning [Kilmainham, 5 May] I heard a slight movement and whisperings in the Major's [MacBride's] cell. I heard the word 'sergeant', a few more whispers, a move towards the door of the cell, then steps down the corridor, down the central stairs. Through a chink in the door I could barely discern the receding figures; silence for a time; then the sharp crack of rifle fire and silence again. I thought my turn would come next and waited for a rap on the door, but the firing squad had no further duty that morning.

Séamus Kavanagh, C Company, 3rd Battalion

. . . a soldier who was a member of the firing party told me that Major MacBride refused the blindfold, stating that he was not afraid, as he had been looking down the barrels of rifles all his life.

Gary Holohan, Fianna Éireann

The Major [MacBride] spent a good deal of his time at their home, and when he was taken prisoner to Kilmainham after the Rising he sent for Mrs Fred [Clara] Allan and she brought him in a change of clothes. It was in Fred's shirt he was executed. His happy, peaceful manner had such an effect on Mrs Allan that she turned Catholic after 1916.

Áine Ceannt, wife of Éamonn Ceannt

I arrived at Kilmainham [on 6 May], was shown in, and found Éamonn in a cell with no seating accommodation and no bedding, not even a bed of straw. The first thing I noticed was that his Sam Browne belt was gone, and that his uniform was slightly torn. A sergeant stood at the door while we spoke, and we could say very little . . . I said to him that the Rising was an awful fiasco, and he replied, 'No, it was the biggest thing since '98.'

Thomas Mallin, brother of Michael Mallin

On the night of 7 May, a military car came to the door, in which were a driver, a British Army corporal and a member of the DMP. The corporal told Agnes that her husband wanted to see her immediately. I got into the car with her. On the way I ascertained from the DMP man that the sentence was death. I spoke to Agnes and told her that even if Mike's sentence was death, she should bear up and not make his sentence harder for him.

We were brought to Kilmainham Jail. In the yard at Kilmainham, Mrs Kent and a man whom I took to be Eamon Kent's brother passed us and the man spoke to me and said: 'Stick it.' Agnes and I were brought into a cell; I went first. Mike was standing at the back wall. There was a small grid in the wall above his head. There was little light. He had an old green blanket around him, and he said it was very cold. He had several days' growth of beard and his eyes appeared to be fixed and glassy. He said: 'Where is Agnes?' She ran towards him and said: 'What is it?' He replied: 'Death.' She collapsed on the floor. When she revived, he said to her: 'We have been married fifteen years, and during that period we have had only one difference, and I hope you are satisfied about my explanation of that one incident. We have three sons and one daughter and another coming into the world. If it is a boy, call it "Michael" after me; if a girl, call it "Mary" after the Mother of God . . . James is now 13 and John is 11. If it is the will of God, I want them to grow up to be big men and look after you. Una and little Joseph, whom I will never hold in my arms again, are dedicated to the Church. I want them in the service of God and for the good of my soul. Try and find the dog. I saw it when I was being brought to the Castle, but I was afraid to call it, in case they would shoot it. I want you to promise me you will never marry again. I would like to see James and John.'

I left immediately to get the two boys. I met the officer in charge of the guard, who said to me, 'I will never forget what I saw in that cell, to hear an aged woman say she was delighted to have her first son die for his country.' . . . The officer was sympathising with her, and she did not want any sympathy, but told him she was delighted to have a son dying for Ireland. I returned with the two boys. Mike spoke to them, and said, 'James, you are 13, John, you are 11.

I have given you as good an education as my father gave me. I am dying in the hope that we have made Ireland a better Ireland for you to live in. I want you to grow up to be big men, to work and keep your mother, and when the time comes, to do as I have done. Tom will look after you . . .'

When I was left alone with him I said: 'Is it worth it?' He replied, 'It is worth it. Ireland is a grand country, but the people in it are rotters. The first Irishman to join the British Army was a bastard. The British Army is made up of them and jailbirds and wasters. Some join through drink and some through lack of work. I will show my guards how an Irishman can die for his own country – in his own country. I can die praying. If these men are sent to France they will die cursing. They will die lying on the ground, moaning, and not able to see their mothers and their sweethearts. Tom, burn the picture with the set of drums. Tom, I have nothing to give. I have my life to give and I will give it for my country. I have many debts. Tell them that by my death I have paid all my debts. Look after Agnes and the children.' He put his arm round my neck, kissed me and put the letter he had written down my breast . . . The priest had entered the cell and I knew the time had come.

Áine Ceannt, wife of Éamonn Ceannt

As I was still in doubt as to the outcome of the morning, I remained up all night with my sister-in-law, and each hour we knelt down and said the rosary. From three o'clock I remained praying until about half past five, when I knew that everything would be over if the executions were to take place. At six o'clock curfew was lifted, and we made our way down to Church Street. It was a glorious summer morning, and when we arrived at the priory I asked for Father Augustine. He sent down another friar, who told me that Father Augustine had only come, celebrated Mass and had gone to his room, but that if I wished he would get up and come down to me. I said no, that I only wanted to know the truth, and this priest said, 'He is gone to heaven.' . . . At about ten o'clock on 8 May my sister-in-law accompanied me to Church Street, where we met Father Augustine. He gave me full details of Éamonn's last moments . . . Father Augustine told me that Éamonn had held his, Father

Augustine's, crucifix in his hands, and the last words he spoke were, 'My Jesus Mercy.' In every case it would appear as if it was necessary for the officer in charge of the firing party to dispatch the victim by a revolver shot.

Father Paddy Browne, friend of Seán MacDermott

About my visit to Seán MacDermott [on 10 May], we talked about everything . . . It was the case of a man who lived for that idea of an insurrection. He also spoke fairly bitterly about the Church in spite of my being present – about the Church and the Fenians. He said he had made his peace with God and had received the sacraments but that he had kept away for a considerable time . . . He was not in a tragic mood. There was not any regret for the Rising. He was really glad to be dying as he was going to die. I could say that with the greatest certainty.

Min Ryan, Cumann na mBan, and girlfriend of Seán MacDermott

We were there at twelve o'clock and remained till three [on 12 May]. He was shot at a quarter to four. The message was brought to us by an army car and we returned in it. They sent word first, I think, that they were calling. Someone came in a car, with an army driver, and handed me a note to say that the prisoner, Seán MacDermott, would like to see me and my sister, if she would like to accompany me. We had to call to the North Circular Road to collect Seán Reynolds and Seán MacDermott's landlady. Seán wanted Seán Reynolds to make his will for him; he had not very much to leave, just a few pounds for Masses. He handed me mementos which I gave to various people – buttons to Máire Cregan and Margaret Browne. We were all there together, listening to each other's conversation. He was very anxious to have the others go. He was much more intimate with us, but there was no budge out of them. 'That is all now,' Seán would say, but there was no budge at all. Then we all came out together.

Nora Connolly, Cumann na mBan, and daughter of James Connolly

One night, we were knocked up at about eleven o'clock [11 May]. There was an ambulance outside the door; and there was a military captain with it. He said the message he brought to us was: James Connolly was very weak, and wanted to see his wife and eldest daughter. Mama had seen him the day before, and he was very weak; and she half believed him; but I guessed what it was. We were brought in the ambulance up to the Castle. I remember it so well. You know the part of the Castle, where there are a porch and pillars outside; there is a staircase landing above, which branches into corridors; they had soldiers on every step of the staircase; and on the landing they had little mattresses; there were soldiers lying on them; and there were soldiers at every door.

We were brought into the room where Daddy was. He lifted his head, and said: 'I suppose you know what this means?' Mama was terribly upset. I remember he said to me – we were talking about various things – he said: 'Put your hand under the bedclothes.' He slipped some paper into my hand. He said: 'Get that out, if you can. It is my last statement.' Mama could hardly talk. I remember he said: 'Don't cry, Lillie. You will unman me.' Mama said: 'But your beautiful life, James,' she wept. 'Hasn't it been a full life? Isn't this a good end?' he said.

Then they took us away; and we got home. We just stood at the window, pulled up the blind, and watched for the dawn; and, after we knew he was gone, the family all came in; and I opened the last statement and read it.

Sergeant Michael Soughley, Dublin Metropolitan Police

The firing parties and staff officers had withdrawn and a mantle of gloom once more hung over Kilmainham prison. The staff of the jail, as well as ourselves, were all delighted that the grim work was finished. We went back to our barracks and about half an hour later were surprised to see a firing party return to the prison as well as staff officers. A four-wheeled general service wagon drawn by two horses came along the old Kilmainham road at a very fast pace, swung to the right and went into the prison. We saw a man sitting in the wagon surrounded by a number of soldiers who were sitting around him. As far as I can remember he was dressed in civilian attire. He did not seem to be wounded that we could see, but as the soldiers were sitting very close to him they could be supporting him with their bodies. A short time after the wagon entered the jail a volley rang out and we later learned that the victim was James Connolly. It would appear as if Connolly's execution was a rushed affair and squeezed in at the last moment.

Robert Barton, Royal Dublin Fusilier

[Major] Heathcote told me he [Connolly] was probably drugged and was almost dead. He was not able to sit upright in the chair on which he was placed and, when they shot him, the whole back of the chair was blown out . . . I gathered from Heathcote that he was quite unconscious. He was a dying man.

Nora Connolly, Cumann na mBan, and daughter of James Connolly

Afterwards, we went to the Castle to demand his body. We knew they would refuse it, but we had to make the request. They refused our request. While we were standing there, a nurse came along, and said: 'Mrs Connolly, I clipped this off your husband's head.' She gave her a lock of his hair. I have that still. Then we met Father Aloysius, who was with him before he was executed. I asked Father Aloysius: 'How did they shoot him?' He told me he had not known Daddy. Of all those men, Daddy was the only one he had not known personally. He felt it was a great favour to have met him before he died. I said: 'How did they shoot him?' He said: 'They came in an ambulance. They carried the stretcher to the yard, and put him in a chair. Before he was executed, I said to your father: "Will you say a prayer for the men who are about to shoot you?"' My father's answer was: 'I will say a prayer for all brave men who do their duty.' Then he was shot.